JUDAISM AND CHRISTIANITY IN FIRST-CENTURY ROME

Judaism and Christianity in First-Century Rome

Edited by

Karl P. Donfried and Peter Richardson

William B. Eerdmans Publishing Company
Grand Rapids, Michigan / Cambridge, U.K.

255 Jefferson Ave. S.E., Grand Rapids, Michigan 49503 /
P.O. Box 163, Cambridge CB3 9PU U.K.

Printed in the United States of America

03 02 01 00 99 98 7 6 5 4 3 2 1

Library of Congress Cataloging-in-Publication Data

Judaism and Christianity in First-Century Rome / edited by
Karl P. Donfried and Peter Richardson

p. cm.

Includes bibliographical references.

ISBN 0-8028-4265-8 (pbk.: alk. paper)

1. Jews — Italy — Rome — History.
2. Judaism — Italy — Rome — History.
3. Christians — Italy — Rome — History.
4. Church history — Primitive and early church, ca. 30-600.
5. Rome (Italy) — Church history.
6. Rome — History — Empire, 30 B.C.–284 A.D.
I. Donfried, Karl P. II. Richardson, Peter, 1935-

DS135.I85R6356 1998

938′.004924 — dc21 98-15906

CIP

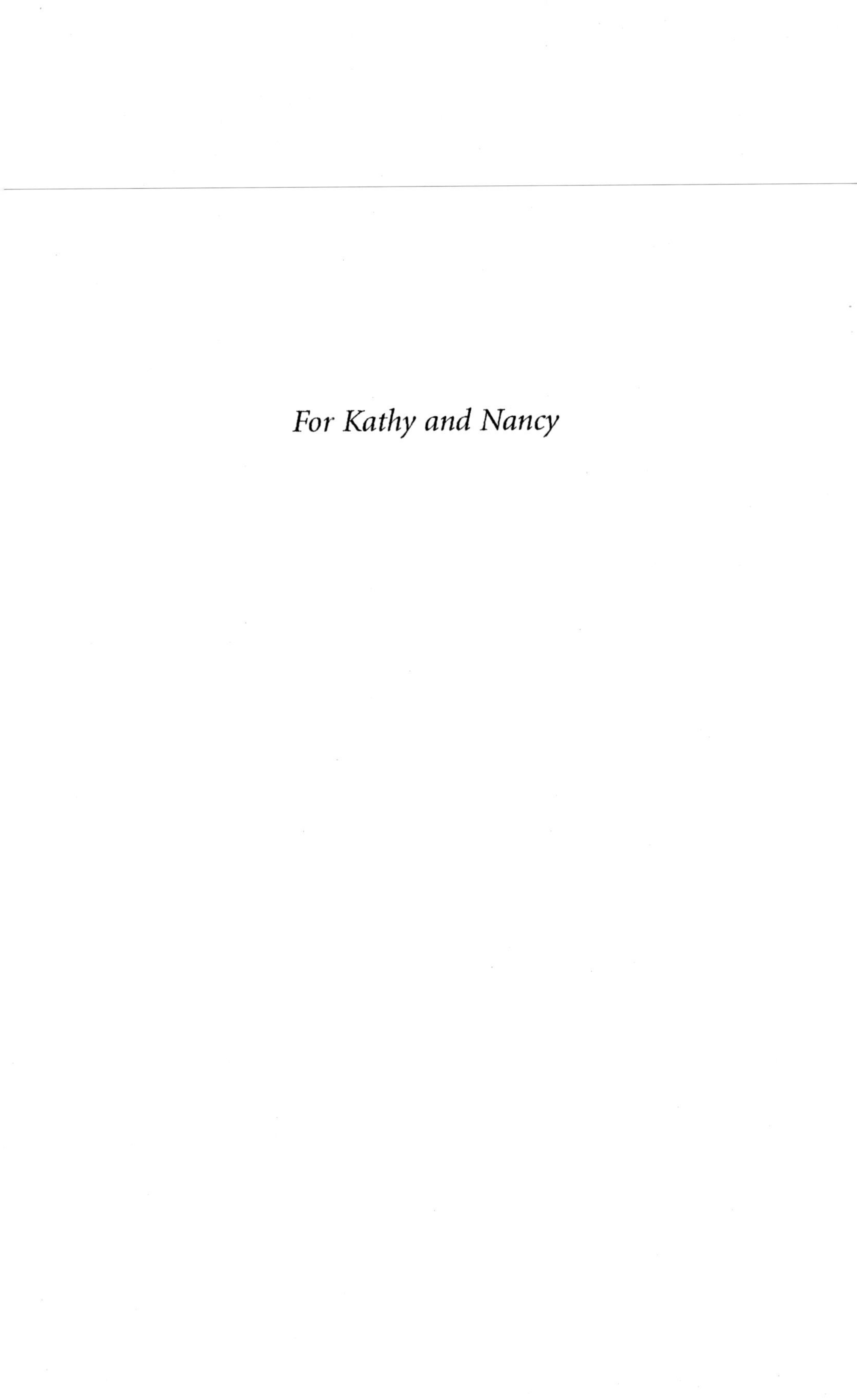

For Kathy and Nancy

Contents

PART 2: SOCIAL-HISTORICAL STUDIES

PART 3: DEVELOPMENTAL STUDIES

Acknowledgments

The papers collected here are revised — substantially revised — versions of papers that were given (except for the editors' contributions) as seminar papers or as responses in meetings of the Studiorum Novi Testamenti Societas (SNTS). It was our privilege to co-chair the Seminar on "New Testament Texts in Their Cultural Environment" from 1990 through 1994, and we are grateful to the SNTS for providing the opportunity to participate in its work in this way. In the first two years of the seminar (1990-91) we focused on Thessalonica, before we turned to Rome (1992-94), the subject of the papers gathered here. To the contributors we owe a special debt of thanks for participating in this collective work, for accepting sometimes intrusive blue-penciling, for expanding or contracting their work so that the result would be more comprehensive and less repetitive. There were more participants and respondents than are represented here; all made helpful contributions to the work of the seminar, shaping the discussions in important ways, and their efforts are not forgotten.

SNTS Seminar on "New Testament Texts in Their Cultural Environments"

Milan (1990)

John Gager, "Judaism and the Earliest Followers of Jesus in Thessalonike"

Wayne A. Meeks, "Is an Ethnography of Early Thessalonian Christianity Possible?"

Helmut Koester, "The Cultural Context of a Pauline Letter: Methodological Issues"

Bielfeld (1991)
Frank W. Hughes, "The Social Settings Implied by Rhetoric"
F. Gerald Downing, respondent
Renée Kieffer, "L'eschatologie en 1 Thessaloniciens dans une perspective rhétorique"
James D. Hester, respondent
Juan D. Chapa, "Consolatory Patterns"
Karl P. Donfried, respondent

Madrid (1992)
L. Michael White, "Synagogue and Society in the Environs of Rome: Archaeological and Epigraphic Evidence from Ostia"
Helmut Koester, respondent
Graydon F. Snyder, "Jewish Catacombs in Rome"
Leonard Victor Rutgers, "The Legal Situation of the Jewish Community in Rome with Special Emphasis on the First Century A.D."

Chicago (1993)
Ekkehard Stegemann and Rudolf Brändle, "The Emergence of the First Christian Community in Rome in the Context of the Jewish Communities"
James S. Jeffers, respondent
Carolyn Osiek, "The Oral World of the Early Jews and Christians in Rome"
Richard Pervo, respondent
J. Paul Sampley, "The Weak and the Strong: Paul's Careful and Crafty Rhetorical Strategy in Romans 14:1–15:13"
Olle Christoffersson, respondent

Edinburgh (1994)
James Walters, "Evolution of the Christian Communities in Rome"
Judith Lieu, respondent
William L. Lane, "Social Perspectives on Roman Christianity"
J. I. H. MacDonald, respondent
Chrys C. Caragounis, "From Obscurity to Prominence"
Beverly Gaventa, respondent

William B. Eerdmans Publishing Company has handled the manuscript expeditiously and sensitively, and we are grateful to William B. Eerdmans, Jr., for the role he has played. We wish to express our gratitude to Tony

S. L. Michael, a doctoral student in the Centre for the Study of Religion at the University of Toronto, who cheerfully standardized all our styles and conventions, unified our discrepant computer programs, dealt with last-minute changes, produced the necessary disks for the press, and compiled the indexes and bibliography.

We acknowledge the permission of *Classical Antiquity* to reprint Leonard Rutgers's article, which first appeared in volume 13/1 (1994). Michael White's chapter appeared in *Harvard Theological Review* 90/1 (1997). Figure 5, the photograph of an Ostian wall of *opus reticulatum*, is by L. Michael White; figures 3 and 4 are also his own work. Figure 1 is adapted from R. Meiggs, *Roman Ostia*, 1973, and is reprinted by permission of Oxford University Press. Figure 2 is from C. Pavolini, "Ostia [Roma]. Saggio lungo la vie Severiana," *Notizie degli Scavi di Antichità*, 8.35, 1981, fig. 1, and is reprinted with permission.

We would like to think that this represents one of the "right" ways to examine questions from antiquity — drawing on the widest possible evidence, asking clear social-historical questions, integrating cross-religious data, and considering ethical and theological questions along with the historical questions. It has been a pleasure to collaborate with such knowledgeable and creative colleagues.

Peter Richardson
Karl P. Donfried

Acronyms and Abbreviations for Journals and Book Series

AB	Anchor Bible
ABD	*Anchor Bible Dictionary*
AIPHOS	Annuaire de l'Institut de Philologie et d'Histoire Orientales et Slaves
AJA	*American Journal of Archaeology*
AJP	*American Journal of Philology*
ANRW	*Aufstieg und Niedergang der Römischen Welt*
ATR	*Anglican Theological Review*
BAGD	W. Bauer, *A Greek-English Lexicon of the New Testament and Other Early Christian Literature,* trans. and adapted by W. Arndt and F. W. Gingrich; 2nd ed. rev. by F. W. Gingrich and F. W. Danker (1979)
BASP	*Bulletin of the American Society of Papyrologists*
BBB	Bonner biblische Beiträge
BDF	F. Blass, A. Debrunner, and R. W. Funk, *A Greek Grammar of the New Testament* (1961)
BEFAR	Bibliothèque des écoles françaises d'Athènes et de Rome
BJRL	*Bulletin of the John Rylands Library*
BJS	Brown Judaic Studies
BNTC	Black's New Testament Commentary series
BR	*Biblical Research*

BZ	*Biblische Zeitschrift*
CahRB	Cahiers de la Revue Biblique
C&M	*Classica et Mediaevalia*
CBQ	*Catholic Biblical Quarterly*
CBQMS	Catholic Biblical Quarterly Monograph Series
CEFR	Collections de l'Ecole française de Rome
CGTC	Cambridge Greek Testament Commentary
CII	*Corpus Inscriptionum Iudaicarum*
CIL	*Corpus Inscriptionum Latinarum*
CIMRM	*Corpus Inscriptionum et Monumentorum religionis mithriacae*
ConBNT	Coniectanea biblica, New Testament
CQR	*Church Quarterly Review*
CRINT	Compendia rerum iudaicarum ad novum testamentum
CSEL	Corpus scriptorum ecclesiasticorum latinorum
CTh	Codex Theodosianus
CTM	*Concordia Theological Monthly*
Ebib	Etudes bibliques
ETL	*Ephemerides theologicae lovanienses*
ExpT	*Expository Times*
HNT	Handbuch zum Neuen Testament
HTR	*Harvard Theological Review*
ICC	International Critical Commentary
ILS	*Inscriptiones Latinae Selectae*
Int	*Interpretation*
JAAR	*Journal of the American Academy of Religion*
JAC	Jahrbuch für Antike und Christentum
JAOS	*Journal of the American Oriental Society*
JBL	*Journal of Biblical Literature*
JETS	*Journal of the Evangelical Theological Society*
JJS	*Journal of Jewish Studies*
JRS	*Journal of Roman Studies*
JQR	*Jewish Quarterly Review*
JSNTSup	Journal for the Study of the New Testament, Supplement Series
JTS	*Journal of Theological Studies*
LCL	Loeb Classical Library
MAAR	*Memoirs of the American Academy in Rome*
MeyerK	H. A. W. Meyer, Kritisch-exegetischer Kommentar über das Neue Testament

MM	J. H. Moulton and G. Milligan, *The Vocabulary of the Greek Testament Illustrated from the Papyri and Other Non-Literary Sources* (1930)
NICNT	New International Commentary on the New Testament series
NovT	*Novum Testamentum*
NovTSup	Novum Testamentum, Supplements
NTS	*New Testament Studies*
P&P	*Past & Present*
PCPS	*Proceedings of the Cambridge Philological Society*
RAC	*Reallexikon für Antike und Christentum*
RB	*Revue biblique*
RE	*Real-Encyclopädie der klassischen Altertumwissenschaft*, ed. Pauly, Wissowa, et al.
Rev. phil.	*Revue de Philologie*
RGG	*Die Religion in Geschichte und Gegenwart*, ed. K. Galling
RSI	*Rivista storica italiana*
RSPT	*Revue des sciences philosophiques et theologiques*
SBLCP	SBL Centennial Publications
SBLTT	SBL Texts and Translations
SBT	Studies in Biblical Theology
SC	Sources chrétiennes
SHA	*Scriptores Historiae Augustae*
SICV	*Sylloge inscriptionum christianarum veterum musei vatiacani*
SNTS	Studiorum Novi Testamenti Societas
SNTU	*Studien zum Neuen Testament und seiner Umwelt*
SR	Studies in Religion/Sciences Religieuses
TAPA	*Transactions of the American Philological Association*
TNTC	Tyndale New Testament Commentary series
TU	Texte und Untersuchungen zur Geschichte der altchristlichen Literatur
VC	*Vigiliae Christianae*
WBC	Word Biblical Commentary
WUNT	Wissenschaftliche Untersuchungen zum Neuen Testament
ZAW	*Zeitschrift für die alttestamentliche Wissenschaft*
ZKT	*Zeitschrift für katholische Theologie*
ZNW	*Zeitschrift für die neutestamentliche Wissenschaft*
ZPE	*Zeitschrift für Papyrologie und Epigraphik*

INTRODUCTION

In the First Century: The Nature and Scope of the Question

Karl P. Donfried

Judaism and Christianity in the first century is a broad topic. All of the essays that follow have their context in the five-year work (1989-94) of the Seminar on New Testament Texts in Their Cultural Environment sponsored by the Studiorum Novi Testamenti Societas. What follows is a brief overview of the issues, queries, and suggestions that the reader will encounter in the various essays included in this volume.

1. Archaeological and Epigraphic Studies

In considering the manifold types of interaction between Judaism and Christianity in Rome during the first century, archaeological insights are critical. In his essay "Augustan-Era Synagogues in Rome," **Peter Richardson** suggests that inscriptions expand considerably our knowledge about synagogues in Rome. Although the evidence for the dating of synagogues in Rome is fragmentary, Richardson proposes that, where they are named after specific persons, it is possible to suggest a date of origin in proximity to that person's influence. So, for example, the "Synagogue of the Augustans" likely honors Augustus, who, as emperor, was instrumental in allowing Diaspora Judaism to flourish, continuing the benevolence of Caesar toward the Jews. Similarly, the "Synagogue of the Agrippans" was named after Marcus Vipsanius Agrippa, a chief lieutenant and heir to Augustus. If this identification is correct, we now have evidence of a synagogue in Rome stemming from the late first century B.C.E. or early first century C.E. Citing another of the five synagogue inscriptions reviewed in this article, Richardson scrutinizes and reconstructs a fragmentary inscription from the Roman catacombs that, in his judgment, refers to a "Synagogue of the Herodians." Although there is a certain ambiguity in this attribution given the antipathy to Herod following his death, he urges that "the simplest view is that he was well known, was active on behalf of Diaspora Jews, and was seen as king of all Jews everywhere."[1] Finally, it is suggested that this naming of at least three synagogues in Rome after high-status individuals, all of whom were friends, may not be accidental since it is just in this period that Jewish privileges were under debate and, in some cases, dispute.

Richardson attempts to strengthen his argument by indicating that it coheres well with the evidence presented by **L. Michael White** in his article, "Synagogue and Society in Imperial Ostia: Archaeological and Epigraphic Evidence." Richardson assumes that the early synagogues in Rome were buildings, not simply communities of Jews. Relying on White's identification of a second-century-C.E. level for the synagogue at Ostia, Richardson urges that while "it is possible to imagine a situation in which Ostia could have a synagogue building while Rome did not, it seems very unlikely; the Ostia synagogue supports the likelihood of synagogue buildings in Rome, perhaps as many as four or five, at this relatively early period."[2] The experts will, no doubt, wish to evaluate the cogency of identifying second-century evidence with that of the first.

An examination of the archaeological and epigraphic evidence in Ostia leads White to conclude that the first edifice, only later used as a Jewish synagogue, was originally part of an *insula* complex built near the beginning of the second century and that it was not *de novo* a Jewish construction. Only toward the middle to late second century did the first renovation take place that permitted synagogal usage. In this early stage the structure resembled a collegial hall or community center, not atypical among Diaspora synagogues. In the late second and early third century, under the continued patronage of Mindis Faustus, this process of renovation and expansion proceeded.

One of the inscriptions found on an inscribed plaque, reused for repair work on the final stage of the synagogue floor and therefore dating

1. Peter Richardson, "Augustan-Era Synagogues in Rome," 28.
2. Richardson, 23.

from the second to third century, reads: "For the well-being of the Emperor. Mindi(u)s Faustus constructed (the edifice or hall) and made it out of his own gifts, and he set up the 'ark' for the sacred law[. . .]." Here there is a direct link with Richardson's discussion of the synagogues of the "Augustesians" and the "Agrippesians," suggesting clientage to members of the imperial household along the lines of a collegial organization.[3] "Such ties," urges White, "would inevitably link Jewish residents of Rome or Ostia directly to the non-Jewish population in important social and economic ways."[4]

White links the significant social location and influence of these Ostian Jews to the later period of synagogue growth and renovation (third and fourth centuries). And so the Ostian evidence suggests a "high degree of acculturation of Jews within the social life of these Italian cities, even as they worked to retain their Jewish cultural identity and religious traditions."[5] And yet, "the aesthetics of the renovated architecture, its decoration, and even the Torah shrine itself show distinctively Roman tastes."[6] But the last word on this matter of acculturation is one of caution. The Ostian evidence comes from one synagogue; in Rome there are at least ten, and thus it is likely that one may find a greater degree of variability in social location and acculturation. "The material evidence from Ostia, Rome, and throughout the Diaspora reflects a high degree of diversity from locality to locality, and even within given Jewish congregations. Thus, we must be cautious about the nature of the Judaism we expect to find, and allow the archaeological, social, and historical evidence to inform our reading of the literary remains."[7]

The theme of inculturation is also a focal point in **Graydon F. Snyder's** essay, "The Interaction of Jews with Non-Jews in Rome." A detailed examination of representative Jewish inscriptions in Rome and symbols linked to the Jews of that city leads to the conclusion that "Jewish inculturation of the Roman world was negligible."[8] Although in the first two centuries C.E. Judaism was defined by a firm symbolic identity and could utilize

3. L. Michael White, "Synagogue and Society in Imperial Ostia: Archaeological and Epigraphic Evidence," 52.

4. White, 52.

5. White, 62.

6. White, 62.

7. White, 63.

8. Graydon F. Snyder, "The Interaction of Jews with Non-Jews in Rome," 77.

Roman symbolic material, it did not assimilate these pagan symbols nor did it infuse them with Jewish meaning. Confirming the work of Richardson and White, Snyder acknowledges the active participation of Jews in the Greco-Roman culture, but this cannot lead to the conclusion that "these symbols became a part of the Jewish iconic conversation."[9] Judaism could and did borrow Roman symbolic material, but it "did not assimilate it."[10]

Not only did Judaism not provide any new symbols for the Roman world, it was also not the source for emerging Christian symbols. The level of interaction of early Christianity with its alien culture is markedly different. Roman Christians did not have any prior identifying symbols; what they found useful they borrowed from the dominant Roman culture, transformed it with new meaning, and, in the process, provided the Roman and eventually the Western world with determinative cultural symbols. Snyder also suggests that the early Christians, by using such symbols as bread, lamb, vine, dove, and Good Shepherd, may themselves have been the agents of Jewish inculturation by allowing Judaism to contribute its worldview in and through these Christian symbols. Most significantly, however, Snyder urges that Jews and Christians, together, "brought to the Roman world their most significant social contribution, a deep sense of community satisfaction through an identifying word: *PAX — shalom.*"[11]

2. Social-Historical Studies

What was Rome's policy toward Jews? Should it be described as tolerant or intolerant? It is to this complex set of issues that **Leonard Victor Rutgers** turns in his essay, "Roman Policy toward the Jews: Expulsions from the City of Rome during the First Century C.E." His work leads him to the paradoxical conclusion that the only constant factor in Rome's policy toward the Jews was that "there was no such constant factor."[12] Roman magistrates responded to situations, and it is only from this perspective that one can understand the expulsions of Jews from Rome.

9. Snyder, 76.

10. Snyder, 96.

11. Snyder, 85.

12. Leonard Victor Rutgers, "Roman Policy toward the Jews: Expulsions from the City of Rome during the First Century C.E.," 110.

Although Rome recognized the distinctiveness of the Jewish people, there was never anything like a "Magna Charta" for them. The *senatus consulta,* a primary form of Roman legal measures, were intended to solve specific disputes; they were ad hoc measures and thus never attained universal validity intending to define the legal status of all Jewish communities in the eastern Mediterranean. The critical factor that determined Rome's policy was its overwhelming desire to maintain law and order. This is the key that allows us to understand Rome's attitude toward the Jews, and whether they are to be considered "tolerant" or "intolerant" is guided by this goal. Thus, when Jews were expelled from Rome, Roman authorities were not exhibiting a systematic ideology of anti-Judaism since other people could and were also expelled under similar circumstances; rather, the authorities were responding to specific disruptions of law and order.

The expulsion of Jews from Rome under Claudius, is, for Rutgers, a clear example of Rome intervening as a result of disturbances; it is not to be seen as an attempt to interfere with the internal affairs of the Jewish community. This approach does not answer all the important questions surrounding this expulsion, but it does provide the overall framework in which they are to be interpreted. The suppression of unrest, not persecution based on Jewish religious practices and beliefs, was the primary motivation for Roman action.

The ambiguous situation of Judaism in Rome is further elaborated by **Rudolf Brändle** and **Ekkehard W. Stegemann** in "The Formation of the First 'Christian Congregations' in Rome in the Context of the Jewish Congregations." The earliest Christian congregations in Rome, it is urged, can only be understood in light of their close association with the Jewish congregations. So closely are they interwoven that non-Jews in Rome would have come into contact with the Christ-faith only if they had had association with Jews. The immediate context of Paul can be situated historically in the "diffusion" of Diaspora Jews in a society that is dominated by a non-Jewish majority. The response of this Roman majority-ruled society to the Jewish minority was varied: on the one hand the response was so positive that it allowed God-fearers and proselytes to flourish; on the other hand the response could be so negative that it fostered xenophobia and anti-Semitism. Simultaneously the Jewish interaction with the pagan world varied widely from apostasy to various grades of acculturation to aggressive antipaganism.

Given this diverse situation, there is little cause for surprise when one observes that the Pauline congregations reacted in divergent ways to Judaism. In Galatia there was a strong tendency to convert to Judaism; in Rome the tendency was quite the opposite: disassociation from and the theological disqualification of Jews. Paul rejects both tendencies. Thus the remarkable thing about "Romans is that Paul calls both Jews and non-Jews to a mutual association with each other (Rom. 15:7-13). In any case, he opposes theological positions that deduce the rejection of Israel from the nonacceptance of the 'Christ-faith' by (the majority of) the Jews; cf. Romans 11:1-24."[13]

Based on Romans 16, the evidence allows the conclusion that there were Jews, both male and female, among the believers in Rome. Although Romans 14–15 suggest a certain degree of social interaction between Jews and non-Jews among the believers in Christ, there is no evidence for any organized church structure comprising Jews and non-Jews, nor for a central meeting place for all Christians. Rather, there existed a variety of house churches.

Brändle and Stegemann also raise questions about the identity of "all the Jews" in Acts 18:2 that had to leave Rome as a result of the Claudius decree. Most likely, they suggest, the text refers to "all Jews believing in Christ."[14] If some Jewish believers in Christ did remain in Rome, it would have created a very tense situation. Further, it is likely that the synagogues would have taken particular measures to distance themselves from the Gentile believers in Christ. Thus, when those who had been expelled are allowed to return to Rome after the death of Claudius, "social contacts existed (again) between the 'called of Jesus Christ' from the ἔθνη"[15] and these returning Jewish believers in Christ. The stage is now set for an explosive situation of tension and hostility, and it is to this situation that Paul must address himself in his letter to the Romans.

What can be said about the private lives of Jews and Christians in Rome? This, rather than the more usual focus on the public organizations of these two groups, takes center stage in **James S. Jeffers**'s work, "Jewish and Christian Families in First-Century Rome." The social location of the Jews and Roman Christians is among the city's poor and less respected

13. Rudolf Brändle and Ekkehard W. Stegemann, "The Formation of the First 'Christian Congregations' in Rome in the Context of the Jewish Congregations," 119.

14. Brändle and Stegemann, 122.

15. Brändle and Stegemann, 123.

foreigners. Although Christians lived in very small apartments or in *tabernae* where their shops were, the house congregations gathered in the first-floor "deluxe" apartments of fellow believers. "If Jews," remarks Jeffers, "were able to congregate in buildings with other Jews, they would have found it easier to practice the dietary and exclusivity demands of their religion. Jews who converted to Christianity would have found their apartment building a natural place to proselytize."[16]

Much like pagan Roman families, Jewish and Christian families were also nuclear in nature, comprising husband, wife, and two or three children at most. Given the fact that most Jewish and Christian marriages were not legal before Roman law in this period, a weakened patriarchy resulted: "husbands may have had less power over their families and the wives more autonomy (in some respects) than in the upper classes."[17] Consequently, these husbands could not rely on the state to reinforce the wife's obedience to the husband; to what extent did the synagogue or Christian house congregation provide encouragement? What the latter community did communicate, in sharp difference from the dominant Roman culture, was a single standard of sexual behavior for both men and women. As Jeffers is quick to acknowledge, his investigations into the nature of the Jewish and Christian families of first-century Rome are only initial probes into an area where much further study is required.

The social character of Roman Christianity is discussed from an insightful and unique perspective in **Carolyn Osiek**'s "The Oral World of Early Christianity in Rome: The Case of Hermas." Hermas himself testifies both to the deep Jewish roots of early Christianity in Rome and to its sociological diversity; he "represents that segment of the majority nonelite population that had some acquaintance with literacy but lived in a world predominantly characterized by orality."[18] The letter-form, on the one hand, represents literacy and thus the social power of an approximate 10-15 percent minority of the Christian population; the narrative of the *Shepherd,* on the other hand, best described as either oral communication or oral dictation, is directed toward the "low" majority culture of orality.

16. James S. Jeffers, "Jewish and Christian Families in First-Century Rome," 129.

17. Jeffers, 145.

18. Carolyn Osiek, "The Oral World of Early Christianity in Rome: The Case of Hermas," 151.

Hermas's audience is one of hearers, not readers, and this explains much of its singular literary form. Because of this peculiarity, the

> *Shepherd* reveals to us something of the thought world of the nonelites of early imperial Rome: direct, present-oriented, yet possessed of an eclectic imagination capable of bringing in bits and pieces of classical tradition: a beautiful woman at her bath, the mountains of Arcadia, allegorical virtues. It reveals, too, something of the piety of the ordinary early Christians of Rome, who were probably much like the author, and who could freely combine Greek and Jewish images and traditions into their new faith. They lived in an oral world little touched by the literate theological developments that preoccupied some of their more highly educated leaders, except in the brief references that occasionally seem to slip in and out of a document like this one.[19]

3. Developmental Studies

James C. Walters, in his essay "Romans, Jews, and Christians: The Impact of the Romans on Jewish/Christian Relations in First-Century Rome," is concerned about the evolving relations between Christians and non-Christian Jews in Rome and how their interactions during the Flavian period, especially under Domitian, were affected by Roman administrative interventions. In harmony with the studies of Lampe and others, it is urged that earliest Christianity in this city was an intra-Jewish phenomenon and that Claudius's decree creates a rupture between Christians and non-Christian Jews in Rome. As a result non-Christian Jews distance themselves from Christians, and this sets the stage for Roman moves against Christians, for example in 64 C.E., as non-Jews.

While the Julio-Claudian period is marked by the distancing of non-Christian Jews from Christians, in the Flavian period "the incentives for distancing belonged equally, if not especially, to the Christians."[20] Such factors as strong anti-Jewish feelings in Rome, resulting from the Jewish rebellion in 66 C.E. and Domitian's "witch-hunt" for Jewish tax evaders in the 90s, certainly contributed to the strain between the Jewish and Christian

19. Osiek, 167.

20. James C. Walters, "Romans, Jews, and Christians: The Impact of the Romans on Jewish/Christian Relations in First-Century Rome," 179.

communities, events that would hardly have encouraged positive interaction between these two groups in the capital. Walters finds support in 1 Peter for what he refers to as "the crystallizing of boundaries"[21] in the Flavian period. This same state of affairs is evident in *1 Clement* as well. Although there are manifold references to Jews and Judaism in the context of Scripture, no engagement with the Jewish communities of Rome contemporary to the writing of this document is suggested. "Whereas the common approach to the Old Testament for early Christian writers was to claim the traditions while attacking the Jewish institutions, Clement used both and attacked neither."[22] Thus, to speak of the "Jewishness" of Christianity in Rome during the time that *1 Clement* was written is not only unhelpful, but it is a "Jewishness" radically different from the situation to which Paul addresses his letter to the church at Rome.

The continuities and discontinuities in Roman Christianity in the period from Nero to Nerva are among the central concerns that are reviewed in **William L. Lane**'s essay "Social Perspectives on Roman Christianity during the Formative Years from Nero to Nerva: Romans, Hebrews, *1 Clement*." He maintains that it is possible to speak of a trajectory since there is a continuum in the development of Christianity from Romans to Hebrews to *1 Clement*.

Roman Christianity is anchored in Judaism, and it was successful in missionizing the Jewish Diaspora community in Rome, which was largely organized in the form of district synagogues. Romans is addressed to a troubled community in Rome, largely the result of Claudius's expulsion of synagogue and church leaders who had been responsible for the disruption of civil peace in the city, and the tensions resultant upon the return of these groups to a church that was now predominantly Gentile. The exegetical key to the letter is to be found in Romans 15:1-13; viz., that Roman Christians, comprised of Jews and Gentiles, are to welcome one another, just as they have been welcomed and accepted by Christ.

The household setting of Roman Christianity provides the social context for the development of leadership structures; many of these church hosts provided leadership, and there appears to be a close relationship between such patronage and developing leadership. While wealthy patrons contributed to the expansion of Christianity, those churches dependent on

21. Walters, 178.
22. Walters, 189.

the households of wealthy patrons also showed signs of fragmentation and dissension. In this way, the theme of reconciliation, referred to by Lane earlier, takes on expanded importance: "One of the purposes of Romans was to urge reconciliation between alienated constituencies of Jews and Gentiles, and to reinforce unity in a fragmented church denied the privilege of common worship."[23] This latter emphasis is not unimportant, given Lane's conviction that there is no evidence for a common meeting of the Christians in Rome, let alone a single church structure.

Hebrews provides independent testimony to Roman Christianity in the decade following Romans. In all likelihood it was directed to one of the several house churches in Rome, the roots of which lie in the life of a Hellenistic synagogue. The audience addressed in Hebrews is, however, distinguished from their leaders, from whom they appear to be alienated; thus the author of the writing has a decided interest in strengthening respect and obedience for those in positions of leadership. Hebrews 13 reveals that the existence of this leadership relies on charismatic endowment and service to the congregation, not on patronage, as was observed in Romans. Since there is not yet any hierarchical structure in the community, this leadership is derived entirely from the authority of the word proclaimed.

The social structure of this community reveals other tensions as well. The household setting continues to contribute to the fragmentation of the church and a "potential for strained relationships existed in the tension between the householder, who as host and patron held prerogatives of social authority, and those who had been recognized as leaders on the basis of charismatic endowment."[24] Given this type of situation, it becomes recognizable why *1 Clement,* a generation after Paul's death, gives evidence "of the institutionalizing forces at work."[25]

Although there are no specific references to house churches in *1 Clement,* the continued household setting of Roman Christianity is alluded to in *1 Clement* 1.2; 10.7; 11.1; 12.1, 3, especially by the emphasis placed on the household virtue of hospitality, and this suggestion is further supported by evidence from *Hermas.* While Christian communities in Rome are able to act and express themselves as a whole, they still consist of a network of

23. William L. Lane, "Social Perspectives on Roman Christianity during the Formative Years from Nero to Nerva: Romans, Hebrews, *1 Clement,*" 210.

24. Lane, 219.

25. Lane, 224.

groups meeting in the home of wealthy fellow believers. It should come as no surprise, therefore, that the writer of this letter remarks that Rome is troubled by the same spirit of competition and strife that plagues Corinth (*1 Clem.* 7.1). As a result, *1 Clement* is valuable for the study of Roman Christianity because it reflects the social setting and the structures of leadership in that city.

"The household structure of the church in Rome under the leadership of wealthy patrons," urges Lane, "would tend to promote a spirit of independence reflected in a variety of Christian cells differing from one another in varying degrees."[26] This situation, coupled with the void left by the death of the apostles and persecutions under Nero, not to mention more general societal pressures, all contributed to the development of more formal and centralized functions of leadership in Roman Christianity during the period of *1 Clement* and *Hermas.* Quite different from the period of leadership marked by charismatic endowment, distinct groups known as "bishops," "presbyters," and "deacons" are now invested with authority through the consent of the wider church in Rome. This maturation is understood as a reflection of the creative will of God, in whom all formal structures of ecclesiology are grounded. Even though formal criteria for leadership are being developed, there is "no explicit evidence for a hierarchy of leadership in the Roman church" according to *1 Clement.*[27] Although *1 Clement* breaks new ground and achieves a formal legitimation for certain ecclesiastical structures that were emerging at Rome (and in Corinth), Lane is insistent that there is a "basic continuity in the development of the church from Romans to *1 Clement.*"[28]

The final essay in this volume, "From Obscurity to Prominence: The Development of the Roman Church between Romans and *1 Clement,*" by **Chrys C. Caragounis,** challenges much of the consensus concerning the social situation of Roman Christianity presented in many of the contributions in this volume and elsewhere.[29] Thus, at key points, Caragounis's conclusions are in striking contrast especially to those of William Lane in the immediately preceding article. Caragounis challenges the thesis that the ecclesial structure in Rome consisted only of a series of house churches and

26. Lane, 238.
27. Lane, 231.
28. Lane, 237.
29. Karl P. Donfried, *The Romans Debate* (Peabody, Mass.: Hendrickson, 1991).

that there was, as a result, no unified ecclesial structure. Furthermore, he rejects the suggestion that the absence of the term ἐκκλησία in Romans supports this perspective. The failure of Paul to use the word ἐκκλησία in the prescript of Romans is irrelevant, as is shown by Philippians. Further, there is no objective evidence for the close proximity of earliest Roman Christianity with the synagogues. Finally, the reference to individual house churches in Romans 16 does not substantiate the thesis that "Roman Christianity consisted entirely of separate house groups. . . . On the contrary, house churches found in other cities than Rome existed side by side with the main city church, and their existence was not owing to divergencies in belief or to conflicting standpoints, but rather to zealous initiative to evangelize, to win one's neighbors."[30] And so, Caragounis argues vigorously, there was "but one church for each city."[31] Ultimately the interpreter of Romans will need to ask which description of the social situations of earliest Roman Christianity offered in this volume allows for the best understanding of the detailed references and issues addressed in the apostle's letter to the Christians in Rome.

Turning to *1 Clement,* Caragounis understands the structure of the Roman church in this period to be in exact continuity with that represented during the Pauline period; viz., one church and no evidence of any house groups. While agreeing with other interpreters in this volume and elsewhere that the Roman church in the late first century demonstrates a far more developed ecclesiastical structure and authority than is found in Romans, Caragounis places an unusual emphasis on the theme of "succession" in his interpretation of *1 Clement* 44.1-2.[32] It is this development, unique to *1 Clement,* that permits such an "imperious tone" in addressing the sister church of Corinth. In light of this challenge one will have to reread the document carefully to see whether it is "succession" or "order" that is being emphasized and, also, whether the tone is one of "imperiousness" or one of affection and humility (cf. 7.1). Is it really ecclesiastical authority or is it a "plea [ἔντευξις] for peace and harmony" (cf. 63.2), based on advice and persuasion, that motivates this letter (cf. 58.2)? And, finally, one will have to ask whether Caragounis does not perhaps present the options too uni-

30. Chrys C. Caragounis, "From Obscurity to Prominence: The Development of the Roman Church between Romans and *1 Clement,*" 255.

31. Caragounis, 256.

32. Caragounis, 271.

laterally. Even if one were to disagree with the type of ecclesiology championed by the author of *1 Clement,* can one simply state that the "letter has nothing new to offer"?[33] Further, can this new ecclesiology alone bear the burden of the conclusion that "*1 Clement* represents the Roman repudiation of Pauline Christianity and its definite embracing of a more static, sacerdotal type of Christianity, patterned on the OT and Judaism"?[34] Finally, will the majority of commentators agree that *1 Clement* represents "the triumph of the Jewish-Christian point of view over the Pauline understanding of Christianity, and this may imply also the long-term failure of Paul's letter among the Roman Christians"?[35]

33. Caragounis, 274.
34. Caragounis, 275.
35. Caragounis, 275.

PART 1

ARCHAEOLOGICAL AND EPIGRAPHIC STUDIES

CHAPTER 1

Augustan-Era Synagogues in Rome

Peter Richardson

1. Judaism in Rome in the First Century B.C.E.

Though Julius Caesar played a key role in assuring the relative freedom of synagogues in the Roman world, the most important figure in shaping the political situation of Diaspora synagogues was Augustus. Writing in about 41 C.E., Philo said Augustus

> did not expel them from Rome or deprive them of their Roman citizenship because they remembered their Jewish nationality also. He introduced no changes into their synagogues, he did not prevent them from meeting for the exposition of the Law, and he raised no objection to the offering of first fruits, . . . [and] if the distribution [of money or food in Rome] happened to be made on the Sabbath . . . he instructed the distributors to reserve the Jews' share . . . until the next day.[1]

Augustus's personal benevolence toward Jews in Rome was paralleled by Rome's institutional tolerance. Synagogues were viewed as collegia[2] by

1. Philo, *Embassy to Gaius* 156-58; cf. 311-17. Philo has an interest, of course, in presenting Augustus in generous terms, yet the impression he gives is confirmed by other evidence.

2. Peter Richardson, "Early Synagogues as Collegia in the Diaspora and Palestine," in *Voluntary Associations in the Ancient World*, ed. John S. Kloppenborg and S. G. Wilson (London: Routledge, 1996), 90-109.

Roman authorities in the first century B.C.E., yet their position was not altogether like that of other collegia. In 64 B.C.E. the Senate prohibited all collegia on principle because of the danger they posed to the state as private institutions;[3] in 58 B.C.E. collegia were permitted again (during the First Triumvirate);[4] in 56 B.C.E. the Senate again dissolved one specific class of collegia, political clubs. Sometime between 49 and 44 B.C.E. Julius Caesar prohibited all collegia empire-wide except the most ancient ones; one exception was Judaism, and this exception appears also to have been empire-wide. During the chaotic period of the civil wars the law against collegia again fell into abeyance. At some unknown date Augustus reenacted it, though synagogues continued to be exempted and to enjoy special privileges.

Jews had probably first reached Rome around the time of a delegation from Judah the Hasmonean to the Roman Senate in the mid–second century B.C.E. (1 Macc. 8:1-32; about 161 B.C.E.), establishing a connection between Rome and the Jews of Judea that was repeated on two later occasions (1 Macc. 12:16; 14:24; about 150 and 139 B.C.E., respectively). During this early period their position in Rome was somewhat tenuous. Numbers increased throughout the early first century B.C.E., accelerated by Pompey's conquests in the East, for many Jews from Syria and Judea came to Rome as slaves as a result of Pompey's settlement of the Eastern questions. Others, perhaps, came on their own because of the opportunities in Rome, following Rome's continued expansion in the East, as it assumed the position of the main Mediterranean power.

Though initially resident aliens and slaves, some Jews gradually acquired freedom and Roman citizenship. Most of the Jewish community

3. "Senatus consulto collegia sublata sunt, quae adversus rem publicam videbantur esse." See Wendy Cotter, "Collegia," in *Voluntary Associations.*

4. Direct insight into the character of the period emerges from Cicero's defense of Flaccus: "There follows that ill-will stemming from Jewish gold. . . . Although it is the practice annually to send gold in the name of Jews to Jerusalem from Italy and all the provinces, Flaccus ordered by an edict that it was forbidden to export it from the province of Asia. . . . 'But,' you will say, 'Gnaeus Pompey, when he captured Jerusalem, although a victor, touched not a thing in that shrine.' In this especially, as in many other matters, he acted wisely, for, in the case of such a suspicious and abusive state, he left no occasion for gossip on the part of his opponents. For I do not think that it was the religion of the Jews and of his enemies that acted as an obstacle to this very distinguished general, but rather his sense of honor" (*In Flacco* 66-69).

lived in the suburbs, initially Transtiberinum, later the Campus Martius and the Subura. By the first century B.C.E. a Jewish community had developed in nearby Ostia, Rome's port city.

Jewish communities such as those in Rome and Ostia, and in other places in Italy, thought of themselves as enclaves of Judaism in a foreign land; while many thought of Jews as outsiders, the state treated their religious activities as collegia or *thiasoi.* Yet they were progressively integrated into the Roman cultural context, to judge from later (second to third century C.E.) evidence, speaking Greek — and to a lesser extent Latin — and only to a very modest degree using Hebrew or Aramaic.[5] To non-Jews, some of their customs seemed odd, others barbaric: circumcision, avoidance of pork, paying a tax to the temple in Jerusalem, and so on.

2. Synagogues in Rome

It is hardly surprising to learn from inscriptions that there were Augustan-era synagogues in Rome. Given the benevolence of leaders such as Caesar and Augustus toward Jews, it was natural for Jews to have made out reasonably well in the imperial city and to have acted so as to cultivate their corporate life.[6] Thirteen synagogues are mentioned in inscriptions dating mostly to the second and third centuries B.C.E., though the synagogues themselves may have been older. The inscriptions are of little help in dating them, since they are typically burial inscriptions and refer only in passing to the name of the synagogue as the deceased's place of worship. None is a building inscription, referring to a benefaction for some building; consequently, the only chronological data that can be derived from the inscriptions have to do with the period of the synagogues' activities. For our purposes, the epigraphic conclusions only determine the period before which the synagogue must have been begun[7] and do not bear on the origins

5. See the essay by Graydon Snyder in this volume.

6. In his account of the events following the death of Herod, Josephus describes hearings before Augustus, attended by the members of the Roman Jewish community; see *War* 2.80. He numbers those participating at eight thousand, which would not be a huge exaggeration perhaps, if he meant adult male members of the Jewish community or some such. Their support went to the delegation arguing for Judean autonomy.

7. The inscriptions themselves can only be dated epigraphically; they do not contain absolute dates.

of the various synagogues. But the inscriptional evidence shows that the Jewish community was visible at the period of the burials and was organized in ways that would have underscored its appearance as a collegium.

It is likely that the earliest of these synagogues was a "Synagogue of the Hebrews," for two reasons:[8] (1) a similarly named synagogue at Corinth provides a sound analogy,[9] and (2) the inherent probability is that the generic name was earliest. Differentiating itself (linguistically?) from the "Synagogue of the Hebrews" was the "Synagogue of the Vernaculars," where Latin may have been spoken.[10]

In addition to these two that may have been named after language groups or places of origin (Vernaculars, Hebrews), Roman synagogues were named after persons (Augustus, Agrippa, and Volumnius), neighborhoods in Rome (Campus Martius, Subura, and Calcaria), and foreign cities (Elea, Tripolis, Skina [?], Arca in Lebanon). There is one quite uncertain designation, a synagogue that may have been named after another person (Herod, or someone with a similar name) or after a place (Rhodes has been proposed).

The evidence for synagogues in Rome is relatively late and imperfect, with neither descriptions of the synagogues themselves nor — with the important exception of nearby Ostia[11] — archaeological remains. Nevertheless, the existence of a large number of synagogues in Rome is impressive, in part because of the casual character of the allusions. When might they have originated? In the cases of those referring to neighborhoods or foreign places, no convincing arguments can be mounted with respect to the synagogue's date of foundation. In the cases of those named after persons, it is plausible to propose a date of origin close to the time of that person's influence.

Augustus's active role with respect to Judaism makes it unsurprising to find a "Synagogue of the Augustans" (or Augustesians).[12] Nothing is

8. On the Roman Synagogue of the Hebrews, see Harry J. Leon, *The Jews of Ancient Rome* (Peabody, Mass.: Hendrickson, 1995 [1960]).

9. The evidence from Corinth comes from a well-known reused lintel (probably from the second century; its original use was probably late first century) with a fraction of the inscription that reconstructed reads ΣΥΝΑΓΩΓΗ ΕΒΡΑΙΩΝ.

10. Synagogue of the Hebrews: *CII* 291, 317, 510, 535; Synagogue of the Vernaculars: *CII* 318, 383, 398, 494.

11. See Michael White's essay in this volume.

12. *CII* 284, 301, 338, 368, 416, 496; see the valuable discussion in Leon, *The Jews of Ancient Rome,* though in the end I disagree with some of his views.

known of the synagogue other than its name:[13] we cannot know certainly its date of origin, the reasons behind its honoring of Augustus, or Augustus's reasons for accepting this dedication. It seems plausible that the synagogue was so named in order to honor Augustus as the emperor under whom Judaism was able to flourish in the Diaspora. It is improbable that Augustus was the patron; it is unlikely that the synagogue was formed by his *libertini* (freed men).[14] The Jewish community must have proposed to name the synagogue while Augustus was still alive, otherwise the point would very largely be lost and permission would hardly have been granted. Since most of the inscriptions come from the Monteverde catacomb, the oldest in Rome, it is likely that the synagogue was located nearby in the oldest Jewish area in Transtiberinum. Two consequences would follow: (1) Augustus approved the naming of the synagogue, vividly underscoring his tolerance of Judaism and its institutions, even in Rome itself; (2) the Jewish community felt sufficient gratitude or had enough political wisdom to name the synagogue after the emperor. There is a partial Egyptian parallel to naming synagogues (or "houses of prayer," to be more correct for the Egyptian analogy): surviving inscriptions almost uniformly suggest the προσευχή was dedicated to one or another of the Ptolemies and consorts.[15]

Another synagogue, a "Synagogue of the Agrippans,"[16] was probably named after Augustus's chief lieutenant and heir, Marcus Vipsanius Agrippa, who died in 12 B.C.E.[17] In this instance, too, the origin of the synagogue was likely to have been in the late first century B.C.E. or during the first century C.E. If it was named after Marcus Agrippa, as I think likely, it would have been because he upheld Jewish privileges in the East, in Asia

13. The form of the name is actually "Augustesians," with minor variants in spelling. Cf. also "Agrippesians" and "Volumnesians."

14. The ending -ησιοι is a Latinism: R. Funk, *Greek Grammar of the New Testament* (Cambridge: Cambridge University Press, 1961), §5 (2), n. 4. It is equivalent to *-enses* in Latin, "belonging to, pertaining to." While it could signify *liberti*, it need not.

15. Richardson, "Early Synagogues," for the texts and comments upon them. They are conveniently displayed recently in David Noy and William Horbury, *Jewish Inscriptions of Graeco-Roman Egypt* (Cambridge: Cambridge University Press, 1992).

16. *CII* 365, 425, 503; again the form is "Agrippesians."

17. It is also possible that it was named after either Agrippa I or Agrippa II, both of whom had deep and lengthy contacts with Rome.

Minor particularly.[18] Like the synagogue of the Augustans, the synagogue of the Agrippans likely stood in the Transtiberinum.

A third synagogue, a "Synagogue of the Volumnians,"[19] was named after Volumnius, a name that Josephus mentions, though he remains a hazy figure (*War* 1.535-42; *Ant.* 16.277-83, 344-69). While Josephus seems to have thought there were two of them, there was probably only one, a military tribune who acted in close association with the governor of Syria. He agreed with Herod's punitive expedition against Syllaeus the Nabatean in 9 B.C.E., and he carried Herod's letter to Augustus about his sons Alexander and Aristobulus. Subsequently Volumnius was present at their trial in Berytus, urging a "pitiless sentence," according to Josephus. So Josephus knows of a Volumnius whose role intersected with the interests of the Jewish community. It is uncertain whether we can identify the Volumnius of the inscriptions with the tribune of Syria from 9 to 7 B.C.E., however; there were other important persons of the same name referred to in the ancient sources. An argument in favor of the association is that no other of the several known Volumnii had even this degree of contact with Jews, so far as can be ascertained. If this Volumnius was the tribune of Syria, there was a third synagogue in Rome named after a person involved in Jewish history.[20] The origin of this synagogue may also have been contemporary with the other two. Since three of the four inscriptions came from the Monteverde catacombs, it was probably located in Transtiberinum and dated from the end of the first century B.C.E. or early first century C.E.

In sum, the earliest synagogue in Rome was simply the "Synagogue of the Hebrews." Two other synagogues were named after the highest officials in the land, Augustus and Agrippa, who together had been instrumental in alleviating the conditions of Jews in the Diaspora. It is more reasonable to imagine that the Jewish community honored the members

18. Peter Richardson, *Herod, King of the Jews and Friend of the Romans* (Columbia: University of South Carolina Press, 1996). See also Peter Richardson, "Herod's Architectural-Religious Policy in the Diaspora," in *Second Temple Studies: The Roman Period,* ed. John Halligan and Philip Davies (Sheffield: JSOT Press, forthcoming).

19. *CII* 343, 402, 417, 523; again the form in three cases is "Volumnesians," in the fourth it is *Bolumni* (in Latin).

20. Leon, *The Jews of Ancient Rome,* has argued vigorously that no Jewish community in Rome would name a synagogue after one who took part in the execution of Herod's two sons. On the contrary, however, Volumnius might be honored for strongly supporting the cause of Judea and Herod against Nabatea and Syllaeus.

of the imperial family than that the synagogues were named after freedmen who were attached to the imperial household. In addition, a synagogue may have been named after Volumnius, tribune of Syria. All four synagogues originate in the period just before or just after the turn of the eras; all four were probably located in the suburb across the Tiber. Jews in Rome at the time of Herod's death would have been attached to these synagogues; some of the debates over Judean affairs in 4 B.C.E. would have been conducted there.

I have tacitly assumed in the above discussion that these early synagogues were in fact buildings, not communities of Jews meeting informally together. The evidence is strong for buildings, especially in the Diaspora, to house the varied activities of Jewish communities; the earliest known *buildings* go back to the late third century B.C.E. in Egypt. Others are attested in second- and first-century-B.C.E. contexts elsewhere in the Diaspora. It is only in the late first century B.C.E. and first century C.E. that synagogue structures are found in Palestine.[21] The synagogue in Ostia has a first- or a second-century level; while it is possible to imagine a situation in which Ostia could have a synagogue building while Rome did not, it seems very unlikely; the Ostia synagogue supports the likelihood of synagogue buildings in Rome, perhaps as many as four or five, at this relatively early period.

3. A Synagogue of the Herodians?

A fragmentary inscription from the Roman catacombs that may refer to a "Synagogue of the Herodians"[22] is more debatable and the arguments about it more vigorous and more convoluted. The question that interests me especially and that bears on this present analysis is whether it alludes to a synagogue named after Herod the Great, and if so, what its significance is. It was found on a large broken marble slab from the Via Appia with

21. Richardson, "Early Synagogues," for the evidence and discussion. I have in mind here the contrary argument of Howard Clark Kee, "The Transformation of the Synagogue after 70 C.E.: Its Import for Early Christianity," *NTS* 36 (1990): 1-24; see the refutation by Rainer Riesner, "Synagogues in Jerusalem," in *The Book of Acts in Its Palestinian Setting*, ed. Richard Bauckham, The Book of Acts in Its First-Century Setting, vol. 4 (Grand Rapids: Wm. B. Eerdmans Publishing Co., 1995), 179-211.

22. *CII* 173.

unusually large lettering for these inscriptions.[23] Only a portion of the text remains, giving parts of four lines, on three of which writing survives:

. . .]X X X
. . .]ΓΩΓΗϹ
. . .]ΡΟΔΙΩΝ
. . .]ΕΥΛΟΓΙΑΠΑϹΙ

The debate over the inscription has taken three forms, though only two seem actively held today. On the one hand, Leon, followed now by David Noy in the most recent publication of the inscription,[24] argues for a personal name, some variant on "Rhodion"; on the other, J.-B. Frey, followed by the most recent museum catalogue,[25] accepts the reference to Herod. A third view proposes to read it as a reference to a place name, specifically the island of Rhodes.[26] The arguments are fairly evenly balanced, and whatever conclusion one comes to cannot be especially secure. I conclude that it is likelier than not to refer to a synagogue of Herodians, and in what follows I offer a rereading of the inscription, with reasons for that conclusion.

1. None of the discussions to date allude to the first line with the three "X's." I begin with two preliminary observations: first, I can find no other inscription in *CII* (nor in Noy's volumes) with a similar device;[27] second, there are cases where the first line of the inscription is a highlighted name and other cases where the first line is bracketed by iconographic devices of one kind or another.[28] I suggest that one of the keys to the correct

23. The slab is 57 cm. long by 45 cm. high. The letters vary from 6 to 9 cm. in height (2½" to 3½"); the size of the lettering is unequaled in the inscriptions from this location.

24. David Noy, *Jewish Inscriptions of Western Europe*, vol. 1 (Cambridge: Cambridge University Press, 1993).

25. Frey, in *CII;* Joan Goodnick Westenholz, *The Jewish Presence in Ancient Rome* (Jerusalem: Bible Lands Museum, 1995).

26. Apparently E. Schürer once held this view; the new Schürer does not deal with this issue but rejects a synagogue of the Herodians. See Emil Schürer, *The History of the Jewish People in the Age of Jesus Christ,* rev. ed., vol. 3.1 (Edinburgh: T. & T. Clark, 1986), 73-81, 97-98.

27. Cf. *CII* 491, however.

28. Highlighted names: *CII* 222, 229, 252, 269, 298, 460 (in each case the name occupies the first line and is clearly intended to do so); decorated ends of first lines: *CII* 213, more dramatically 283, 299, 340, 354 (generally decoration comes at the bottom or in the middle, sometimes right at the top).

reading of the inscription is to read the "X's" as a design motif decorating the first line, at both ends, with a name between either in the dative[29] or, more likely, in the nominative.[30] The first line, I suppose, was thus:

X X X NAME X X X

This supposition helps to establish the limits for the size of the original marble slab (the first line may — but need not — have been centered; it need only have been prominent);[31] it was probably just over a meter wide.

2. Several inscriptions that highlight the name in one line go on in the next to name a position: e.g., ἄρχων, γερουσιάρχης, γραμματεύς, also in the nominative,[32] and this analogy works well here. Line 2 must have read something such as ἄρχων (τῆς) συναγωγῆς, γραμματεύς (τῆς) συναγωγῆς, or πατήρ (τῆς) συναγωγῆς.[33] Using the first as an example, notice how the relative position of the "X's" and the surviving letters -γωγης is just about right; lines 1 and 2 then read:

X X X NAME X X X
[αρχωντησσυνα]ΓΩΓΗC

3. Immediately before the letter *rho* in]ΡΟΔΙΩΝ is the vertical stroke of either an *iota* or an *êta*.[34] Leon reads an *iota* and interprets it as the final letter in a dative of the deceased's name, while he takes "Rhodion" as the name of the donor setting up the inscription.[35] Frey reads *êta* and recon-

29. Though most gravestones begin with ἐνθάδε κειτε, it is not rare to find inscriptions beginning with a name in the dative.

30. No inscription in *CII* has this exact combination of name between decorative elements. But, as just noted, each part is fairly commonly found.

31. Note especially the space available for the first line relative to the right side and bottom.

32. *CII* 221, 277, 284, 353.

33. The genitive of συναγωγή requires some word such as ἄρχῶν before it; supplying this word establishes the line length (which then fits neatly with the definite article τῶν in the next line).

34. Examination of the photograph of the inscription and comparison of the vertical stroke and serifs with the other *iotas* (there are two) and the *êta* (only one) leads to the conclusion that the missing letter is likelier to be an *êta*. I have not been able to examine the inscription itself.

35. H. J. Leon, "The Synagogue of the Herodians," in *JAOS* 49 (1929): 318-21.

structs the middle line of text as ΗΡΟΔΙΩΝ. Against Frey's reconstruction are two difficulties. First, while one might have expected ἡρωδείων, an influence from the Latin and the way the name was pronounced might well give ἡροδείων.[36] Second, in the surviving letters the first "O" is an *omicron,* not an *omega,* as "Herodians" (ἡρωδίων) would require.[37] Two facts soften this latter difficulty: first, one Augustus inscription misspells his name,[38] so the misspelling of Herod — in Rome a less commonly heard name — is not much of a problem; second, there is evidence that the name Herod was in fact occasionally spelled in this fashion.[39] While it is impossible to prove that there has been a similar error here, it is not implausible.

Following Frey, then, line 3 should be completed with a reference to "the Herodians," in the genitive plural. This reading does not fill the whole line, and it is obvious that the carver was not under any pressure to squeeze his letters at the end of line 3. This suggests strongly a space on the left,[40] which I propose to fill with a menorah (a symbol very frequently found, and not infrequently on the lower left) or some such, following Frey's suggestion and numerous examples in the corpus.[41]

4. Line 4 preserves the final encomium, but it can easily be seen that the carver misjudged his line length and had to squeeze the letters as he neared the end. My reconstruction proposes reference to the deceased's age before the final blessing, a standard feature that would account for the decreasing space of the letters at the end of the line.[42] The final blessing is

36. This is analogous to the Latinisms in "Augustesians" and "Agrippesians." It is worth noting that the form is not "Herodesians," parallel to the other named synagogues, suggesting perhaps a different relationship to Herod.

37. Leon argues strongly against this view.

38. Since the Greek of the inscriptions is barbarous, a misspelling is not unexpected. The misspelling of "Augustus" is found in *CII* 368; there is also a misspelling of "Volumnius" in 417.

39. For example, a coin type of Herod of Chalcis has the name misspelled in the same way with an omicron; illustration in A. Reifenberg, *Ancient Jewish Coins,* 3rd ed. (Jerusalem: Rubin Mass, 1963), #70 (p. 47) and plate V. One inscription also misspells Herod's name.

40. There is generous spacing on lines 2 and 3, which speaks against Leon's argument for long lines. Line 4 is, however, very squeezed, indicating that the left edge of the text is constrained in some way, as by a drawing of some sort.

41. For the layout, with a menorah on the lower left, see *CII* 396; see also 97, 111, 150, 161, 193, and less clearly, 50, 51, 89.

42. See also *CII* 176.

usually "in peace your sleep"; the simple form of blessing found here, though not unique, is very rare. In over five hundred inscriptions there is only one that is somewhat similar (*CII* 204);[43] it, too, has a menorah.[44] This suggests:

ετη??]ΕΥΛΟΓΙΑ ΠΑCΙ

The result of these observations is a revised reconstruction of the missing portion of the text (the empty space on the lower left would be occupied by a drawing of a menorah or some such Jewish symbol).

X X X name X X X	X X X n a m e X X X
[αρχωντησσυνα] ΓΩΓΗC	[ruler of the syna]gogue
[τωνη] ΡΟΔΙΩΝ	[of the He]rodians
[ετη??] ΕΥΛΟΓΙΑΠΑCΙ	[age??] A blessing to all

This reconstruction gives a grammatically correct and sensible result without straining the evidence, as Frey, Leon, and Noy all must do.[45] The result conforms in all its details to other evidence from the same catacombs. If this reasoning is correct, a fourth person was honored in an early synagogue inscription in Rome — Herod the Great, who was influential in Diaspora affairs and familiar to the Roman Jewish community. This would then be the only known dedication of a synagogue to Herod,[46] and it would add an otherwise unknown element to his portrait.[47] Why the Roman

43. See also *CII* 652, 694, and 515 — a gold glass inscription.

44. A few inscriptions have lettering that can be compared to this: *CII* 155, 196, 365, 440, among others; cf. also 417.

45. Attractive as Frey's reconstruction is, referring to a "place of the synagogue of the Herodians," it would be unparalleled and poses problems of reconstruction and layout. Leon's views require too large a slab.

46. Richardson, *Herod,* chap. 8; Richardson, "Herod's Architectural-Religious Policy."

47. I have followed the usual view that Herod never built a synagogue himself, though it is possible that the room below the present synagogue at Masada was also a synagogue, a Herodian one. For arguments against, see Ehud Netzer, *Masada III* (Jerusalem: Israel Exploration Society, 1991). Attention is now being paid to Herodian baths as indicative of Herod's religious attitudes; the baths at both Masada and Cypros include cold pools that may have functioned as *mikvaoth.* If so, his religious views were more traditional than is usually thought.

community honored him in this way, especially in light of their antipathy to him (according to Josephus) following his death, is less clear. The simplest view is that he was well known, was active on behalf of Diaspora Jews, and was seen as king of all Jews everywhere.[48]

4. Augustus, Marcus Agrippa, and Herod

This proposal about "Herodians" adds a fifth late-first-century-B.C.E. synagogue to the other four from the same period. At least three were named after persons instrumental in bettering the conditions of Jews in the Diaspora. These three were good friends who knew each other well and were well disposed to the maintenance of the Jewish communities.[49] This may not be incidental, for the naming of synagogues after these high-status individuals comes exactly at the time when Jewish privileges were a matter of debate or dispute.[50] Since other evidence links Augustus, Agrippa, and Herod to the welfare of the Diaspora, the evidence is mutually confirming.[51]

The persons most active in supporting Jewish rights in the Diaspora correlate closely with the named synagogues in Rome. Roman Judaism's actions in naming synagogues after Augustus, Agrippa, and Herod (and possibly Volumnius should be included) was a deliberately conceived response to the important roles these persons played in guaranteeing the rights and privileges of the various Jewish communities.

48. It is conceivable that even if the burial inscription has been correctly reconstructed and that it refers to a Herod, that Herod could be other than Herod the Great — e.g., Agrippa I or II. In such a case, the number of synagogues might fall by one, since the synagogue of the Agrippans could also refer to a synagogue named after Agrippa I or II. Either or both of these conclusions would not materially affect the main point of this paper.

49. Josephus comments, exaggeratedly, that Herod was Augustus's best friend after Agrippa, and Herod was Agrippa's best friend after Augustus.

50. The collections of decrees in Josephus show that many features of Jewish Diaspora life were controversial and unpopular; there must have been unhappiness at the special concessions given to the Jewish communities, especially those dealt with repeatedly in the decrees, such as exemption from military service.

51. This situation was not unique to the Diaspora or to the period of Augustus. It is reported that a second-century synagogue in the Galilee (at Qatzyon) had a mosaic inscription on the floor referring to the emperor.

5. Conclusion

The synagogues in Rome that I have discussed attest the vigor of the Jewish community at the end of the first century B.C.E. and the beginning of the first century C.E. The community was large enough to have (probably) five synagogues in the capital city. It was self-confident enough and sufficiently closely connected politically that it named two of these five after the most powerful men in Rome, Augustus and his son-in-law Marcus Agrippa.[52] Another honored Herod, king of Jews; a fourth may have referred to a tribune of Syria; the fifth was the original synagogue of Hebrews.

There may have been more, though most of the other eight synagogues probably developed in the second and third centuries C.E. Despite the paucity of evidence, especially the total absence of synagogue remains, the result is more impressive than is usually realized. Rome, consistent with its size and diversity, had a substantial Jewish population, which was served by a number of synagogues datable to the first century B.C.E. and first century C.E. This evidence dovetails neatly with the other evidence for Diaspora synagogues and reinforces the view that synagogues developed in the Mediterranean Diaspora under the benign influence of Augustus, Marcus Agrippa, and King Herod.[53]

52. It should be observed that there is no synagogue of the Tiberians or Claudians or Neronians or Vespasians. The ones who are honored are exactly the persons who, on historical grounds, we should expect to have been honored.

53. While the physical remains of pre-70 or pre-100-C.E. synagogues are still relatively slim, they are growing. What is most intriguing about them is that the evidence is growing both in the homeland and in the Diaspora.

CHAPTER 2

Synagogue and Society in Imperial Ostia: Archaeological and Epigraphic Evidence

L. Michael White

> It is now generally acknowledged that no one can understand the peculiar form of early Christianity we call Pauline without first gaining some understanding of contemporaneous Judaism. But what kind of Judaism?[1]

1. Jewish Groups in Rome and Ostia: "What Kind of Judaism?"

The purpose of this study is to present and analyze evidence for the social location and organization of Jewish groups in the environs of Rome, specifically evidence from the port city of Ostia. It has generally been recognized that the presence of a thriving Jewish community in Rome, as elsewhere in the eastern Mediterranean, is a crucial element to understanding developments in the Christian movement throughout the first centuries. Such discussions have become more common in recent studies.[2] Still, one will

1. Wayne A. Meeks, *The First Urban Christians* (New Haven: Yale University Press, 1983), 32.

2. So, for example, E. P. Sanders, *Paul, the Law, and the Jewish People* (Philadelphia: Fortress, 1983), 183-90; Peter J. Tomson, *Paul and the Jewish Law,* CRINT III.1 (Assen: Van Gorcum; Minneapolis: Fortress, 1990), 51-55; Philip F. Essler, *Community and Gospel in Luke-Acts,* SNTS-MS 57 (Cambridge: Cambridge University Press, 1987),

look long and hard in New Testament and early Christian studies for direct discussion of the primary data for the Jewish communities of urban Rome.

This omission is perhaps a natural result of the nonliterary nature of the evidence and the previous traditions of literary interpretation. The nonliterary evidence for early Judaism in the city of Rome consists almost exclusively of epigraphic remains, predominantly funerary inscriptions. The basic collection and discussion of these materials were drawn primarily from J.-B. Frey's *Corpus Inscriptionum Iudaicarum*.[3] A systematic analysis of the 534 Jewish inscriptions from Rome was first done by H. J. Leon in 1960.[4] Since then considerable new work has been done in terms of updating, revising, and expanding the epigraphic collection for the Jews of ancient Rome.[5] To date, however, there has been no systematic treatment of the Ostian evidence.

A limitation of using either Frey's or Leon's work arises from the fact that no identifiable architectural remains of a synagogue have ever been found in the city of Rome, and the discovery of the synagogue building at Ostia (1961) came only after their work was complete. Thus, while Leon identified eleven (and possibly fourteen) synagogue communities from the inscriptions, we know little of their actual social setting.[6] Most of what we can guess comes from conjectures based on the names of the groups, some hints as to topographical location within the city, and other prosopographic

30-34, 65-70, and passim; Peter Lampe, *Die stadtrömischen Christen in den ersten beiden Jahrhunderten,* WUNT 2/18 (Tübingen: Mohr-Siebeck, 1987), 26-29.

3. J.-B. Frey, *Corpus Inscriptionum Iudaicarum,* 2 vols. (Rome: Pontificio Instituto di Archeologia Cristiana, 1936); hereafter cited as *CII.* For Rome see esp. 1:lvi-cxvii. See also George La Piana, "Foreign Groups in Rome during the First Centuries of the Empire," *HTR* 20 (1927): 183-403, esp. 341-93.

4. Harry Joshua Leon, *The Jews of Ancient Rome* (Peabody, Mass.: Hendrickson, 1995 [1960]), 73-74. Leon's groundbreaking work was done while he was professor and chair of classics at the University of Texas at Austin.

5. For example, the prolegomenon and corrections to the second edition of *CII,* vol. 1, ed. Baruch Lifshitz (New York: KTAV, 1975), 21-97; cf. Lawrence H. Kant, "Jewish Inscriptions in Greek and Latin," *ANRW* II.20.2:672-713; P. W. van der Horst, *Ancient Jewish Epitaphs* (Kampen: Kok-Pharos, 1991). The most recent work has been done by Leonard V. Rutgers, "Archaeological Evidence for the Interaction of Jews and Non-Jews in Late Antiquity," *AJA* 96 (1992): 101-18, and *The Jews in Late Ancient Rome: Evidence of Cultural Interaction in the Roman Diaspora* (Leiden: E. J. Brill, 1995), passim.

6. Leon, *The Jews of Ancient Rome,* 135-66. On the question of certainty see esp. 159-65 (though corrected to ten by van der Horst; see n. 8 below).

data in the inscriptions. From these clues Leon derived significant information for the demographic features of the Jewish population of Rome as well as titles to be used in reconstructing the organization of the synagogues.[7] Nonetheless, the tendency has been to read later rabbinic or talmudic norms into these materials, norms not necessarily operative in the Diaspora of the early to middle Principate.[8] When archaeological remains of synagogue buildings have been found in other areas of the Diaspora, they have often run counter to expectations based solely on supposed rabbinic norms. So, too, new work has brought revisions and new insights, especially with recent research into social world studies.

Most notably, this new research has opened again debates over social and cultural issues in Diaspora communities. The degree to which such Jewish groups participated in or were acculturated to the social life of Roman cities has been a continuing question sparked especially by the work of E. R. Goodenough and others.[9] When Jonathan Z. Smith surveyed the Jewish inscriptions from Rome (alongside those from Venosa and Beth Shearim), he concluded that some traditional marks of Jewishness, such as circumcision, were noticeably lacking in their taxonomy of self-definition.[10] Other studies have shown that traditional assumptions regarding the role and status of women do not apply, particularly in the Diaspora. Jewish women are seen in active social leadership positions within the synagogue and participating in larger arenas of social life.[11] These new historical and social perspectives, seen

7. Leon, *The Jews of Ancient Rome,* 167-94, 229-56.

8. Cf. van der Horst, 73-84, and esp. 88-89; Kant, 2:694.

9. E. R. Goodenough, *Jewish Symbols in the Graeco-Roman Period,* 13 vols. (New York: Bollingen, 1952-65), esp. vols. 1-3.

10. Jonathan Z. Smith, "Fences and Neighbors: Some Contours of Early Judaism," in *Approaches to Ancient Judaism,* ed. W. S. Green, vol. 2, BJS (Missoula: Scholars Press, 1980), 1-25; reprinted in Smith's *Imagining Religion: From Babylon to Jonestown* (Chicago: University of Chicago Press, 1982), 1-18.

11. Bernadette J. Brooten, *Women Leaders in the Ancient Synagogue: Inscriptional Evidence and Background Issues,* BJS 36 (Chico: Scholars Press, 1982), passim, for Rome, esp. 58-62, 68-70, 75-76; cf. Ross S. Kraemer, "A New Inscription from Malta and the Question of Women Elders in Diaspora Jewish Communities," *HTR* 78 (1986): 431-38; "Non-Literary Evidence for Jewish Women in Rome and Egypt," *Helios* 13 (1986): 85-101; cf. van der Horst, 102-9. In his recent work, however, Leonard Rutgers has questioned some of Brooten's conclusions regarding the nature of this "leadership." Nonetheless, it is clear that women are seen in much more prominent social positions within the Roman Jewish congregations, and this includes significant patronage.

especially through the epigraphic evidence, have been substantiated further with new discoveries and analysis of synagogue buildings from the Diaspora. Here, too, traditional assumptions have been significantly revised in the light of the social interaction of these synagogue communities with their local environments.[12] What has become increasingly clear is that traditional assumptions of the static nature of Diaspora Judaism, whether in relation to the later development of the rabbinic tradition or in relation to the emergence of the Christian movement, must be discarded. Instead, we see a diverse and socially active Jewish life in the Diaspora, where the competing social and cultural pressures of self-definition and assimilation are held in a creative tension by local congregations.

My own earlier work on Rome and Ostia came out of this revisionist perspective. It focused on social factors in the development of places of worship with special attention to the Diaspora synagogues and the origins of Christian architecture.[13] Two main conclusions arise from this work. The first concerns the fact that many of the smaller "foreign" religious groups

12. See especially Eric M. Meyers and Alf Thomas Kraabel, "Archaeology, Iconography, and Nonliterary Written Remains," in *Early Judaism and Its Modern Interpreters*, ed. R. A. Nickelsburg and G. W. E. Nickelsburg, SBLCP (Atlanta: Scholars Press, 1986), 175-210; A. T. Kraabel, "Impact of the Discovery of the Sardis Synagogue," in *Sardis from Prehistoric to Roman Times: Results of the Archaeological Exploration of Sardis, 1958-1975*, ed. G. M. A. Hanfmann (Cambridge: Harvard University Press, 1983), 178-90; "The Roman Diaspora: Six Questionable Assumptions," in *Essays in Honor of Yigael Yadin*, ed. G. Vermes and J. Neusner (*JJS* 33, nos. 1-2 [1982]), 445-64; "The Diaspora Synagogue: Archaeological and Epigraphic Evidence Since Sukenik," in *ANRW* II.19.1 (1979), 477-510; "The Social Systems of Six Diaspora Synagogues," in *Ancient Synagogues, the State of Research*, ed. J. Gutmann, BJS 22 (Chico: Scholars Press, 1981), 79-93; "Unity and Diversity among Diaspora Synagogues," in *The Synagogue in Late Antiquity*, ed. L. I. Levine (Philadelphia: ASOR, 1987), 49-60; Andrew R. Seager, "Ancient Synagogue Architecture: An Overview," in *Ancient Synagogues*, ed. Gutmann, 39-48; L. Michael White, "The Delos Synagogue Revisited: Recent Fieldwork in the Graeco-Roman Diaspora," *HTR* 80 (1987): 133-66. Most recently see J. Andrew Overman and Robert S. Mclennan, eds., *Diaspora Jews and Judaism: Essays in Honor of, and in Dialogue with, A. T. Kraabel* (Atlanta: Scholars Press, 1992), passim (this work contains many of the previously published articles of Kraabel cited above), and Dan Urman and Paul V. M. Flesher, eds., *Ancient Synagogues: Historical Analysis and Archaeological Discovery* (Leiden: E. J. Brill, 1995), passim.

13. See my *Building God's House in the Roman World: Architectural Adaptation among Pagans, Jews, and Christians* (Baltimore: Johns Hopkins University Press, 1990), esp. 60-101; "The Delos Synagogue Revisited"; and the volume cited in n. 17 below.

that moved into the Roman world (and here I would also include groups other than Jews or Christians, such as Mithraists) tended to adapt existing buildings, especially homes and other nonpublic architecture, for their religious usage. This observation is, of course, directly related to the development of the house church known from numerous New Testament texts, but it is significant for our understanding of early Diaspora Judaism as well. For the evidence indicates that most, if not all, of the earliest synagogues were renovated from existing buildings, usually houses. Of course, the best-known example is Dura-Europos. My study also suggests that this rather common process of architectural adaptation and renovation has significant social implications. Hence, the second main conclusion to note here in passing is the role of private patrons in sponsoring the social progress as well as the architectural adaptation within these religious groups.

The Ostia synagogue building is of special importance in this light, since it is the only synagogue site from the Diaspora for which it has been claimed that the building was a *de novo* construction dating from the first century C.E. and designed explicitly for Jewish usage.[14] As part of my ongoing fieldwork, therefore, I undertook a new investigation of the Ostia remains. In the present study I will examine the archaeological evidence in three parts. First, I will present an analysis of the physical remains of the synagogue structure and suggest an architectural and social history of the building. Second, I will examine the two Jewish inscriptions from Ostia both epigraphically and in relation to the synagogue structure. Third, with some contextual clues drawn from other inscriptional evidence of proximate Italian provenance, I will draw some conclusions from the epigraphy about the nature, the social location, and the development of the Ostian Jewish community.

2. Archaeological Analysis of the Ostia Synagogue Building

The architectural remains of the synagogue were first unearthed in 1961 during construction on the main expressway (Via della Scafa) leading from Rome to Fiumicino and Leonardo da Vinci Airport. Ironically, this construc-

14. This was the conclusion reached by the principal Italian excavator, Maria Floriani Squarciapino (see n. 15 below), and this conclusion was followed by Kraabel in his earlier work on this subject (cf. "The Diaspora Synagogue," *ANRW* II.19.1:498).

tion, originally planned to skirt the archaeological zone of Ostia Antica, resulted in expanding it. The new finds lay in a previously unexcavated area several hundred meters south of the excavated quarter of suburban sprawl outside the western or Porta Marina gate (Reg. IV. viii-x). (See fig. 1.) The building stood near the ancient shoreline and faced onto the Via Severiana, the main Roman road running south from Portus, across the Isola Sacra, to the Porta Marina gate of Ostia, and on to Laurentium. Excavation of the site was conducted through 1962 under the direction of Maria Floriani Squarciapino, then superintendent of the Ostia Excavations.[15] Unfortunately, since the original report of the finds little further analysis (and no final excavation report) has been published. Continued excavation work at Ostia (especially during 1977-78) has uncovered other buildings along the Via Severiana in the area between the synagogue site and the extramural (in Italian, *f.l.m.*) quarter of the Porta Marina gate.[16] (See fig. 2.) Perhaps because none of these other buildings has exhibited explicitly Jewish artifactual remains or identification, no further attempts have been made to correlate the new discoveries with our understanding of the architectural and social makeup of this area of Ostia.

15. The primary publications of the excavations to date are as follows: Preliminary reports of the discovery were made by Maria Floriani Squarciapino, "La sinagoga di Ostia," *Bolletino d'Arte* (1961): 326-37; "La sinagoga recentemente scoperta ad Ostia," *Rendiconti della Pontificia Accademia Romana di Archeologia,* ser. 3, 34 (1961-62); "Die Synagoge von Ostia antica," *Raggi: Zeitschrift für Kunstgeschichte und Archäologie* 4 (1962): 1-8; and H. L. Hempel, "Synagogensfunde in Ostia Antica," *ZAW* 74 (1962): 72-73. The most complete report (following the 1962 season) is that of M. Floriani Squarciapino, "La sinogaga di Ostia: secondo campagna di scavo," in *Atti di VI° Congresso internazionale di archeologia cristiana,* 1962 (Rome: Pontifical Press, 1965), 299-315; also published as *La sinagoga di Ostia* (Rome, 1964); an extensive English summary of this same article was published as "The Synagogue at Ostia," *Archeology* 16 (1963): 194-203 (but it is weak in documentation and detail). Other brief reports of the find were made by Russell Meiggs, *Roman Ostia,* 2nd ed. (Oxford: Clarendon, 1973), 587-89; Rachel Wischnitzer, *The Architecture of the European Synagogue* (Philadelphia: Jewish Publication Society, 1974), 5-7 (and fig. 3); and Hershel Shanks, *Judaism in Stone: The Archaeology of Ancient Synagogues* (New York: Harper, 1979), 162-69; however, these are generally derivative of the summary in *Archeology* and are full of errors. The most complete discussion based on Squarciapino's reports after the second season (noted above) is that of A. T. Kraabel, "The Diaspora Synagogue," *ANRW* II.19.1 (1979), 497-500. The reference system for Ostia divides the city into five regions (I-V), with each block in lowercase Roman numerals and each building in Arabic numerals.

16. See Carlo Pavolini, "OSTIA (Roma): Saggi lungo la via Severiana," in *Notizie degli Scavi di Antichità* VIII.35 (1981), 115-43. Figure 2 is taken from Pavolini's figure 1.

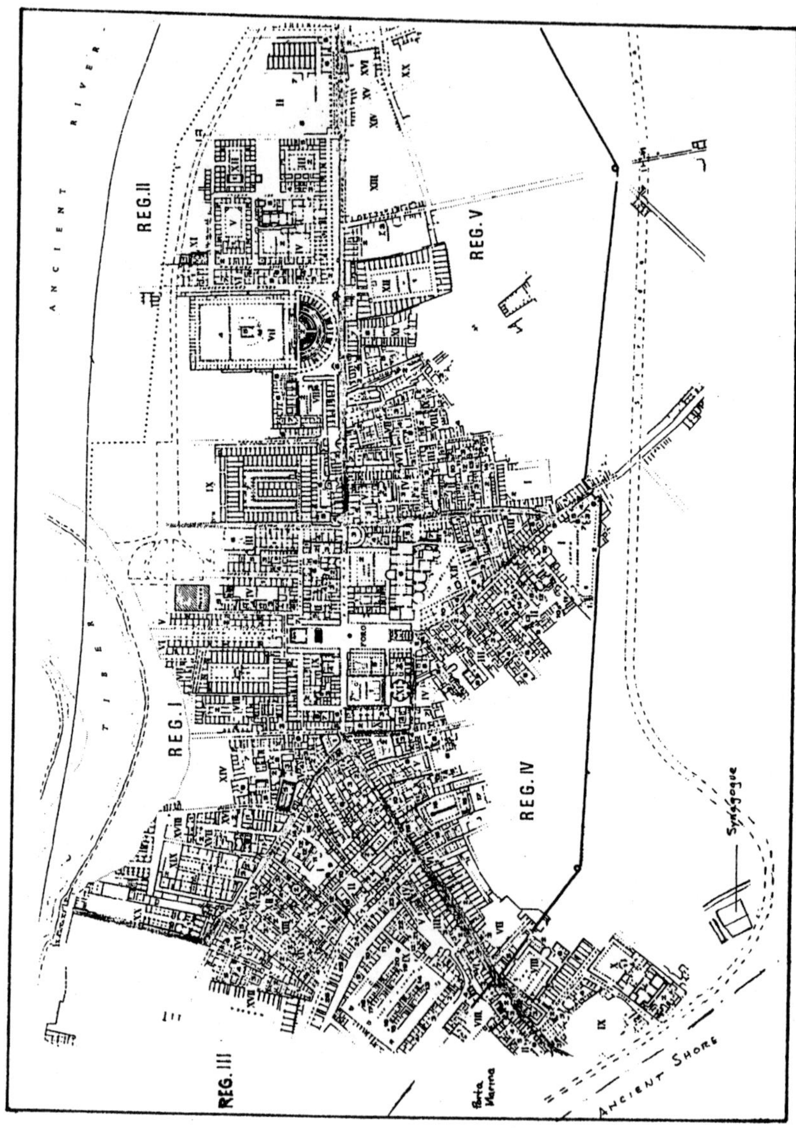

Figure 1. Ostia. General Plan of the Archaeological Zone.

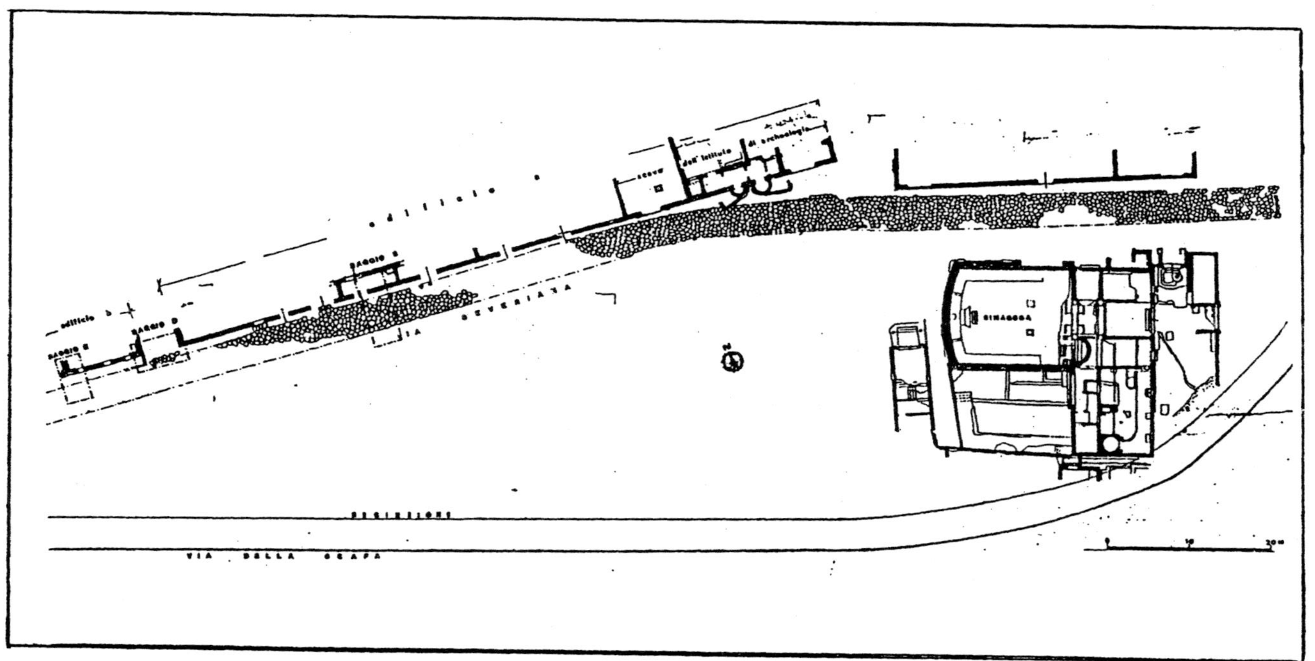

Figure 2. Ostia. The Excavated Areas along the Via Severiana. (From C. Pavolini in *Notizie degli Scavi di Antichità* VIII.35 [1981], Figure 1)

From the perspective of the architectural and urban development of Ostia, however, these buildings bear directly on the construction history of the synagogue edifice.[17]

The architectural remains of the synagogue edifice clearly indicate that the building was in Jewish usage in its final stages, as there was a menorah relief inscribed on each of the extended corbels of the architraves of the apsidal niche on the south side of the main hall. The masonry work of the edifice suggests several distinct phases in the construction of the building. (See fig. 3.)

The core of the original edifice of the synagogue was constructed in *opus reticulatum* with brickwork framing. (See fig. 4.) This type of masonry was common at Ostia in the Flavian period (later first century C.E., beginning especially under Domitian) and down through the reigns of Trajan (98-117) and Hadrian (117-138) but was no longer used after the mid–second century. Notably, the architectural expansion of the Porta Marina *(f.l.m.)* quarter was primarily a product of Trajanic and Hadrianic periods.[18] Thus, it is safest to date the original construction of the synagogue edifice to the early second century, though perhaps as early as the last decade of the first century C.E.[19] The masonry work of the later stages (seen in the

17. My own field observations and analysis are also reported in my book, *The Social Origins of Christian Architecture,* vol. 2, *The Christian Domus Ecclesiae in Its Environment,* Harvard Theological Studies (Philadelphia: TPI, 1996), nos. 83-85. The discussion is based primarily on the second season reports (in Italian and English) of Squarciapino and on the discussion of Kraabel, together with the author's own field survey, conducted in stages from 1983 to 1994. See also the discussion in my *Building God's House,* 69-71, 79.

18. Cf. R. Meiggs, *Roman Ostia* (Oxford: Clarendon, 1960), 539-48 and 133-41. For further discussion of this type of masonry, cf. M. E. Blake, *Roman Construction in Italy from Tiberius through the Flavians* (Washington, D.C.: Carnegie Institute, 1959), 66 (and s.v. in index). The most recent work on Roman brickwork has been done by J. S. Boersma, *Amoenissima civitas* (Leiden: Brill, 1987).

19. I am intentionally taking a cautious approach to the dating, since the secondary literature often cites the synagogue simply as "from the first century," thereby leaving a faulty impression (so Shanks, 162, following Squarciapino, "The Synagogue at Ostia," 196). On the basis of the masonry type employed in the core of the building, it is very unlikely that the edifice was constructed prior to the Flavian period (i.e., not before the 70s-80s) and is most likely later, especially from the time of Trajan or even Hadrian. This dating is now supported by Pavolini's work on the buildings across the street from the synagogue edifice, and, significantly, these buildings show a mix of masonry work, reflecting phases of renovation, similar to that in the synagogue itself. See Pavolini, 124.

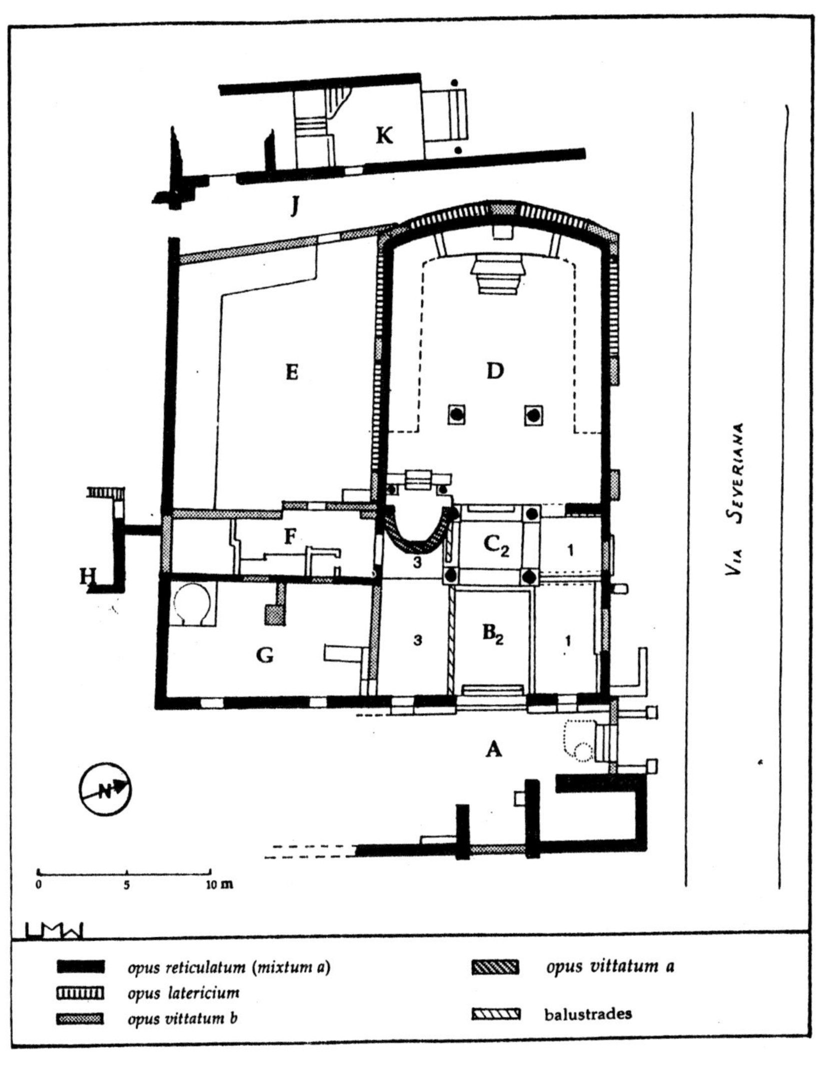

Figure 3. Italia, Ostia. Synagogue, ca. 2nd-4th centuries. Plan restoration, composite, showing types of construction.

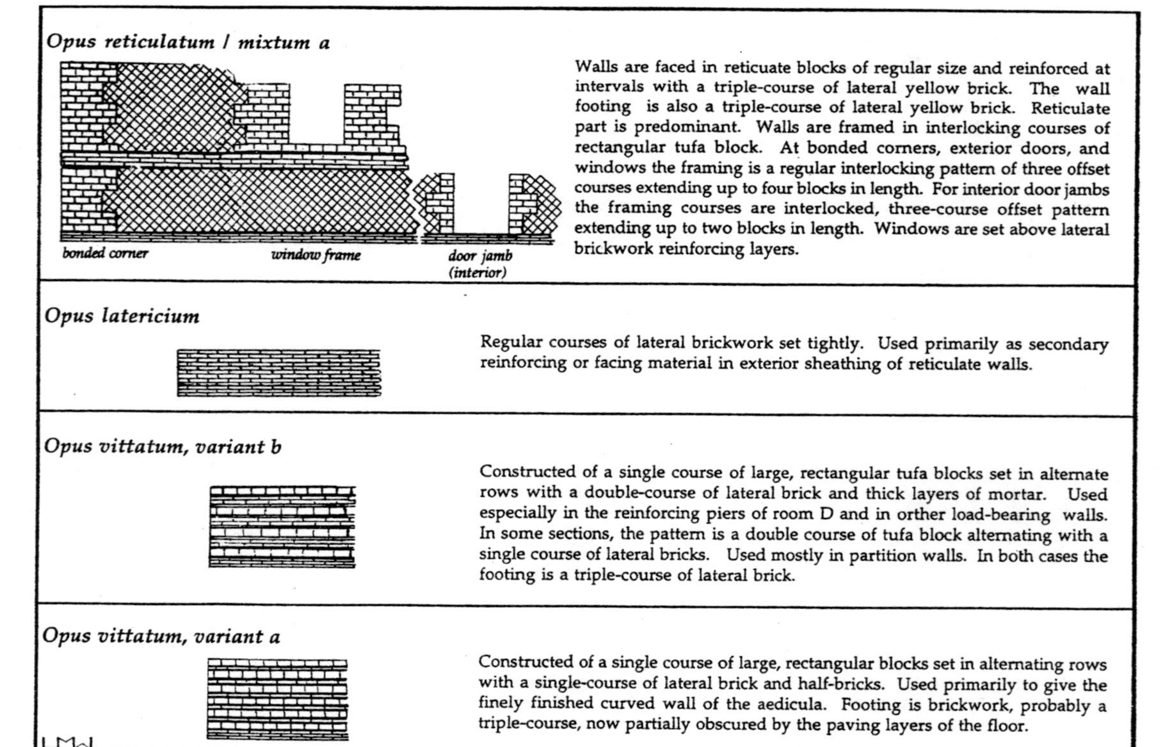

Figure 4. Types of Masonry in Wall Construction of the Ostia Synagogue.

construction of the apsed niche itself and other areas to be noted) is of a lateral "brick-and-block" masonry type known as *opus vittatum mixtum simplex* (with some *opus listatum*). (See fig. 4.) It was typical of the later empire, especially in the late third and fourth centuries, and is quite common from this period in Ostia's urban development. This date is also indicated for the use of *opus sectile* floors as seen in the entry areas of the later synagogue building.[20] The building seems to have been abandoned by the later fifth century (consistent with the period of Ostia's decline), so that we have fairly clear termini for its architectural history (early second to late fifth centuries). In order to establish more clearly the construction history of the edifice, we must work backward from the final form of the building, when it was clearly used as a synagogue.

a. The Later Synagogue

In its final form (fig. 3) the synagogue building was a large complex, measuring 36.60 × 23.50 meters. The entry was through a group of rooms or vestibule (Area A: ca. 23.50 × ca. 3.80 m.) down steps from the Via Severiana. This entrance was likely a later addition, since it employs *opus vittatum* in the frame of the steps and it blocked a cistern, which had been covered over with a stone slab. From this vestibule the main hall was entered through a central doorway, flanked by two narrower ones. Inside was an inner court (Area B) subdivided into three chambers or aisles corresponding to the three doorways (B_1: 5.85 × 3.37 m.; B_2: 5.37 × 4.15 m.; B_3: 7.40 × 3.35 m.). These areas had a fine mosaic floor in sections.

Area B opened onto an inner "gateway" (Area C), also divided into three parts. Area C_2 (4.30 × 3.20 m.) contained an imposing structure of

20. Cf. Meiggs, *Roman Ostia*, 544-45, 550-53. One edifice cited by Meiggs as clearly dating from this later period is the House of Cupid and Psyche (Reg. I.xiv.5), which likewise employs *opus sectile* floors (cf. 259-62). Another example of fourth-century renovation worth noting is found in the House of the Fortuna Annonaria (Reg. V.ii.8), built originally under Antoninus Pius. There is both *opus listatum* and *opus vittatum* brickwork in the building. Cf. Meiggs, 254, 545, and pl. XIVb. See also the excavation reports from this region by Giovanni Becatti, *Scavi di Ostia, Volume VI: Edificio con Opus Sectile fuori Porta Marina* (Rome: Instituto poligrafico dello Stato, 1967), passim.

four columns of gray marble (probably spoils)[21] on a raised platform to serve as a main axis into the hall of assembly proper (Room D). The main hall (Room D: 14.31 × 12.50 m.) was paved in *opus sectile.* Two more columns of the same type as that in C_2 stood in Room D, although not precisely on the same line as those of the "gateway" structure. The west wall is slightly curved, and against it was set a tiered *bema* (width: 6.20 m.; depth: 1.25 m.; height: 0.79 m.), faced by a smaller platform and steps.

At some stage, the triportal entry and inner court were further modified. The southernmost aisle (Areas B_3 and C_3) was blocked off by the construction of the apsidal Torah shrine abutting the southwest column of the inner "gateway" (C_2).[22] The apse was *opus vittatum* on a raised podium faced by a stair of four steps. From the top of the apse sidewalls architraves (ending in corbels) extended to two small colonettes. The architraves probably carried a pediment that reached to the ceiling (at the same height as the columns in C_2), making the entire apse structure an *aedicula,* undoubtedly to serve as an *aron* or Torah shrine. There is evidence of other later modifications to the *aedicula* structure.[23] At the same time as the construction of the *aedicula,* several other partitions were constructed: Areas B_3 and C_3 were blocked off from B_2 and C_2 using balustrades; Area C_1 was fitted with a gate into Room D. As a result of these modifications, the central aisle (B_2-C_2) became the only access to the hall of assembly (D).

From the left aisle (B_3) a door opened to the other rooms of the complex. Prior to the construction of the *aedicula* and partitions noted above, this doorway would have been accessible directly from the main entryway in Area B_2. After the *aedicula* was introduced, the only access to this door was from the vestibule (A) through the flanking door into B_3.

21. It appears that one of the columns was broken in antiquity and repaired before being used in the renovation of the later synagogue. I am grateful to Leonard Rutgers for this observation.

22. The construction of the *aedicula* podium is clearly secondary to the column and its footing, around which it is carefully built.

23. When the niche structure was first built, these colonettes rested on the floor and framed the podium steps. At some later point, the podium was enlarged, so that the steps were no longer freestanding, and the colonettes were framed into the podium. For discussion of the form of the *aedicula,* see Squarciapino, "The Synagogue at Ostia," 198, and Kraabel, "The Diaspora Synagogue," 498, citing the inscription from Side, Pamphylia, for a structure in the synagogue called a "*simma*" (i.e., Greek lunate *sigma*). See also L. Robert, "Inscriptions grecques de Side," *Rev. phil.* 32 (1958): 36-47.

The presence of *opus reticulatum* masonry in Room G shows that the area was part of the original building, as was the shell of the vestibule A and the main hall (Areas B, C, D). Probably at the same time as the construction of the *aedicula,* a partition wall (also in *opus vittatum*) was constructed between G and B_3, while several openings between G and F were likewise blocked (using *opus vittatum*), thus creating the two narrow rooms.

Room G (6.20 × 10.32 m.) was accessible by two doors from vestibule A. It contained a marble table near the door and an oven in the southwest corner, and is thereby identified as some sort of kitchen. In its final state the floor of G was covered with a layer of ash, earth, and mixed marble and terra-cotta fragments. Under this floor level, however, was found a mosaic floor arranged in sections, similar to that found in Area B. Room F (2.73-3.23 × 10.50 m.), after the partitioning, seems to have been little more than a storage pantry and corridor leading to Area E; among the appurtenances in F was a low bench. Room E (13.90 × 10.18 m.) was a large hall, with its west wall set askew. A low bench (depth: 1.83 m.) ran along the south and west walls, terminating at a small doorway in the west wall (and opening onto an alleyway J outside the edifice). The south wall of Room E is in *opus reticulatum* and seems to be from the same phase of construction as the core of Room D, but the west wall of Room E is in *opus vittatum,* a product of later renovation. This room appears to be some sort of dining or social hall, and the floor was decorated with mosaic.

b. Evidence of Earlier Stages

The evidence for the earlier stages of the building is fragmentary apart from the indications of the masonry itself (as indicated in the plan, fig. 3). Taken together, however, they point to renovation of the building in several phases before it reached its final form. The question that must still be addressed is whether the building was a synagogue from the beginning (as the excavators supposed) or was at some point converted to synagogue use.

The original structure in *opus reticulatum* included the areas of Room D, the entry court area (B + C), and the "kitchen" (G). Portions of the east wall of the vestibule A and the entire south wall of Room E were also part of the original phase of construction. The contiguous structures (H and K) to the south of Room E and to the west of the alleyway (J) are also in the same masonry type and may be an integral construction with the south wall of

Room E. It is likely, however, that neither the vestibule (Area A)[24] nor the area in E was part of the original building (at least not in this form); both were incorporated or spatially reconfigured later through subsequent renovation.

Further indication of this earlier stage is found in the lower floor level in Areas B and C. The earlier floor was of *cocciopesto* (a packed floor of crushed earthenware mixed with plaster); it extended over the entire Area B/C without any lateral aisles or divisions. There was also a layer of *cocciopesto* flooring beneath the mosaic floor (and the latest ash floor) in Room G. This fact indicates that the subdivisions of B and C to match the triportal entry come from the later renovations. The use of a different type of brickwork facing indicates, moreover, that the two flanking doors from A (into B_1 and B_3, respectively) were later insertions into an existing *opus reticulatum* wall, while the main door in B_2 also seems to have been widened. Hence, the entire triportal entrance scheme (including the doors from A and the interior aisles of B/C) was the conscious product of a secondary renovation.

The original entrance to the main building seems to have been directly from the Via Severiana at Area C. On the north wall of Area B/C two openings appear in the *opus reticulatum* masonry, but these were later sealed with *opus vittatum*. These were likely the original entrance to the edifice.[25] Area B/C, then, would have been the entry chambers of the edifice until the *opus vittatum* renovation phase.[26] The remnant of an *opus reticulatum*

24. This conclusion is supported by the fact that an existing cistern was blocked by the creation of the new entrance from the Via Severiana at the steps down into A. The marble well that stands beside the steps was most likely installed at this time. Thus, while the east wall of Area A contains some elements in the earlier *opus reticulatum* masonry, it does not appear to have been an integral construction with the original east wall of Areas B and G.

25. The L-shaped spur on the exterior of B_1 may well substantiate this. Also there is a surviving wall-spur in *opus reticulatum* between C_1 and D that indicates some elements of internal partitioning in this area dating from the period of the earliest structure. This, too, would be consistent with Area B or C as the original entrance to the building directly from the Via Severiana and physically partitioned from Area D.

26. It is noteworthy, then, that the dominant axial orientation of the entire complex in the earliest *opus reticulatum* phase(s) seems to be north-south, that is, from the Via Severiana toward the seashore. This axial orientation can be seen in the parallel lines of the alleyway J, the original passageway from C through F, the original passageway from B through G, and the alleyway (?) A. As seen in figure 2, there were other contiguous structures of integral construction with the *opus reticulatum* phase to the south side of Room E, and which seem to connect also to the rear areas of the edifice at K (and perhaps also to Area A). Given that the south wall of Room F was sealed only in the

wall between C_1 and D indicates that Area D would have originally been separate. The excavators found some remnants of earlier benches in D that had been removed or covered over in the later renovations. The *bema* at the western end of D also seems to be from an earlier phase. Floriani Squarciapino dated these to the construction of the original edifice; however, they might as easily belong to a middle stage of renovation focused primarily on the interior of Room D.

One more piece of evidence is particularly significant in this vein but has (to my knowledge) never been treated in other discussions of the synagogue building. In her original report, the excavator mentions in passing the existence of a low "bench" construction (width: 1.93 m.) of an "earlier masonry type" (presumably meaning *opus reticulatum*) found beneath the later *aedicula* platform (and now no longer visible for inspection). She speculated that this was an earlier Torah shrine, which she equated with the evidence of the Mindis Faustus inscription.[27] Subsequent excavations in the areas immediately west of the synagogue edifice have revealed another adjacent building with contiguous walls (indicated as Areas J and K in my plan, fig. 3, and also shown in fig. 2). This edifice was constructed in the same *opus reticulatum* with brickwork framing as in the synagogue edifice. Significantly, the entrance to this building (K) was down a narrow hall on the north side, entered directly from the Via Severiana; in other words, precisely parallel to the north-south axial orientation suggested above for the earlier entrance (Area C) to the synagogue edifice. The entry hall in K leads to a set of stairs which gave access to a second story.

In anticipation of further analysis, I will suggest here that the "bench" construction in C_3 noted by Floriani Squarciapino (admittedly, prior to the discovery of this adjacent building K) may be the remnant of a stairway from the first stage of the edifice, later removed owing to the design of subsequent renovations. Thus, much like other *insulae* at Ostia, one would expect that the original entrance to the building from the Via Severiana would have included a separate passage for the first-floor rooms (in Area C_1) and an access to the upper-floor stair. Given the external wall footing

---

later renovation, it might have also provided access to these southern rooms in the earliest phases. It appears that the axial orientation of Room D was east-west from some early stage, and this became the basis for the later orientation of the building.

27. Squarciapino, "La sinogaga di Ostia: secondo campagna di scavo," 314-15. For discussion of the inscription see below.

along the street front in Area B_1, it would appear that B could have been used as a street-front shop, and functionally segregated from other areas of the building, again a pattern typical of Ostian *insula* architecture. The adjacent edifices in Areas H, J, and K, moreover, seem to be integral with the construction of the first edifice and bear directly, in my view, on our understanding of its character as a typical Ostian *insula* complex. Similarly, the earliest phases of the mostly commercial buildings directly across the Via Severiana use the same masonry and come from this period, suggesting that all this construction (including the synagogue edifice itself) occurred as part of a larger pattern of general urban expansion along the Via Severiana. These points will become significant in later discussion.

c. An Architectural Chronology

On the basis of early analysis, Floriani Squarciapino developed the following chronological scheme for the synagogue structure:[28]

1. First century: the *opus reticulatum* structure, consisting of three rooms (D, B/C, and G), was built *de novo* for a synagogue, as indicated by the presence of the curved wall in D and the presence of the *bema.*
2. Late second to early third centuries: remodeling of the synagogue included division of the areas in B/C and the construction of the Torah "ark" (mentioned in the Mindis Faustus inscription).
3. Fourth century: substantial renovation produced the present plan, with the addition of Rooms A, E, and F along with interior decoration.
4. Late fourth century: further remodeling and addition of the present Torah *aedicula.*

A. T. Kraabel, however, has questioned this scheme.[29] While essentially following her scheme for stages 1 and 2, he questions the continuity, espe-

28. Squarciapino, "The Synagogue at Ostia," 197-98.

29. Kraabel, "The Diaspora Synagogue," 499-500. This would result in making the subsequent enlargement of the *aedicula* podium (not discussed by Kraabel) part of stage 4. The crucial piece of evidence here is that the plaque on which the Mindis Faustus inscription occurs was found reused in the floorwork of the final synagogue. Since the Mindis Faustus inscription is dated to the late second or early third century by Squarciapino, this yields an important series of steps in the process.

cially with regard to the evidence correlated with her third and fourth stages. He would prefer to place the construction of the present Torah *aedicula* in stage 3, integral with the fourth-century renovation. With such qualification we may basically agree on the general four-stage building history, but there are further indications of renovation that need to be taken into account.

The renovations associated with *opus vittatum/listatum* construction seem to me to represent not only some changes in the basic ground plan but also a monumentalization of the structure from its earlier form. Most notable in this regard are the six columns in C_2 and D, which must have been used to carry a ceiling more than 6 meters in height (including the orders) spanning the entire area of C and D (and perhaps B). These do not appear to me to be integral with the original form of the building (as suggested by the excavator), but were added later. The original edifice was a two-story building with a segregated upper chamber over at least much of the building.

In keeping with this, it should be noted that at some point in the later renovations the original *opus reticulatum* walls on the north, west, and south sides of Room D were reinforced by encasing them in a brickwork shell that doubled their thickness. This included both *opus vittatum* and *opus listatum* masonry, but is largely consistent with the masonry work of the later additions in Areas A, E, and F and in the blocking of the earlier doorways in B_1 and C_1.[30] Additional buttressing was also introduced by adding exterior piers that helped to support the new roof.[31] What has not been noticed previously is that this exterior reinforcement also blocked several large windows on the second-floor level of Area D (as indicated in a remaining section of the wall from the northwest corner; see fig. 5).[32] The construction of this north wall of D is important because it shows a lower wall course in *opus reticulatum* with an upper border of lateral brickwork

30. Significantly, the row of buildings across the Via Severiana and the adjacent edifice K show the same type of later masonry in renovations.

31. Also noted by Squarciapino, "La sinogaga di Ostia: secondo campagna di scavo," 306-7.

32. Again, a systematic excavation report has not taken this evidence into its account of the building's construction history. This remaining section of the north wall of Room D is the only portion of the building that still exists at a height more than circa 1.5 meters from the floor. In the excavations it was found toppled into Room D, and has since been restored. Numerous other fragments of these walls were found, but have not (to my knowledge) ever been studied carefully to see if more of the upper wall construction can be determined.

Figure 5. Ostia. The Synagogue. View of the north wall of Room D, the Hall of Assembly, showing the position of earlier upper-level windows blocked by later renovation. *(Photo, L. M. White)*

at a height of 3.20 meters from the current floor level. Above this brickwork band extends another level of *opus reticulatum* in which one can see two vertical windows framed in lateral brickwork. These windows, then, are integral with the original construction of the edifice and seem to reflect a second-story room (or rooms). They were sealed with *opus vittatum* brickwork at the same time that the exterior wall was reinforced with the *opus vittatum* shell and *listatum* piers.[33]

This reinforcing of the exterior walls, I would suggest, occurred at the same time as the introduction of the six columns as a result of the removal of the second floor.[34] (This is consistent with my suggestion above of an earlier stairway.) Given the similarity of plan and *opus reticulatum* masonry to the recently excavated adjacent building (K) to the west (which also has a second floor and a baking establishment in the rear, reached by the alleyway J beside Room E), I do not think the first edifice was exclusively a synagogue or a *de novo* Jewish construction. The evidence suggests a private *insula* complex containing both domestic quarters and shops (or work space, as indicated by the ovens to the south). A collegial hall is also possible as part of such an *insula* complex. It seems to me entirely possible that the two buildings were in some similar usage (or perhaps part of one larger complex) prior to the renovation of the synagogue. They may have remained related afterward, as the open access of Room E to the alleyway (J) and the adjacent building (K) indicates. Thus, I would suggest the following construction history for the building:

Phase 1: Construction of an *insula* complex as part of the general expansion of the Porta Marina *(f.l.m.)* quarter to the south down the Via Severiana, near the beginning of the second century C.E.

Phase 2: First renovation for synagogue usage. These were probably minimal internal modifications, as no major structural changes seem

33. It also appears that there were some original windows or apertures in the west and south walls of Room D which were sealed at the time of the *opus vittatum* renovation.

34. An unanswered question exists regarding a source of lighting for assembly hall D in this renovated form, since all the earlier windows were blocked. It may well be that the columns, which were used to support the interior elevation, carried a kind of shallow clerestory construction to allow for interior lighting. Unfortunately nothing of the roofing or ceiling treatment was preserved to indicate such.

to be indicated at this time. The nature of the renovation likely included the layout of an assembly hall (D) with benches lining the sidewalls and the *bema* on the western end. The "ark" would have been set up on this *bema.*

It appears that this project occurred in the middle to later second century and continued under the patronage of Mindis Faustus (as indicated in the inscription), probably in the late second to early third century. The fact that the name Mindis Faustus is secondary on the inscription[35] may suggest, however, that there were two distinct stages of renovation (perhaps to be designated 2a and 2b). While it is possible that the building was used by the Jewish group in Phase 1, no clear evidence of a formal synagogue structure can be detected prior to the renovations of Phase 2.

Phase 3: The major renovation project of the building. It included expansion of the plan (to incorporate Areas A, E, F); the monumentalization of the hall of assembly by raising the ceiling through the second-story level; installation of the columns (and other supports); and creation of the triportal entry from A through Areas B/C. The side benches in Room D were removed, but the layout of Room E may be thought to take their place. This project dates to the late third or early fourth century. It is also possible that this was the project commemorated in the Mindis Faustus inscription.

The full Torah *aedicula* was most likely introduced as an afterthought, since it blocked the third aisle (B_3-C_3) of the triportal entry. We should likely place it either in a secondary stage (3b), or as the impetus for the subsequent renovations of stage 4. Prior to the construction of the new *aedicula,* the Torah "ark" of Mindis Faustus (located on the western *bema* in D) must be assumed to have remained in use.

Phase 4: Further embellishment and decoration, including the introduction and/or subsequent enlargement of the *aedicula* podium. (Hence this may be designated stages 4a and 4b.) There were also

35. See the discussion of the epigraphic evidence below, at n. 46.

further floor treatments and other minor alterations in the later stages of usage. Dates to the middle or later fourth century and continuing to the abandonment of the building.

This building history points to an incremental process of renovation that gradually transformed the original edifice into a formal, liturgically articulated, synagogue building. In its earlier stages (Phase 2) of Jewish usage, however, the form of the renovations more resemble a collegial hall, or community center, styled after local norms of architectural planning and use, but such is not atypical among Diaspora synagogues.

Three final points may now be made regarding the implications of this building history. First, it should be noted that the introduction of a fixed or architectural Torah shrine is generally a later innovation in synagogue architecture *and* liturgy. It does not appear before the last quarter of the second century C.E., and it did not become common until after the mid–third century.[36] The Ostia evidence, outlined above, is consistent with the pattern found in other Diaspora synagogues and shows some important developments in synagogue architecture and liturgy. It appears to me that the first Torah "ark" (as described in the Mindis Faustus inscription, discussed below) was set up on the *bema* at the west end of the hall D. There are no remains, of course, but the first *aron* (ark) could easily have been a small wooden chest for the scrolls, of a type regularly depicted in artwork from the Jewish catacombs of Rome.[37] The later renovations must have had a bearing on the spatial orientation of the community's worship. The enlargements of Phase 3 suggest an expansion of the assembly space by turning the orientation of the entire building on an east-west axis and extending the longitudinal axis of Room D to carry through the triportal (Areas B and C). The continuity of the axis in Room D proper, however, suggests that it was the original hall of assembly of

36. See White, *Building God's House,* 95 and n. 126.

37. For depictions of this type of "ark" or *aron* in the context of the Roman Jewish inscriptions, see *CII* 315, 327, 337, 343, 401, and 460. The stylized depictions found in Rome are in my view remarkably consistent in type, and may represent a distinctive local development. Also a number of decorated glass plates show similar depictions; cf. *CII* 515-22. The ark for scrolls does not seem to have been introduced prior to the mid–second century. The shift from a portable wooden chest to a fixed architectural implacement (in which the chest might still be used) represents a significant advancement in synagogue planning.

the congregation and served as the core around which the later monumental design of the renovation was ordered. Later, however, introduction of the new Torah *aedicula* suggests a reorientation toward the east (at least in relation to use of the Torah itself) and further internal modifications of the assembly space. While these changes were relatively late, they too are consistent with patterns of reorientation found elsewhere in the Diaspora.[38]

Second, such major renovation projects as reflected at Ostia suggest substantial social energy on the part of the Jewish community, as well as the role of local patron figures. Just as with Mindis Faustus, such leading figures were most likely involved in the later periods as well, but their names are lost. Third, these monumental changes in the building suggest that the community itself was growing, in both numbers and economic strength, and was finding a general degree of social acceptance in the local environment. As noted, the construction style itself followed the fashion of fourth-century architectural trends seen elsewhere in the city.[39] Such a renovation project as that reflected in the later stages could not have gone unnoticed by the local population of Ostia. The monumentalization of Room D was a complex construction project; not only would it have entailed extensive exterior scaffolding (to erect the encasing wall and piers) but it would also have meant the removal of the entire roof. The casual traveler along the Via Severiana had to have been aware of the scale of this type of construction project. While we have no evidence of external artistic symbolism of a Jewish character, the use of the menorah carvings on the architraves of the Torah *aedicula* reflect a robust and self-consciously Jewish identity. Moreover, the location and the hints of a continued relation with the adjacent buildings may be taken to suggest some of the lines of the social location of this particular Jewish community at Ostia. In this light, we may now turn our attention to detailed analysis of the epigraphic remains.[40]

38. That eastern orientation (or toward Jerusalem) was not normative in earlier periods is one of the recent conclusions from the archaeological work. Nonetheless, both the Sardis and Ostia synagogues reflect this later reorientation to the east.

39. See above, n. 20. Cf. Kraabel, "Social Systems," 87.

40. A hitherto little-known inscription suggests that there may have been another Jewish community at nearby Porto (the imperial harbor). Cf. M. Floriani Squarciapino, "Plotius Fortunatus archisynagogus," *Rassegna mensile di Israel* 36 (1970): 183-91. Also note that there are several other Jewish inscriptions assigned to the area of Porto. These

3. The Epigraphic Evidence and Its Social Context

Two inscriptions bear directly on the Ostia synagogue community. The first was found in the excavation of the synagogue building itself; the second was displaced but seems to belong to the Jewish community of Ostia. So, lacking evidence of any other synagogue congregation in Ostia proper, we may safely discuss both in this context.

a. Inscription 1: The Donation of Mindi(u)s Faustus

The text is on an inscribed plaque found reused in repair work on the final stage of the synagogue floor. It seems to date, therefore, from the second to the third century, well before the final renovation of the edifice. To date it has not been formally published, but a simple transcription was given by M. Floriani Squarciapino in her report of the second season, though no other pertinent data were given.[41] The following transcription is taken from the author's observations of the plaque at the Ostia Museum and of a cast now housed in the Museum of the *Comunità Ebraica di Roma*.[42]

---

include *CII* 534a (from Lifshitz's prolegomena in the 2nd ed., 44) and a number of funerary monuments (*CII* 535-51). However, it should also be noted that at least two of these indicate some possible connections either to a synagogue community known from Rome proper (*CII* 537: "synagogue of the Carcaresians [*sic*]," cf. Leon, *The Jews of Ancient Rome*, 142-44) or to another inscription from Ostia itself (*CII* 551a: the name *Iustus*, cf. *CII* 533, discussed below). More generally on Porto, cf. H. J. Leon, "The Jewish Community of Porto," *HTR* 45 (1952): 165-75, though this study must certainly be updated in the light of recent work.

41. Squarciapino, "La sinogaga di Ostia: secondo campagna di scavo," 314; cf. Kraabel, "The Diaspora Synagogue," 498. Another publication of the inscription by Floriana Squarciapino, issued in *La rassegna mensile di Israel*, has been unavailable to me.

42. Cf. my *Christian Domus Ecclesiae*, no. 84a. I am grateful to Signora Anna Blie, director of the Jewish Museum of Rome, for allowing me the opportunity to study the cast. The stone measures: length: 54.5 cm.; height: 29.9 cm. Letter height by line: line 1: 4.1 cm.; lines 2-3: 3.5 cm.; lines 4-5: 3.0 cm.; lines 6-7: 3.2 cm. The stone is cracked vertically along the middle, and the bottom line is lost except in the very center of the stone. Lines 6-7 show signs of an erasure, with letters recut in a second hand for most (but not all) of line 6.

Pro Salute Aug(usti)[43]
οἰκοδόμησεν κὲ αἰπό-[44]
ησεν ἐκ τῶν αὐτοῦ δο-
μάτων καὶ τὴν Κειβώτον[45]
ἀνέθηκεν νόμῳ ἁγίω
Μίνδι(ο)ς Φαῦστος ΜΕ[46]
[. . . . .] ΔΙΩ [. . . .]

Translation:
For the well-being of the Emperor. Mindi(u)s Faustus [. . . DIO? . . .][47]

43. The following notes (43-48) are epigraphical annotations to the text:
Line 1 is in Latin while the rest is in Greek, but the hand is the same for both, down to line 6.

44. Lines 2-3: For KE (lapis) read καί; for AIΠO/ΗΣΕΝ (lapis) read ἐποίησεν.

45. Line 4: For ΚΕΙΒΩΤΟΝ (lapis) read Κιβώτον, meaning "ark." See also Kraabel, "The Diaspora Synagogue," 498, with parallel references on the usage.

46. Lines 6-7: These lines show an erasure corrected in a distinctively second hand. Most notable is the change from a square "M" in the first five lines to a curved form (U), especially in the name Mindi(u)s Faustus. However, the lunate "E" at the end of line 6 seems to be from the first hand, and was only slightly damaged by the erasure. It is difficult to speculate, therefore, on the cause of the erasure and the nature of the original wording of the text.

47. I have corrected the name to Mindius based on other inscriptions from the immediate environs of Ostia. It must have been a fairly common name. It occurs in a list of the members of the Corporis Fabrum Navalium, an association of shipwrights at Ostia (found at Portus, *CIL* 14.256, line 246). Two texts from Isola Sacra bear special notice in this regard. For the texts see especially Hilding Thylander, *Inscriptions du port d'Ostie,* Skrifter Utgivna av Svenska Institutet i Rom (Lund: C. W. K. Gleerup, 1952). Thylander No. A181 (from tomb N. 73) gives the name L. Mindius Diocas (and his wife Julia Zoe) and is datable to the time of Antoninus Pius. Thylander No. A182 (from tomb C) gives the name L. Mindius Dius (and his wife Genucia Tryphaena) and is datable to the time of Hadrian. The complete text of the latter is as follows:

L. Mindius Dius
fecit sibi et Genuciae
Tryphaenae coniuji
incomparabili cum qua
vixit annis xxiiii mens iii
et Lucceiae Ianuariae ma-
ritae et Anniae Laueriae contuverna-
li suae santissimae et libert(is) libertab(usque) suis pos[ter(is)q(ue)] eor(um)
h(oc) m(onumentum) e(xterum) h(eredem) n(on) [s(equetur)].
In fronte p(edes) xxx, in agro p(edes) xxxi.

constructed (the edifice or hall) and made it out of his own gifts,[48] and he set up the "ark" for the sacred law [. . .].

Given the location of the find and the wording of the text, it can hardly be read as anything but a building inscription. It seems to me that the text refers to two distinct acts as indicated by the verbs, both of which were sponsored by the donor (Mindi[u]s Faustus in the corrected version of the text). The first is a construction project (using the verbs οἰκοδόμησεν and ἐποίησεν), which I take to refer to the edifice itself, rather than to the

In addition to the onomastic similarities, the form of this epitaph will also be useful for the discussion of the second Jewish inscription, below nn. 61-63. While both inscriptions are in Latin, the names of both wives have clear Greek influences. The mid–second-century dating for both is significant. Moreover, we may note the names Dius and Diocas (which could even be related cognates) in the light of the badly damaged portions of lines 6 and 7 in our Jewish text, which yield portions of two more words, Me[. . .] and Dio[. . .]. The similarity to the two names from Isola Sacra is striking. There is, of course, no way of being certain, but it would be typical of the form of such inscriptions if lines 6-7 would have given the name of important relatives (or patrons). It is not impossible that our Mindius Faustus was somehow related or attached to the families of Mindius Diocas and Mindius Dius. Thus, it should be noticed that L. Mindius Dius (in the epitaph above) had three wives: the first, a legal marriage, was to Genucia Tryphaena (termed *coniux*), who was deceased at the time of the dedication of the tomb. Mindius Dius was still living with Lucceia Januaria, to whom he was married (but here using *marita* instead of the more usual *coniux*), and he also had a *contubernalis* (a "domestic partner," usually meaning a slave or freedwoman, where there was no legal status to the marriage) named Annia Laveria, most likely a freedwoman. Mindius Dius might have had children by all three, and their familial position and inheritance could be quite variable, depending on his wishes. Mindius Faustus could be a Jewish freedman, or the descendant of a freedman, from such a complex family, but such a restoration must remain highly speculative.

48. Line 3: δομάτων would normally mean "gifts," but could be read as the derived meaning "funds" (presumably given for the project). Still, the use of this term is unusual and another option suggests itself. Given the generally poor orthography found in the text, we might well read the *omicron* for an *omega*, hence δωμάτων, a variant found in some papyri (cf. P. Petr. III. 42, so Moulton-Milligan). This orthographic variant is also common among Greek epitaphs from Rome (cf. van der Horst, 26). This spelling would seem a natural substitution also in a Latin context, given the regular use of the loanword *domus* in Greek as δόμος. Read in this way, then, the phrase would refer to the house or rooms from which the synagogue was renovated. A similar use of the term δώματα as "rooms" associated with a synagogue building (as hostelry) may be found in the Ophel synagogue inscription (*CII* 1404 = *Christian Domus Ecclesiae*, no. 63). Finally, in either case it is not possible to read the ἐποίησεν merely as an auxiliary verb with ἀνέθηκεν (as suggested by Squarciapino, "The Synagogue at Ostia," 203).

Torah shrine. The second refers to the erection and dedication (using the verb ἀνέθηκεν) of the Torah "ark" itself, probably as the capstone of the entire project. Consequently, I would read this text to refer to the renovation of the existing private edifice for use as a synagogue. It should be correlated then with the archaeological evidence for internal renovation to create the assembly hall D (as suggested above, Phase 2b), and dated to the later second or early third century.[49] As suggested earlier, I think the "ark" set up by Mindi(u)s Faustus was a portable chest placed on the *bema* at the west end.

In this light, two points of social data arise from the text. First, it should be noticed that the inscription is in Greek. It probably suggests something of the ethno-cultural background of the donor and perhaps others in the congregation. We may guess that there was already an existing Jewish community, but where it had been meeting prior to this renovation cannot be ascertained. Private meetings in someone's home (as found elsewhere) are not ruled out. The use of Greek, however, should not be surprising, since 68-70 percent of the Jewish inscriptions from Rome were likewise in Greek.[50] Also, a number of orthographic features of the text are quite consistent with Jewish patterns of pronunciation and spelling of Greek in the Latin context of Rome.[51]

Second, an outstanding feature of the inscription is the use of the Latin invocation *Pro salute Augusti* as an introductory formula. This is a common formula at Ostia and elsewhere, of course, and is especially featured in the Antonine period.[52] It is also found in Ostian Mithraic

49. Cf. White, *Building God's House,* 77-85. It is also possible to identify the work with Phase 3a, dating to the middle or later third century. See also Baruch Lifshitz, *Donateurs et Fondateurs dans les Synagogues juives,* Cahiers de la Revue Biblique 7 (Paris: Gabalda, 1967), passim.

50. Leon, *The Jews of Ancient Rome,* 76-77, had earlier estimated 76 percent, but these numbers have subsequently been revised through the work of Heikki Solin, "Juden und Syrer im westlichen Teil der römischen Welt. Eine ethnisch-demographische Studie mit besonderer Berüksichtigung der sprachlichen Zustände," *ANRW* II.29.2 (1983), 590-789, esp. 701-2. Van der Horst, 22 (following Solin), gives the following breakdown: 68 percent Greek, 18 percent Semitic, 12 percent Latin, and 2 percent bilingual (usually with Greek as one of the languages).

51. Leon, *The Jews of Ancient Rome,* 76-77, 79-89; cf. van der Horst, 25-34.

52. The formula is found in earlier periods (including late Julio-Claudian and Flavian), but much more rarely than in the Antonine period. For first-century examples, see *CIL* VI.918, 940, 2042, and 3751. By itself it cannot be used to date the inscription absolutely.

building inscriptions in a strikingly similar usage.[53] Still, it would traditionally be thought out of place among Jews (unless one were to hark back to the Jewish inscriptions from Ptolemaic Egypt). It is significant, therefore, that the ordinary salutary formula is often used by groups or individuals who are clearly in some way clients (or dependents) of the emperor.[54] Here we must remember that the names of at least two of the synagogue communities known from Rome (the "Augustesians" and the "Agrippesians") suggest just such clientage to members of the imperial household along the lines of a collegial organization.[55] Such ties would inevitably link Jewish residents of Rome or Ostia directly to the non-Jewish population in important social and economic ways. Does this suggest a similar connection for either Mindius Faustus or the congregation at Ostia? The second inscription gives further evidence in this direction.

b. Inscription 2: Honors for C. Julius Justus, Jewish Gerusiarch

This Latin inscription (*CII* 533) is on a marble plaque found originally at Castel Porziano, south of Ostia on the Via Severiana, and first published in 1903. Recent work by the British School at Rome has begun to examine

53. Cf. Maarten J. Vermaseren, *Corpus Inscriptionum et Monumentorum religionis mithriacae* [*CIMRM*], 2 vols. (The Hague: Martinus Nijhoff, 1956-60), from Ostia: no. 273 (from the Planta pedis mithraeum, Reg. III.xiii.2, in the Porta Marina quarter, probably under Marcus Aurelius); from Rome: no. 510 (= *CIL* 6.727, under Commodus).

54. Thus, note also the Mithraic inscription from Noricum: *CIMRM* 1438 (= *CIL* 3.4800, dated in the year 239), which seems to come from members of the imperial bureaucracy who were also patrons of the local Mithraic cell. Cf. White, *Building God's House*, 56-57. For Rome, note also the salutary to the emperor Septimius Severus and his sons (datable to 207/8), probably by an imperial client, *CIL* 6.3768:

> Pro Salute et Victoria et Reditu
> Impp . Caesar . L . Septimi . Severi . Pii
> Pertinacis . et . M . Aureli Antonini Augg
> [[et P Septimi Getae nobilissimi Caesaris]] et Iuliae
> Aug m(atris) k(astrorum) totiusq(ue) domus divinae numeroque eorum
> L . Accius Iustus ex voto d(onum) d(at) c(um) s(uis).

55. For the inscriptions and discussion see Leon, *The Jews of Ancient Rome*, 140-42.

other Roman architectural remains from Castel Porziano that suggest at least some elements of an elite life from imperial times. These findings, however, are as yet in a very early stage. This inscription has traditionally been associated directly with Ostia. Unfortunately, the left third of the stone is now completely lost. According to the reconstructed text, it refers directly to a Jewish community "dwelling in the colony of Ostia" (line 2). As we shall see, the names in the text support this identification. The transcription below is based on *CII,* with some emendations by the author.[56]

[Collegium ?][57] **Iudeorum**
[in col. Ost. commor]antium qui compara-
[verunt ex conlat]ione[58] locum C. Iulio Iusto
[gerusiarchae ad m]unimentum struendum
[donavit rogantib]us Livio Dionisio patre et
[col(legii) patro]no[59] gerusiarche et Antonio
[. . . . . diab]iu anno ipsorum consent(iento) ge[r]-
[us(iae), C. Iulius Iu]stus gerusiarches fecit sibi
[et coniugi] suae lib(ertis) lib(ertabusque) posterisque eorum
[in fro]nte p(edes) XVIII, in agro p(edes) XVII.

Translation:
The Community (? Collegium or Synagogue) of the Jews dwelling in the

56. Cf. White, *Christian Domus Ecclesiae,* no. 85. The stone is now in the Museo Nazionale della Therme in Rome.

57. The following notes (57-60) are epigraphic annotations to the text:

Line 1: The term *universitas* was supplied by Frey. Given the tone of the text, I suspect that either *collegium* or even *synagoga* (meaning "congregation") might as easily fit. My own preference (since certainty is out of the question), given the tone of the rest of the text and the kind of honors being bestowed, would lean toward *collegium,* which may also be restored below in line 6.

58. Line 3: [*ex conlat*]*ione* (from the collection) is Frey's restoration. The reading *ex compositione* (by agreement) would also fit the space and the sense, if the preceding verb were abbreviated *comparaver.* (vel sim.).

59. Line 6: Frey proposed no reconstruction for the lacuna at the beginning, though the sense is clearly understood in his translation: "père (de la communauté) et de——— gérousiarque" (p. 393). I propose to read *patro]no* for the partially preserved word, making the titulature a double reference "father and patron of the collegium" and "gerousiarch" (an ablative in apposition with *patre,* instead of supplying a missing genitive).

colony of Ostia, who from the collection acquired[60] a place (or plot) for C(aius) Julius Justus, gerusiarch, so that he might construct a monument, (hereby) have donated it to him at the request of Livius Dionysius, father (and patron of the collegium?), gerusiarch, and of Antonius (? archon) for life, in the year of their office, by consent of the gerusia. C. Julius Justus, gerusiarch, made (this monument) for himself and his wife, together with their freedmen and freedwomen and their descendants, in width, 18 feet; depth, 17 feet.

Frey dated the inscription to the early part of the second century. A Hadrianic to early Antonine date (ca. 117-160) is confirmed by the form of the text in comparison with other funerary monuments from the immediate vicinity (i.e., Ostia, Isola Sacra, and Portus).[61] If we assume that Frey's restored reference to Ostia (line 2) is correct and that it comes, therefore, from the larger Jewish community now known through the architectural remains, then several social and historical conclusions may be drawn. We must guess that the size (reflected by a gerusiarchy of several men), the social status, and economic strength of these individuals are to be associated with the renovation (Phase 2) of the synagogue building, but it seems to be contemporaneous with or to antedate slightly the donation of Mindius Faustus. While a direct connection with the synagogue edifice remains conjectural, the social implications of this inscription deserve further discussion.

The basic form and style of this inscription are quite common. The epitaph takes the form of a *titulus*, a standardized type of inscribed title plaque affixed to the front of the houselike tombs in the extramural necropolises of Rome and Ostia.[62] Other recent work on the form and

60. If we use the alternative reconstruction of lines 2-3 suggested above (n. 56), it would yield a slightly different meaning: "who by agreement provided a plot for . . ." (thus suggesting a gift or purchase of property owned by the Jewish community itself). This latter reconstruction is, in my view, supported by similar formulaic legal provisions found in other *tituli*, so see n. 65 below. The plot could also have been donated by Livius Dionysius himself, and the deed transfer was mediated through the collegial organization.

61. Compare the similar inscription from Isola Sacra in n. 47 above.

62. See the important work of Werner Eck on the form and dating of funerary inscriptions in the environs of the city of Rome: "Inschriften aus der vatikanischen Nekropole unter St. Peter," *ZPE* 65 (1986): 245-93; "Römische Grabinschriften. Aussageabsicht und Aussagefähigkeit im funerären Kontext," in *Römische Gräberstrassen*, ed.

character of such epitaphs indicates that they were usually set up by donors during their own lifetime and designated for use by various members of their own extended family, including freedmen and slaves.[63]

The Jewish *gerusiarch* C. Julius Justus (lines 8-10) set up this *titulus* out of his own testamentary bequest; it displayed formally an honorific (lines 1-7) bestowed on him by the Jewish community. It does not appear that this was a posthumous honorific for Julius Justus, nor is there any mention of deceased family members in the text. In other words, the occasion of the text was the acquisition of the property and the construction/dedication of the tomb. The *titulus* served as a public deed and legal instrument on the property. In this case, the legal terms included a decree of the *gerusia,* under the leadership of Livius Dionysius and Antonius, to allow Julius Justus to use the plot of land for his family's funerary monument. The land was either the property of the Jewish community or purchased out of the communal treasury; Julius Justus was given the land as an honor for his services to the gerusiarchy.[64] The honorific of the Jewish community is cited in the text to establish the legal claim of Julius Justus to the property for himself and his heirs.[65] Such special recognition is not

H. von Hesberg and P. Zanker, Abhandl. des Bayerisch. Akad. Wiss (Munich: Akademie Verlag, 1988), 61-83; and "Inschriften und Grabbauten in der Nekropole unter St. Peter," in *Die Antike im Brennpunkt,* ed. P. Neukam (Munich: Bayerischer Schulbuch-Verlag, 1991), 26-58.

63. On the formulaic nature and the social relationships reflected in these inscriptions, based on a careful study of the tombs and texts from Isola Sacra, see the article by Hanne Sigismund Nielsen, "The Physical Context of Roman Epitaphs and the Structure of the Roman Family," *Analecta Romana instituti Danici* 23 (1996): 35-62. I thank Dr. Nielsen for allowing me to use a draft of this article and for other assistance in the analysis of the Ostian inscriptions.

64. The difference of interpretation here is based on the reconstruction of lines 2-3, as noted above in nn. 58 and 60. The lacuna at the beginning of line 3 makes it impossible to be sure.

65. Other funerary *tituli* regularly mention the legal provisions for the acquisition of the land on which the monument was built. Compare the wording of the Hadrianic-period *titulus* of an imperial slave from Tomb 94 at Isola Sacra (Thylander No. A251):

Dis Manibus
Trophimus Caes(aris) n(ostris) ser(vus) et Claudia
Tyche sibi et Claudiae Saturninae
filae pientisimae quae vixit ann(is)
xv mensibus vi dieb(us) xiii, et libertis
libertibus(que), posterisque eorum.

uncommon among collegial organizations for prominent members, especially leaders, who displayed special service or beneficence to the group. Unfortunately, no mention is made of what actions by C. Julius Justus merited such an honorific, except that he had served as *gerusiarch.*

The *gerusia* was not a central council of elders serving for all the local Jewish congregations, as is sometimes argued.[66] Instead, it reflects the self-definition of a Jewish group that organized itself, at least in public terms, as a typical collegium, club, or religious and craft association. The *gerusia* would have been a commonly recognized term for the governing board or trustees of the collegium. Here we must remember that the earliest form of the synagogue edifice (Phase 2) would have appeared much like other collegial halls at Ostia. The titles *pater* and *patronus* (if my reconstruction of lines 5-6 is correct) for Livius Dionysius indicate that the office of

---

Comparato loco a Valeria
Trophime p(ro) p(arte) IIII huius monumenti.

The woman Valeria Trophime (lines 7-8) appears to be a client or relative of Trophimus to whom as a legal provision he allocated a quarter of his tomb monument. The formula here is comparable to that found in line 2 of the Julius Justus inscription. Compare also the wording of Thylander No. A189 (dating from the time of Antoninus Pius):

Octavius Felixs [. . . .]
Maxima et Iunia E[. . . .]
comparaberunt [. . . .]
loco concessu
Iulio Zotico et A[. . . .]
Artemidora itu amb[itu . . . .]
D

66. For *gerusiarchs* (or *gerousiarchs*) at Rome, cf. Leon, *The Jews of Ancient Rome,* 180-83. I am in complete agreement with Leon (168-70, following Schürer and Frey) that the *gerusia* did not represent a central council of elders over all the Jewish congregations in a city (except perhaps Alexandria), and especially not in the city of Rome. Instead, it seems that it represents the volition of individual congregations to adopt for themselves a collegial organization (and appropriate titles) in imitation of other collegial groups in their immediate locality. For patronage roles and titles in synagogue communities, see White, *Building God's House,* 77-85. For comparable honorific Jewish texts see Lifshitz, *Donateurs,* passim; cf. White, *Christian Domus Ecclesiae,* nos. 64 (= Lifshitz, *Donateurs,* 100), 65 (= *CII* 766), 68 (= *CII* 738), and 71b (= White, "The Delos Synagogue Revisited," *HTR* 80 [1987]:141-44). See also for the title *pater/mater* and other social implications the discussion by Brooten, 57-72 (the Castel Porziano inscription is discussed on p. 70).

gerusiarch carried substantial leadership and patronal functions within the collegial organization. Both C. Julius Justus and Livius Dionysius would appear to be individuals of some stature in Ostian society. Though not likely among the highest echelon of the aristocracy, they were nonetheless well connected socially and upwardly mobile. Hence, their social location begins to reflect on some of the social connections of the larger Jewish community in Ostian society.

One marker of social status for both men is their names. Both appear to be Roman citizens and to carry names that reflect a comfortable position in the pagan society of Ostia. Moreover, both names are common among the aspiring and socially mobile freedmen of Ostia. After one generation, the families of the most prominent of these freedmen entered the ranks of the Roman citizenry, with a boost on the social ladder compared to others. It may be the case that both of the Jewish leaders were descended from freedmen families that had moved into the ranks of the free citizens of Ostia. Julius Justus now has his own network of familial slaves and freedmen as well.

The onomastic C. Julius at Ostia may indicate direct linkage to imperial freedmen. At Ostia, at least four individuals with this onomastic held the office of *Augustalis,* the highest rank among freedmen.[67] The onomastic Livius similarly indicates linkage through freedmen of the aristocratic Ostian family, the A. Livii, which held magistracies under Trajan and Antoninus Pius. More than forty individuals are known at Ostia from this family, and six of these were *Augustales;* however, the name is not attested at Rome.[68] Such aspiring freedmen were not admitted to the decurionate in the first genera-

67. John H. D'Arms, *Commerce and Social Standing in Ancient Rome* (Cambridge: Harvard University Press, 1981), 127, 137 n. 82 and App. 1, nos. 62-65 (cf. *CIL* 14.369, 461, and 5322). At least two of these (nos. 63 and 65) also married outside of their *gentilicium,* which gives further testimony to their social prestige; cf. D'Arms, 134 and App. 2. Given the second-century date of our text, it is important to note that such familial names passed on through layers of freedmen; they tended "to cluster and repeat themselves, especially within the *collegia*" (so D'Arms, 137; cf. Meiggs, *Roman Ostia,* 2nd ed., 323). In general on the problems of onomastic changes in the later empire, see Benet Sałway, "What's in a Name? A Survey of Roman Onomastic Practice from c. 700 BC to AD 700," *JRS* 84 (1996): 124-51. On the problems of Jewish names see especially Heikki Solin, "Die Namen der orientalischen Sklaven in rom," in *L'Onomastique latine,* ed. N. Nuval (Paris: Centre Nationale de la Recherche Scientifique, 1977), 205-9.

68. Meiggs, *Roman Ostia,* 2nd ed., 202; D'Arms, 138 and App. 1, nos. 68-74. Of these, three (nos. 70, 72, and 74) married outside their *gentilicium;* cf. App. 2.

tion after manumission, but their children might have been. Consequently, their acts of public beneficence were important to social mobility. The office of *Augustalis,* prominent in both the imperial cult and civic life, required a substantial fortune to finance public acts of benefaction. These acts are well attested in Ostian inscriptions. The descendants of freedmen, especially the *Augustales,* might be admitted to the decurionate, hold magistracies, and serve as leading civic patrons.[69] Within another generation they could become part of the local aristocracy. One finds, too, that such aspiring freedmen also created tentacular networks of social dependency through serving as officers of guilds or collegia and through patronage of cultic groups.[70] They also had layers of their own freedmen and other clients, who were especially important in trade and commercial ventures.[71] Thus, the names of our two Jewish *gerusiarchs* indicate contacts or clientelism to these higher levels of pagan society at Ostia.[72]

69. The office of treasurer of the *Augustales* alone cost HS 10,000. Two Ostian *Augustales* established foundations in the amount of HS 40,000 and HS 50,000. See D'Arms, 129; Meiggs, *Roman Ostia,* 2nd ed., 221. See also Richard Duncan-Jones, *The Economy of the Roman Empire: Quantitative Studies* (Cambridge: Cambridge University Press, 1974), 176.

70. D'Arms, 133. Such freedmen were widely represented in the guilds and collegia of Ostia, especially those associated with building and shipping. Usually, the freedmen *Augustales* held the highest offices in these collegia, while the patrons of the same collegia were from the decurionate. In other words, here is another mechanism for establishing and maintaining the social connections. Cf. Ramsay MacMullen, *Roman Social Relations* (New Haven: Yale University Press, 1974), 97-100. For the use of private benefactions to foreign cults as a mechanism in this upward mobility, note the case of N. Popidius Celsinus at Pompeii (discussed in my *Building God's House,* 31).

71. D'Arms, 40-45, 132. On the upward mobility of freedmen (especially of non-Italian background) into the decurionate at Pompeii, with implications for population growth and socioeconomic conditions, see the study by Willem Jongman, *The Economy and Society of Pompeii* (Amsterdam: Gieben, 1988), 284-311. More generally on slaves and freedmen in the economic and social activities of the Roman world, see also Susan Treggiari, *Roman Freedmen during the Late Republic* (Oxford: Clarendon, 1969), esp. 205-6 (for Jewish groups and collegia); and Keith Hopkins, *Conquerors and Slaves* (Cambridge: Cambridge University Press, 1978), 64-74, 163-72.

72. Here we may note two other family tombs from Isola Sacra, since they reflect similar names. The following inscriptions come from a closely connected set of families, and they were buried closely as well:

Tomb 88 (Thylander No. A160, dated under Hadrian):

c. Further Epigraphic and Social Observations

In this connection we may notice some comparative evidence from the other main port city of Italy, Puteoli. Ostia and Puteoli have a number of important similarities, especially in regard to the status and mobility of these freedmen and foreign trading groups.[73] The growth of Ostia, especially in the second to fourth centuries, must have been matched by substantial demographic changes, in addition to the massive building programs that are evidenced. Here we may expect commercial contacts and the role

---

Iuliae C. f. Quintae et
M. Antonio Hermeti
fili parentibus
piissimis

Tomb 89 (Thylander No. A180, dated under Antoninus Pius or Marcus Aurelius):

D. M. Coniugi
carissimo Messia
Candida fecit et sibi
et libertis libertabus-
que posterisque eorum
locus concessus ap
Gavinis II, Chresimo
et Eutycho et ap Antonis
II, Iuliano et Polione
itu ambitu introitum
liberum.

73. In general, Puteoli may have reached its zenith a little earlier than Ostia, though both continued to be commercially significant for shipping throughout the Principate. Ostia seems to have been boosted in importance especially after construction began on Trajan's harbor. It inclined to its peak in the second to the fourth centuries but declined after the time of Constantine, when the commercial interests shifted to Porto. Cf. Meiggs, *Roman Ostia*, 64-82. Significantly, Puteoli was set up on the model of and with contacts from the famous Hellenistic commercial center of Delos, where there were both Jewish and Samaritan enclaves. Moreover, it seems rather clear in the case of the Samaritan group that trade and shipping played a part in their activities. A number of other immigrant enclaves (such as the Poseidoniasts from Berytus) on Delos were also organized as commercial agencies or cultic collegia. See my "The Delos Synagogue Revisited," 144-46, 152-53. Also at Puteoli, there is the well-known case of the Tyrian merchants dedicated to Helios Seraptenos. See A. D. Nock, *Conversion* (Oxford: Clarendon, 1933), 66-67; cf. White, *Building God's House*, 31-32. On the comparison of Puteoli and Ostia see also D'Arms, 122-26.

of freedmen and clients to have been a factor for Jews moving into these areas. A good example is the Jewish freedman P. Claudius Akiba from Puteoli. In addition to his own monument (dedicated with the pagan formula *Dis Manibus*), he also set up a monument to his patron, one P. Caulius ([*sic*] ? Claudius) Coeranus, whom he calls a merchant *(negotiator)* in ironware and wine.[74] This Jewish freedman, like most others, took his patron's name. The patron's name, however, suggests that he too had descended from the family of an aspiring freedman, much as suggested for Julius Justus above. P. Claudius Akiba's memorial to his patron and the mention of the commercial activities probably mean that Akiba himself was involved in these same business affairs. Patron and client, pagan and Jew, were part of a layered social relationship. It is likely, too, that Akiba's own economic success came as a result of the support of his former master, to whom he continued to be loyal. Thus, we have other evidence for Jewish freedmen participating in the active social and commercial life of these Roman cities. Such tentacular networks of social relations need to be examined more fully to understand the diffusion of Jews and Christians in the Roman environment.[75]

The name C. Julius Justus shows the same kind of mobility a generation or so later; there are now social connections going in both directions. He was in all probability connected socially to the family of the C. Julii or one of their early freedmen, and was himself, in all likelihood, the descendant of an aspiring Jewish freedman or client. Now he is a Roman citizen and serves as patron of the Jewish community. So, too, he had freedmen and freedwomen clients who were noted in his funerary bequest (line 9). Even the size of the plot and the provisions of the bequest give further testimony of social standing and mobility. Among many of the funerary inscriptions from Ostia, especially of the higher social classes, it was common to announce in the *titulus* the size of the plot, both as a legal provision and as a sign of prestige. The tomb of C. Julius Justus (line 10) measured 18 × 17 Roman feet, or 306 square Roman feet. In size this would compare

74. The two inscriptions are, respectively, *CII* 76* (= *CIL* 10.258) and 75* (= *CIL* 10.1931). Frey's listing indicates he considered the Jewish identity of Akiba dubious, despite the name. Others would disagree. On the use of the formula *D M (Dis manibus)* in clearly Jewish contexts, see Kant, 2:683; cf. van der Horst, 42-43.

75. See my article "Finding the Ties That Bind: Issues from Social History," in *Social Networks in the Early Christian Environment: Methods and Issues for Social History*, ed. L. M. White, *Semeia* 56 (Atlanta: Scholars Press, 1991), esp. 15-21.

favorably, though on the small side, with the average tomb size (ca. 800 Roman square feet) among prominent Ostian freedmen, as known from a survey of the epigraphic remains. It should also be noted that average tomb sizes tended to decrease over time as prices increased, especially in the third and fourth centuries. In contrast, the tombs of *Augustales* and the decurions were considerably larger, averaging circa 1,250 and ranging as large as 2,400 Roman square feet.[76] Here again, we see evidence of an active participation in the social life of the city. In addition to the synagogue building itself, this may be one of our clearest indicators of the relative social position of the Jews within Ostian society. Their social location and apparent affluence must be related to the growth and later renovation (Phases 3 and 4) of the Ostia synagogue. At the same time, it must be noted that this growth seems to have carried the social and architectural identity from its earlier collegial form into a more formal liturgical form.

4. Conclusions: Jews in Ostian Society

C. Julius Justus and Livius Dionysius, the *gerusiarchs* of the Ostia synagogue community, were socially connected and upwardly mobile. There are many other things we would like to know which we are simply not told by the epigraphic remains. For example, how did they come to Ostia? Were they brought as slaves? Did they come voluntarily through commercial contacts or the imperial service?[77] Or were they locally born? In either case one

76. D'Arms, 130; Eck, "Römische Grabinschriften," 61-83.

77. A tantalizing glimpse of the centripetal pull of provincials into this social mix is seen in a casual reference from a private letter from Egypt, in which it is reported that "Herminos went off to Rome and became a freedman of Caesar in order to receive offices" (Ερμῖνος ἀπῆλθεν ἰς Ρώμ[ην]/καὶ ἀπελεύθερος ἐγένετ[ο]/Καίσαρος ἵνα ὀπίκια λάβ[ῃ]). The text is from P.Oxy. 3312, lines 11-13 (ed. J. R. Rea); for the text and discussion see G. H. R. Horsley, *New Documents Illustrating Early Christianity* 3 (1983), 7-9. The letter is variously dated between the first and third century. Note that the Greek word ὀπίκια (line 13) is a Latin loanword *(officia)*. This text clearly deals with a case of a local man who has gone to Rome to join the *familia Caesaris*, the imperial bureaucracy made up of freedmen and slaves. It is noteworthy, however, that there is no mention of his becoming a slave, only a freedman. As an imperial freedman he would have achieved a significant boost on the social ladder at Ostia or Rome. In general Leon was very skeptical of the notion that most of the Jews of Rome had come originally as slaves; therefore, he tended also to discount the idea of Jewish freedmen (*The Jews of Ancient*

senses that they were tied socially both to other Jews and (as clients) to non-Jews in Ostian society. For Livius Dionysius, even though his name suggests some Greek heritage, the *gentilicium* of the prominent A. Livii was indigenously Ostian. Is it possible that he could also be related to the Greek-speaking Jewish patron Mindius Faustus? Were their freedmen and freedwomen also members of the Jewish community?[78] Was the synagogue community part of their functional social network and thus an integral part of their social mobility? How did they make their fortunes? Did the baking establishment and the dining hall attached to the synagogue building have anything to do with these commercial activities, or were they primarily for the social functions of the collegial association of the synagogue? Does the mix of Latin and Greek signal a further social transformation in the life of the Jewish community through the arrival of other Jewish residents in the second and third centuries? Would that we knew the answers to even a few of these questions.

What the Ostian evidence does reveal is the high degree of acculturation of Jews within the social life of these Italian cities, even as they worked to retain their Jewish cultural identity and religious traditions. Both the architectural and the epigraphic remains attest to numerical growth and social mobility for the Jewish community. Just as C. Julius Justus was an aspiring Roman citizen in Ostia's social arena, so too the elaborate renovation of the later synagogue building suggests a higher degree of public awareness and acceptance for the Jewish congregation. Yet, the reverence for Torah as "sacred law" is there in the dedication of Mindius Faustus and later in the installation of the *aedicula* in the synagogue hall. It attests to further elaborations and/or reorientations of the synagogue liturgy over time. Nonetheless, the aesthetics of the renovated architecture, its decoration, and even the Torah shrine itself show distinctively Roman tastes.

Generally, Ostia has been viewed as a microcosm of Rome itself. Our evidence points to one congregation. In Rome the same dynamics were operating in at least ten, probably with a greater range of variability in

---

Rome, 142). But see also Gerhard Fuks, "Where Have All the Freedmen Gone? On an Anomaly in the Jewish Grave-Inscriptions from Rome," *JJS* 36 (1985): 25-32. A recent study of slavery and manumission practices among Jews and Christians has been done by J. Albert Harrill, *The Manumission of Slaves in Early Christianity* (Tubingen: J. C. B. Mohr [Paul Siebeck], 1995).

78. Note *CII* 551a, which gives the name Iustus (in Greek) in a Jewish epitaph from Porto.

social location and degree of acculturation. The Ostian evidence, however, probably corresponds best to the Roman congregations of the "Augustesians" and "Agrippesians." But we must remain somewhat cautious in the use of these materials, since they tend to point to a date from the second century and later. What becomes increasingly clear through much of the archaeological evidence is the relatively late date for a distinctive Jewish synagogal organization and social life at Ostia and Rome (just as elsewhere), even though we know from other sources that there were Jews in Rome and Ostia from the middle of the first century. For the first century, greater attention must be paid to the role of household organization (or "house synagogues"), small ethnic enclaves, and collegial organization in the diffusion of Jewish groups. The material evidence from Ostia, Rome, and throughout the Diaspora reflects a high degree of diversity from locality to locality, and even within given Jewish congregations.[79] Thus, we must be cautious about the nature of the Judaism we expect to find, and allow the archaeological, social, and historical evidence to inform our reading of the literary remains.

79. Cf. Kraabel, "The Roman Diaspora," *JJS* 33 (1982): 457-58; Smith, "Fences and Neighbors," in *Imagining Religion,* 17-18.

CHAPTER 3

The Interaction of Jews with Non-Jews in Rome

Graydon F. Snyder

The interaction of religion and culture has increasingly become a major problem as deconstructed Western Christianity attempts to determine how faith may be shared with persons in other cultures without also exporting a Western culture which no longer serves as a universal system. The key rubric has become inculturation, best defined perhaps by Pedro Arrupe as

> the incarnation of the Christian life and of the Christian message in a particular cultural context, in such a way that this experience not only finds expression through elements proper to the culture in question, but becomes a principle that animates, directs and unifies the culture, transforming and remaking it so as to bring about "a new creation."[1]

In light of this concern we can note the several ways in which Christian "culturization" does occur.

1. Definitions[2]

In the course of religious history, faith (religious myth) has approached other cultures in a variety of ways. It is important that we define these.

1. Pedro Arrupe, "Letter to the Whole Society on Inculturation," in *Other Apostolates Today: Selected Letters and Addresses of Pedro Arrupe*, ed. J. Aixala, vol. 3 (St. Louis: 1981 [1978]), 172-81.

2. Works consulted on inculturation and interaction: David J. Bosch, *Transform-*

a. Assimilation/Acculturation

Assimilation and acculturation are the same dynamic seen from different perspectives. When two cultures meet, or when a new myth contacts a culture, the host culture may assimilate the foreign culture, or assimilate a heretofore unknown myth. From the perspective of the invasive culture or myth, when assimilation occurs it has been acculturated. Needless to say, as we shall frequently note, the process can be one of mutual, though seldom equal, assimilation and acculturation.

Assimilation occurs within a specific social matrix which, by definition, must manifest at least some cultural characteristics. Assimilation of a religious myth is often simply putting social flesh on the more ethereal soul. For the most part a social matrix, in order to exist at all, *must* articulate certain sociological elements. A social matrix must care for its own sense of community, and for families within that community. It must look to a common authority to guide the community and the individual's participation. It must develop common times and styles of celebration. Finally, it must define, in some way, the relationship of community to nature (specifically, land). For the purpose of this study a social matrix will be defined as a community which shares a common ethos in regard to community formation, family, authority, celebrations, and nature. In that sense we will, with some trepidation, speak of a Jewish social matrix and a Roman social matrix. We believe we can describe the elements of an earlier, or extinct, social matrix by examining its artifacts.[3] In any case, culture then will be defined as the commonly accepted manner in which a specific social matrix

---

ing Mission (Maryknoll: Orbis, 1991); Ray O. Costa, ed., *One Faith, Many Cultures: Inculturation, Indigenization, and Contextualization* (Maryknoll: Orbis, 1988); Bolaji Idowu, *Towards an Indigenous Church* (London: Oxford, 1965); Robert Redfield, *The Little Community* (Chicago: University of Chicago Press, 1955); Lamin Sanneh, *Translating the Message: The Missionary Impact on Culture* (Maryknoll: Orbis, 1989); Peter Schineller, *A Handbook on Inculturation* (New York: Paulist, 1990); Robert Schreiter, *Constructing Local Theologies* (Maryknoll: Orbis, 1985); Aylward Shorter, *Toward a Theology of Inculturation* (Maryknoll: Orbis, 1988).

3. Culture may be defined as a social network for dealing with common structural realities (Clifford Geertz, *The Interpretation of Cultures: Selected Essays* [New York: Basic Books, 1973], 89), or in a more archaeological way as occupants of archaeological sites with like artifacts (Bruce Trigger, *Gordon Childe: Revolutions in Archaeology* [New York: Columbia University, 1980]; Vere Gordon Childe, *The Danube in Prehistory* [Oxford: Clarendon, 1929], vi).

expresses itself. Myth will be understood as the religious or philosophical conviction which holds together the component parts.

b. Enculturation

Within the social matrix there must be a method for establishing the validity of the dominant culture and its mythology. Children born into the matrix will be formed and educated to accept the dominant system. We call that enculturation. More complicated than the formation of children would be the enculturation of adult converts. For example, once Christian communities were established, how did they enculturate non-Christians? Obviously, Paul addresses this question when he advises the Corinthian Christians not to eat meat offered to idols (1 Corinthians 10). New converts needed to be aware of a cultural shift even though there was no theological basis for "belief" in idols or meals eaten with such nonentities.

c. Cultural Domination

Though destruction of another culture was not an option for either Jew or Christian in the early centuries of the Roman Empire, eventually, and especially in the nineteenth century, domination became the rule. The procedure is well known and widespread. A more dominant power forces the less dominant culture to give up its characteristics and its method of enculturation. The Christianity of the more powerful culture then replaces the "pagan" culture of the oppressed group.[4] Cultural domination normally occurs in situations where the Christian power holds a military or political advantage. However, there are other possibilities. A superior patronage system can make it advantageous for persons in the disadvantaged culture to "convert." Though less obvious, there are, of course, historical moments when the infrasystem of the dominant culture — intellectual clarity, moral superiority, or linguistic universality — makes it advantageous for the less useful system to be discarded.

4. Note the discussion of Jewish cultural domination by Eliezer Ben-Rafael, *The Emergence of Ethnicity: Cultural Groups and Social Conflict* (Westport, Conn.: Greenwood Press, 1982), 13-19.

d. Inculturation

In recent years a new term has surfaced to describe a style of cultural interaction which allows for an aggressive promotion of an *outside* myth without seeking to dominate or destroy an invaded culture. As noted above, Pedro Arrupe of the Society of Jesus has defined inculturation as an experience which not only finds expression through elements proper to the culture in question, but becomes a principle that animates, directs, and unifies the culture, transforming and remaking it so as to bring about a beneficial "new creation." While Arrupe moves more toward an intentional result than is appropriate for our investigation, the perception is correct. As we shall see, in the case of the Roman social matrix the Jesus tradition entered the social matrix, used the cultural elements, and created a new culture which expressed the Christian faith for that matrix.

We look primarily to the New Testament for the way Christian inculturation began. The Jesus tradition, lacking specific cultural components, infiltrated the Mediterranean world in such a way that eventually a Christian civilization was formed out of Greco-Roman ingredients. The New Testament canon reflects, then, that process of fusing the Jesus tradition with the culture(s) of the Mediterranean social matrix.

The issue is a critical one in New Testament scholarship. In recent years those who espouse a "Jesus tradition" have reduced the canonical Jesus tradition, by means of redaction criticism and form criticism, to a more universal, deculturized Jesus. The premise that the real Jesus tradition should be devoid of prior Jewish materials and later Christian materials has essentially made the historical Jesus an acultural person. Of course, that cannot be true. Jesus was a Jew of the first century, and nearly all of the first Christians were Jews. Granted the Jewish beginning of the Jesus tradition, still the process of further inculturation can be seen quite clearly.

We do not know what Jesus said. We have only the tradition of the first witnesses.[5] According to some, especially Burton Mack, these sayings were first used by specific Jewish communities (centered around Q, around the *Gospel*

5. The Jesus tradition begins with the Jewish people who first heard him. See Willi Marxsen, *Jesus and the Church: The Beginnings of Christianity* (Philadelphia: Trinity Press International, 1992), xxii, 4; and James H. Charlesworth, "Christian Origins and Jesus Research," in *Jesus' Jewishness: Exploring the Place of Jesus in Early Judaism,* ed. Charlesworth (New York: Crossroad, 1996 [1991]), 78.

of Thomas, around miracle stories, around pronouncement stories, and around leading Jerusalem tradents). For Mack, at least, the Gospels and the genuine letters of Paul, as we have them, are indeed already inculturations of these early tradition communities.[6] In the first letters of Paul we find the Jesus material inserted into Jewish apocalypticism. That apocalyptic motif eventually resulted in the identification of the death and resurrection of Jesus as the defining symbol of Christianity.[7] As with the Jesus tradition, the first letters of Paul spawned Pauline communities which might also stress issues of law/freedom, or spiritualism, or even proper church order. In Mark the Jesus tradition was inserted into another Jewish framework, the narrative myth of the suffering righteous.[8] In Matthew the Jesus tradition was inserted into yet another Jewish narrative myth about the righteous who were persecuted. In Luke the Jesus tradition was inserted into a Jewish teleological framework found in the Priestly document (promise and fulfillment). In both Paul and the Gospels there were also elements that paralleled Hellenistic motifs, such as the dying and rising god and the cult meal. These made the early Christian message something which could be inserted into the culture of the Roman world.

At least one Gospel redactor recognized the problem of inculturation — that a Jesus tradition inextricably caught in Jewish cultural patterns (or even Hellenistic cultural patterns) could not be universal. So the Gospel of John was written primarily to deculturize Jesus. In the Fourth Gospel there is no ethic but love, there is no dogma, no community organization. The death and resurrection myth has been shifted to a sign of God's love, and the cultic meal has been rejected in favor of assimilation of the incarnate Jesus. The author of the Fourth Gospel made Jesus available to all cultures.

e. Cultural Interaction

Of course, any cultural interchange must result in a mutual influence. The radical, charismatic revelation of the prophet will need to be adapted to any given social matrix, and, at the same time, that social matrix will be

6. Burton Mack, *Who Wrote the New Testament? The Making of the Christian Myth* (San Francisco: HarperCollins, 1995), 99-121.

7. Luke Timothy Johnson, *The Real Jesus: The Misguided Quest for the Historical Jesus and the Truth of the Traditional Gospels* (San Francisco: HarperCollins, 1995), 134.

8. Mack, chap. 6.

altered in the process. Divine revelation itself may be permanently modified. While the Jesus tradition so altered the Greco-Roman culture that a Christian empire was formed, at the same time the Jesus tradition became a creedal formulation which we have come to call Christian orthodoxy — an orthodoxy which did not exist in the first century of the faith.

When we speak of possible Jewish inculturation of early Rome, it has been conventional to speak of the Jews as strictly isolated, primarily in the Trastevere, without influence on the dominant Roman culture and without assimilating the life of their immediate neighbors.[9] To think of Judaism as an enclosed entity would be highly inappropriate. One can see in the Judaism of Elephantine,[10] or later in Ethiopia,[11] that essential Judaism does interact with and enter into other cultures. In regard to Rome, however, the argument that the Jews of Rome did not interact with Roman culture has depended to a large extent on literary sources and historical data. To be sure, literary sources are the product of a culture and reflect the social matrix from which they originated, but they usually reflect the discrete opinion of one person. In order to assess cultural changes the broader, popular data of symbols and

9. Leonard Victor Rutgers, "Archaeological Evidence for the Interaction of Jews and Non-Jews in Late Antiquity," *American Journal of Archaeology* 96 (1992): 101-18; also *The Jews in Late Rome: Evidence of Cultural Interaction in the Roman Diaspora* (Leiden: Brill, 1995). Rutgers traces the consensus thesis that the Jews lived in isolation (*Jews*, pp. 43-49), and proposes that the issue should be studied primarily in light of archaeology. He shows considerable interaction between Jews and non-Jews. I have used the same method and some of the same data, but my concern is inculturation, not assimilation. That is, I am not asking if the Jews adapted Roman culture, but to what extent the Jews influenced and altered Roman culture. The literary history is well summarized by Harry J. Leon, *The Jews of Ancient Rome* (Peabody, Mass.: Hendrickson, 1995 [1960]), 1-43.

10. The fifth-century-B.C.E. Jews of Elephantine Island, in an Egyptian culture and presumably with only an oral "Moses tradition," developed in a way quite different from Second Temple Jews in Palestine. See A. Cowley, *Aramaic Papyri of the Fifth Century B.C.* (Oxford: Oxford University Press, 1923), xxv-xxvii.

11. Ethiopian Jews or Falasha are so integrated with Ethiopian culture that it has become a matter of continual national debate in Israel as to whether the Beta Israel is actually Jewish or Ethiopian with a Jewish inculturation. See Steven Kaplan, *The Beta Israel (Falasha) in Ethiopia: From Earliest Times to the Twentieth Century* (New York: New York University Press, 1992), 13-32. The complexity of forming a new Israel *(mizug galuyot)* out of so many "acculturations" or "inculturations" exhibits the many ways in which Judaism has fully joined with another culture. The issue has been well described by Ben-Rafael, *The Emergence of Ethnicity.*

inscriptions provide a sounder basis. Although many of us disagree with his conclusions, it is the prodigious work of E. R. Goodenough[12] which demonstrates both the richness of resources and the validity of the symbolic method. In this study I will examine the question of interaction by means of inscriptions, symbols, and language.[13] I will consider how, in the early centuries, the Jews of Rome interacted with Roman culture, how the first Christians of Rome interacted with the same culture, and to what extent these first Christians were themselves the agents of Jewish inculturation. In order to assess the Jews in Rome, I include here a small sample, the inscriptions and symbols found in the Vatican Museum.[14] The symbols are noted by name in brackets. When appropriate, the number in Leon (which corresponds to the *CII* numbers) has been used to catalogue the inscription.[15]

2. Representative Early Jewish Inscriptions in Rome

1. Leon #540

ἐνθάδε κῖτε	Here lies
Μαρτινα	Martina
ἐν ἰρήνη	In peace
ἡ κοίμησις	the sleep
αὐτης	of her
[menorah]	

2. Leon #306

Ἀστήρ	Esther
[bird/grapes menorah bird/grapes]	

12. Erwin R. Goodenough, *Jewish Symbols in the Greco-Roman Period* (New York: Pantheon, 1953 [vols. 2 and 3], 1954 [vol. 4]).

13. The multivolume study of Goodenough has been helpfully abridged by Jacob Neusner, ed., *Jewish Symbols in the Greco-Roman Period* (Princeton: Princeton University Press, 1988). In his introduction Neusner agrees with Goodenough that the religion and its interaction with cultures can best be understood through symbols (p. xvii). In this study we agree with Goodenough that symbols are prior to language and should not be considered decorations. But we do not see symbols as universal in nature (p. xviii). They have a socio-contextual meaning.

14. At the SNTS meeting in Madrid, these specific inscriptions were shown to the seminar by video.

15. Leon, *The Jews of Ancient Rome.*

3.		Leon #477		
		Sabbati-		Sabbatius
		us in pace		In peace
4.		Leon #467		
		Iobinu [menorah]		Jovinus
		qui vix(it) an(nos) XXX V		who lived 35 years
5.		Leon #406		
		ἐνθάδε		Here
		κεῖτε		lies
		Στράτων		Straton
6.		Uninscribed fragment		
7.		Frey, *CII* 451		
		οσειωνως		For devout Noah
		ετ		years
8.		Leon #335		
		[ἐνθάδε κ]εῖτε Εὐφράσεις		Here lies Euphrasius
		ἐτῶν γ μήῶν ι [menorah]		3 years, 10 months
		θάρει Εὐφράσει		Be courageous, Euphrasius
		οὐδεὶς ἀθ[ά]νατος		No one is immortal
9.		Leon #385		
		ἐνθάδεν		Here
		κεῖτε		lies
		Πρεμειτι-		Primiti-
	[ethrog,	βα μετὰ	[flask,	va with
	lulab,	τοῦ ἐγγό-	menorah,	the grand-
	menorah	νου αὐτῆς Εὐ-	lulab,	mother of her
	flask]	φρένοντος	ethrog]	Euphrenon
		ἐν εἰρήνη κοί-		In peace
		μησις αὐτῶν		their sleep
10.		Leon #325		
		ἐνθάδε		Here
		κεῖτε ’Ετη-		lies Etetus
		τος μελλά(ρ)-		almost
		χων ἐν εἰρή-		archon. In peace
		νη ἡ κοίμη-		the sleep
		σις αὐτοῦ		of him
		[menorah]		

11.	Leon #300	
	[two lamps]	
	ἐνθάδε κ-	Here
	εῖτε Ἀννι-	lies Annia
	α ἐπόσε-	Made
	ν σύμβιος	husband
12.	Leon #290	
	אניה חתנה	Annias son-law
	רבר כולברוה	Of Bar-Colbruah
13.	Leon #369	
	ἐνθάδε κεῖτε	Here lies
	Λεοντία	Leontia
	ἐτῶν κ [menorah]	20 years
14.	Leon #374	
	ἐντάδε κῖτε Μαρία γυ-	Here lies Maria
	νὴ Σαλουτίου ὅστις	wife of Salutius, who
	καλως ἔζησεν με-	lived well with
	τὰ τοῦ ἄνδρος αὐτῆς	her husband.
	ἐν ἰρήνῃ ἡ κοίμησις	In peace her sleep.
	[shofar, ethrog, menorah, lulab]	
15.	Leon #361	
	ἐνθάδε κεῖντε 'Ιστασία γυνὴ	Here lies Istasia wife of
	Ἀμαβιλίου ἐτῶν ξ καὶ	Amabilius, 60 years, and
	Πριμα	Prima,
	θυγάτηρ φλαβίας ἐτῶν	daughter of Flavia, years
	ε ἐν ἰρήνῃ ἡ κοίμισις	5, in peace sleep
	αὐτῆς καὶ τῆς Πρίμας	of her and of Prima.
	[matzoh (?), scroll, menorah,	
	ethrog, shofar, flask, lulab]	
16.	Fragment	
17.	Leon #296	
	ἔνθα κῖτε Ἀμμι-	Here lies Ammias,
	ὰς 'Ιουδέα ἀπὸ	a Jewess from
	Λαδικίας ἥτις	Laodicea, who
	ἔζησεν ἔτη [menorah]	lived years
	שׁ πε לם	85
		peace

18. Leon #381

ἐνθάδε κεῖτε	Here lies
Νωμητωρα	Nometora,
παρθαίνος	a virgin,
ἐτῶν ιη	1 years
ἐν εἰρήνη	In peace
ἡ κοίμισις αὐτῆ[ς]	her sleep

3. Symbols and Interaction

In this particular set of inscriptions we find the following symbols: menorah, ethrog, lulab, shofar, and flask. According to Jacob Neusner's study of Jewish discourse in iconic form, the four major Jewish symbols found in early synagogues are, indeed, menorah, ethrog, lulab, and shofar.[16] Granted the mathematical limitations of a small sample, a chart of extant Jewish symbols used will be helpful in assessing the symbolic interaction in Rome.

Twenty-eight sites from the second and third centuries have been identified. In these we find the following distribution of symbols:

Symbol	Sites	Instances
Amphora	2	3
Birds	4	7
Cross	3	3
Crown	1	1
Eagle	7	7
Ethrog	5	6
Flowers	2	2
Genii	3	4
Geometric	1	1
Grapevine	3	3
Hercules knot	2	2
Incense shovel	2	2
Laver	3	3

16. Jacob Neusner, *Symbol and Theology in Early Judaism* (Minneapolis: Fortress, 1991). The archaeological tables, based on the remains of early synagogues, were prepared by Andrew G. Vaughn and revised by James F. Strange.

Lions	3	4
Lulab	3	3
Meander	1	1
Menorah	13	26
Oil jug	1	1
Plant motif	3	3
Rosette	7	7
Shell	4	4
Shofar	5	5
Swastika	1	1
Torah shrine	3	4
Torus	1	1
Vine	8	8
Wheel	2	2
Wreath	5	5

While the menorah clearly appears as a definitive mark of a pre-Constantinian, third-century Jewish synagogue, other symbols are not so obvious. That is, symbols such as the amphora or flask, birds, the cross, an eagle, genii, lions, rosettes, shells, wreaths, and others are just as prevalent as patently Jewish symbols such as the ethrog, lulab, and shofar. Neusner does not include the Torah shrine in his Jewish foursome, though in his list it is the only other definitively *Jewish* symbol. Using the historical criterion of dissimilarity, and assuming the others in Neusner's list are simply decorations held in common with Roman culture, there are indeed just five Jewish symbols in the Roman catacomb list:

1. Ethrog. One of the Four Species *(arbaah minim)* carried and shaken in the Feast of Tabernacles; it is presumed to be the "fruit of goodly trees" of Leviticus 23:40.
2. Lulab. Another of the Four Species, the branches of palm trees, like the ethrog, are mentioned in Leviticus 23:40.
3. Shofar. A ram's horn blown on ceremonial occasions. It was blown at the beginning of the Jubilee Year, the Day of Atonement (Lev. 25:9), the anointing of a new king (1 Kings 1:34), and other high occasions.
4. Menorah. A seven-branch candelabrum used at Hanukkah. See Exodus 25:31-40 for a description of the temple menorah and 1 Kings 7:49 for its use.

5. Torah shrine. An ark topped by a triangular pediment with doors opened to show the scrolls of the Torah.[17]

Derivations for these five symbols are difficult to determine, but as seen in synagogues of the Diaspora they function to make the worshiper a participant in the Jewish holy days.

Artistic symbols serve four distinct functions.[18] (1) Primarily a symbol is a basic form of communication, or an iconic conversation in which a complex set of meanings is conveyed to those who share the same symbol field. In Judaism one thinks of a vineyard or a lamb. In Christianity one thinks of a fish or a dove. (2) A symbol may become sufficiently stereotyped that it actually attaches to a written or oral text and therefore acts as an illustrative recall to bring to the viewer the story found in the text. Judaism had little illustrative art at the time of early Christianity, but in Dura-Europos one does find likenesses of great Jewish leaders, such as Abraham, Isaac, Jacob, Moses, and David. These pictures did not honor the great leaders but symbolically recalled the biblical narratives. One finds illustrations first used in Christianity in S. Maria Maggiore in Rome. (3) Symbols can also capture a myth in such a way that they become an identifying mark for a particular culture. For Judaism that has become the Star of David, while for Christianity it is the cross. (4) Finally symbols can serve simply as common cultural language without any particular meaning. We often think of these as decorations or ornamental art, but actually most of them do identify the user with a particular time, place, and culture.

In their synagogues Jews of the first centuries of the Christian era were quite willing to use a large number of Greco-Roman decorations and symbols. Some, like Goodenough, see in such symbols signals of a more mystical Judaism. Others assume Jewish leaders had no choice but to use ateliers which offered, as a matter of course, pagan decorations, or ornamental art, and other generally accepted cultural symbols.[19] Or, in terms

17. Romano Penna assumes the five are the identifying symbols of Roman Judaism. Romano Penna, "Les Juifs à Rome au temps de l'apôtre Paul," *NTS* 28 (1982): 334.

18. The discussion of symbols by Goodenough (*Jewish Symbols* [1988]) is most instructive even though eventually his mystical/eschatological meanings become too abstract and complex for an average adherent (250-51). In the abridged edition the discussion of symbols occurs on pp. 36-78.

19. Goodenough, *Jewish Symbols* (1988), 38, and excerpts from the interpretive conflict between Goodenough and Kraeling, xx-xxvii.

of interaction, Jews were willing to utilize the decorations and symbols of their non-Jewish neighbors. By so doing they indicated their active participation in Greco-Roman culture. But *none* of these symbols became a part of the Jewish iconic conversation. In that sense, by the first two centuries of the Christian era Judaism had developed a firm symbolic identity. It could accept and utilize pagan symbolic material, but did not assimilate it. Likewise, Judaism of that time did not contribute any symbols to the Roman world, nor, as far as we can determine, did it infuse Roman symbols with a Jewish meaning. That is, Jewish inculturation of the Roman world was negligible.

By looking again at the Vatican collection of Jewish inscriptions, the above conclusion can be confirmed. On their funerary *tituli,* where only a bare minimum of iconic conversation was possible, the Jews of Rome utilized their primary identity symbols: menorah, shofar, ethrog, lulab, and the Torah shrine. As symbols of major events and festivals these five carried intense religious meanings, but they also had become marks of identity. Where one of these five symbols appeared, Jews were present. It could be that the flask (amphora or vase?) also served as a Jewish ceremonial symbol, but such items are too common to make a sure identification.[20] To expand the Vatican sample, Leon lists 534 Jewish inscriptions from Rome. Of these, 144 show the menorah, 34 the lulab, 27 the ethrog, 27 a flask, 14 the shofar, and 6 (all from Monteverde) the Torah shrine.[21] Other items such as birds and branches are very occasional.

In sharp contrast to the Jewish symbolic interaction, the earliest Christian communities came to Rome with no firm identifying symbols. Their earliest examples were all taken, with varying degrees of popularity, from Roman culture. The issue now becomes complex. What did these earliest Christian symbols convey, what meaning was inculturated, and to what extent is that meaning also Jewish? The earliest were:

1. Lamb. The meaning of the lamb has suffered the intense overlay of an illustrative meaning. In Christian history it rather quickly symbolized

20. There are no examples of Torah shrines in the Vatican *tituli.*

21. Leon, *The Jews of Ancient Rome,* 196. Carolyn Osiek, in her revision of Leon's *The Jews of Ancient Rome,* lists 41 more inscriptions, 32 of which were found in the Villa Torlonia catacomb, and were first published by Umberto Fasola ("Le due catacombe ebraiche di Villa Torlonia," *Rivista Archeologia Cristiana* 52 [1976]: 7-62). In Osiek's additional 41 examples, 3 inscriptions from the catacomb of Villa Torlonia include a Torah shrine or ark (#4, #13, #14).

the faithful protected by the Good Shepherd. Representations of the Good Shepherd conveyed the care of Jesus Christ for the believer. As such it appears in many Christian burial locations and, of course, with considerable visibility in Ravenna, both in the Saint Apollinare in Classe and the Mausoleum of Galla Placida.[22] As an illustration it refers to John 10 and Psalm 23. But as iconic conversation it has no Jewish or Christian history. The rich multicultural history of the Good Shepherd as caregiver, as well as the lamb with Orpheus, was sufficiently compatible with nascent Christianity that it assimilated the lamb symbol from Greco-Roman culture.

2. Anchor. Unlike the lamb, the anchor has no illustrative function. Without any particular history it would appear that it carries the iconic meaning of security in an alien environment. Since the Roman culture is that alien environment, then the anchor must express the Jewish-Christian apocalyptic tradition as expressed in the early Jesus tradition. It either recognizes the incompatibility of the faith community with the Roman culture or, more likely, any mass culture at all.

3. Vase. The vase or flask (see Jewish symbols above) may actually simply be a generic decoration. If it carries a more complex meaning, that would be as a symbol of wine at the table fellowship, the meal for the dead (or *refrigerium*), the wine of the Eucharist and the cup of the Passover meal.

4. Dove. The dove has a rich tradition as the bird that brought the deliverance message to Noah and that descended on Jesus at baptism. The dove is a messenger from God, so to speak. Both of these biblical scenes appear fairly often in early Christian art but do not endure as major illustrations (the ark of Monreale near Palermo and the baptism of Jesus in the Cathedral Baptistery at Ravenna are marvelous exceptions). It is seldom that we know the linguistic equivalent of a symbol, but in this case we do. Frequently the dove appears with the word *PAX* or even *EIRENE.* Often an orante and an olive branch occur with the dove, primarily in catacomb art.[23] Clearly we have a highly significant, complex symbol that conveyed the primary message of early Christianity. We cannot easily determine whether it occurred only in funeral art. We do know that the phrase *IN*

22. Giuseppe Bovini, *Ravenna: An Art City* (Ravenna: Edizioni A. Longo, 1967), 21, 153.

23. See the chart in Graydon F. Snyder, *Ante Pacem: Archaeological Evidence of Church Life before Constantine* (Macon, Ga.: Mercer University Press, 1985), 17; also "Early Christian Art," *ABD,* I, 458.

PACE became an identifying mark of Christian burials, as did the term ἐν εἰρήνῃ ἡ κοίμησις αὐτοῦ and *shalom* in Jewish inscriptions. The Jewish sense of covenant *shalom* entered the Western symbol system primarily through the Christian use of the dove symbol and its concomitant sense of peace.

5. Boat. Like the anchor, the boat has no particular iconic significance in either Judaism or Christianity. Granted, it might have funeral significance as the boat for the dead, but there is no literary reason for supposing either Judaism or Christianity entertained such a belief. The early Christians adopted the boat as a significant symbol to express, along with the fish and the anchor, a sense of distance from or even alienation with the dominant culture. Following the peace of Constantine the boat never became either an identifying symbol or a major illustration.

6. Olive branch. Like the dove, the olive branch does appear in pre-Constantinian representations of Noah's ark, but as a symbol it appears more often simply in the beak of the dove. Like the dove, it must be taken as an iconic expression of peace or *shalom*. As such it derives from Judaism and continues through early Christianity. It did not survive as either an illustrative symbol or an identifying mark.

7. Orante. The orante, or praying woman with uplifted hands, has no Jewish or Christian precedent and did not survive either as an illustration or identifying mark. It is strictly a Greco-Roman symbol found on coins and in burial situations. Its iconic value cannot be easily determined. In early Christian art it is often found in the *PAX* complex, and in pictorial representation as the person delivered in such threatening situations as Noah in the ark, the sacrifice of Isaac, Daniel in the lions' den, the three young men in the fiery furnace, and Susanna and the elders. She always appears female even when the person delivered is male. Since her primary identification occurs with the dove and the olive branch, we must assume that she also represents the Jewish, early Christian sense of covenantal *shalom*. The use of the orante on coins with the term *pietas*, an apparent call for trust and loyalty to the emperor, suggests even more that the orante, in difficult situations, including death, calls for the Christian to live by trust in God. So a basic complex of Judeo-Christian meanings is signified by the Greco-Roman icon, though it did not continue after Constantine as an illustration of these well-known biblical passages.

8. Tree. The tree has symbolic significance in all the involved cultures. Though it occurs in early representations, such as Adam and Eve, it probably

serves more as a general culture symbol used for decoration and as a boundary line between pictures.

9. Bread. In Judaism bread not only signifies the fellowship meal, including festival meals (Feast of Unleavened Bread), but also the divine gift of life, as, for example, the manna in the wilderness. Early Christians kept the same sense of bread as a symbol of covenant fellowship and as a divine gift of life. It is impossible to discern what iconic communication occurred between the Christian and Roman cultures. But bread certainly beamed a powerful statement (it not only appears by itself, but also with other meal symbols such as the fish or even the flask). Yet bread did not become an identifying mark for Christianity, and as an illustration it occurs only in the Eucharist.

10. Good Shepherd. Like the lamb, the Good Shepherd has important biblical roots (Psalm 23, John 10), so that as a visual symbol it goes back at least to the ninth century B.C.E.; yet it was also common in the Roman world. Though not present in Jewish symbolism, it appears early and often in early Christian art, both at burial sites and meeting sites. The Good Shepherd picked up the sense of caring and development of community. As such these meanings were expressed in the ancient figure of a shepherd carrying a sheep. Eventually the lamb narratives of the Bible were also inserted into the Good Shepherd so that the shepherd became Jesus caring for the flock. The Good Shepherd became an illustrative symbol for these biblical materials and was an identifying mark of Christianity second only to the cross (and also prior to the cross).

11. Fish. Like the Good Shepherd, the fish was one of the most important identifying marks of early Christianity. Ostensibly the fish was important because of the acrostic meaning of the Greek word ΙΧΘΥΣ, Jesus Christ, Son of God, Savior. That can hardly be the case. In the first place, highly significant symbols do not derive from verbal concepts; the opposite is true.[24] And secondly, there are far more important symbolic meanings which would take precedence over any dogmatic, verbal meaning. Fish are used extensively in much the same fashion as, and sometimes in conjunction with, the anchor. Like the anchor and the boat, the fish conveyed the meaning that real life existed in a realm other than the Roman culture. Furthermore, the fish was, with the bread, the primary symbol for the

24. P. Berger and T. Luckmann, *The Social Construction of Reality* (Garden City, N.Y.: Doubleday, 1966).

Eucharist, the meal that developed, maintained, and celebrated the new community of faith. There is no portrayal of the Christian meal other than fish and bread (wine). There must be a meaning connection with Jesus feeding the five thousand (with pieces left over for the poor and hungry). At this point early Christians must have broken with Passover symbolism, yet — still using Jewish apocalypticism — they made their primary symbol of fellowship one that signified distance from the Roman world. After Christianity became the accepted religion, the fish was no longer a primary or even identifying symbol. Christianity no longer lived in an alien environment. The fish did remain in illustrative portrayals of the Last Supper.

12. Vine/grapes. The vine, the vineyard, and the grape are highly significant symbols for both Judaism and Christianity. On a verbal level the vineyard conveys the meaning of the people of God (Isa. 5:1-10). Sometimes the people (Israel) may simply be a vine (Hos. 10:1; Ps. 80:8-19). In the New Testament the parable of the vineyard (Mark 12:1-10) assumes, by redaction, that the vineyard is Israel. But early Christians obviously considered themselves a valid extension of Israel, so they, too, were the vineyard (1 Cor. 3:5-9; Rom. 15:7-13; John 15:1-8; *Shepherd of Hermas, Similitude* 2). Given the importance of the symbol, it is surprising that it never became an illustrative symbol or identifying mark. Or, perhaps it is so more than we can realize. The vine was a general decoration in the Roman world, and its rather frequent use in catacomb art as an apparent decoration may well have carried more meaning than suspected. The vine and grape occurs more frequently in Jewish symbols than anything except the menorah (see above). For Christians the vine passed into iconic conversation as the glass of wine in the Eucharist. It would still signal the formation of the people of God, even as it did in Jewish festivals.

All of these became identifying symbols for the first Christians, though the anchor, vase, boat, olive branch, orante, and tree took a secondary role after the peace of Constantine. All were "pagan" symbols infused with a new meaning by the early Christian community and the Jesus tradition. None of the early Christian symbols indicates a direct relationship to the early Jewish symbols. As far as iconic conversation is concerned, the Jews of Rome had developed a set of identifying symbols. While they may have been willing to utilize other decorations and symbols,[25] they did not

25. For example, note the Season sarcophagus. See Adia Konikoff, *Sarcophagi from the Jewish Catacombs of Ancient Rome: catalogue raisonné* (Stuttgart: Steiner, 1986).

adapt any as marks of identification, they did not infuse any pagan symbols with new meaning for themselves, they did not provide any new symbols to the Roman world, and they did not serve as a source for nascent, graphic Christian symbols. In contrast, the Roman Christians had no prior identifying symbols, they adopted all their symbols from the Roman world, they infused them with new meaning, and they provided the Roman (Western) world with major cultural symbols.

4. Language and Interaction

The above-mentioned samples from the Vatican are mostly written in Greek, with 2 in Latin and 1 in Hebrew. Leon's larger sample lists 405 (76 percent) in Greek, 123 (23 percent) in Latin, and only 3 in Hebrew.[26] There is nothing surprising here. Diaspora Jews spoke primarily Greek, some Latin, and practically no Hebrew or Aramaic.[27] While language could be an issue of interaction of Jews with non-Jews in Rome, there is no reason to suppose the data for Jews in Rome would be significantly distinctive. It is not clear where and at what point Jews adopted the *lingua franca* of the Roman world.

The same is true of names, though perhaps more can be learned because the use of names does not necessarily reflect the absolute need to communicate with the dominant culture. According to Leon, however, the Jews of Rome did not attempt to maintain identity by means of names. Of his 551 names, only 72 (13.1 percent) are Semitic. In fact, Latin has become predominant with 254 examples (46.1 percent), followed by Greek with 175 examples (31.8 percent). The predominance of Latin names found in inscriptions which are primarily Greek indicates that the Jews of Rome spoke the common language of the Mediterranean world but named their

26. At least two of which came from the same Monteverde catacomb which had the five Torah shrines.

27. Wolfgang Wiefel assumes the Jewish congregations must have spoken in Greek ("The Jewish Community in Ancient Rome and the Origins of Roman Christianity," in *The Romans Debate*, ed. Karl Donfried [Peabody, Mass.: Hendrickson, 1991], 90). Tessa Rajak notes that the balance between Latin and Greek varies according to the catacomb, so that so-called Romanization may well have differed from synagogue to synagogue ("Inscription and Context: Reading the Jewish Catacombs of Rome," in *Studies in Early Jewish Epigraphy*, ed. Jan Willem van Henten and Pieter Willem van der Horst [Leiden: E. J. Brill, 1994], 232-33).

children according to the custom in Rome.[28] In terms of interaction the Jews did not contribute their symbols to the Western world, did not contribute a language, but did contribute many favorite names, such as Esther, Jacob, Jonathan, Isaac, Mary, Martha, Rebecca, Samuel, Sara, and Simon.[29]

Again, the first Christians of Rome did not bring with them names which would mark their identity. So most of their names are Roman or the virtue-names of slaves (such as Fortunatus). When Christians did begin to develop identifying names, they produced four types:[30] (1) biblical names and names of early martyrs; (2) names incorporating names for God; (3) calendar names; (4) Christian virtues. In the larger collection of Christian inscriptions found in the Vatican (*SICV*), there is only one example of a name taken from the Hebrew Scriptures — Susanna. Two of the New Testament names have Hebrew roots (Johannes and Maria), but, in any case, only three other New Testament names are used (Andreas, Paulus, and Petrus). It is possible that the name Laurentius refers to the early martyr. God-names appear in such appellations as Theophilus, Timotheus (or is it a New Testament name?), Theonis, and Cyriacus/Cyriace/Cyriacete. Calendar names have Jewish roots. The *SICV* examples are Paschasius and Sabbatius/Sabbatia. As for virtues, it is difficult to tell whether frequent names such as Elpis and Irene are actually Christian. Probably Anastas, Redempta, Renatus/Renata are of Christian origin. Nevertheless, the one certain Christian virtue name was Agape, though one cannot claim uniqueness.

Perhaps it is not the names themselves that are most important. It is somewhat remarkable that the lasting names of the Western world include a large number from the Hebrew Scriptures and names of Jews who were primary figures of the New Testament. Even more important, though, is the process of name democratization. The formal male name in the Roman world contained three names, while the formal female name contained two. Of the 541 names listed by Leon, only 3 are triple and only 49 are double. Of the names listed in the *SICV*, 20 percent are proper Roman names.

28. In Osiek's revision of Leon's *The Jews of Ancient Rome*, 20 of the 41 names are Greek (49 percent), 15 are Latin (37 percent), and 3 are Semitic (7 percent). See xv-xvi.

29. See Gerard Mussies, "Jewish Personal Names in Some Non-Literary Sources," in *Studies in Early Jewish Epigraphy*, 250.

30. According to Iiro Kajanto, "Les Noms," in *Sylloge inscriptionum christianarum veterum musei vaticani*, ed. Henrik Zilliacus, Acta instituti romani finlandiae, vol. I:2 (Helsinki, 1963), 68-71; hereafter cited as *SICV*.

Although chronology is, unfortunately, uncertain for most of these inscriptions, it is quite clear that Roman names took a sharp drop after the peace of Constantine. By the sixth century only 4 percent of the men and 2 percent of the women had proper Roman names. Jews and Christians in Rome participated in (caused?) a sociological shift which obviated the social distinctions between noble, artisan, and even slave.[31]

In terms of the vocabulary itself, there is much to observe. In the Jewish collection from the Vatican museum nearly every inscription is introduced by the terms ἐνθάδε κεῖτε. This simple statement about the presence of the deceased in the tomb contrasts sharply with the nearly universal introduction on Roman inscriptions: *DM,* or *dis manibus* (to the spirits).[32] Christians dropped the *DM,* sometimes in favor of *BM, bene merenti,* or *depositus/deposita,* meaning, one supposes, that the deceased is here only temporarily. Both ἐνθάδε κεῖτε and *depositus/deposita* break with the sense that the deceased is now among the spirits or daimons.

Both Jewish and Christian burial inscriptions are frequently marked by the key word "peace."[33] In the Vatican Jewish inscriptions, numbers 1, 3, 9, 10, 14, 15, 17, and 18 end with some form of the acclamation "in peace." The final phrase follows this formula: (1) the acclamation "in peace"; (2) the condition wished, "sleep"; (3) a pronoun reference to the deceased person. A typical example would be number 15, ἐν ἰρήνη ἡ κοίμισις αὐτης, or number 10, ἐν εἰρήνη ἡ κοίμησις αὐτοῦ. Of the 294 complete inscriptions described by Leon, 239 open with ἐνθάδε κεῖτε and 167 end with ἐν εἰρήνη. Of the 167 ending with "in peace," 136 contain the complete phrase, in varying forms, ἐν εἰρήνη ἡ κοίμησις αὐτοῦ.[34] In addition, at least 10 of the remaining examples mention sleep in some form.

31. An observation so lamented by Jérôme Carcopino, *Daily Life in Ancient Rome* (New Haven: Yale University Press, 1963).

32. See also Rutgers, *The Jews,* 269-72.

33. Erich Dinkler, "Shalom-Eirene-Pax: Jüdische Sepulkralinschriften und ihr Verhältnis zum frühen Christentum," *Rivista Archeologia Christiana* 50 (1974): 121-44.

34. Leon, *The Jews of Ancient Rome,* 122. Of the 41 additional inscriptions listed by Osiek in the revised edition of *The Jews of Ancient Rome,* 3 include the complete set of formulas, 4 others have the closing formula "in peace, sleep," and 2 include the opening formula "here lies" and the closing "in peace." Of the remaining, 4 close with "in peace" and 12 open with "here lies." Or, put another way, 17 open with "here lies" and 13 close with "in peace."

Several speak of sleep with the saints, e.g., μετὰ τῶν δικέων ἡ κύμησις αὐτοῦ (number 110). While one cannot deduce from a few epexegetical phrases that the sleep always refers to rest or peace with the faith community, it would be difficult to avoid this intent. The ending phrase was an identity mark for Jewish graves. The sleep referred to continued existence within the boundaries of the community, likely even the specific synagogue that used that catacomb. The quality of sleep with the righteous was, it was hoped, *shalom.*

Likewise, *in pace* became the identifying mark of a Christian burial. Of the 350 examples in the *SICV,* 107 utilize *in pace* at some point. The origin and meaning of the phrase has been much debated.[35] Like *vivas,* it appears as an acclamation, used perhaps at meals or other times of conviviality. *In pace* offers a wish that the person will find joy and satisfaction in the corporate (meal) setting. Christians followed the Jews by using the term *shalom.*[36] Instead of death as a time of individual wandering, Jews and Christians expressed faith in a continued existence *(depositus)* among the believing community.

5. Conclusion

According to the data available, it is clear that Jewish inculturation of Roman culture was slight. While Jews utilized common decorations, they did not accept any major symbols from the Roman world, nor did they contribute any. In regard to language the picture is different. Jews did take on the language of the Romans and used Roman names. While Hebrew or Aramaic never became a significant element in the language of the Western world, the Jews did contribute many personal names.

Christians, on the other hand, in order to express themselves to each other and to the Roman world adopted their symbols directly from the

35. For references see Patrick Bruun, "Symboles, Signes et Monogrammes," in *SICV,* 76-79.

36. Dinkler ("Shalom-Eirene-Pax") doubts that early Christians derived their acclamation "in peace" from Jewish burial practices. He prefers a separate development that depends on early Christian worship (he notes John 14:27; 20:19, 21, 26; Eph. 2:14). In any case, the source for the peace acclamation and its communal meaning would have been Judaism.

dominant culture. Sometimes the symbol already carried what the Christian wished to say (Good Shepherd, orante, and lamb), while at other times Christians infused the symbol with their own meaning (fish, bread, vine, and dove). Sometimes the symbol signified a desire to remain aloof from the dominant culture (anchor, boat, and fish). While Judaism did not contribute symbols directly to the Roman world, it did indirectly contribute its worldview through Christian symbols (bread, lamb, vine, dove, and Good Shepherd).

In regard to language the story is different. Jews almost totally adopted the language of Rome and used Roman names, but not the name system. In terms of interaction, however, Jews contributed a large number of personal names to the Western world. Christians also adopted the language of the Roman world. Likewise, they used Roman names, but not the system. They apparently contributed very few personal names to the Western world.

Together Jews and Christians brought to the Roman world their most significant social contribution, a deep sense of community satisfaction through an identifying word: *PAX* — *shalom.*

Finally, the Jews of Rome built an identity vis-à-vis Roman culture. Christians, on the other hand, infused the symbols of Rome with new meaning and created new ones. That inculturation created a new culture.

PART 2

SOCIAL-HISTORICAL STUDIES

CHAPTER 4

Roman Policy toward the Jews: Expulsions from the City of Rome during the First Century C.E.

Leonard Victor Rutgers

> Tant de causes secrètes se mêlent souvent à la cause apparente, tent de ressorts inconnus servent à persécuter un homme, qu'il est impossible de démêler dans les siècles postérieures la source cachée des malheurs des hommes les plus considérables, à plus forte raison celle du supplice d'un particulier qui ne pouvait être connu que par ceux de son part.
>
> Voltaire, *Traité sur la tolérance* (1763)

In this essay I want to discuss the evidence for expulsions of Jews from the city of Rome in the first century C.E. Scholars have long been interested in the reasons underlying these expulsions. Because the ancient literary sources regarding such expulsions are scanty and often contradictory, no generally accepted explanation for the rationale behind these events has hitherto been offered. We, in fact, often lack even the most basic kind of information. Not infrequently it remains obscure, for example, how many Jews were expelled by Roman authorities and to what social class they belonged. Similarly, we simply cannot tell whether expulsions of Jews from Rome were at all effective in the long run.

Rather than studying individual expulsions of Jews in isolation — as several scholars have done recently — I have opted in this essay for a more comprehensive approach. In order to explain Rome's decision to remove Jews from the capital of its empire, it is necessary to study the question of the position of the Jews in the Roman Empire in general. In addition, it is necessary to study the evidence for expulsions of people other than Jews. Finally, we also need to establish if (and if so, how) Romans were tolerant of other non-Roman peoples.

1. The First Roman Legal Measures regarding the Jews: The *Acta Pro Judaeis*

Although the Jews of both Palestine and the Diaspora had steadily moved into the orbit of the Roman world in the course of the second century B.C.E., Rome did not develop a substantial body of laws regarding the Jews until the second half of the first century B.C.E. Only then, in the fifty-odd years from Caesar to Augustus, did Roman magistrates pass a number of decrees aimed at protecting the free exercise of Jewish religion. They decreed that Jews might gather freely in *thiasoi,* observe the Sabbath and the Jewish festivals, send money to the temple in Jerusalem, and enjoy autonomy in their communal affairs. Jews were also absolved from compulsory enrollment in the Roman military.[1]

Josephus, our only ancient source on these decrees, indicates that by passing legal measures in favor of the Jews, Rome acted in its own interest but not of its own initiative. In the later first century B.C.E., Roman law on the Jews developed primarily in response to the requests of the Jewish communities of the Aegean, Asia Minor, and other parts of the Near East, including Cyrenaica, to help them protect their traditional Jewish way of life against the constant attacks of their Greek neighbors.

Roman legal measures normally took the form of *senatus consulta* that were sent to individual Greek cities of the East in order to settle specific disputes between Jews and Greeks. Because the rulings contained in these

1. Josephus, *Ant.* 14.190-264; 16.162-73. For later measures taken by Claudius, see Josephus, *Ant.* 19.278-91; 19.299-311; 20.1-14. 1 Maccabees 15 claims that Rome became a guarantor of Jewish religious liberty throughout the Mediterranean as early as the second century B.C.E. But there is no convincing evidence to substantiate this claim; see J.-D. Gauger, *Beiträge zur jüdischen Apologetik: Untersuchungen zur Authentizität von Urkunden bei Flavius Josephus und im ersten Makkabäerbuch* (Cologne: Hansten, 1977), 299f. The enrollment of the Jews in the *formula amicorum et sociorum* of the Roman People in 140 B.C.E. did not oblige the Romans to protect the rights of individual Jews living in the Diaspora; see Gauger, 188f., 205, 229f., 253f., 324.

senatus consulta never attained universal validity, it is not correct to regard such senatorial decrees as a Magna Charta or formal document that aimed at defining the legal status of all Jewish communities in the eastern Mediterranean once and for all. The *senatus consulta* regarding the Jews were essentially ad hoc measures that related to geographical units of much smaller dimension.[2] That this was so should not surprise us: a variety of sources indicates that in the later Republic and early Principate Rome tried to leave the constitutions of the Greek cities intact as far as possible.[3]

Scholars have often wondered whether the documents presented by Josephus are at all genuine. Josephus is the only ancient author to mention these decrees. We furthermore also know that Josephus's text suffers from serious textual corruptions. Finally, numerous mistakes in chronology and in the names of serving magistrates further complicate the interpretation of this already problematical text.[4] All this is true. Yet, instead of focusing exclusively on the more formal characteristics of Josephus's account, we rather need to ask whether textual difficulties suffice to discredit altogether the evidence presented by Josephus as regards the substance of these decrees. The answer to this question is negative. For example, it is well known from sources other than Josephus that attacks on Jewish property were punished immediately by the Roman authorities.[5] It is likewise well known that anyone who attempted to confiscate money destined for the (Second) Temple in Jerusalem was liable to prosecution.[6] Last but not least,

2. Earlier literature in L. H. Feldman, *Josephus and Modern Scholarship* (Berlin: de Gruyter, 1984), 273-76. T. Rajak, "Jewish Rights in the Greek Cities under Roman Rule: A New Approach," in *Approaches to Ancient Judaism*, vol. 5, *Studies in Judaism in Its Greco-Roman Context*, ed. W. S. Green (Atlanta: Scholars Press, 1985), 23; T. Rajak, "Was There a Roman Charter for the Jews?" *JRS* 74 (1984): 107-23.

3. L. Mitteis, *Reichsrecht und Volksrecht in den östlichen Provinzen des römischen Kaiserreichs* (Hildesheim: Olms, 1963), 85-109; R. Bernhardt, *Polis und römische Herrschaft in der späteren Republik (149-31 v. Chr.)* (Berlin: de Gruyter, 1985), 219f., 227f.

4. These problems are discussed in detail by H. R. Moehring, "The *Acta pro Judaeis* in the *Antiquities* of Flavius Josephus," in *Christianity, Judaism, and Other Greco-Roman Cults: Studies for Morton Smith at Sixty*, ed. J. Neusner (Leiden: Brill, 1975), 124-58. More recently, C. Saulnier, "Lois romaines sur les juifs selon Flavius Josèphe," *RB* 87 (1981): 161-98.

5. Hippolytus, *Haeres.* 9.1-9.

6. Witness Cicero, *Pro Flacco* 66-69; and cf. Philo, *Embassy* 156. For evidence from Cyrenaica, see M. W. Baldwin Bowsky, "M. Tittius and the Jews of Berenice," *AJP* 108 (1987): 509.

evidence for Jews serving in the Roman military is virtually nonexistent.[7] Such evidence suggests uniformly that when Roman magistrates intervened in disputes involving Jews, they were enforcing decrees very similar to the ones Josephus claims the Romans issued. There thus exists little circumstantial evidence to suggest that Josephus invented these decrees to insert them in his *Antiquities* for purely apologetic purposes.

From a Jewish perspective, the first series of Roman senatorial decrees concerning the Jews was above all important in that they gave the various Jewish communities under Roman rule something to fall back on when under pressure from their non-Jewish neighbors.[8] From the Roman point of view, the *senatus consulta* were significant in terms of both administration and law: these decrees quickly assumed the role of legal precedents to which provincial governors and indeed emperors could refer in order to justify their decisions when confronted with disputes over Jewish rights.[9] For the ancient historian, finally, an analysis of Josephus's account is particularly interesting in that it helps to place into a long-term perspective the question of the expulsions of Jews from Rome during the first century C.E. Josephus's description serves to illustrate that Roman policy toward the Jewish community of Rome during the first century C.E. was not a new phenomenon but rather followed patterns that had already been established in the later republic. The most salient feature of this policy (at least for the purpose of this article) was that Rome did not have a standard policy toward the Jews: Roman magistrates responded to situations.

7. Jews could serve in the Roman army (cf. *CTh* 16.8.24; 12.1.100; 16.8.16), but it is not clear if they ever did so in large numbers. Two epitaphs of soldiers published by A. Scheiber (*Jewish Inscriptions in Hungary: From the Third Century to 1686* [Leiden: Brill, 1983], nos. 4 and 6) contain names that are Semitic but not necessarily Jewish. The same is true of the names in V. A. Tcherikover et al., *Corpus Papyrorum Judaicarum* 3 (Cambridge: Harvard University Press, 1964), no. 465. Further references in L. Cracco Ruggini, "Note sugli ebrei in Italia dal IV al XVI secolo," *RSI* 6 (1964): 932 n. 21.

8. See, e.g., Josephus, *Ant.* 16.172.

9. Josephus, *Ant.* 16.173; 19.282-83; 19.304-6; V. A. Tcherikover et al., *Corpus Papyrorum Judaicarum* 2 (Cambridge: Harvard University Press, 1960), no. 153, col. V, lines 86-87. Edicts issued by an emperor remained in force after his death: F. Millar, *The Emperor in the Roman World (31 B.C.–A.D. 337)* (Ithaca: Cornell University Press, 1977), 252-53; *RE* 5 (1905): 1947.

2. The Civic Status of the Jews of Rome

In order to understand the legal aspects of the expulsions of Jews from Rome during the first century C.E., we need to know something about the civic status of those Jews.

Philo says the Jews of Rome were mostly slaves who had become Roman citizens after manumission.[10] This seems to be fairly close to the truth. Jews may have reached Rome as early as the middle of the second century B.C.E.[11] Whether they arrived there as free *peregrini* or whether they descended from manumitted slaves who had first reached Rome through the slave markets of the eastern Mediterranean (such as Delos) is impossible to tell.[12] After Pompey's victories of 63 B.C.E. in Syria and Palestine, new Jewish slaves were brought in, this time directly from Palestine. We do not know how many of these prisoners of war actually reached Italy or what percentage of them ended up as slaves in the city of Rome.[13] What is clear, however, is that by the time of their arrival a Jewish community was already well established in Rome. It must have counted free immigrants among its members as well as the many who were slaves or freedmen.

That a not inconsiderable number of Jews in Rome had become *cives Romani* by the time of Augustus can be inferred from their participation in the monthly doles;[14] exact figures, however, cannot be given. Not every slave of Jewish origin automatically became a Roman citizen upon manumission, since not all manumissions were formally carried out, that is, *testamento, vindicta,* or *censu.* Informal manumission led, at least after 19

10. Philo, *Embassy* 156.

11. E. M. Smallwood, *The Jews under Roman Rule: From Pompey to Diocletian* (Leiden: Brill, 1976), 130; Harry J. Leon, *The Jews of Ancient Rome* (Peabody, Mass.: Hendrickson, 1995 [1960]), 3-4; H. Solin, "Juden und Syrer im westlichen Teil der römischen Welt: Eine ethnisch-demographische Studie mit besonderer Berücksichtigung der sprachlichen Zustände," *ANRW* II.29.2 (1983), 607.

12. The enrollment in the *formula amicorum et sociorum* (cf. A. N. Sherwin-White, *Roman Foreign Policy in the East, 168 B.C. to A.D. 1* [Norman: University of Oklahoma Press, 1983], 58-77) resulted in all Jews on Roman territory who were not Roman citizens or slaves automatically becoming *peregrini;* see Kübler in *RE* 19 (1937): 639-55, s.v. "peregrinus."

13. Josephus, *Ant.* 14.78; Plutarch, *Vita Pomp.* 45.1-2; Appian, *Mith.* 117.571; Eutropius, *Breviarum a.u.c.* 6.16.

14. Philo, *Embassy* 158; A. N. Sherwin-White, *The Roman Citizenship,* 2nd ed. (Oxford: Clarendon Press, 1973), esp. 221f.

C.E., to a status inferior to that of the Roman citizen, namely, to that of the Junian Latin.[15] Of course, such *Latini Iuniani* could become *cives Romani* — for example, by serving in the police or by supplying Rome with corn for a period of time — but once more, it is not clear whether this was common or even whether achieving the status of Roman citizen was considered desirable.[16] Cicero remarks that prisoners of war should be freed after six years of slavery, but this cannot be taken to mean that Jewish (or non-Jewish) slaves were always quick to acquire their freedom.[17]

Under Roman law Jews in Rome during the first century C.E. belonged to one of the three following categories. (1) Some were slaves. Although lacking legal personality, slaves were subject to criminal law. In case of criminal offenses they could be punished either by their master or by the Roman state. (2) Some were free *peregrini* or *Latini Iuniani.* As such they were largely outside the sphere of the *ius civile* and subject to the *coercitio* of the magistrates. They could be chased out of the city without any form of trial.[18] (3) Some were Roman citizens, who could only be expelled after they had been found guilty of a criminal offense in a Roman court.[19] Yet, even after having been convicted, a Roman citizen had the right to appeal *(provocatio)* to a higher authority, in the present case the emperor.

3. The Expulsion of Jews from Rome under Tiberius

Various authors relate how in 19 C.E. Jews as well as worshipers of Isis were expelled from Rome. The sources disagree as to why these expulsions took

15. A. Watson, *Roman Slave Law* (Baltimore: Johns Hopkins University Press, 1987), 24f. On formal manumission, see Gaius 1.17.

16. Watson, *Roman Slave Law;* P. R. C. Weaver, "Where Have All the Junian Latins Gone? Nomenclature and Status in the Early Empire," *Chiron* 20 (1990): 275-305, esp. 303f.; R. MacMullen, "Notes on Romanization," *BASP* 21 (1984): 167.

17. Cicero, *Phil.* 8.32.

18. Examples of limited legal protection provided to *peregrini* in *RE* 10 (1919): 1229-30, s.v. "Ius Gentium."

19. When someone's guilt was beyond doubt, however, or when someone was a *confessus,* no trial was necessary: cf. W. Kunkel, "Prinzipien des römischen Strafverfahrens," in *Kleine Schriften: Zum römischen Strafverfahren und zur römischen Verfassungsgeschichte* (Weimar: Böhlaus, 1974), 17f.

place and who was responsible for them.[20] That the problems that had arisen were serious is, however, beyond doubt: the incident was scandalous enough for the Senate to deal with it directly rather than leaving it to the intervention of the city prefect.[21]

Because of the contradictory statements in the primary sources, scholars have offered differing accounts of what actually happened. Some argue that Jews and devotees of Isis were expelled for religious reasons, while others contend that Rome acted merely to maintain law and order.[22] Let us consider these two views in turn.

From Josephus's account it seems to follow that in 19 C.E. Jews were expelled from Rome for religious reasons. Josephus writes that a few Jews deceived an aristocratic female proselyte called Fulvia by stealing the "purple and gold" Fulvia had intended as gifts to the temple in Jerusalem, and that it was this that led to the expulsion. This rather detailed account is highly interesting, but it cannot be taken at face value. In dealing with the Isis worshipers the Roman authorities punished only the *auctores seditionis,* who were found guilty of seriously maltreating an aristocratic woman:[23] why, then, on being confronted by a less serious offense committed by a few Jews, should they have punished the whole Jewish com-

20. Tacitus, *Annals* 2.85.4-5; Suetonius, *Tiberius* 36.1; Josephus, *Ant.* 18.63f.; Dio Cassius 57.18.5a; Philo, *Embassy* 159-61. Cf. also Philo, *Against Flaccus* 1. I do not believe that the evidence provided by Philo suggests two separate moves against the Jews in Tiberius's reign, contra Smallwood, 208f., and Solin, 688 n. 218b.

21. See, in general, P. Garnsey, *Social Status and Legal Privilege in the Roman Empire* (Oxford: Clarendon Press, 1970), 30-33.

22. References to earlier literature in M. H. Williams, "The Expulsion of the Jews from Rome in A.D. 19," *Latomus* 48 (1989): 765, to which should be added Solin, 686-89, and the uncritical essay by G. Marasco, "Tiberio e l'esilio degli ebrei in Sardegna nel 19 d.C.," in A. Mastino, ed., *L'Africa romana: Atti del VIII convegno di studio, Cagliari, 14-16 XII 1990* (Sassari: Gallizzi, 1991), 649-59.

23. In case of the Isis worshipers, the charge is most likely to have been adultery; so, correctly, Garnsey, *Social Status,* 22. Cf. also M. Malaise, *Les conditions de pénétration et de diffusion des cultes égyptiens en Italie* (Leiden: Brill, 1972), 88f. The adultery laws promulgated by Augustus continued to be valid under Tiberius and later emperors; see the list of adultery prosecutions in S. Treggiari, *Roman Marriage: Iusti Coniuges from the Time of Cicero to the Time of Ulpian* (Oxford: Clarendon Press, 1991), 509-10. On the importance of adultery cases in later Roman penal law in general, see T. Mommsen, *Römisches Strafrecht* (Graz: Akademische Druck- und Verlagsanstalt, 1955), 528f. and 691f. On the Roman practice of punishing accomplices to a crime, see Mommsen, 100-103; and on the *auctor seditionis,* Mommsen, 564.

munity of the city? Given Rome's generally moderate policy toward the Jews, and given the fact that Roman magistrates took the trouble of issuing a special *senatus consultum,* it is hardly possible to accept Josephus's view that the Roman authorities blamed the entire Roman Jewish community for the misdeeds of a handful of culprits.[24] It is quite possible, therefore, that Josephus inserted the story of Fulvia in order to absolve the Jews from any real responsibility for the expulsion of 19 C.E.[25]

Some scholars who reject the deception of Fulvia by a few impostors as the reason for the expulsion of Jews from Rome suggest, along with Dio and possibly Tacitus, that the reason for expelling the Jews must be sought in the fact that in general the Jews of ancient Rome were all too successful in making new converts.[26] Tacitus observes that "another debate dealt with the proscription of the Egyptian and Jewish rites," and then continues by remarking that four thousand men *libertini generis* were sent to Sardinia to help suppress brigandage there; all others had to leave Italy "unless they had renounced their impious rites by a given date."[27] Dio writes that "as the Jews had flocked to Rome in great numbers and were converting many of the natives to their ways, he [i.e., Tiberius] banished most of them."

The interpretation of these passages raises several problems. Tacitus nowhere states that Jews were found objectionable because they tried to win over new converts. He observes only that the Senate decided to expel all practitioners of Judaism and of "Egyptian rites." By adding that all those who were willing to give up their "impious rites" did not have to leave Italy, he implies that the offense of those to be expelled had to do with their

24. Note that also Philo, who is likewise somewhat apologetic about what happened, remarks that the people who were really guilty were few in number (*Embassy* 161).

25. *Pace* M. H. Williams, "Expulsion," 775-77, and contra Marasco, 652, 654. But Williams's suggestion that the men who carried out the deceit became folk heroes is farfetched. Malaise, 88, considers even the story involving the Isis priests an invention.

26. Leon, 19; Smallwood, 203-4; M. Stern, *Greek and Latin Authors on Jews and Judaism,* 3 vols. (Jerusalem: Israel Academy of Sciences and Humanities, 1974-84), 2:70; Solin, 687; K. A. D. Smelik, "Tussen tolerantie en vervolging," *Lampas* 22 (1989): 181; Suetonius, *Tiberius* 36.1.

27. On the translation of this expression, see Solin, 687-88. L. Feldman, "Jewish Proselytism," in *Eusebius, Christianity, and Judaism,* ed. H. W. Attridge and G. Hata (Leiden: Brill, 1992), 372-408. Nothing, however, warrants the conclusion that these people were "proseliti ebrei," contra Marasco, 649.

religious customs rather than with regular offenses of a criminal nature.[28] Yet, Tacitus never elaborated in any detail on the rationale behind this measure. In his eyes the Senate's decision was too self-evident to need a more specific explanation.[29]

Dio, by contrast, is very explicit as to why Jews were expelled from Rome: Jews were proselytizing on too large a scale.[30] Although this explanation is straightforward, it is nevertheless not very plausible. The passage in Dio's *Roman History* is only a casual reference inserted into an account written roughly two hundred years after the expulsion. It is even more problematical that evidence pointing to widespread conversion of non-Jews to Judaism under Tiberius is extremely weak. It is true that Jewish proselytism was one of the favorite subjects of first-century authors who wrote about the Jews,[31] though the remarks are rather stereotypic. It is also true that in the first century C.E. some upper-class Romans felt attracted to Judaism, not improbably because of its "lofty moralism with high moral codes."[32] Yet, as a result of the inclusivist character of Roman religion, as opposed to the exclusivist tendency of Jewish and, later, early Christian monotheism, sympathy for Judaism could also take forms other than conversion. From a Roman perspective there was nothing strange about integrating the Jewish god into a larger, non-Jewish pantheon.[33] Furthermore,

28. Suetonius says of the astrologers only that those who gave up the practice of their art were permitted to stay.

29. Mommsen thought that the practice of Judaism by *cives Romani* (even Jewish ones) constituted an abandonment of Roman religion ("Der Religionsfrevel nach römischem Recht," in *Gesammelte Schriften* 3 [Berlin: Weidmann, 1907], 403-6, 413), but this is too rigid and less convincing. Mommsen (p. 418) believed that before 70 C.E. the "Jewish privileges" did not apply to a Jew who became a Roman citizen.

30. This passage is, in my view, not superior to all other accounts, contra Smallwood, 208. I agree with M. H. Williams, "Expulsion," 767-78.

31. Sources in Stern, vol. 3, index, s.v. "proselytism."

32. Smallwood, 205.

33. E.g., *SHA*, *Alex. Sev.* 29.2. Other good examples in E. Bickermann, "The Altars of the Gentiles: A Note on the Jewish 'Ius Sacrum,'" in *Studies in Jewish and Christian History* 2 (Leiden: Brill, 1980), 339-40. See in this context also M. H. Williams, "*Theosebes gar en* — The Jewish Tendencies of Poppaea Sabina," *JTS* 39 (1988): 97-111, esp. 104-5; S. J. D. Cohen, "Crossing the Boundary and Becoming a Jew," *HTR* 82 (1989): 13-33; J. Reynolds and R. Tannenbaum, *Jews and Godfearers at Aphrodisias*, Cambridge Philological Society Suppl. vol. 12 (Cambridge, 1987); and A. F. Segal, *Paul the Convert: The Apostolate and Apostasy of Saul the Pharisee* (New Haven: Yale University Press, 1990), 95f.

to think that many conversions to Judaism took place because Roman religion had become petrified by the early first century C.E. is grossly to oversimplify the situation. Recent studies have shown that in the early Principate the Roman cults of old had far from disappeared. In this period many Romans were *not* desperately looking elsewhere for spiritual guidance.[34] In this context we should also consider, once more, Josephus's story of the proselyte Fulvia. Even if the story as a whole is probably fictional, it contains valuable information in its details. According to it, the Jews of Rome were punished only for stealing the "purple and gold" Fulvia wanted to send to the temple in Jerusalem. Nowhere does Josephus indicate that Jews were penalized for converting a member of the ruling class to Judaism.[35] On the basis of these considerations, then, it is simply impossible to maintain that in early first-century Rome conversions to Judaism were taking place on a large scale;[36] nor, more important, can one tell whether Roman authorities thought such conversions were actually taking place. Inscriptions from the third- and fourth-century Jewish catacombs cannot, of course, be used to demonstrate that the number of proselytes in the first century C.E. was either large or small.[37]

Another explanation for the expulsion of the Jews from Rome in 19 C.E. favors political over religious concerns. The evidence for this thesis, however, is even more scanty than that for a religious one. H. Solin, unsatisfied with Josephus's explanation of the event, designates the Jews of Rome as a "ständiges Ferment der Unruhe," but he does not offer any evidence in support of this judgment. There is no such evidence in the

34. K. Latte, *Römische Religionsgeschichte* (München: Beck, 1960), 327f.; Smallwood, 205. With special emphasis on the Isis cult, Malaise, 152f., esp. 155; 357f. For different views, A. Momigliano in *Ottavo contibuto alla storia degli studi classic e del mondo antico* (Rome: Edizioni di storia e letteratura, 1987), 234; A. Wardman, *Religion and Statecraft among the Romans* (London: Granada, 1982), 23f., 42f., 113-14; J. H. W. G. Liebeschütz, *Continuity and Change in Roman Religion* (Oxford: Clarendon Press, 1979), 27f.

35. Esp. Josephus, *Ant.* 18.81-83.

36. Tacitus, *Histories* 5.5, does not, in my view, support the inference that Jewish proselytism was successful, contra Segal, 86, a book that contains an otherwise very useful discussion of conversion. M. H. Williams, "Expulsion," 771-72, shows that Tacitus is misleading with his designation *ea superstitone infect.*

37. Contra M. H. Williams, "Expulsion," 771 and n. 32, and contra Smallwood, 205 n. 14. For the dating of the Jewish catacombs, see L. V. Rutgers, "Überlegungen zu den jüdischen Katakomben Roms," *JAC* 33 (1990): 140-57.

ancient sources. To anyone familiar with the so-called *Berliner Antisemitismusstreit* it need hardly be pointed out that in reality Solin's phrase is nothing but a condensed and somewhat garbled version of the phrase that sparked this controversy. It may be found in the third volume of Mommsen's *Römische Geschichte:* "Auch in der alten Welt war das Judentum ein wirksames Ferment des Kosmopolitismus und der nationalen Dekomposition usw."[38]

In a recent study, Williams independently arrives at a conclusion very similar to that of Solin.[39] She, too, tries to show that the Jews of Rome were guilty of unruly behavior. In order to prove her case she refers to a passage in Suetonius and to the account of a famous *repetundae* case of 59 B.C.E. written by Cicero in defense of the propraetor of Asia of the year 62 B.C.E., L. Valerius Flaccus. A closer look at both sources, however, reveals that these references do not support Williams's point. Cicero, it is true, depicts the Jews of Rome in his *Pro Flacco* as a disorderly lot, but his remarks are not trustworthy. In other defense speeches Cicero discredits non-Jewish opponents using exactly the same kind of expressions he applies to the Jews on this occasion.[40] It is obvious, therefore, that Cicero's negative comments on the Jews of Rome are rhetorical devices too stereotypical to be of much evidential value.[41] In addition, even if these comments are correct, they predate the events of 19 C.E. by some eighty years. The passage from Suetonius is likewise useless as evidence for the idea that Jews were a disturbing element in Rome. To infer that in 19 C.E. Jews in Rome were notorious troublemakers from the fact that in 44 B.C.E. Jews were among those who had most intensely lamented the death of Caesar, flocking to the Forum for several nights in succession to see the dictator's bier, is in fact too ridiculous to merit further comment.[42]

Williams suggests, furthermore, that the real reason why the Roman

38. Solin, 686, sim. 690 n. 224. T. Mommsen, *Römische Geschichte,* 8th ed. (Berlin: Weidmannsche Buchhandlung, 1889), 3:550. On this controversy, see C. Hoffmann, *Juden und Judentum in den Werken deutscher Althistoriker des 19. und 20. Jahrhunderts* (Leiden: Brill, 1988), 87-132.

39. M. H. Williams, "Expulsion," 780.

40. Examples in B. Wardy, "Jewish Religion in Pagan Literature during the Late Republic and Early Empire," *ANRW* II.19.1 (1979), esp. 604f.

41. This also explains how in other contexts the same Cicero argues in a much more conciliatory tone (*Off.* 3.6.28; *Fin.* 5.23.65).

42. Suetonius, *Julius* 84.5.

Senate expelled Jews in 19 C.E. was to suppress the unrest caused by a deficiency in Rome's corn supply in that same year. This cannot be proven, as she herself admits, but the suggestion certainly has its merits. It was quite common for the Roman authorities to expel easily identifiable groups from Rome in times of political turmoil. Such expulsions were ordered not for religious reasons, but rather to maintain law and order. It is conceivable that the expulsion of both Jews and worshipers of Isis in 19 C.E. is just another example of such a policy.[43] But as a result of the piecemeal information provided by the ancient sources, several of the most basic questions remain unanswered. Why, for example, were *the Jews* chosen to be expelled for reasons of law and order? What had *the Jews* done to interfere with the law? How would an expulsion of *Jews* (as opposed to any other group of the city populace) have aided the reestablishment of law and order? One simply cannot tell.

What we do know is that the measures taken by the Roman state were confined to the Jewish community in Rome and not directed against the Jewish population in other parts of the Roman Empire.[44] As in the case of other troublemakers, the verdict was *relegatio* but not *deportatio*.[45] Jews were banished from Rome, but it appears that their civic or religious liberty was not otherwise impeded. In fact, it is conceivable that they did not have to move very far away from the capital. The decision to conscript Jews, probably in auxiliary units, was made in order to expel a significant number of Jewish *cives Romani* and *Latini Iuniani* without having to go to the trouble of convicting each one individually.[46] The action could not have encompassed all Jewish citizens living in Rome at this time. Women, children, and those above or

43. M. H. Williams, "Expulsion," 783. Different and unconvincing is Marasco, 657-58. Exile as a punishment for committing *vis publica* of one sort or another is well documented in Roman legal sources: see Garnsey, *Social Status,* 113.

44. Tacitus writes that Jews were expelled from Italy, while Josephus and Suetonius talk about an expulsion from Rome only. The latter authors are probably correct. Solin's argument that Josephus must be believed because Josephus of all people "hat die Strafe sicher nicht unterschätzt" is incorrect (p. 686 n. 212; sim. Smallwood, 204). After all, it is conceivable that Josephus would have attempted to play down the extent of the expulsion had it concerned the whole of Italy. Note that in dealing with the expulsion of astrologers and actors from Rome, Tacitus likewise always talks about expulsions from the whole of Italy: *Annals* 2.32; 4.14; 15.52; 13.25; *Histories* 2.62. Is this a coincidence?

45. Garnsey, *Social Status,* 116, 119.

46. Note that freedmen were not normally admitted to the legions: *RE* 5.1 (1923): 604, and esp. 612-22, s.v. "dilectus."

below military age were not legally affected by these measures. In fact, one wonders how individual Jews were at all identified.[47] Yet, even though some Jews escaped direct punishment, it was clear to everyone that in taking such harsh measures Rome was determined to restore law and order.

4. The Expulsion of Jews from Rome under Claudius

During the reign of Claudius, the Jewish community and the Roman authorities clashed once more. The sources yield even less information than they do for the events of 19 C.E.[48]

In their accounts of these events both Suetonius and Dio indicate that Claudius intervened because he wanted to maintain law and order. Suetonius, in a famous phrase, writes that Jews were expelled because "they constantly made disturbances *impulsore Chresto* [at the instigation of Chrestus]." Acts 18:2 confirms that Claudius banished Jews from Rome, but does not specify why. According to Dio, Claudius did *not* banish the Jews from Rome because there were too many of them. In Dio's version, Claudius rather permitted the Jews to continue to live their traditional Jewish way of life. At the same time, however, he suppressed all gatherings, whether of Jews or of non-Jews, because he considered such gatherings a potential source of unrest.

Because the interpretation of Suetonius's phrase *impulsore Chresto* is difficult, opinions differ as to what caused these disturbances. Some see in *Chrestus* an otherwise unknown individual by that name,[49] while others consider *Chrestus* to be a synonym for Christianity and consequently believe it was the preaching of Christianity that led to all this commotion.[50] Most

47. Did Roman officials proceed as aggressively as they did later under Domitian (Suetonius, *Domitian* 12.2)? Similarly, one wonders how the worshipers of Bacchus who were expelled in 186 B.C.E. (Livy 39.17.5) were identified in the first place. (Through informers? Cf. Livy 39.17.1.)

48. Suetonius, *Claudius* 25.4; Dio Cassius 60.6.6; Acts 18:2; Orosius, *Adversum Paganos* 7.6.15.

49. Solin, 659, 690, following E. Koestermann, "Ein folgenschweres Irrtum des Tacitus (*Annals* 15.44.2f.)?" *Historia* 16 (1967): 456-69.

50. Smallwood, 211, and P. Lampe, *Die stadtrömischen Christen in den ersten beiden Jahrhunderten: Untersuchungen zur Sozialgeschichte* (Tübingen: Mohr, 1989), 6, interpret the term as misapprehension on the part of Suetonius.

recently, Slingerland has argued forcefully that a Christian interpretation of the evidence provided by Suetonius is wrong because it is based exclusively on arguments *ex silentio.*[51] Slingerland's observations, while not new, are correct. Yet, though it cannot be proved, the idea that the appearance of Christianity created unrest within the Roman Jewish community still remains, in my view, an attractive possibility.[52]

Whatever upset the Jews of Rome, however, there can be no doubt that Rome intervened because there were disturbances and not because it wanted to meddle in the internal affairs of the Jewish community of Rome. We would like to know the nature of the disturbances referred to by Suetonius, and how an expulsion of Jews would affect the reestablishment of law and order. Were the Jews really responsible for these disturbances, as Suetonius claims? Or were they just a convenient group whose expulsion could serve as an example to reestablish peace and quiet among the city populace at large? Why the Jews? Even though the passage from Suetonius can be interpreted to mean that only a small group and not the entire community was expelled, one also wonders how many Jews were expelled, or what legal machinery was used to achieve this purpose.[53] We have no answers to these important questions.

5. Problems under Domitian

Dio Cassius recounts that under Domitian, "many who drifted into Jewish ways were condemned." The charge against these people was atheism. From Dio's remarks it is not clear what kind of attachment to Judaism these people displayed, nor do we know who was responsible for familiarizing them with

51. D. Slingerland, "Chrestus: Christus?" in A. J. Avery-Peck, *New Perspectives on Ancient Judaism* 4 (Lanham, Md.: University Press of America, 1989), esp. 143.

52. Cf. Lampe, 8-9.

53. Leon, 24; Solin, 690; Lampe, 7. Smallwood, 210f., has suggested that under Claudius measures against the Jews of Rome were taken on two separate occasions, but there are several reasons for believing that Jews were expelled only once; cf. Stern, 2:116; Solin, 689-90; Smallwood, 216; Lampe, 8; see also D. Slingerland, "Suetonius *Claudius* 25.4 and the Account in Cassius Dio," *JQR* 79 (1989): 305f., esp. 320; and see the discussion in Slingerland, "Suetonius *Claudius* 25.4, Acts 18, and Paulus Orosius' *Historiarum Adversum Paganos Libri VII:* Dating the Claudian Expulsion(s) of Roman Jews," *JQR* 83 (1992): 127-44.

Jewish beliefs and practices. Even though it may very well have been an additional factor, we cannot even be sure whether attraction to Judaism was the real reason for prosecution. It is certainly conceivable that the charge "Jewish ways" offered nothing but a convenient excuse for the autocratic Domitian to eliminate all those suspected of conspiracy. Punishments were heavy. They varied from the confiscation of property to the death penalty.[54] Despite such rigorous actions against those who felt an affinity for Judaism, the Roman Jewish community as a whole was left undisturbed under Domitian. The *fiscus Iudaicus* was rigorously extracted in these days,[55] but no one who was born a Jew seems to have been banished from Rome.[56]

6. Further Reflections on the Expulsions of Jews from First-Century Rome

Was Rome's policy toward the Jews in first-century Rome determined by religious concerns, by the wish to maintain law and order, or by a combination of the two?

Analyzing the expulsions of Jews from Rome under Tiberius and Claudius, I have shown that there is only very little ancient evidence to suggest that in the first century C.E. Roman Jews were persecuted because of their religious practices and beliefs.[57] Insofar as the sources indicate at all why Roman authorities decided to act, they all suggest that the main motive was the wish to suppress unrest. The fact that Roman authors use disparaging terms such as *superstitio* and "impious [*profani*] rites" in describing these events reflects a general antipathy to un-Roman religious practices.[58] In the case of Tacitus and Suetonius, the choice of a depreciative vocabulary in respect

54. Dio Cassius 67.14.1-3.

55. Most recently, M. H. Williams, "Domitian, the Jews and the 'Judaizers' — A Simple Matter of Cupiditas and Maiestas?" *Historia* 39 (1990): 196-211, esp. 209.

56. The evidence in the apocryphal Acts of John and rabbinic evidence cannot be used to document an expulsion of Jews from Rome under Domitian (contra Smallwood, 383-84).

57. Correctly seen by A. Momigliano, "Freedom of Speech and Religious Tolerance in the Ancient World," in S. C. Humphreys, *Anthropology and the Greeks* (London, 1978), 189, 193.

58. Tacitus, *Annals* 2.85; Suetonius, *Tiberius* 36. See, in general, S. Calderone, "Superstitio," *ANRW* II.1.2 (1972), 377-96.

to Jews may, in addition, have been caused by Rome's bitter experiences during the Jewish Revolt of 66-70/73 C.E. The use of such verbal aggression, however, should not mislead us into believing that Roman magistrates expelled Jews from first-century Rome for religious reasons. At best, a dislike for Judaism served to justify on a subconscious level decisions that had essentially been reached on the basis of administrative and legal considerations.

Other data further support the idea that Rome's measures concerning the Jews had straightforward political causes. For example, Roman law of this period never prescribes expulsion as the penalty for un-Roman religious practices. Of course, irreligious behavior could be exploited in the courts,[59] yet neither *impietas* nor *superstitio* was considered a criminal offense. Before the fourth century, no technical legal term for religious crimes seems to have existed.[60] To my knowledge, there is no evidence to support Mommsen's view that in the early Principate Roman citizens who converted to Judaism were liable for capital punishment.[61]

If the objective of the authorities in first-century Rome really was systematically to stamp out Judaism as a religion, why then, one might ask, did they simultaneously protect the free exercise of Jewish religious practices in other parts of the empire? The many senatorial decrees issued at the end of the republic, the measures concerning the Jews in Alexandria taken by Claudius,[62] and the fact that, during the First Jewish Revolt, Titus was unwilling to abrogate privileges that had been accorded to the Jewish inhabitants of Antioch[63] are all expressions of a policy aimed at guaranteeing the unimpeded observance of Jewish cult practices.

Rome was of course capable of treating the Jews harshly, but usually it had good reasons when it did so. Under Vespasian the Jewish temple at Leontopolis in Egypt was destroyed. This happened, in the words of

59. J. A. North, "Religious Toleration in Republican Rome," *PCPS* 25 (1979): 85, 98 n. 2.

60. This was already noted by Mommsen, "Religionsfrevel," 399-400, 406-7; cf. also A. Watson, *The State, Law, and Religion* (Athens: University of Georgia Press, 1992), passim.

61. The sources cited by Mommsen, *Römisches Strafrecht*, 574 n. 3, do not prove his point. The evidence for this does not predate the second century C.E. (Stern, 2:625). Nor have I found evidence that citizenship was bestowed on the basis of religious preference (so Segal, 89).

62. Josephus, *Ant.* 19.278f.

63. Josephus, *War* 7.100-111.

Josephus, because Vespasian was "suspicious of the incessant tendency of the Jews to revolution."[64] Similarly, during the Jewish Revolt of 66-70/73 C.E. Rome treated her adversaries without clemency.[65] In Rome itself one of the more prominent commanders of the same revolt, being a *hostis* of the Roman people, was put to death without formal trial.[66] Yet, it is clear that these were special measures that were dictated by the war. They did not have any lasting effect on Rome's general policy toward the Jews.[67]

Josephus mentions the expulsion of Jews from Rome in 19 C.E. in direct conjunction with an expulsion of devotees of Isis. This connection is not accidental. In repeatedly expelling the devotees of this Egyptian goddess during the first centuries B.C.E. and C.E., Roman magistrates had concerns very similar to the ones that prompted them to banish the Jews from Rome.[68] Measures against the cult of Isis were not taken out of fear of non-Roman religion per se. They occurred rather in times of general political unrest, as in 58 B.C.E. when Clodius manipulated religion for factional purposes.[69] On such occasions restrictive measures such as forbidding Isiac cult practices from taking place inside the *pomerium* quickly followed. Yet, significantly, Isis worship outside the *pomerium* was not prohibited, nor were its practitioners ever severely persecuted.

In the first and early second centuries C.E. astrologers formed another group that was chased out of Rome at regular intervals. Like the actions against Jews and worshipers of Isis, such expulsions took place without exception in times of political turmoil. Yet, again, an edict forbidding astrology throughout the Roman Empire was never issued, at least not before the time of Diocletian.[70]

64. Josephus, *War* 7.420.

65. M. Goodman, *The Ruling Class of Judaea: The Origin of the Jewish Revolt against Rome, A.D. 66-70* (Cambridge: Cambridge University Press, 1987), 231, 235-36.

66. Josephus, *War* 7.154. In that sense a *hostis* was similar to a *confessus;* cf. Kunkel, 22. On the Roman law of war, Mommsen, *Römisches Strafrecht,* 59.

67. Cf. Josephus, *War* 7.100-111, 447-50; *Ant.* 12.124; *Life* 424.

68. Tacitus, *Annals* 2.85; Suetonius, *Tiberius* 36. Cf. H. Last, "The Study of the Last 'Persecutions,'" *JRS* 27 (1937): 84-88; G. E. M. de Ste Croix, "Why Were the Early Christians Persecuted?" *P&P* 26 (1963): 24-25, 28.

69. Dio Cassius 53.2.4 (28 B.C.E.); Malaise, 78, 369f., 378; Latte, 282f.; F. Coarelli, "I monumenti dei culti orientali in Roma," in *La soteriologia dei culti oriental nell'impero romano,* ed. U. Bianchi and M. J. Vermaseren (Leiden: Brill, 1982), 33-67, esp. 53f.

70. F. H. Cramer, "Expulsion of Astrologers from Ancient Rome," *C&M* 12 (1951): esp. 10, 12, 21, 49; Liebeschütz, 119f.

The Roman response to the events surrounding the Roman Jewish community in the first century C.E., then, did not differ essentially from the way Rome treated Isis worshipers and astrologers: when law and order were seriously disturbed, expulsion was used as a means to suppress disorder. In dealing with such situations, Roman authorities systematically applied a well-tried formula that can be traced back as far as the Bacchanalia affair of 186 B.C.E. In that year, which followed a period of general unrest, the Senate took vigorous action against the worshipers of Dionysos. These not only had shocked their Roman contemporaries by immodest and promiscuous behavior, but were also alleged to have committed crimes such as the forging of wills and even murder. What most upset the *Patres*, however, was that the number of these worshipers "was so great that they almost constituted a state in the state."[71] In Roman eyes, then, the cult of Bacchus appeared above all as a politically dangerous *coniuratio*.[72] The Senate reacted by punishing those held responsible for conspiracy. Worship of Bacchus was forcefully discouraged, but, significantly, it remained possible under certain conditions.[73]

All the elements one later encounters in Rome's actions against Jews, Isis worshipers, and astrologers are thus present in Livy's account of the Bacchanalia affair: when law and order were disturbed, Roman authorities interfered because they feared the possible political consequences of such disturbances. The scope and actual effectiveness of the measures taken tended to be limited. Interventions were most likely to occur in periods of general civil unrest. Religious concerns played only a subordinate role; that is, intervention was not generally aimed at suppressing religious practices as such, but was usually carried out because specific criminal offenses that could be formally prosecuted had been committed.

71. Livy 39.8.8; cf. 14.16.2f.; 39.13.14. North, 86f.; P. Garnsey, "Religious Toleration in Classical Antiquity," in *Persecution and Toleration*, ed. W. Shiels, Studies in Church History 21 (Oxford, 1984), 8-9; J. M. Pailler, *Bacchanalia: Répression de 186 av. J.-C. à Rome et en Italie: Vestiges, Images, Tradition*, BEFAR 270 (Rome: École Française, 1988), esp. 247f.; R. A. Bauman, "The Suppression of the Bacchanals: Five Questions," *Historia* 39 (1990): 334-48.

72. Livy 14.17.6. North, 91, maintains that it is impossible to distinguish between political and religious issues.

73. Livy 39.18.7-9; *CIL* 1 (2d ed.) 581; North, 91; Pailler, 821; Bauman, 342-43, 347.

7. Were the Romans Tolerant?

It has long been customary to see in Rome's dealing with the Jews aspects of tolerance or intolerance. For example, Rajak considers the expulsions of Jews from first-century Rome a sign of a Roman intolerance not dissimilar to the intolerance displayed by the Greek cities of Asia Minor half a century earlier. Williams regards the forcible undressing of a ninety-year-old Jew reported by Suetonius as indicative of persecution, while Wardman defines persecution by the test of "a government's will or reluctance to take steps which it knows will be offensive to a significant group" and concludes that in Judea, Alexandria, and indeed in the entire Diaspora Jews felt persecuted.[74] Does the evidence justify such conclusions?

To label Rome's policy toward its subjects as tolerant or intolerant is misleading when such terms are not clearly defined. The word "tolerance" can mean the mere willingness to allow people to practice their religion, provided that there is no particular reason to stop them. But in other contexts, as for example in Voltaire's *Traité sur la tolérance* (1763), the word has wider implications. It is used to indicate a policy of tolerance; that is, a policy based on the belief that people have a *right* freely to practice their religion (whatever it may be).[75]

Roman laws of the first century C.E. that relate to Jews give the impression that tolerance or intolerance was nothing but a by-product in the formulation of a given policy. Conscious efforts to be tolerant or intolerant do not seem to have been frequently made.[76] Rome was interested in keeping the urban masses under control and in checking initiatives of too political a nature. For the rest, Roman authorities just let people be. The first definition of "tolerance" is thus more appropriate than the second to characterize Roman policy toward the Jews.

Further evidence likewise illustrates that tolerance was only a by-product of Rome's administrative measures. The reaffirmation of Jewish privileges in Asia Minor by the Senate in the last half of the first century

74. Rajak, "Jewish Rights," 28; Suetonius, *Domitian* 12.2; M. H. Williams, "Expulsion," 205, 209, 211; Wardman, 125-27.

75. Voltaire, *Traité sur la tolérance* (Paris: Flammarion, 1989 [1763]), passim; Roger Williams, *The Bloudy Tenent of Persecution for Cause of Conscience Discussed* (1644), as cited in S. Ettinger, "The Beginnings of the Change in the Attitude of European Society towards the Jews," *Scripta Hierosolymitana* 7 (1961): 201.

76. Contra Smelik, 179.

B.C.E., for example, was primarily an organizational measure aimed at reestablishing peace and quiet on the local level. It was not the expression of a policy whose main objective was to ensure religious freedom. That the motive behind Rome's confirmation of Jewish privileges during the first centuries B.C.E. and C.E. did not result from a policy of tolerance also follows from the fact that most, if not all, senatorial and imperial decrees regarding the Jews were not initiated by the Romans themselves but were the result of initiatives taken by individual Jewish communities.[77] Comparably, during the First Jewish Revolt (66-70/73 C.E.) Rome showed little mercy to the Jewish insurgents. Yet no repressive measures were taken against the Jews of the Diaspora. Again, this happened not because Romans were generally tolerant, but simply because such measures were not necessary. Later, early in the third century C.E., the decurionate was imposed on Jews wealthy enough to carry the financial burdens connected with this office.[78] Once again, such an act is not indicative of specifically pro- or anti-Jewish feelings on the part of Roman authorities. Rather, it was the economic situation of the empire that necessitated the measure. All these examples suggest that Roman policy toward the Jews was often guided by purely pragmatic concerns rather than by an ideology of tolerance.

There were many areas where Roman authorities did not regulate. Once more, it is not correct to equate such nonintrusion with tolerance. In first-century Rome, shrines dedicated to gods of foreign extraction were springing up throughout the city.[79] Urban officials do not seem to have interfered with this development. Clearly, such officials did not display tolerance. They were just being indifferent. Even when it came to persecuting the earliest Christian communities in the course of the second century C.E., an element of noninterference did not disappear completely: the emperor Trajan decided that Christians should be punished, but he simul-

77. Garnsey, "Religious Toleration," 11. On the pattern of "petition and response" in general, see Millar, 541-44.

78. *Dig.* 50.2.3.3; 27.1.15.6.

79. See Coarelli, 33-67, esp. the map between pp. 38 and 39 (the evidence partly postdates the period addressed in this article); S. M. Savage, "The Cults of Ancient Trastevere," *MAAR* 17 (1940): 26-56; M. Le Glay, "Sur l'implantation des sanctuaires orientaux à Rome," in *L'urbs: Espace urbain et histoire,* CEFR 98 (Rome: École Française 1987), 545-57. On the ad hoc character of urban development in first-century Rome, see D. G. Favro, "The Urban Image of Augustan Rome" (Ph.D. diss., University of California, Berkeley, 1984).

taneously made it clear that no efforts should be made to track them down.[80]

Much of what has been said with regard to tolerance also holds true in respect to intolerance. After the First Jewish Revolt the temple tax was converted into the *fiscus Iudaicus*. It has been suggested that a punitive element played a role in this conversion, but there is little ancient evidence that points in that direction.[81] It is not correct to infer that the Romans wanted to penalize the Jews from the fact that some Jews viewed the Jewish tax as a punishment.[82] It is much more likely that Rome construed this measure as an ingenious redirecting and systematization of an already existing tax. Especially when seen in the larger context of Vespasian's taxation policy, the institution of the *fiscus Iudaicus* ceases to appear as an act of vindictiveness that was aimed at the Jews because they were Jews. In the 70s C.E. various forms of taxation were enforced with great rigor among all subjects of the empire.[83] To their disappointment, even the opportunistic Alexandrians had to pay the same heavy taxes as everyone else.[84] Thus, for Vespasian, it was not merely privy money that did not stink; no money did.[85]

Earlier Roman measures concerning the Jews can likewise not be said to reflect an ideology of intolerance. Julius Caesar, the great benefactor of the Jews, had doubled taxation in kind in Judea, but this was not a specifically anti-Jewish measure.[86] Little less than a century later, Claudius confirmed the existing rights of the Jewish community of Alexandria in 41 C.E. but abolished the last remnants of the Jewish state following the death of Agrippa I three years later. Again, decisions like these were reached on the

80. For "accusatory" as opposed to "inquisitorial," see de Ste Croix, 15. Cf. also Voltaire, 69-76.

81. S. W. Baron, *A Social and Religious History of the Jews* 2 (Philadelphia: Jewish Publication Society of America, 1952), 106, believes Vespasian instituted the tax to demonstrate to the rebels in Gaul and Germany that Rome was powerful enough to curb revolts.

82. A. Carlebach, "Rabbinic References to Fiscus Judaicus," *JQR* 66 (1975): 57-58.

83. Suetonius, *Vespasian* 16. Carlebach, 61, is not aware of this.

84. Dio Cassius 65.8.2-4.

85. Suetonius, *Vespasian* 23. On the conceptual background of this tax as interpreted by Josephus, see M. Simon, "Jupiter-Yavhé," *Numen* 23 (1976): 56-57, 65-66; cf. also C. Saulnier, "Flavius Josèphe et la propaganda flavienne," *RB* 96 (1986): 545-62.

86. On the rate of this tax, R. Duncan-Jones, *Structure and Scale in the Roman Economy* (Cambridge: Cambridge University Press, 1990), 189-90.

basis of administrative concerns. They were not influenced by pro- or anti-Jewish sentiments, but must rather be seen within the larger framework of the ruling of the empire.

From the moment they had first encountered Jews onward, upper-class Romans had grown used to making a distinction between practical considerations and ideas of a more theoretical nature. In Latin literature of the first century C.E., negative remarks on Jews and Judaism went hand in hand with a tendency to confirm rather than to abrogate Jewish privileges. From a Roman perspective, there was nothing anomalous about this combination of maintaining the legal status of the Jewish community on the one hand with strong verbal abuse of this same community on the other. Several centuries later we encounter the same phenomenon once more, this time in the laws dealing with Jews contained in the *Codex Theodosianus* of 430 C.E.[87] Such a state of affairs shows that in unconditionally calling Roman attitudes toward the Jews tolerant or intolerant, one is making a complex set of issues too simple. In the early fifth century, as in the first, verbal "intolerance" could very well be combined with practical "tolerance," at least as far as the Jews were concerned. Now, as then, attitudes to religion and way of life did not directly or automatically affect decisions of a political or administrative nature.

8. Conclusions

The evidence discussed in this article warrants the conclusion that the constant factor in Roman policy toward the Jews was that there was no such constant factor. In the Republican period, as in the early empire, Rome's "Jewish policy" remained in essence a collection of ad hoc measures with often limited effectiveness in both space and time. The *senatus consulta* of the late first century B.C.E. and the expulsions of Jews from Rome a few decades later are examples of a policy that responded to situations. The ad hoc character of Roman policy toward the Jews resulted from the fact that both the Jewish communities of the Mediterranean and the policies of individual emperors were subject to change. In the earlier Roman Empire,

87. Listed but not interpreted by A. Linder, *The Jews in Roman Imperial Legislation* (Detroit and Jerusalem: Wayne State University Press and the Israel Academy of Sciences and Humanities, 1987), 60-61.

there never was a standard Roman "Jewish policy," let alone a Magna Charta for the Jews.

To call Rome's treatment of the Jews either tolerant or intolerant is to misunderstand the nature of Rome's dealings with the Jews. Rome readily acknowledged the distinctiveness of the Jewish people and, when they were under attack, was willing to help the Jews protect it — witness, for example, the series of *senatus consulta* dating to the later first century B.C.E. In general, however, Roman magistrates remained hesitant to supervise too closely the practices that expressed aspects of this distinctiveness. In fact, most of the time they saw no reason to do so.[88] Thus, Roman magistrates treated the Jews the way they did, not because they were consciously tolerant, but simply because they had no reason to hinder the free exercise of Jewish religious practices. It is not necessary, therefore, to suppose that Rome treated the Jews reasonably in explicit response to Jewish *beneficia.* Nor is it correct to state on the basis of the limited number of attested Jewish *beneficia* that "toleration of the Jews was sporadic because their loyalty to the empire was an uncertain factor."[89] The opposite is true: well into late antiquity, nontoleration (or, better, interference with) rather than toleration of the Jews was sporadic.

Study of the expulsions of Jews from first-century Rome serves to illustrate the central concern that profoundly determined Rome's measures concerning its Jewish subjects: the wish to maintain law and order. When law and order were maintained (in the eyes of the Roman authorities), Jews had nothing to fear. When they were disturbed, as in 19 C.E. or under Claudius, legal and administrative measures were taken. In addition to being aimed at remedying the situation, such measures frequently also resulted in impeding the free exercise of religious practices. Interventions by Roman authorities were usually not isolated events. More often than not, Rome intervened in periods characterized by an atmosphere of general unrest among the city populace. In such cases, the emperor or the Senate normally followed a pattern first developed while resolving the Bacchanalia affair of 186 B.C.E.: expulsion of those who on the basis of their un-Roman rituals and practices could easily be represented as threatening the boundaries of Roman society.[90] In the first century C.E. this happened to at least

88. Cf. Garnsey, "Religious Toleration," 12. Contra Smelik, 179f.

89. Garnsey, "Religious Toleration," 11, 25; cf. also Rajak, "Jewish Rights," 116-18.

90. On the possible influence of the Bacchanalia on Pliny's famous *Letter* 96, Pailler, esp. 759-70; Bauman, 342-43.

segments of the Jewish community of Rome; before and after it happened in a more or less identical fashion to other groups such as Isis worshipers and astrologers. Why *Jews* were chosen to be banished from Rome on at least two occasions during the first century C.E., it is impossible to tell. In placing the expulsions of Jews from first-century Rome within the larger framework of Roman Republican and early imperial administration, we unfortunately perceive only the how, not the why. But this much is clear: the expulsion of Jews from first-century Rome cannot be regarded as an example of a specifically "Jewish policy" on the part of Roman officials: people other than Jews could be and were expelled under circumstances comparable to those under which the Jews had to leave the city at least twice in the first half of the first century C.E. Thus, in banishing Jews from Rome, Roman officials did not display a systematic ideology of anti-Judaism; they merely gave expression to general administrative concerns as they had arisen unanticipated at specific points in place and time.

CHAPTER 5

The Formation of the First "Christian Congregations" in Rome in the Context of the Jewish Congregations[1]

Rudolf Brändle and Ekkehard W. Stegemann

1

When one wants to talk about the beginnings of the "Christ-faith" in Rome, one generally talks about the beginnings of a "Christian congregation" there. In the title of our essay we have followed this convention. Right from the start, however, we would like to draw attention to this terminology as an anachronism. It is, of course, true that believers in Christ were recognized at an early stage by those outside as a separate group, and thus could become victims of measures taken by the Romans in the course of their power politics. In our opinion, this happened at the latest under Nero. But the term "Christians" (Χριστιανοί; Lat. *Chrestiani* or *Christiani*) only became tangible in documents after the year 70 (Acts 11:26; Tacitus, *Ann.* 15.44; Suetonius, *Nero* 16.2).[2] Of note is the fact that in the reference by Suetonius to the Claudius edict[3] ("As

1. A paper read on 10 August 1993 in the course of the seminar "NT Texts in Their Cultural Environment" from the meeting of the SNTS in Chicago. The initial feedback from Dr. Jim Jeffers and the following discussion set a number of new emphases.

2. M. Karrer, *Der Gesalbte. Die Grundlagen des Christustitels* (Göttingen: Vandenhoeck & Ruprecht, 1991), 81ff.

3. *Claudius* 25.4; according to M. Hengel, *Zur urchristlichen Geschichtsschreibung*, 2nd ed. (Stuttgart: Calwer, 1984), 91, Augustine's reference (*Ep.* 102.8) that the "law of the Jews" had come to Rome under Caligula is to "the Jewish sect of the Christians."

the Jews under their leader Chrestos were continually causing unrest, he expelled them from Rome"), the believers in Christ were reckoned ethnically and religiously as belonging totally to the Jews. We shall come back to this text, but would like to point out already that Suetonius, in any case, does not mention any "Christians" under Claudius in Rome. We certainly agree with those scholars who assume that *Chrestus* is the same as *Christus* here, i.e., Jesus (Christ). On the basis of Suetonius's note, we can thus assume that under Claudius there were already adherents to the "Christ-faith" in Rome. M. Stern is nevertheless right when he writes, "However, the words of Suetonius could convey the impression that Christus himself was present in Rome at that time, and that the disturbances were instigated by him personally, while Tacitus, indeed, was better informed on the whereabouts of Christus."[4] Suetonius first mentions *Christiani* under Nero, but the "Christ-faith" or followers of Christ already under Claudius. This explains, once again, why it is advisable to be cautious with the use of the term "Christian" when referring to the beginnings of the "Christ-faith" in Rome. It also has consequences for any sociological assessment. For if the note by Suetonius is correct, then the beginnings of the "Christ-faith" in Rome must be looked for within the bounds of the Jewish community. We shall demonstrate a little further on that this assumption can be related well to Romans 16 and Acts 18. In the following we shall also refrain from using the term "heathen Christians," much less the term "Jewish Christians." We would, rather, endeavor to show that the beginnings of the "Christ-faith" in Rome must be understood in the context of the encounter between Jews and non-Jews in Rome, an encounter which had already been taking place over a longer period of time. From this assumption we would thus formulate our thesis: Non-Jews in Rome only came into contact, initially, with the "Christ-faith" if they had already come into contact with Jews, and therefore lived as proselytes or God-fearers in more or less close communication with the Jewish community.

4. M. Stern, *Greek and Latin Authors on Jews and Judaism,* 3 vols. (Jerusalem: Israel Academy of Sciences and Humanities, 1974-84), 2:116.

2

According to Valerius Maximus,[5] Jews were expelled from the city in 139 B.C.E., so there must have been Jews in Rome at least since the middle of the second century B.C.E. It is, however, not certain how reliable his statement is. A sure date is 63 B.C.E., when Pompey conquered Palestine. As a result many Jews were forced to emigrate, or were sold as slaves, and thus ended up, among other places, in Rome. The first Jews in Rome could therefore have been prisoners of war or slaves. The widespread assumption that Jews also came to Rome as merchants cannot be verified. Moreover, it is based on problematic conceptions regarding ancient long-distance trade. Numerous slaves were soon set free and settled in Trastevere, where others from the East had also settled. It is also there that we find the oldest Jewish cemetery in Rome, which was discovered by Bosio in 1602. The Coemeterium Monteverde is situated on the right-hand side of the Tiber before the Porta Portuensis; its beginnings could well reach back to the first century C.E.[6] Philo writes in *Embassy to Gaius* 155, 157, that Augustus "knew that a large area of Rome beyond the river Tiber, had been taken over and inhabited by Jews. Most of them were Roman slaves who had been given their liberty, after having been brought as prisoners of war to Italy . . . he [Augustus] neither expelled them from Rome nor took away their Roman citizenship" (τὴν Ρωμαϊκὴν αὐτῶν πολιτείαν). According to Juvenal, Jews settled as beggars in the vicinity of the Nympheum of the spring-nymph Egeria, situated in front of the Porta Capena to the southeast (*Saturnalia* 3.12-16). Three Jewish cemeteries near the Via Appia, although probably only laid out in the third century C.E., would seem to indicate this area as well.[7] Epigraphic proof for synagogues on the Campus Martius and

5. Stern, *Greek and Latin Authors*, 1:358; Harry J. Leon, *The Jews of Ancient Rome* (Peabody, Mass.: Hendrickson, 1995 [1960]); H. Wolff, "Die Juden im antiken Rom," in *Minderheiten im Mittelmeerraum*, ed. K. Rother (Passau: Passavia Universitätsverlag, 1989), 35-62, here 37-38.

6. R. Penna, "Les Juifs a Rome, au temps de l'apotre Paul," *NTS* 28 (1982): 321-47, here 326.

7. P. Lampe, *Die stadtrömischen Christen in den ersten beiden Jahrhunderten*, 2nd ed. (Tübingen: J. C. B. Mohr [P. Siebeck], 1989), 27; cf. H. Lichtenberger, "Josephus und Paulus in Rom. Juden und Christen in Rom zur Zeit Neros," in D.-A. Koch and H. Lichtenberger, *Begegnungen zwischen Christentum und Judentum in Antike und Mittelalter. Festschrift für Heinz Schreckenberg* (Göttingen: Vandenhoeck & Ruprecht, 1993), 245-61, here 247-48.

the Subura stems from a later period. In summary, it is certain that in the first century C.E. there were Jews living in Trastevere, between Porta Collina and Porta Esquilina, as well as in front of Porta Capena.[8]

A quick glance should be taken at the sources relating to the history of the Jews in Rome. Penna divides them into four groups: (1) Authors before Paul: Cicero, Horace, Ovid, Valerius Maximus, Philo; their opinion of the Jews, apart from Philo, of course, tends to be tainted negatively or expressed in an ironic manner. (2) Contemporaries of Paul: Seneca, Persius, Petronius, Quintilian, Martial, Juvenal, Flavius Josephus; with the exception of Flavius Josephus, these authors also write in a somewhat sarcastic tone. (3) Later authors: Tacitus, Suetonius, Dio Cassius; M. Stern suspects, especially with regard to Tacitus, that his severely anti-Jewish polemic is the reaction of a conservative patrician against the diffusion of Jewish conceptions even into upper-class Roman society.[9] (4) Epigraphic material: this originates for the most part from the seven presently known Roman catacombs, which only go back, however, to the third century at the earliest.

Statements about the number of Jews in Rome at the time of Paul can be nothing more than estimates. Important leads are given in Josephus (*Ant.* 17.299-303; cf. *War* 2.80), who says that in 4 B.C.E. eight thousand Roman Jews accompanied a Jewish delegation from Palestine to appear before Augustus. According to another report, four thousand Jews capable of taking up arms were deported to Sardinia under Tiberius (Suetonius, *Tiberius* 36; Josephus, *Ant.* 18.81-84; cf. Tacitus, *Ann.* 2.85).[10] These figures allow for a guess that there were around twenty thousand Jews in Rome at the time of Nero.[11] We know nothing about the social composition and

8. Lampe, 28.

9. M. Stern, "Sympathy for Judaism in Roman Senatorial Circles in the Period of the Early Empire," *Zion* 29 (1964): 155-67 (Hebrew). J. G. Gager, *The Origins of Anti-Semitism: Attitudes toward Judaism in Pagan and Christian Antiquity* (Oxford: Oxford University Press, 1983).

10. Wolff, 39-40.

11. The estimates range between fifteen thousand and fifty thousand. H. Solin, "Juden und Syrer im westlichen Teil der römischen Welt: Eine ethnisch-demographische Studie mit besonderer Berücksichtigung der sprachlichen Zustände," *ANRW* II.29.2 (Berlin, 1983), 587-789 and 1222-49, here 700, mentions the number fifteen thousand. Wolff, 39-41, reckons as probable numbers between twenty-five thousand and thirty thousand.

level of education within these Jewish communities. From general considerations of social history,[12] it would seem probable that the Jews were considered lower-class citizens, although they may have had sympathizers among non-Jews even up into the Roman upper class.[13]

3

The immediate context in which Paul, as well as early Christianity in general, can be situated historically is the "diffusion" of Diaspora Jews within a society dominated by a non-Jewish majority. Menachem Stern, Shimon Applebaum, and John Gager, among others, have described accurately the process which took place in the first century C.E. of pagan conflict with the Jewish way of life, a conflict marked by antipathy as well as sympathy.[14] Indeed, Paul was relegated by this conflict to a life on the borderline, with his own peculiar dialectic of limitation and openness which had an effect on both sides. For, as in a Roman majority–ruled society the reaction to the Jewish minority was not only characterized by indifference, xenophobia, and anti-Semitism but also by interest, even to the point of the forming of a circle of sympathizers by the so-called God-fearers and some converts (proselytes), so amongst Jews there was an exceedingly wide and differentiated spectrum of reaction. It reaches, in a parallel manner, from apostasy (i.e., the conversion of some to the Roman way of life; Tiberius Alexander, Philo's nephew, is a well-known example), through more or less extensive acculturation (as, for instance, in Hellenistic Jews of the Diaspora) or an attitude of indifference, to aggressive antipaganism derived from bitter, historical experience of oppression and persecution.[15]

12. Cf. E. Stegemann and W. Stegemann, *Urchristliche Sozialgeschichte. Die Anfänge im Judentum und die Christusgemeinden in der mediterranen Welt* (Stuttgart, 1995), 249ff.

13. Under Domitian, Titus Flavius Clemens, a relative of the emperor, was sentenced to death for atheism and inertia (cf. Suetonius, *Domitian* 15.1). Was Clemens a God-fearer?

14. Cf. Stern, *Greek and Latin Authors;* Gager, *The Origins of Anti-Semitism;* S. Applebaum, *Jews and Greeks in Ancient Cyrene* (Leiden, 1979).

15. H. Frohnhofen, ed., *Christlicher Antijudaismus und jüdischer Antipaganismus. Ihre Motive und Hintergründe in den ersten drei Jahrhunderten* (Hamburg: Steinmann & Steinmann, 1990).

One can find at the same time very different theoretical definitions of the relationship between Judaism and paganism, as well as different practical types of behavior toward non-Jews.

It now seems little more than a truism that early Christianity was a product of this diffusion of Judaism into a society dominated by non-Jews. Its origins, to be sure, lie in an apocalyptic esoteric movement within Palestinian Judaism. However, it gained its effective historical form, theologically and socially, in the tension-filled encounter between Jews and non-Jews in the Mediterranean urban centers. Indeed, it seems reasonable to say that the "Christian" movement, as it was named in the final quarter of the first century, at the latest, to distinguish it from the Jews, was a new, self-supporting, although somewhat unstable form of reaction to the encounter between Jews and pagans. In substance it could perhaps best be characterized as a messianic-apocalyptic and charismatic movement in the gray area between Jews, proselytes, and God-fearers. The instability of the movement can be demonstrated, for instance, in the fact that members of the Galatian congregations, which were founded by Paul, had obviously taken, or were intending to take, the path already laid out for God-fearers of conversion to Judaism, whereas in Rome, in a congregation not founded by Paul, exactly the opposite tendency of disassociation from and theological disqualification of the Jews seemed to be at work (Romans 9–11; 14–15). Moreover, there were very different viewpoints concerning these things amongst the Judeo-Christian missionaries. Once again the epistle to the Galatians, but also Philippians and perhaps 2 Corinthians, reveal that Paul had to deal with apostles in his own congregations who favored conversion to Judaism. This conflict, as is well known, determined at a very early stage his relationships with Peter and Barnabas and the early apostles in Jerusalem. Paul, it would seem, had a disposition for involvement in the formation of this new movement. Although a Hellenistically acculturated Jew of the Diaspora, he was indifferent neither to his Jewish identity nor to a society dominated by a majority of non-Jews. His great commitment to his origins reveals itself, not least, in the fact that according to his own record he shared in the Pharisaic observance of the Torah. Whether that means that he was a member of a Pharisaic group and possibly received a Jewish education in Jerusalem, as we are told in Acts, is a matter of controversy, though here of little importance. Decisive is his undisputed self-identification with his Judaism. This showed itself before his calling, with regard to non-Jews, in that he tended to advise sympathizers to convert rather than to keep the intermediate identity of God-fearers. This, it would seem, is to be taken from Galatians 5:11, where Paul says that in earlier days he had been "preaching circumcision." Presumably it is also in the background of his initially highly critical reaction to the missionary activities of the older Jesus movement amongst non-Jews. After his call, Paul obviously decided that the God-fearers, who had come to faith in Christ, should not convert to Judaism. The reason for this is most likely found in the fact that he saw the existence of the believer in Christ already shaped by the pneumatic gift from heaven of adoption as a child of God, an adoption which transcended every historical identity (κατὰ σάρκα) and thus also that of the Jews. Believers in Christ are, through the power of the Spirit, already the seed of Abraham in eschatological quality and legitimacy (cf. Galatians 3). Thus it is understandable why Paul stands up against the tendency to conversion in Galatia, while opposing the tendency to disassociation from the Jews or the context of the synagogue in Rome. The especially remarkable thing about the epistle to the Romans is that Paul calls both Jews and non-Jews to a mutual association with each other (Rom. 15:7-13). In any case, he opposes theological positions that deduce the rejection of Israel from the nonacceptance of the "Christ-faith" by (the majority of) the Jews; cf. Romans 11:1-24.

4

The oldest document which testifies to the "Christ-faith" in Rome is Paul's epistle to the Romans.[16] Written in the second half of the 50s,[17] this epistle presupposes that there are κλητοὶ Ἰησοῦ Χριστοῦ (Rom. 1:6) in Rome. The question is, Who are these "called of Jesus Christ" and in what type of social form do they express their faith in Christ? Paul would lead us, in Romans, to understand these κλητοὶ Ἰησοῦ Χριστοῦ as belonging to the ἔθνη, as he reckons them in Romans 1:5, to be within the sphere of his apostleship. This apostleship is described quite specifically in verse 5 as leading to obedience that comes from faith among all the ἔθνη. The κλητοὶ

16. A. J. M. Wedderburn, *The Reasons for Romans* (Edinburgh: T. & T. Clark, 1988).

17. For a Pauline chronology see R. Jewett, *A Chronology of Paul's Life* (Philadelphia: Fortress, 1979).

'Ιησοῦ Χριστοῦ are then counted in verse 6 amongst these ἔθνη. It can also be deduced from other passages that non-Jews are being addressed in the epistle. Above all we would make reference to Romans 9–11, and there specifically 11:13: Ὑμῖν δὲ λέγω τοῖς ἔθνεσιν. ἐφ' ὅσον μὲν οὖν εἰμι ἐγὼ ἐθνῶν ἀπόστολος, τὴν διακονίαν μου δοξάζω.

Alongside that, the passage in Romans 7:1 should be noted, which regards those receiving the epistle as people who know the *nomos*. This means that here either Jews are being addressed or Paul is speaking to non-Jews with regard to their knowledge of the Torah. Such knowledge of the Torah by non-Jews can, however, only be presupposed if they had, in turning to the Jewish religion, become God-fearers. We assume that God-fearing non-Jews are indeed meant in Romans 7:1. At the same time we would not exclude the possibility that Paul knew Jews, male or female, in Rome who were believers in Christ. This would, in any case, seem to follow from Romans 16. We agree with recent research that this chapter — probably with the exception of the polemic against heretics and the doxology — originally belonged to the epistle.[18] Paul here gives his regards to the married couple Prisca and Aquila, who were Jews (Acts 18:2; 18:26; 1 Cor. 16:19; 2 Tim. 4:19). In addition, in the list of those to be greeted, Andronicus, Junia, and Herodion are specifically indicated as being Jews (Rom. 16:7, 11). We do not rule out the possibility that there were other Jews, male or female, on the list of those to be greeted, although we cannot state it with any certainty. Perhaps the names Mary and Aristobulus[19] could point to this. We hold, therefore, that there were Jews, male and female, amongst those who believed in Christ in Rome.

The question now, however, is how Paul can reckon the κλητοὶ 'Ιησοῦ Χριστοῦ as belonging to the ἔθνη if there really were male and female Jews amongst the Roman believers in Christ. First of all, we presume that quantitatively there were clearly more non-Jews making up the numbers of the believers in Rome. Moreover, it is important that we put aside certain conceptions concerning the organization of those believers. There is no evidence at all of any organized structure of a church composed of Jews

18. Cf. recently J. D. G. Dunn, *Romans 9–16*, WBC 38B (Waco: Word, 1988), 884ff.

19. H.-J. Klauck, *Hausgemeinde und Hauskirche im frühen Christentum* (Stuttgart: Verlag Katholisches Bibelstudien, 1981), 28, thinks Aristobulus did not belong to the believers in Christ.

and non-Jews, in the sense that, similar to the organization of synagogues, different offices, a constitution, and something identifiable as a body of members could be found. Rather, the mention of a house church in Romans 16:5, and that especially in regard to the couple Aquila and Prisca, would seem to lead to the conclusion that those who believed in Christ met together in various house churches in Rome.[20] The analogy that 1 Corinthians 16:19 obviously assumes for Ephesus would seem to point to this as well, once again hardly accidentally connected with the names Aquila and Prisca. House churches would also have existed in Corinth.[21] Whether these house churches were made up of a mixed group of Jews and non-Jews, we cannot state with any certainty. Admittedly the problems reflected in Romans 14–15 seem to point to a certain amount of social interaction between Jews and non-Jews amongst the believers in Christ.[22] We must therefore reckon with the fact that at the time of the sending of the epistle to the Romans, there existed no concrete social form of any uniformly organized Christian congregation, apart from loosely organized house churches. The observation that the early Roman church at the turn of the first century had a presbyterial constitution points in the same direction. This fits the conclusion that there was at the time no central meeting place for all the Christians in Rome, but that there existed a number of house churches. Later on these may have been topographically identical with churches carrying the same titles. Roman Christianity developed a monarchical structure only at a much later date.

Having then posed the question of how Paul came to reckon the "called of Jesus Christ" in Rome as belonging to the ἔθνη, we must now juxtapose this with the fact that, according to Acts 18:2 and Suetonius, *Claudius* 25.4, there is no mention of non-Jews with regard to the followers of Christ. We are of the opinion that the Claudius edict was the cause of the development of the "Christ-faith" in Rome, ascertainable in the epistle to the Romans. Our assumptions with regard to the Claudius edict are the following: (1) The edict is most probably to be dated to 49 C.E. (as the

20. Klauck, 26-30; Lampe, 301ff.

21. G. Theissen, "Social Stratification in the Corinthian Community: A Contribution to the Sociology of Early Hellenistic Christianity," in *The Social Setting of Pauline Christianity* (Philadelphia: Fortress, 1982), 69-119; Stegemann and Stegemann, 231ff.

22. Cf. the detailed discussion of these chapters in K. P. Donfried, ed., *The Romans Debate*, 2nd ed. (Peabody, Mass.: Hendrickson, 1991).

tradition according to Orosius has it)[23] and not to 41 C.E. (as Dio Cassius has it). Acts 18:2 would also seem to indicate 49 C.E. (2) Further, we hold that, contrary to Acts 18:2, not all the Jews in Rome[24] were expelled. (3) We assume that all the sources — Acts, Suetonius, Dio Cassius (although he may have meant a different measure in the year 41), and Orosius — refer to the same event.

If, however, Aquila and Prisca came to Corinth as a consequence of the Claudius edict, the question must be asked: To what degree was the edict actually carried out? Were, for instance, only "ringleaders" expelled? Or was the edict adjourned after a number of initial expulsions? Or does Luke, in Acts 18:2, mean all Jews believing in Christ when he writes "all the Jews"?[25] We suggest that the latter interpretation should seriously be taken into consideration.

In any case, the Claudius edict presupposes that at the end of the 40s there were conflicts amongst Jews about Christ, which made police measures necessary. These conflicts could only have developed, of course, if the Jews who believed in Christ had already had a certain resonance within the synagogues or within the associated circles of God-fearers. Suetonius appears to have had such a course of events in mind. Assuming that our suggestion for an interpretation of Acts 18:2 is correct, there would only have been believers in Christ from the ranks of God-fearers left in Rome after the expulsion of those Jews who believed in Christ. But even if a few Jewish believers in Christ had been able to remain in Rome, we can assume that the relationship between the believers in Christ and the synagogues was very tense, if it had not, indeed, already broken down. In this process, it is quite possible that the synagogues, or those responsible in them, also took measures to distance themselves from those believers in Christ who were remaining in Rome. These traumatic circumstances would seem to supply the background to the theological developments amongst the God-fearing believers in Christ in Rome, the same developments which Paul has to deal with in Romans, especially in chapters 9–11 and 14–15. The possi-

23. Lampe, 7.

24. W. Wiefel, "The Jewish Community in Rome," in *The Romans Debate,* 84-101, takes the view on p. 93 that all the Jews were affected by the imperial expulsion.

25. Stern thinks the edict initially ordered the expulsion of all Jews but was then modified to a ban on all public meetings. See Dio Cassius 60.6.6; Stern, *Greek and Latin Authors,* 2:116.

bility cannot be ruled out that, after the return of the Jewish believers in Christ to Rome, new tensions may have sprung up, whose victim Paul himself may possibly have been.[26]

Romans presupposes that believers in Christ who were Jews also returned to Rome after a number of years, amongst them Prisca and Aquila. When Romans 16 emphasizes that they organized a house church in their home in Rome, one could perhaps conclude that they brought their whole house church from Ephesus to Rome with them. Important, though, is the fact that social contacts existed (again) between the "called of Jesus Christ" from the ἔθνη and these Jewish believers in Christ.

5

Finally, we must ask the question of how the "Christ-faith" happened to come to Rome at all. Paul certainly did not bring it there. As we can conclude from Romans, Paul had undertaken to evangelize in Rome himself. He was, however, hindered in the execution of his plan, and in the meantime the "Christ-faith" came to be preached there without him. His own intentions, which he communicated in Romans to those addressed, had then changed. Romans, however, also presupposes that Paul and his missionary endeavors in Rome were not unknown. There are indications in Romans 3:8 that certain negative opinions of Paul were well known in Rome.

We can only speculate as to the identity of the person or persons who first brought the "Christ-faith" into the capital city of the empire. In our opinion, it is plausible that either Jewish believers in Christ from Palestine or the Diaspora took up residence in Rome, or that Roman Jews, perhaps in connection with a pilgrimage to Jerusalem, came into contact with the "Christ-faith" and then started propagating it on their return to Rome. No intention of missionary activities by believers in Christ purposely directed toward Rome, apart from Paul's, is known to us.

26. *1 Clement* 5–6.

CHAPTER 6

Jewish and Christian Families in First-Century Rome

James S. Jeffers

1. Introduction

Studies of early Judaism and Christianity generally focus on the public lives and organizations of Jews and Christians rather than on their private lives. This is due in part to a scarcity of evidence. But we cannot claim to understand the lives of first-century-C.E. Jews and Christians in the city of Rome without an appreciation of their concepts of the family and their family practices. Relatively little has been written about the family life of early Jews, still less about that of early Christians, so a great deal of work remains to be done.

This essay seeks to begin a history of Jewish and Christian families in first-century Rome, within the context of Roman family concepts and practices. We have very little direct evidence of Jewish and Christian family life in this period, so we must make use of several lines of investigation to suggest what family life was like for them. For example, recognizing the social status of most Jews and Christians in Rome tells us something about how their families would have had to operate. Understanding the location and nature of their housing tells us a bit more. Examining the ideas and practices of the pagan Roman family, about which we have more information, should provide insights, since many first-century Christians came from pagan homes and the practices of Jews of the Diaspora seem to have been affected by the surrounding cultures. Jewish and Christian literature from this era prescribing proper family relationships and practices can give us some sense of what was and was not possible. We also can learn from the testimony of epitaphs left by lower-class Romans and by Jews in the city of Rome.

I will argue that family life among the Jews and Christians in first-century Rome did not differ much from family life among pagan Romans among the lower classes at the time. The key differences probably were a stronger emphasis on religious education along with heightened ethical demands. I believe that most first-century Jews and Christians can be found among the non-Roman lower classes of the city. I will not look at the poorest of the poor in Rome, since we have no direct evidence for them, but will focus on those families representing low social status, whose economic condition was somewhere between bare subsistence and subsistence with a margin of comfort.

Terminology can become quite involved when studying the family in antiquity. For the sake of clarity, I will normally use the term "family" as equivalent to the Roman term *familia.* I will discuss only those terms from Roman law which have a bearing on understanding the marriages of non-Romans in the lower classes, which were not legal under Roman law.

2. Social and Economic Status

The social statuses of Jews and Christians in Rome place them for the most part among the lower classes. The lower classes in Rome included some poor Roman citizens, but they were largely composed of noncitizen, Greek-speaking slaves, former slaves, and freeborn non-Romans. From the second century B.C.E. non-Romans made up a large portion of the city's population. Those who came voluntarily to Rome from the East generally brought with them their means of livelihood. They may have been respected, honored members of their former locales, but in Rome they were considered noncitizen foreigners, only a little better than slaves. Most foreigners came to Rome involuntarily, as slaves, but often they were able to gain freedom during their lifetimes. By the first century C.E. non-Romans and their descendants made up a large part, if not the majority, of the common people of the city, a large population of free resident aliens, and the entire slave class.

About forty thousand to fifty thousand Jews lived in the city of Rome by the first century C.E., making them one of the largest foreign groups in the city.[1] They had the right to assemble freely to worship and perform other rites specific to Judaism. The primary language used in the Jewish funerary inscriptions discovered in Rome, as late as the third century C.E., was Greek.[2] Any chance for upward mobility in ancient Rome would depend in part on fluency in Latin.

The *lingua franca* of earliest Roman Christianity was the Greek of the common classes. Latin did not supplant Greek among the Christian congregations of Rome until late in the second century. Roman Christianity's surviving documents are all composed in Greek, as are most of the burial inscriptions of its adherents. It appears that the majority of early Christians were persons of non-Roman stock, with roots in the Hellenized East. Unlike Judaism, Christianity was not recognized by Rome as a licensed religion. Though Rome had not specifically forbidden the practice of Christianity at this time, it considered the practice of any religion not directly authorized by the government as sedition.

The economic condition of Roman Jews and Christians in the first century also locates them among the lower classes. Jewish families in Rome probably came mostly from poorer socioeconomic classes; non-Romans, from very poor to subsistence level to modestly successful. A few were wealthy enough to endow local synagogues, and a few upper-class Romans found Judaism attractive. Roman authors scorn Roman Jews for their poverty.[3] The Jewish catacombs tend to bear out the notion that Jews were at the lower end of the economic scale. Thousands of the grave sites are plain, unmarked by epitaph or with only a brief notice crudely painted or scratched on the stucco enclosures. Some were unskillfully carved in faulty grammar on discarded pieces of marble. The grammar of the inscriptions points to a low degree of literacy. A few grave sites are finely decorated, although not on a level with those of upper-class Romans.[4]

Roman Christianity was located for the most part among the city's poorer and less respected foreigners. Most of those who were not Jews were

1. Tacitus, *Annals* 2.85.5; Cassius Dio, *History* 57.18.5a; Josephus, *Ant.* 18.81-84; and Suetonius, *Tiberius* 36. See E. Mary Smallwood, "Some Notes on the Jews under Tiberius," *Latomus* 15 (1956): 314-29.

2. Harry J. Leon, *The Jews of Ancient Rome* (Peabody, Mass.: Hendrickson, 1995 [1960]), 240-41.

3. Martial 12.57.13; Cicero, *Pro Flacco* 69; Juvenal, *Satires* 3.2, 14; 6.542-48; 14.105-6.

4. Leon, 233-35.

Gentiles originally from the Greek-speaking East. A number of the earliest converts to Christianity in the cities of the empire, according to the NT, were Gentiles who had first been attracted to Judaism. This was probably true in Rome as well.[5] Many were slaves of the Roman Empire or the descendants of slaves. Few were Roman citizens, and fewer still enjoyed any measure of status in the larger society. Romans 16, although not necessarily representative of Roman Christians, suggests a strong connection between Roman Christians and the Hellenized East. The fact that some Christians in the first century sold themselves into slavery to help out fellow believers suggests the poverty of the Christian community as a whole (*1 Clem.* 55.2).

3. Housing

Since most Jews and Christians in first-century Rome had low social and economic status, we may deduce something about their families by examining the location and nature of their homes. New immigrants from virtually all of the Roman provinces around the Mediterranean and western Europe continued to come to Rome during the first and second century C.E. Roman tenement buildings were usually the only places open to them. Persons of the same nationality tended to congregate in individual apartment buildings as new arrivals sought the companionship of established compatriots.

Even more than other foreign groups, the Jews lived together. The oldest and largest settlement of Jews was in Transtiberinum (modern Trastevere), across the Tiber River from the center of Rome. The majority of Roman Jews continued to live here into the Middle Ages. The oldest Jewish catacomb is just outside this area. Leon thinks that over half of the Jewish synagogues we know about were located here. Its narrow, crowded streets and towering apartment buildings thronged with poor, unassimilated immigrants crammed hundreds to a building. It is likely that a number of the free Jews living here worked at the nearby docks on the Tiber. Over time, Jews expanded from Transtiberinum to other areas.[6] Since most early

5. George La Piana, "Foreign Groups in Rome during the First Centuries of the Empire," *HTR* 20 (1927): 183-403, here 390-91.

6. Leon, 136-37; Hermann Vogelstein, "The Jews in Ancient Rome," bk. I in *Rome,* trans. M. Hadas (Philadelphia: Jewish Publication Society of America, 1941), 18.

Christians were Jews or lower-class Romans, we should expect to find many first-century Christians in Transtiberinum as well.

From the second century B.C.E., Rome began erecting multistory apartment buildings *(insulae)*. Packer believes the *insula* originated in Rome to address the housing needs of its rapidly growing population. They were typically built around an inner courtyard that provided light and air to the rooms above. Small shops *(tabernae)* were often built into the outer ring of the first floor of the *insula*. Families who operated such small shops often lived in them as well. There was sometimes a back room behind or a mezzanine above the main room, offering a bit of privacy for the family. A few "deluxe" apartments might be found behind these shops, facing the inner courtyard. These apartments contained a number of rooms, including accommodations for servants, and were suitable for hosting small social gatherings. They generally lacked kitchens and latrines.[7]

Above the *tabernae* were usually three to five floors of apartments. The absence of elevators and the poorer construction of the higher stories meant that the cheapest apartments were on the upper floors. These were mostly one- and two-room apartments. Interior rooms, probably used for sleeping, received no natural light or fresh air. Families either cooked on charcoal braziers located near an outside opening or went out for hot meals. They used public latrines, the small spaces under stairs, or chamber pots. Privacy would have been rare. Within the individual apartment, several unrelated families might have separate sleeping rooms but share a common sitting room. These apartments were too small to allow for socializing with friends, let alone for Christian house congregations. Those who lived in such apartments would have to do most of their eating and socializing in public places.[8]

Slaves in Rome typically lived in the homes of their masters. Some residences had slave quarters, but frequently slaves were expected to sleep in the kitchen or wherever they could put down a cot. Masters encouraged their slaves to form families, and those who did were more likely to be assigned separate quarters.[9] Once a slave had gained his freedom, he nor-

7. James E. Packer, *The Insulae of Imperial Ostia* (Rome: American Academy, 1971), 43; John E. Stambaugh, *The Ancient Roman City* (Baltimore: Johns Hopkins University Press, 1988), 166-67.

8. Stambaugh, 175-78; Packer, 72-73.

9. Keith R. Bradley, *Slavery and Rebellion in the Roman World, 140 BC–70 BC* (London: Oxford University Press, 1989), 52-53.

mally continued to serve his former master and sometimes continued to live in the master's home, but some were allowed to maintain separate residences near the master's home. Those who moved out of the home almost certainly ended up in the kind of homes just described.

While we have no remains of private homes of Jews or Christians in Rome, it seems clear that the majority of Jews and Christians of necessity would have lived either in tiny apartments several stories above ground floor, in the homes of their masters or former masters, or in *tabernae* where their shops were located. Did Jewish and Christian families practice religious rituals in such homes? If so, what kinds of rituals did they practice and what did their neighbors think of them? Christian house congregations which met in the homes of believers probably met in the first-floor "deluxe" apartments. If Jews were able to congregate in buildings with other Jews, they would have found it easier to practice the dietary and exclusivity demands of their religion. Jews who converted to Christianity would have found their apartment building a natural place to proselytize.

4. Marriage

a. Forms of Marriage

Not all marriages in Rome were recognized by Roman law. Only when both partners were Roman citizens could a legal marriage *(matrimonium)* normally be formed. By the late republic, the most common form of legal marriage was "without *manus*" *(sine manu)*. The wife did not come under her husband's complete authority; her father remained her *paterfamilias*, so she did not belong to her husband's family. This meant, for example, that the dowry she brought into the marriage would usually be refunded to her family if the marriage was dissolved.[10]

Other "marriages" were informal, not governed by Roman law. In contrast with later cultures, Rome did not consider such unions immoral; it simply did not offer them the protection of the law. Children born to an

10. Archie C. Bush, *Studies in Roman Social Structure* (Washington, D.C.: University Press of America, 1982), 95; Beryl L. Rawson, "The Roman Family," in *The Family in Ancient Rome: New Perspectives*, ed. Beryl L. Rawson (London: Croon Helm, 1986), 19.

informal marriage were illegitimate and took their status from the mother, the father having no legal rights over them. The fact that the wife could not be accused of adultery may have given her greater freedom than women in legal marriages. Slaves typically initiated informal marriages with other slaves, usually within their master's *familia,* though with permission a slave might marry a slave from another *familia.* Slave marriages involved little security, since either partner or the children might be sold at any time. Despite this, many slave marriages survived over long periods of time, regardless of changes in habitation or changes in status from slave to free of one or both partners. In the epitaphs slaves refer to each other as husband and wife.

b. Marriage Traditions

Roman law made twelve the minimum marriage age for girls, fourteen for boys. Typically, the age of first marriage for free Roman girls was between twelve and eighteen. Men married for the first time as late as thirty, but in Roman culture a five-year difference between man and woman seems to have been most common. The age of first marriage seems to have been within the same range for slaves as for free men and women. Weaver believes the majority of children born to slaves were born prior to the mother's manumission.[11]

A principal basis for contracting a marriage among the lower classes was mutual suitability, as determined by the parents. Political alliance was not a factor, so the pattern of successive marriages and divorces among the upper class is not likely to be found in the lower. The inscriptions show that some old Roman ideals of marriage were embraced by the non-Roman lower classes: marriages were of long duration and women were lauded for having married only once.[12]

The age of first marriage for Jewish girls probably was also between twelve and eighteen. Epigraphical and papyrological evidence suggests an

11. Richard P. Saller, "Men's Age at Marriage and Its Consequences in the Roman Family," *Classical Philology* 82 (1987): 21-34; Rawson, 21; P. R. C. Weaver, "The Status of Children in Mixed Marriages," in *The Family in Ancient Rome,* 155-56.

12. Sarah Pomeroy, *Goddesses, Whores, Wives, Slaves: Women in Classical Antiquity* (New York: Schocken Books, 1975), 204.

average age of fifteen, while rabbinic sources generally assume an age of twelve, with betrothals earlier. The average age for men was older. Evidence suggests that thirty was not unusual. Philo of Alexandria considered a man "ripe" for marriage between twenty-eight and thirty-five (*On the Creation of the World* 103). The Mishnah gives eighteen as the proper age for a young man to marry (*Abot* 5:21). The Roman Jewish inscriptions tend to confirm these ages of first marriage.

5. Family Structure

The Roman *familia* is a classic example of a patriarchy. It is composed of the group, including relatives by blood and marriage, slaves and freedmen, over whom the male head (the *paterfamilias*) has power. Women who married without *manus* stayed under their father's authority, and thus were a part of his *familia*. The *paterfamilias* was normally the only member of the family who could own property; this power was not broken until his death. Despite this, his sons set up their own households when they married.[13] As a result, the Roman *familia* often consisted of several households under the legal authority of the *paterfamilias*.

Each Roman household was nuclear in form, normally composed of husband, wife, unmarried children, slaves, freedmen, and other clients. Bigamy was illegal. Examples of several conjugal units living under the same roof appear to be the exception, not the rule. Cicero described the family unit as the married couple and children. Brothers and cousins, who could not be expected to live in the same household, formed their own households as colonies of their parents' home (*De officiis* 1.53).

The nuclear family tended to be small at all social levels. Few families had as many as three children who survived infancy. The epitaphs from lower-class families seldom record more than two children.[14] Inscriptions at Rome also mention a number of single-parent families (only one parent is named on the inscription). The frequency of divorce and of the early death of one parent must have led to frequent remarriage, and thus to stepchildren and blended families. Grandparents seem not to have been prominent in the Roman family, due in part to a shorter life expectancy

13. Stambaugh, 158.
14. Rawson, 8-9.

than in modern times. Verner believes that the intact households in one- and two-room apartments in Rome and Ostia consisted of husband, wife, one or two children, and no slaves.[15]

Saller and Shaw believe that Roman slave family structures did not differ substantially from the family structures of the free populace.[16] Many slaves in Rome in this era could hope to win their freedom: if they were owned by Roman citizens they would normally be granted Roman citizenship when they were freed or manumitted. The Lex Aelia Sentia of 4 C.E. set thirty as the minimum age of manumission, but exceptions were allowed. Females were likely to be freed earlier than males, in part because masters had to free them in order to marry them. While marriage to a slave by lower-class freeborns was perfectly acceptable, it was a cause for censure among the wealthy. Since a slave had no father in the eyes of Roman law, when he or she was freed the former master was recognized as legal father.[17]

Unlike Roman law, Jewish law allowed polygamy, but we know of no examples of polygamy among Jews in Rome. It is likely that here, as in other cities of the Greco-Roman world, Jews adopted the marriage practices of the culture around them. Reinhartz believes that the structure and problems of Jewish families differed little from those of non-Jewish families in the Hellenistic world at this time.[18]

Like Roman families around them, the Jewish household probably consisted of two, sometimes three, generations of kin by blood and marriage. Most Jewish families in Rome probably did not own slaves. Unlike the Roman *familia*, those that included slaves probably did not include freedmen, since freedmen owed no continuing service to former masters who were not Roman citizens.

It is likely that the structure of Christian families in Rome mirrored that of Jewish and pagan families. First-century Christian adults were either first- or second-generation converts, and thus not far removed from their Jewish or pagan origins. The NT and other early Christian writings include

15. Rawson, 14; David C. Verner, *The Household of God: The Social World of the Pastoral Epistles* (Chico: Scholars Press, 1983), 61.

16. Richard P. Saller and Brent D. Shaw, "Tombstones and Roman Family Relations in the Principate: Civilians, Soldiers and Slaves," *JRS* 74 (1984): 124-56, here 145-51.

17. Rawson, 12-13.

18. Adele Reinhartz, "Parents and Children: A Philonic Perspective," in *The Jewish Family in Antiquity*, ed. Shaye J. D. Cohen (Atlanta: Scholars Press, 1993), 87.

a number of codes of household ethics *(Haustafeln)*. Those originating in the city of Rome include 1 Peter 2:13-21; 3:1-7; *1 Clement* 1.3; 21.6-8; and the *Shepherd of Hermas* (*Man.* 8.10). 1 Peter probably was written from Rome between 65 and 90 C.E.[19] *1 Clement* was authored ca. 93-97 C.E., while the *Shepherd of Hermas* was written between ca. 95 and 135 C.E.[20] 1 Peter addresses only wives, husbands, and slaves. Balch believes that social tensions between Christian wives and slaves on the one hand and non-Christian husbands and masters on the other motivated the writing of this code; that is why 1 Peter has nothing to say to masters or to children.[21]

The NT provides information about Prisca and Aquila, two of the Roman Christians greeted in Romans 16. They were tentmakers who worked in Rome, Corinth, and Ephesus, indicating a high degree of mobility. The fact that Aquila and Prisca could afford to rent residences capable of seating a dozen or two worshipers shows that they were able to live well above a subsistence level. Their wealth, though modest, exceeded that of most residents of Rome and, therefore, probably that of most other Roman Christians. Perhaps they were able to rent a "deluxe" apartment. It also is possible that a house church could have met in the work area of their *taberna*.[22]

Scholars in general accept the self-identification of Hermas, the author of the early second-century-C.E. *Shepherd of Hermas* (*Vis.* 1.1.1). He was raised by a man who brought him to Rome and sold him to a Roman woman named Rhoda. He apparently gained his freedom a number of years before he met Rhoda again. In the meantime, he had become "rich" and then lost his wealth (*Vis.* 3.6.7). Hermas has a wife and grown children (*Vis.* 1.3.1; 2.2.2-3).[23]

19. David L. Balch, *Let Wives Be Submissive: The Domestic Code in I Peter* (Chico: Scholars Press, 1981), 138.

20. James S. Jeffers, *Conflict at Rome: Social Order and Hierarchy in Early Christianity* (Minneapolis: Fortress, 1991), 90, 112.

21. Balch, 109. Quotations from the NT are from the *New American Standard Bible;* quotations from *1 Clement* and the *Shepherd of Hermas* are from the Loeb Classical Library edition, trans. K. Lake.

22. Acts 18:2-3, 18, 26; 1 Cor. 16:19. Peter Lampe, *Die stadtrömischen Christen in den ersten beiden Jahrhunderten* (Tübingen: J. C. B. Mohr, 1987), 156-62.

23. Lampe, 182-200; Carolyn Osiek, *Rich and Poor in the Shepherd of Hermas* (Washington, D.C.: Catholic Biblical Association, 1983); William Jerome Wilson, "The Career of the Prophet Hermas," *HTR* 20 (1927): 21-62; Kirsopp Lake, "The Shepherd of Hermas and Christian Life in Rome in the Second Century," *HTR* 4 (1911): 25-46.

Jewish and Christian families, because of their socioeconomic condition, their physical space, and their contact with the larger Roman culture, probably were structured much like the other lower-class families in Rome. They would have constituted a weakened patriarchy. But the patriarch's low social status would tend to undermine his power; moreover, since marriage for most Jews and Christians was not legitimate in the state's eyes, Roman law, which served to reinforce the patriarchy, would not aid Jewish or Christian men. The small size of their dwellings and their economic status would keep the household small: husband, wife, and two or three children.

6. Husband-Wife Relationships

a. Nature of the Marriage Relationship

Both Roman and Jewish marriages typically were arranged by the parents of the prospective spouses, sometimes with the latter's assistance. In the absence of evidence to the contrary, it seems likely that Christian parents would have arranged the marriages of their children as well. Marriages were arranged more for the sake of the family than for the individuals involved.[24] Among the upper classes, they took into account the social and economic benefits an alliance with the other family would bring and the suitability of the prospective spouses for each other. Among the lower classes, social alliances can hardly have been much of a factor. Here the emphasis would have been on finding a spouse suitable for one's son or daughter. Faithfulness to the relationship and harmony within the marriage were ideals, and constituted a kind of love. The need to raise children to continue the family line was considered a basic obligation. Traditionally, marriage among Jews was brought about by a contract agreed upon by two men, the father of the bride, and the groom or his father (Tobit 7:12-14).[25] Few women would have reached the age of twenty unmarried.

At least some Romans valued "togetherness" in marriage. In 21 C.E. the Roman Senate considered preventing wives from accompanying their husbands when they served as governors in the provinces. Tacitus reports that

24. Gillian Clark, "Roman Women," *Greece and Rome* 28 (1981): 193-212, here 203.

25. Verner, 44.

one senator said wives "share most aspects of life with their husbands." He calls their wives "their partners in prosperity and adversity." For many Roman couples, marriage was a close relationship between husband and wife, as important as — perhaps more important than — producing children.[26]

The standardized expressions of sentiment in the Jewish inscriptions in Rome tell us what qualities in a spouse, parent, or child the community of the person setting up the monument expected: a good reputation, religious piety, and devotion to family members.[27]

b. Husbands

As noted above, the head *(paterfamilias)* of the Roman *familia* held almost absolute power over all the members of his household. This power, which included even the power of life and death, was called *patria potestas;* it had diminished considerably by the first century C.E., though the Roman husband and father still held total control of the family property. While even his adult sons owned nothing legally before his death, in practice many adult sons lived lives quite independent of their fathers. In any case, many fathers did not live long into their children's adulthood. The transition to marriage without *manus* meant a lessening of the husband's power over his wife. Plutarch, writing around the turn of the second century C.E., tells newlyweds, "Every activity in a virtuous household is carried on by both parties in agreement, but discloses the husband's leadership and preferences" (*Advice on Marriage* 139A). This appears to suggest that the couple's decisions should be based on consensus, though Plutarch clearly believes that the wife must subordinate herself to the husband's governance (142E). He encourages husbands to teach their wives the most useful parts of philosophy (144F).

A sexual double standard existed in Roman marriage. While husbands and wives both were told to avoid sexual infidelity, women were more severely chastised for it by society. Plutarch cautions against sexual infidelity by husbands, but suggests the bride overlook her husband's sexual affairs (*Advice on Marriage* 144D, 143F).

Philo, a Jewish intellectual of the upper classes in Alexandria, wrote

26. Tacitus, *Annals* 3.33-44; see Rawson, 27-29.

27. Leon, 127-32.

about the proper Jewish family during the early first century C.E. Although he was far removed socially and geographically from lower-class Jews in Rome, his ideas may have reflected or influenced the thinking of at least some Roman Jews. Philo says the family is based on three features: an indissoluble bond of love and kinship, the inherent superiority of parents, and the hierarchy of male and female which associates women with the senses and men with the mind.[28]

1 Peter tells Christian husbands to live with their wives "in an understanding way, as with a weaker vessel, since she is a woman," and to grant her honor as a fellow heir of salvation (3:7). This suggests a more or less traditional hierarchical relationship softened by the recognition of her equivalent position before God. This would not have required much adjustment by former pagans or Jewish Christians.

Clement gives all his instructions directly to the male head of the household (*1 Clem.* 1.3; 21.6-8), implying that he is responsible to see that all of the family members mentioned live up to the ideals presented. Clement does not present the proper behavior of husbands and fathers toward the family beyond their responsibility to govern its conduct, which fits well with the Roman concept of the *paterfamilias.* The emphasis on instruction in these codes is similar to Philo's statements in *Apology for the Jews* 7.14, in which he says husbands, fathers, and masters are to provide wives, children, and slaves with a knowledge of the law.

The *Shepherd of Hermas* presents Hermas as the head (κεφαλή) of his household (οἶκος) (*Sim.* 7.2). He has direct responsibility for the sinfulness of his family and bears God's anger as a result (*Vis.* 1.3.1). If he obeys God's commands and corrects them in piety, they will be saved (cf. *Sim.* 5.3.9). These passages seem to give Hermas the absolute power of a spiritual *paterfamilias,* but that power is limited. Hermas is in a sense held hostage by the behavior of his family. He is told that he is being punished harshly because his family "cannot be punished in any other way, than if you, the head of the household, be afflicted" (*Sim.* 7.3), probably referring to economic deprivation. Hermas is also chastised for fantasizing about being married to Rhoda, his former owner (*Vis.* 1.1.2). We do not know how well Roman Christians in general lived up to a strict sexual ethic.

This emphasis on the power of the *paterfamilias* is similar to what we see in the Pastoral Epistles of the NT, in which the "householder exercises

28. *Special Laws* 2.124; quoted in Reinhartz, 86.

authority over his wife, children, and slaves and ultimately must account for their behavior." Verner thinks the Pastorals depart from the larger society only in their strict sexual ethic, "which holds up a single standard of behavior for husbands and wives."[29]

c. Wives

Plutarch and Juvenal told their upper-class readers how wives should and should not behave. Plutarch says wives should not initiate lovemaking, should accept their husbands' friends, avoid "queer rituals and outlandish superstitions" and accept their husbands' gods, be content to stay at home, and remain silent except to address their husbands (*Advice on Marriage* 140C-F, 142C, D). He refers to wives who dominate their husbands using sexual manipulation or magic and to women who are unfaithful to their spouses (139B). Writing in late first-century Rome, Juvenal gives us a portrait of the ideal wife: one who does not cheat on her spouse but puts up with his affairs, who does not reject his friends, who does not leave behind his gods for foreign religions, who does not make a public spectacle of herself but manages his household.[30]

It is not clear to what degree, if at all, women in the lower classes experienced greater freedom in the marriage relationship in this era. The necessities of life in the lower classes would have exerted a curb on the possibilities for social freedom among lower-class women. For example, women in the lower classes did more physical labor and earned more of the family's income than women in wealthier families. On the other hand, women in nonlegal marriages could leave a relationship without interference by the state. Such women were far more likely to get custody of their children, since Roman law recognized the mother as the only legitimate parent in an illegitimate relationship. By contrast, the divorcing father in a legal Roman marriage almost always was awarded custody of the children, since they were his heirs. Many lower-class families were fatherless, requiring the mother to take full responsibility to provide for and raise her children, thus acquiring the rights and duties of a head of household.

Jewish wives living in Rome would have had more freedom in some

29. Verner, 145.
30. Verner, 68-70.

respects and less in others than women who lived under Jewish law. In cities such as Rome, they were freer to engage actively in society outside their homes. They would have found it easy to divorce their husbands, whether or not their marriage was legal in the eyes of Rome. Under Jewish law, a wife could not divorce her husband unless she prosecuted him and the court ordered a divorce (*m. Ned.* 11:12) and the wife's guardianship transferred from her father to her husband at marriage. On the other hand, Jewish law allowed women to take legal actions without the assistance of a guardian, to own property, and to control property without interference by their husbands.[31] Leon finds no evidence in Rome that in the life of the Jewish family women had a position in any way inferior to that of men: "Jewish mothers, wives, and daughters were apparently regarded with no less respect and affection than fathers, husbands, and sons."[32]

The references to Plutarch and Juvenal (above) illustrate the Roman belief that a wife should adopt her husband's gods; a wife's conversion to Judaism or Christianity could lead to serious conflict within the family. 1 Peter devotes almost half its section on household codes to this problem, telling wives to be submissive to their husbands so that those who are not Christians may be won over by their behavior. This behavior was to include being chaste, respectful, and having a gentle and quiet spirit, which its author considers a better adornment than any physical kind, and the model is the obedience of Sarah to her husband Abraham. According to Rengstorf, "to be submissive" as a duty of the wife is a specifically Christian concept.[33]

1 Clement also devotes a disproportionate amount of space to the duties of wives. Clement's instructions are concerned with regulating the behavior of women rather than with delineating their privileges and responsibilities. They are to act from a pure conscience, show the proper affection and obedience to their husbands, show equal affection to all Christians, manage their household with the proper attitude, exhibit purity and meekness, and speak little. This passage implies that Christian wives were expected to manage their households, as were pagan and Jewish wives.

The only comment about wives in the *Shepherd of Hermas* regards the sins of Hermas's wife, primarily her inability to control her tongue:

31. Verner, 45-46.

32. Leon, 232.

33. Karl Heinrich Rengstorf, *Mann und Frau im Urchristentum* (Köln: Westdeutscher, 1954), 25-46.

"For she does not refrain her tongue . . ." (*Vis.* 2.2.3; 2.3.1). Once again, the emphasis is on regulating behavior.

Why the strong emphasis on wives in 1 Peter and *1 Clement*? Perhaps it reflects a decline in the power of the *paterfamilias*, accompanied by a rise in the power and independence of women (assuming that this change affected the lower classes in Rome as well). Perhaps slave and freed women known by these authors were imitating the more independent behavior of their mistresses.

Were Christian wives unwilling to countenance a sexual double standard, in contrast with advice to Roman wives? Clearly the NT does not allow for such a double standard, nor does Hermas. Verner asserts that the ideals of the household in the Pastoral Epistles "directly and uncritically reflect the dominant social values of the larger society"; its ideal departs from the norm in only one area — its strict sexual ethic, which allowed one standard of behavior for men and women. The honor ascribed to men and women who chose not to remarry after the death of a spouse ran counter to the Greek notion that they should remarry and raise more children in order to strengthen the *polis.*[34]

7. Parent-Child Relationships

a. Fathers

The Roman author Seneca believed that fathers show their love for their children by imposing structure: waking them up early so that they are productive, not allowing them to be idle, and drawing effort from them (*De providentia* 2.5). The father is generally depicted as stricter than the mother; Seneca portrays this strictness as genuine love, because its purpose was to oversee the real interests of the child. Roman fathers were able to show affection and tenderness, however. In the literature they cherish children whether beautiful or ugly, healthy or sick, and they take an interest in their sons' education. Epictetus tells of a father who was distraught over his daughter's illness (1.2.4ff.).[35] Unfortunately, we do not know how typical were these feelings.

34. Verner, 145.

35. Emiel Eyben, "Fathers and Sons," in *Marriage, Divorce, and Children in Ancient Rome,* ed. Beryl Rawson (Oxford: Clarendon, 1991), 117-23.

For Jews, having children was itself an obligation, based on the command "be fruitful and multiply" in Genesis 1:28, in harmony with the Roman belief that the principal function of marriage was to continue the family line. The general consensus was that this requirement was for men only.[36]

The fundamental obligation of Jewish parents, according to Jewish literature, was to feed and clothe their children. Failure to do this was the worst type of neglect (*Ep. Arist.* 248). According to Philo, the father is primarily responsible for financial support, from redeeming the firstborn to providing a dowry for daughters and an inheritance for sons, to basic food, clothing, education, and health care (*Special Laws* 2.233).[37] The rabbis considered it a paternal obligation to teach a son a trade.

Jewish parents, especially fathers, were to discipline their children. Corporal punishment was the primary means of discipline. Parents must not play or laugh with their children or risk spoiling them (Sir. 30:1-13). At the same time, they should not be too harsh in disciplining their children; to avoid this, *Pseudo-Phocylides* recommends that a father whose child offends him should allow the mother, the elders of the family, or the chiefs of the people to discipline him (207-9).[38]

Clement's instructions for children in *1 Clement* 21.6-8 differ from those in the NT codes of household ethics. The latter focus on obedience and respect to parents and elders, while *1 Clement* focuses on instruction in the Christian faith. Clement applies this to two age groups: "children" (τέκνα), probably anywhere from early childhood to youth, and "the young" (νέους), probably from youth to young adulthood, with no distinction between the education of boys and girls. This focus on education could reflect an increased concern among second-generation Christians that the received faith be transmitted to the new generation. It may also reflect the high value placed on religious education by Jews.

Hermas is told that his lack of discipline has led to his children's sins: "But you are indulgent, and do not correct your family, but have allowed them to become corrupt." He is instructed to not cease correcting his children so that they will repent and be saved (*Vis.* 1.3.1, 2).

36. O. Larry Yarbrough, "Parents and Children in the Jewish Family of Antiquity," in *The Jewish Family in Antiquity*, 41.

37. Reinhartz, 45, 72.

38. Reinhartz, 74-77.

b. Mothers

According to Dixon, the Roman mother was viewed mainly as the transmitter of traditional morality. She was ideally a firm disciplinarian, not a source of undiscriminating tenderness. As a result, tasks such as nursing infants were better left to others if possible. At the same time, Roman women are praised for their close watch over the moral development of children and grandchildren.[39] The Roman mother was almost fully responsible for her daughter's education, since daughters were educated primarily in domestic skills.

The fact that daughters married earlier than sons and tended to live closer to their husband's family than their natal family suggests that the affective bond between mother and son was stronger than that between mother and daughter. Kraemer thinks that Jewish mothers, like Greco-Roman mothers, had a closer emotional attachment to their sons than to their daughters.[40]

Philo taught that the physical nurturing of a child is primarily the mother's responsibility. Due to maternal affection and the physical need to breast-feed, mothers who are separated from their infants will suffer great distress. A wife owed her husband the obligation of nursing infants (*m. Ned.* 5.5), who were weaned between the eighteenth and twenty-fourth months (*m. Git.* 7.6).[41]

Marriage is depicted as the fulfillment of a woman's life, and the mother is especially associated with helping prepare for it. This is the case in the first-century-C.E. retelling of the biblical account of the sacrifice of Jephthah's daughter in Pseudo-Philo's *Biblical Antiquities* (40.6). In Tobit, Sarah's mother Edna prepares the bridal chamber for her daughter's upcoming marriage (7:15-17).[42]

39. Suzanne Dixon, *The Roman Mother* (Norman, Okla.: University of Oklahoma Press, 1988), 233-35.

40. Kraemer, "Jewish Mothers and Daughters," in *The Jewish Family in Antiquity*, ed. Shaye J. D. Cohen (Atlanta: Scholars Press, 1993), 94.

41. Reinhartz, 71, 86-87; Yarbrough, 46.

42. Kraemer, "Jewish Mothers and Daughters," 93-94.

c. Children

The period of childhood was short and often grim for the lower classes in Rome. Children in poorer families went to work early in their lives. The fact that many humble Roman families lived in a combined home and workshop would make it impossible to focus home life on the children. Children seem to have been exposed to many influences besides that of their parents. If this was intentional, if reflects a view of the family's place in the broader social context.

Children born to former slaves of Roman citizens, after the parents were freed, were freeborn Roman citizens. Mixed-status marriages sometimes show several stages in the parents' changing status, and successive children could have status different from one another. In a regular Roman marriage, children took their status from their father at the time of their conception. In extralegal marriages, they took it from their mother at the time of their birth.

The obligations of Jewish children may be summed up by the command to "honor your father and your mother" (Exod. 20:12). Closely related to honor was the obligation to obey, a major theme in the Wisdom tradition (e.g., Prov. 1:8; 6:20), though 4 Maccabees says that obedience to the law takes precedence over obedience to parents (2:10). The rabbis also believed one may disobey a parent's unlawful request (e.g., *m. B. Mes.* 2.10; *b. Yebam.* 5b-6a). Probably the discussions of honoring parents and the limits to this have in mind grown children.[43]

Philo wrote that children owe their parents obedience, fear, courtesy, care, and nurture.[44] They remain beholden to their parents even after they have reached adulthood. Once a child is married, his relationship with his parents shifts from receiving support to giving support, as his parents grow old.

The Jewish inscriptions in Rome show that Jewish parents rarely gave their children the names of biblical patriarchs. A number of Semitic names do show up, but they are often translated into or adapted to Greek or Latin equivalents. Overall, Greek and Latin names predominate, including a smattering of names derived from pagan deities (such as Aphrodisia and Dionysias). These latter names may have been given be-

43. Yarbrough, 51-53.

44. *Special Laws* 2.235, 237; *Decalogue* 117; Reinhartz, 78-81.

cause they were popular in the wider society, with no thought of their literal meanings.[45]

A number of epitaphs give the ages of Jewish children in Rome at their deaths, the largest number being between birth and ten. Comparatively large numbers also mention ages between ten and twenty-nine. It is probable that the age of one who died young was more likely to be recorded, yet the age of infants dying before completing their first year is recorded only twice (*CII* 108, 348). Is this because such an early death, though regrettable, was not considered particularly unusual or surprising?[46]

Hermas's children are criticized for a variety of sins. Due to the nature of their errors, and from what we know of Hermas's life, they probably were adults. They had "blasphemed the Lord," "betrayed their parents," committed "wanton deeds and piled up wickedness" (*Vis.* 2.2.2; see also *Vis.* 1.3.1, 2). The exact nature of their sins cannot be determined from these references, but the penalty for them is the most severe: if they do not repent, they will not be saved.

8. Master–Slave/Freedman Relationships

It is hard to determine how slaves were treated by Roman masters; they were considered property, to be used however masters wished. We know that slaves were mistreated even when such treatment conflicted with the economic interests of the owners. Roman men commonly engaged in sex with their slaves; Roman women did so as well, but probably less frequently. On the other hand, the literature and epitaphs give examples of apparently genuine affection of masters for their slaves; it was not too uncommon for a master to grant a slave freedom so that he could legally marry her.

We have evidence of Jewish slave owners and of Jews as slaves in a number of places, including Italy. Josephus mentions several times that thousands of Jews captured from Palestine were sold into slavery around the Mediterranean, many of whom ended up in Rome (*War* 3.304-6, 540-42; 6.418). Other writers refer to Jewish slaves and freedpersons in Rome.[47]

45. Leon, 119-21.

46. Leon, 230.

47. Philo, *Embassy to Gaius* 155; Tacitus, *Annals* 2.85; Josephus, *Ant.* 17.141; Martial 7.35.2-3. See Dale B. Martin, "Slavery and the Ancient Jewish Family," in *The Jewish Family in Antiquity,* 120.

Jewish slaves in Rome faced the same basic challenges as Gentile slaves (e.g., breakup of the family, difficulty in practicing their religion), while they would have found it virtually impossible to abstain from certain foods and to limit contact with Gentiles.

First Peter tells slaves to "be submissive to your masters" regardless of the masters' nature. Slaves will find favor with God if they patiently bear unjust punishment. The letter implies that slaves might do something worthy of harsh treatment (2:20), so they are encouraged to emulate Christ, who endured suffering with great patience (2:21-24). Balch believes that the instructions to slaves in 1 Peter, like those to wives, were inspired by social tension. The unwillingness of Christian slaves to practice the religion of their non-Christian master was a source of conflict, but Balch does not think that the intent of the behavior encouraged by 1 Peter was to convert the masters. After all, their model is the martyred Christ. As in the case of wives, slaves are not given the standard Greco-Roman instruction to submit themselves to the gods of their masters. Balch believes that 1 Peter gives no instructions to masters because the point of the passage is to address social tensions in divided households. This was not an issue when the master was a Christian.[48]

It is difficult to explain Clement's omission of slaves and masters in his household code. He does make a few references to slavery: he laments the fact that the patriarch Joseph fell into slavery (4.9) and refers to Roman Christians who had sold themselves into slavery for the sake of others (55.2).

That Hermas was purchased by Rhoda, not her husband, suggests that she was not married at the time. Hermas's fantasies about his mistress may not have been all that rare among slaves (*Vis.* 1.1.1-2). A number of Hermas's parables allude to slavery. He writes of a slave who disappoints his master and of one who was faithful to his master and who consequently was honored by him (*Mand.* 12.2.1; 5.2.2-9). Hermas identifies himself and other Christians as the slaves of God (*Vis.* 1.2.4; 4.1.3; *Mand.* 3.4; *Sim.* 8.6.5). The implication of these passages is that Christians owe God the same obedience that masters require of their slaves.

None of these Christian writings condemns slavery outright or instructs Christian slave owners to free their slaves. Although they prefer freedom to slavery, their acceptance of the institution of slavery indicates

48. Balch, 108-9.

that they do not challenge the basic categories of Roman society. Christian slaves would simply have to make the best of their situation as they sought to establish and maintain a family.

9. Conclusion

I have sought to show that Jews and Christians in first-century Rome were for the most part poor, noncitizen, Greek-speaking foreigners, slaves and former slaves. Their tiny apartments or *tabernae* living spaces made privacy difficult and would have limited the kinds of family religious observances that could take place. They would also have limited the size of their families, making it very unlikely that many relatives beyond the conjugal unit could have lived together. Slaves had virtually no privacy and would have found it difficult to live with family members beyond the conjugal unit. Since most Jewish and Christian marriages in first-century Rome were not legal before Roman law, the husbands may have had less power over their families and the wives more autonomy (in some respects) than in the upper classes. Girls married during their late teens, boys a few years later. The literary and epigraphical sources help confirm what the archaeological sources suggest, that first-century Jewish and Christian families, like pagan Roman ones, were nuclear in nature, composed of husband, wife, and children (often in blended families due to divorce and death). The number of children living at any one time was probably low by premodern standards: two to three seems most likely. Slaves did their best to emulate the families of free Romans. The fact that slave couples tended to stay together after gaining their freedom suggests that those Jews and Christians who were or had been slaves shared the family ideals of free persons and tried to make them work.

We see many parallels in the roles of family members and relationships among pagan, Jewish, and Christian families. We know from a variety of sources, in particular Alexandria, that Jews throughout the Greco-Roman world tended to adopt the practices of the surrounding culture, especially when those practices did not conflict with their religious beliefs. Jews and Christians in Rome found ideals in the pagan family which were not all that different from those asserted by their religious leaders. The husband and father was the head of the family, with the responsibility to provide for his children, treat them with love but without an excess of affection, educate them, and discipline them when necessary. But Jewish and Christian husbands could not rely on the state to reinforce this authority. It would be useful to know to what degree the synagogue or Christian house congregation provided such reinforcement. The wife was to submit to her husband's authority, even obey him. She managed the household, which in the lower classes probably meant overseeing the children. Despite the division of responsibility implied in some of the literature, the Jewish or Christian mother in Rome probably shared many of the duties usually given to the father, such as providing financial support, educating, and disciplining. When the marriage dissolved, she probably kept the children. If she did not remarry, she would assume full responsibility for the children. In the case of mixed-religion marriages, the Christian husband would probably expect his wife to convert. If the wife was the Christian, her faith would have caused real problems in her marriage. 1 Peter makes clear that the Christian congregations had contact with such women, but we do not know to what degree the congregation was able to help them. Children were obliged to obey their parents, even after attaining adulthood.

Many of the first-century Christians in Rome were first-generation believers who were raised in pagan homes. Others were slaves in pagan households. Still others were Jewish converts who brought with them Jewish family concepts, influenced by Hellenistic and Roman beliefs.

Much work remains to be done before we can say that we understand the Jewish and Christian families of the first century. This is especially true with regard to the Christian family, about which very little has been written. Space limitations prevent this essay from exploring topics such as family rituals, divorce, and infanticide. Detailed studies of other cities also are needed.

CHAPTER 7

The Oral World of Early Christianity in Rome: The Case of Hermas

Carolyn Osiek

The last few years have seen the appearance of a surprising amount of writing on the *Shepherd of Hermas*. Other than text criticism, linguistics, and commentary,[1] most of it has concentrated on social aspects, magic, and Christology, and has focused on the *Visions* or the fifth *Similitude*.[2] This paper will focus attention somewhat differently: after briefly situating Hermas in his social context (part 1), it will discuss some of what is known about levels and types of literacy and orality in his world (part 2), then explore the characteristics of oral culture and their influence on the literary structure of the *Shepherd* (part 3), in order to argue that the written text shows evidence not only of being close to oral thought patterns, but also of being originally intended for oral proclamation.

1. Antonio Carlini, ed., *Erma: Il Pastore (Ia-IIIa visione)*, Papyrus Bodmer 38 (Cologny-Genève: Fondation Martin Bodmer, 1991); David Hellholm, *Das Visionenbuch des Hermas als Apokalypse. Formgeschichtliche und texttheoretische Studien zu einer literarischen Gattung*, vol. 1, *Methodologische Vorüberlegungen und makrostrukturelle Textanalyse*, ConBNT 13:1 (Lund: Gleerup, 1980); Norbert Brox, *Der Hirt des Hermas*, Ergänzungsreihe zum Kritisch-exegetischen Kommentar über das Neue Testament 7 (Göttingen: Vandenhoeck & Ruprecht, 1991).

2. On social reality, Martin Leutzsch, *Die Wahrnehmung sozialer Wirklichkeit im "Hirten des Hermas"* (Göttingen: Vandenhoeck & Ruprecht, 1989); on Christology and *Similitude* 5, Philippe Henne, "A propos de la christologie du *Pasteur* d'Hermas," *RSPT* 72 (1988): 569-78; "La véritable christologie de la *cinquième Similitude* du *Pasteur* d'Hermas," *RSPT* 74 (1990): 182-204.

This in turn will tell us something of the life of Roman Christians at the time.

Indeed, precisely those literary characteristics of the *Shepherd* that modern readers find tedious indicators of poor literary quality can be seen from orality studies as characteristic of oral composition and oral performance. These two elements are what is intended by "orality" in this discussion, rather than oral tradition, the more usual designate in early church studies. The further implication of these conclusions is that we have in the *Shepherd* not so much a theological peculiarity as an expression of the syncretistic and practical religion of ordinary Christians, in this case at Rome at the turn of the first century, a form of early Christian belief and piety that is otherwise relatively unknown to us.

1. Hermas as Early Second-Century Roman Christian

The debate about the historical reliability of the biographical information in the *Shepherd* has stretched through most of this century. While some earlier scholars held to its complete historical trustworthiness,[3] others argued that the autobiographical details in the narrative are strictly literary embellishments, or that Hermas's family is a metaphor for the community.[4] More recent assessments lean in the direction of cautious assent to historical reliability, but always with an eye to how the biographical material functions in the text.[5] On

3. William J. Wilson, "The Career of the Prophet Hermas," *HTR* 20 (1927): 21-62; Roelof Van Deemter, *Der Hirt des Hermas: Apokalypse oder Allegorie?* (Delft: W. D. Meinema, 1929); Ake von Ström, *Der Hirt des Hermas, Allegorie oder Wirklichkeit?* Arbeiten und Mitteilungen aus dem neutestamentlichen Seminar zu Uppsala 3 (Uppsala: Wretmans, 1936).

4. Martin Dibelius, *Der Hirt des Hermas,* HNT supp. vol., Apostolischen Väter 4 (Tübingen: J. C. B. Mohr [Paul Siebeck], 1923), 419-20 and passim; Robert Joly, *Hermas le Pasteur,* SC 53 (Paris: Cerf, 1958), 17-21; Erik Peterson, "Kritische Analyse der fünften Vision," in *Frühkirche, Judentum, und Gnosis* (Freiburg: Herder, 1959), 275-77, 282-84; Graydon Snyder, *The Shepherd of Hermas,* ed. Robert M. Grant, Apostolic Fathers 6 (Camden, N.J.: Nelson, 1968), 29-30.

5. Leutzsch, 22; Peter Lampe, *Die stadtrömischen Christen in den ersten beiden Jahrhunderten,* WUNT 2/18 (Tübingen: Mohr [Siebeck], 1989), 182-86; J. Reiling, "Hermas," *RAC* 108/109 (1988): 682-83; Carolyn Osiek, *Rich and Poor in the Shepherd of Hermas: An Exegetical-Social Investigation,* CBQMS 15 (Washington, D.C.: Catholic Biblical Association, 1983), 8-10.

the question of single versus multiple authorship, the pendulum is swinging from the multiple-author theories of Hilgenfeld, Giet, and Coleborne to the assumption of a single author working with many sources.[6]

The present investigation assumes the following data about the author, drawn mostly from the *Visions.* He was a freedman, abandoned as a child and raised as a slave, a common phenomenon.[7] He wrote in the early part of the second century in Rome, probably in several stages: first *Visions* 1–4, then *Vision* 5 and the *Mandates,* then the *Similitudes,* probably in several sections. The information about Hermas's family is based on fact but elaborated in part for literary and theological effect. The opening scene of Rhoda's bath in the Tiber (*Vis.* 1.1), replete with both biblical and classical overtones,[8] is fictional, though Rhoda as the former owner of the freedman Hermas is not. As a freedman, he is quite possibly a Roman citizen. Hermas is engaged in some kind of business, not unusual for a freedman, and has recently suffered some kind of setback in his family's honor and finances (*Vis.* 2.3.1; 3.6.7). He is probably head of a household *(domus);* it is possible that his domicile is in a modest *insula,* or apartment building, but the seeming extent of his business dealings makes that less likely. Except for his religious connections and his status as freedman rather than son of a freedman, we may have a model for the likes of Hermas in a figure known at Pompeii in

6. So already Dibelius; more recently: J. Paramelle, "Hermas," *Dictionnaire de spiritualité* (Paris: Beauchesne, 1969), 7:316-34, here 316; A. Hilhorst, "Hermas," *RAC* 108/109 (1988): 682-701; P. Henne, *L'unité, du Pasteur d'Hermas,* CahRB 31 (Paris: Gabalda, 1992); Luigi Cirillo, "Il pastore di Erma e la storia," in *Miscellanea di Studi storici* 2 (1982): 35-58, here 56; A. W. Strock, "The Shepherd of Hermas: A Study of His Anthropology as Seen in the Tension between Dipsychia and Hamartia (Repentance)" (diss., Emory University, 1984); Harry O. Maier, *The Social Setting of the Ministry as Reflected in the Writings of Hermas, Clement, and Ignatius,* Dissertations SR 1 (Waterloo, Ontario: Wilfrid Laurier University Press, 1991), 58.

7. A. Cameron, "*THREPTOS* and Related Terms in the Inscriptions of Asia Minor," in *Anatolian Studies Presented to William H. Buckler* (Manchester: Manchester University Press, 1939), 27-62; T. G. Narni, "Threptoi," *Epigraphica* 5-6 (1943-44): 45-84; John Boswell, *The Kindness of Strangers: The Abandonment of Children in Western Europe from Late Antiquity to the Renaissance* (New York: Pantheon, 1988).

8. Leutzsch (31-39) counts nine scenes of mortal men surprising goddesses at their bath, eighteen references to the ritual washing of goddess statues or pictures, nine erotic scenes connected with bathing, three biblical or intertestamental: Ruben and Bilha (*T. Rub.* 3.11-15), David and Bathsheba (2 Sam. 11:2), and Susanna.

the previous century through his personal records, Lucius Caecilius Jucundus.[9]

Hermas is not a presbyter, but he does claim some kind of spiritual authority on the basis of his visions (*Vis.* 2.4.3).[10] It is possible that he is already recognized as a prophet, the lack of allusion to him under this title in the text notwithstanding. *Mandate* 11, on criteria for true and false prophecy, indicates that the role of prophet is taken for granted in this community. If the author were already recognized in that capacity, there would be no reason to restate it. It is also possible that he is a deacon if the allusion to his διακονία in *Mandate* 12.3.3 means more than entrustment with the revelatory message, but other than the reference to his placement with the presbyters in *Vision* 2.4.3, there is no other indication that the author is an official of the church.

His educational level is limited, and perhaps that of the house church to which he belongs is just as limited, in contrast to that of, for example, Clement.[11] There is no evidence that the congregation meets in his house,

9. *CIL* 4.3340, presumably the son of a freedman, Lucius Caecilius Felix (probably the same as *CIL* 10.891, *minister Augusti* in 1 B.C.E.), owned an extensive house to which he or his agent returned after the eruption of Vesuvius to try to rescue his business records, 153 waxed tablets tied in triptychs and diptychs, all stored in a wooden chest, detailing receipts for 137 sales and sixteen rents from 351 people, all but one transacted between 52 and 62 C.E. The chest was discovered not at ground level, but well above it, so that someone tried unsuccessfully to extricate it after the volcanic ash had covered the house: Caroline E. Dexter, "The Casa di L. Cecilio Giocondo in Pompeii" (Ph.D. diss., Duke University, 1974), 187-223; Jean Andreau, *Les affaires de monsieur Jucundus*, Collection de l'Ecole Française de Rome 19 (Rome, 1974). Also, for example, the sumptuous and well-known house of the Vettii at Pompeii was owned by A. Vettius Restitutus and A. Vettius Conviva, probably two freedmen and possibly merchants: Lawrence Richardson, Jr., *Pompeii: An Architectural History* (Baltimore: Johns Hopkins University Press, 1988), 324.

10. However, *Vis.* 3.1.8, in which Hermas bids the πρεσβύτεροι to sit first on the couch beside the woman church, is no evidence for his status in the church; it is only his way of indicating that she (called πρεσβύτερα in *Vis.* 2.4.1, etc.), as a person of higher status, should sit first (against most commentators; with Kirsopp Lake, "The Shepherd of Hermas," *The Apostolic Fathers* 2, LCL [London and Cambridge: Harvard University Press, 1913], 29 n. 1). If, on the other hand, the reference is to presbyters, all the more does Hermas not see himself among them. Both Clement and Grapte, however (*Vis.* 2.4.3), could be presbyters or deacons. If they are known historical figures in the community, like Maximus (*Vis.* 2.3.4), there would be no need to identify them by title.

11. The thesis of James Jeffers, *Conflict at Rome: Social Order and Hierarchy in*

unless one accepts Dibelius's theory that his "family" is a metaphor for the community;[12] probably it meets in the house of a leading presbyter. His theological education is equally limited, but his interest in the application of theology and faith to everyday life is a major preoccupation, and his acquaintance with theological themes is wide if superficial.

Hermas belongs to a Christian group with deep Jewish theological roots, and his writing is an important witness to the variety of early Christianity at Rome. He is most likely, though not necessarily, of Jewish origin himself; it is not clear whether he is a convert or one born into a Christian family. The Jewish character of early Christianity at Rome is widely attested, and its influence is evident here.[13] He represents that segment of the majority nonelite population that had some acquaintance with literacy but lived in a world predominantly characterized by orality.

2. Orality and Literacy in the Ancient World

Studies of the implications of orality and literacy in the ancient world continue to multiply, but few have been applied to Christian literature except in the study of the development of oral tradition, and then primarily to certain canonical texts, notably the Gospel of Mark.[14] Moreover, the

Early Christianity (Minneapolis: Fortress, 1991), that Hermas represents more "ordinary" people while Clement represents the imperial civil service and imperial viewpoints, thus two different educational and social levels of freedmen/women's house churches, is an intriguing one.

12. The problem with this theory is that Hermas is held responsible for their deeds (*Vis.* 2.2.2; 2.3.1), which accords with Roman law for a *paterfamilias;* it does not accord with his otherwise apparent lack of governing authority in the community. The woman church must give the authorization at *Vis.* 2.4.3 for him to proclaim the revelation with the presbyters; this is not Hermas's normal place.

13. It is unnecessary to go as far as Pedro Lluis-Font, "Sources de la doctrine d'Hermas sur les deux esprits," *Revue d'Ascétique et de Mystique* 39 (1963): 83-98, and suggest that Hermas is a converted Essene, but ethical/theological Judaism must be a strong factor in his education and environment.

14. Werner Kelber, *The Oral and the Written Gospel* (Philadelphia: Fortress, 1983); Joanna Dewey, "Oral Methods of Structuring Narrative in Mark," *Int* 53 (1989): 32-44; "Mark as Interwoven Tapestry: Forecasts and Echoes for a Listening Audience," *CBQ* 53 (1991): 221-36; "Mark as Aural Narrative: Structures as Clues to Understanding," *Sewanee Theological Review* 36 (1992): 45-56; Barry W. Henaut, *Oral Tradition and the*

corresponding characteristics of oral and literate thinking continue to be the object of study by social scientists, and these studies are becoming more and more nuanced. The ongoing interest in literacy and orality in the ancient world has been reflected in biblical studies largely in the form of interest in the transmission of oral tradition. It is now clear, for instance, that in the case of an oral teacher such as Jesus there was no "original form" of his sayings, even during his lifetime, for oral teaching is necessarily contextual, adapted in each situation to a different audience. The concern here is not about the transmission of oral tradition, but about oral thought processes, oral performance, and the social implications of orality and literacy.

Eric Havelock argued long ago that the transition to literacy in ancient Greece was the beginning of a new style of conceptuality and the ability to think abstractly and synthetically in particular ways.[15] Thus the first- and second-century Mediterranean world, in which literacy at certain higher social levels was fairly widespread while at other levels nearly nonexistent, was what could be characterized as a "residually oral" culture, even as our own is becoming "residually literate."[16] This means that while literacy was present and was the medium for most official transactions, ancient Mediterranean culture was characterized more by oral than literate thinking.

Walter Ong has done the pioneering formulation of the characteristics

---

Gospels: The Problem of Mark 4, JSNTSup 82 (Sheffield: JSOT, 1993). Already in 1961, Charles H. Lohr, "Oral Techniques in the Gospel of Matthew," *CBQ* 23 (1961): 403-35, studied Matthew out of the early work of Parry and Lord (see next note). See also David L. Barr, "The Apocalypse of John as Oral Enactment," *Int* 40 (1983): 243-56.

15. Eric Havelock, *Preface to Plato* (Cambridge: Harvard University Press, 1963); *The Literate Revolution in Greece and Its Cultural Consequences* (Princeton: Princeton University Press, 1982); *The Muse Learns to Write: Reflections on Orality and Literacy from Antiquity to the Present* (New Haven: Yale University Press, 1986). At the same time, Milman Parry and his student Albert B. Lord were relating ancient epic poetry to contemporary examples. For a discussion of their work, see Henaut, 76-86, passim. For an assessment of where studies of orality are going, see James Paul Gee, "Orality and Literacy: From *The Savage Mind* to *Ways with Words,*" *TESOL Quarterly* 20/21 (1986/87): 719-46.

16. For the current transition from literacy to the new orality, see Robin Tolmach, "Some of My Favorite Writers Are Literate: The Mingling of Oral and Literate Strategies in Written Communication," in *Spoken and Written Language: Exploring Orality and Literacy,* ed. Deborah Tannen, Advances in Discourse Processes 9 (Norwood, N.J.: Ablex, 1982), 239-60.

of the thinking processes of oral cultures, and his is the most comprehensive description in a format accessible to the historian.[17] All subsequent studies must take his work into account, even if they produce different conclusions. These characteristics will be discussed and applied in part 3 below.

Later assessments of Ong's work have been somewhat more cautious, but unable to disprove the basic lines of the argument.[18] What especially requires further nuancing is that the arrival of a basic level of literacy among the elites or a select group in a society does not immediately or necessarily produce a changed consciousness in the individual. Rather, such changes happen only slowly and socially, in interaction with cultural forces.[19] No culture ever becomes completely literate; oral modes of thinking and operating continue, so that cultures cannot be divided between oral and literate, but rather between completely oral and oral-plus-literate in varying degrees.[20] Even the most highly literate society will have segments of its population that, although they may be considered literate, still live in a predominantly oral culture. Literate modes of thinking, however, do begin to take form among those segments of a society that rely heavily on literacy, and these modes of thinking also begin to influence nonliterates indirectly.[21]

17. Walter Ong, *Orality and Literacy: The Technologizing of the Word* (London and New York: Methuen, 1982). Ong's work presumes earlier psychological and sociolinguistic studies, among those not mentioned elsewhere in this paper: Aleksandr R. Luria, *Cognitive Development: Its Cultural and Social Foundations* (Cambridge, Mass., and London: Harvard University Press, 1976); Lev S. Vygotsky, *Thought and Language*, rev. ed. (Cambridge: MIT Press, 1986; original 1962); *Mind and Society: The Development of Higher Psychological Processes* (Cambridge: Harvard University Press, 1978).

18. E.g., Albert B. Lord, "Characteristics of Orality," *Oral Tradition* 2, no. 1 (1987): 54-72.

19. Jack Goody, *The Interface between the Written and the Oral* (Cambridge: Cambridge University Press, 1987), 205-16; Goody, ed., *Literacy in Traditional Societies* (Cambridge: Cambridge University Press, 1968); Goody, *The Domestication of the Savage Mind* (Cambridge: Cambridge University Press, 1977); *The Logic of Writing and the Organization of Society* (Cambridge: Cambridge University Press, 1986); also "Alternative Paths to Knowledge in Oral and Literate Cultures," in *Spoken and Written Language*, 201-15.

20. Goody, *Interface*, xii.

21. Goody, *Interface*, 114. A good discussion of the question of the influence of aristocratic literacy on the lower classes of the Greco-Roman world is F. Gerald Downing, "A bas les aristos. The Relevance of Higher Literature for the Understanding of the Earliest Christian Writing," *NovT* 30 (1988): 212-30.

One way this must have happened in the culture that concerns us is through the promulgation of official and legal documents which had an effect on the lives of the majority of the populace. Other ways for Jews and Christians included the public proclamation of sacred texts[22] and the use of the circular letter, which seems to have been a literate composition intended for oral proclamation to communities that were either predominantly nonliterate or did not have access to a written copy. One of the functions of such letters is the assertion of authority. The letters of Paul, Ignatius, and Clement of Rome are obvious examples. Most striking is the assertion: "All over the world, the techniques of writing have been used to acquire, that is, to alienate, the land of 'oral' peoples. It is a most powerful instrument, the use of which is rarely devoid of social, economic and political significance, especially since its introduction usually involves the domination of the non-literate segment of the population by the literate one, or even the less literate by the more. Where writing is, 'class' cannot be far away."[23]

The same author goes on to argue that in cultures where literacy is present, there is an inevitable stratification between literate (high) and nonliterate (low) groupings, and that the result of mass literacy "is to spread the devaluation, including the self-devaluation, of knowledge and tasks that are not gained through the book but by experience," as well as to create "a hierarchical differentiation of speech into proper and colloquial forms."[24] Literacy is social power.[25]

22. Probably such proclamations were often accompanied by visual representations of the stories or scenes described, such as frescoes or handheld placards. Warren G. Moon, "Nudity and Narrative Observations on the Frescoes from the Dura Synagogue," *JAAR* 60, no. 4 (1992): 587-658, here 595-610, contextualizes the paintings of the Dura-Europos synagogue as accompaniments to the corresponding narrative proclamations, and suggests that Gal. 3:1 alludes to the same practice.

23. Goody, *Interface,* xv. The same idea is echoed in studies of literacy specifically in the ancient Mediterranean: Mary Beard, "*Ancient Literacy* and the Function of the Written Word in Roman Religion," in *Literacy in the Roman World,* ed. J. H. Humphrey, *Journal of Roman Archaeology* Supp. Ser. 3 (Ann Arbor: University of Michigan, Department of Classical Studies, 1991), 35-58, here 56-58; Keith Hopkins, "Conquest by Book," *Literacy in the Roman World,* 133-58, here 142-43, 157.

24. *Literacy in the Roman World,* 161-64, 265.

25. The usual way in which this power is exercised is by literates over nonliterates. But see Kathleen Rockhill, "Gender, Language, and the Politics of Literacy," in *Cross-Cultural Approaches to Literacy,* ed. Brian V. Street, Cambridge Studies in Oral and

What, then, were the levels of literacy in the ancient Mediterranean population, and how can we assess how these social dynamics may have been at work? The authoritative study to date, that of William V. Harris,[26] is very conservative in its estimates of levels of literacy, suggesting that in the countryside only elites and their select dependents were literate, while in the cities there was never anything like massive widespread literacy but rather simply a larger minority of literates. All evidence points to a much lower rate of literacy for women than for men. The material evidence of widespread use of graffiti at Pompeii, the evidence for high rates of literacy in the army (both among legionaries and auxiliaries), and that of the business records in the Egyptian papyri must be carefully considered. Even so, the most sanguine estimates rarely reach 50 percent. The authors of a collection of essays assembled in explicit response to Harris quibble with some of the interpretation of data but cannot invalidate his overall findings.[27] More recently, Harry Y. Gamble estimates literacy in the Christian population — as typical of the general population — at 10-15 percent.[28] In the church, as in society at large, the power of literacy was concentrated among educated elites, their direct supporters, and males. But movements such as Judaism and Christianity, so deeply based on written texts, also allowed the formation of new scribal elites because of the power of literacy.

There are, of course, many levels of literacy.[29] The ability to sign one's

---

Literate Cultures (Cambridge: Cambridge University Press, 1993), 156-75. She argues that even the extension of literacy as a way of social emancipation in a modern context can become a means of greater social control precisely through the dissemination of propaganda possible with general literacy.

26. William V. Harris, *Ancient Literacy* (Cambridge: Harvard University Press, 1989).

27. Humphrey, *Literacy in the Roman World.* One of the corrections most apposite to the scholarship of early Christianity is the reminder that having a third party represent one signer of a contract does not necessarily indicate illiteracy; the use of agents and secretaries was common (cf. Rom. 16:22): Harris, 262; James L. Franklin, Jr., "Literacy and the Parietal Inscriptions of Pompeii," in *Literacy in the Roman World,* 77-98, here 80 n. 9. The discussion is apropos of L. Caecilius Jucundus of Pompeii (*CIL* 4.3340), of whose seventeen male creditors, eleven wrote for themselves and six through an agent; of his five female creditors, all were represented by an agent.

28. Harry Y. Gamble, *Books and Readers in the Early Church: A History of Early Christian Texts* (New Haven and London: Yale University Press, 1995): "not more than 10%" (p. 5); no more than 10-15 percent (p. 10).

29. Gamble, 8; Harris, 3-8.

name to a legal document, to scribble a graffito on a wall, or to keep a list of business records is not the same as the ability to compose literary works or to think habitually in ways associated with literacy. The percentage of the population that did think habitually in those ways must have been very small indeed.

3. The Oral and Literary Character of the *Shepherd of Hermas*

Within the context of the above considerations, we now turn to the *Shepherd.* In spite of the fact that it is a very long written text, the presuppositions behind it are largely oral; that is, the narrative setting is either oral communication or oral dictation. The opening scenes of the *Visions* are accounts of visions and oral exhortation, in which first Hermas's former owner Rhoda, then another mysterious female figure, later identified as the church, instruct Hermas on his responsibility regarding his family (1.1.1–3.1-2). Then the female apparition reads aloud to him (1.3.3-4). Only a year later is Hermas given a written text, which it takes him two weeks of prayer and fasting to understand (2.1.3-4; 2.2.1). The rather brief text of the written document is then given (2.2.2–3.4). Hermas is to make two copies of this message for written dissemination to other churches via Clement and to the widows and orphans via Grapte (2.4.3). All of *Visions* 3–4 are supposed to consist of visual revelation and oral explanation by the woman church, with no command to write. Only in 5.5, under the direction of the newly appeared shepherd, does writing reenter the narrative, this time again as oral dictation, for the purpose not of private reading but of oral proclamation: "I command you [sing.] first to write the commandments and the parables, so that you [sing.] can at once read them aloud ἵνα (ὑπὸ χεῖρα ἀναγινώσκῃς αὐτάς) and keep them" (5.6; cf. *Sim.* 9.1.1), followed immediately by the author's exhortation to the hearers in the plural, to listen and keep the commandments (5.7).

In the narrative context, there is a direct connection between the instructions Hermas receives, to write what is orally dictated to him, and the use of what he writes for a wider audience of hearers, not readers. The directive to write is always for the purpose of proclamation to a larger group, and the singular directive to the recipient is always linked to a widened social context (compare *Vis.* 3.3.1; *Sim.* 5.5.1). The whole of the *Mandates* and through the eighth *Similitude* that follows, therefore, is given within the narrative framework of oral dictation to be written and then communicated by reading aloud, not an unusual occurrence in revelatory literature.[30] Thus the proclaimer attains twofold status in a predominantly nonliterate community: as recipient of revelation and public reader. It is quite likely that the supposedly dictated heavenly message (*Vis.* 2.2.2–3.4) and didactic material were intended and used in their original context not as transcripts to be read verbatim but as aids for oral proclamation.

We see the envisioned context for such oral proclamation in *Vision* 2.4.3: after giving written copies of the revelation to Clement and Grapte, Hermas is to read the text with the presbyters in the assembly. This "reading" is not confined to a written text but is interpreted as it progresses, and the expanded version of the interpretation may be the rest of the book. A comparable example is Nehemiah 8:2-8, where Ezra read from the law all morning in the square by the city gate, accompanied by Levites who "helped the people to understand the law. . . . So they read from the book, from the law of God, with interpretation. They gave the sense, so that the people understood the reading" (NRSV).

If such oral proclamation is the context for the *Shepherd*, two conclusions follow. First, what has survived as the manuscript is not the whole message but a more or less full outline. Second, there never was an original version, since each successive proclamation would alter the content slightly as appropriate to the context.[31]

30. Compare Rev. 1:11, 19; 2:1, etc., with blessings on the reader and hearers, 1:3; 4 Ezra 15:2; *2 Bar.* 50.1; 77.12, 19; 78.1; 86; 87. Gamble (108-9) refers to this writing activity as an example of the "bookish aspect of apocalyptic literature," but misses the point that the purpose of the writing is oral proclamation.

31. As argued by Kelber about Mark (p. 30). Gregory Nagy, "Homeric Questions," *TAPA* 122 (1992): 17-60, notes that at the time of the introduction of literacy into Greek culture, it had to be established that the written word should have the same authority as the spoken word, the opposite of the modern assumption. For epic poetry, writing then became used as an *equivalent* of performance, not as a *means* for performance. Later, the written text became an *aid* to performance, but not a means. A transcript, by contrast, is a *means* for performance (pp. 34-44). The same preference for oral communication over written is reflected in early Christianity in Papias's comment that collecting what remained in his day of oral tradition was of more benefit than information from books (Eusebius, *Hist. eccl.* 3.39.4). Gamble is correct (30-31) that this does not mean Papias the writer was anti-books, but it does mean that he thought he had access to reliable oral tradition. If a preference for oral rather than written information was "a topos in certain contexts," that was because of the oral nature of popular culture.

The author Hermas may have fit the known type of the literate slave, trained to do business transactions, serve in a secretarial capacity, and keep records. Beyond record keeping, however, he can compose basic prose narrative and deal with a certain level of abstraction in the paraenetic traditions he uses. His text contains structured chiasms and sequential patterns (e.g., the triad of *Man.* 1.2 is developed explicitly later in *Mandates* 6–8), which, however, are also possible in complex oral structures. The text also exhibits the literary ability to speak abstractly of virtues and vices (though in a semipersonified way) and to itemize lists of virtues and vices (e.g., *Vis.* 3.8; *Mandate* 8), a topos common to the Jewish and Christian paraenetic literary tradition. "An oral culture has no vehicle so neutral as a list,"[32] but the decontextualizing of items into a list is a primary use of literacy.[33] Yet the *Shepherd* is more evidently the product of oral thinking. Its structure continues to elude literary analysis, and its length and repetitiveness continue to be obstacles to the synthetic, abstract modern mind. "To label a text incoherent if one does not understand its source and its purpose is simply ethnocentric. A pragmatically oriented analysis begins with the assumption that most linguistic productions are not inept or pathological or primitive, and that those which appear foreign, even if they are in the language of the analyst, probably are."[34]

Walter Ong gives nine characteristics of orality,[35] and most of them can be seen operating in the *Shepherd.* An examination of these characteristics in the text of the *Shepherd* shows that much of what is seemingly rambling and repetitious, inexact and obscure to the literate mind, is evidence of "residual orality" and of oral thought patterns.

First, oral communication is additive rather than subordinative: statements and whole sections accumulate one after the other with no apparent subordination of one thought to another. The primary mode of linkage is paratactic. In the *Shepherd,* new additions occur wherever, and it would be very difficult to diagram the whole piece to show the interrelationship of the parts. A good example of this paratactic structure occurs in *Vision*

32. Ong, 42.

33. Goody, *Interface,* 274-75.

34. Dennis Jarrett, "Pragmatic Coherence in an Oral Formulaic Tradition: I Can Read Your Letters/Sure Can't Read Your Mind," in *Coherence in Spoken and Written Discourse,* ed. Deborah Tannen, Advances in Discourse Processes 12 (Norwood, N.J.: Ablex, 1984), 155-71, here 155.

35. Ong, 37-57.

3.7.4-6, at the conclusion of the explanation of the various kinds of stones rejected for the building of the tower. The woman church who is interpreting it all ends her explanation in verse 4 — explicitly; but there is still another question to address: whether any of the rejected stones will have another chance. So a new question is asked at verse 5 to that effect, and a very different kind of explanation given in verse 6, suggesting a temporary place of torment from which they will be released after an appropriate change of heart.[36]

Another example is the meaning given to the couch on which the rejuvenated woman church sits in *Vision* 3.13.3. The woman who is the church has appeared younger in each successive appearance. The content of the narrative up to that point is explanation of the successive stages of her rejuvenation. But suddenly the fact that she sits on a couch with four legs means security, since the world is controlled by four elements. Another example is the pattern of the *Mandates: Mandates* 1–4 deal with faith, simplicity, truth, and chastity.[37] *Mandates* 5–12 develop, sometimes explicitly, sometimes obscurely, a theological dualism: two spirits (5); two paths, two angels, two kinds of faith (6); the Lord and the devil, two kinds of fear (7); two kinds of restraint (8); doubt and faith (9); sadness and joy (10); two kinds of prophets (11); two kinds of desire (12). Yet only in 8.1 is a general "introductory" statement about dualism made.

Still another example is *Mandate* 7.5. Verse 4 ends with the usual formulaic conclusion: "whoever does . . . will live to God." But in verse 5 a new question is asked about the statement, and the answer given is a general statement that could belong with any of the *Mandates.* Again, the fifth *Similitude* begins with a lesson on fasting (1), illustrated and explained by

36. The interpretation by Adhémar D'Alès, *L'édit de Calliste. Etudes sur les origines de la pénitence chrétienne* (Paris: Beauchesne, 1914), 62; Bernhard Poschmann, *Paenitentia secunda: die kirchliche Busse im ältesten Christentum bis Cyprian und Origenes* (Bonn: Hanstein, 1940), 195-96, and others, that this passage refers to penitents at the door of the church in an already full-blown penitential discipline, has rightly found little favor.

37. *Man.* 4.2-3 is a further discussion of conversion that has nothing to do with 4.1 and 4 on marital chastity and adultery. Redactionally, it may be an interpolated or misplaced text, but as a residually oral piece it is simply an excursus on the central theme. It is an error to assume from its placement that Hermas is preoccupied with sex, as is sometimes done. Other than this passage, the opening bath scene of *Vision* 1, and the command to prophetic encratism meant only for Hermas (*Vis.* 2.2.3), sex is seldom mentioned outside conventional contexts in passing (e.g., *Man.* 6.2.5).

the parable of the son and the slave (2-4), to which the christological and anthropological interpretations (5-7) are joined in a way that simply adds them on as new interpretations of the parable.[38]

Second, oral communication is aggregative rather than analytic: the text "carries a load of epithets and other formulary baggage which high literacy rejects as cumbersome and tiresomely redundant because of its aggregative weight."[39] Formulaic expressions and clichés are valued as connectors and memory implementers, a characteristic that fits not only ancient oral cultures but contemporary eastern Mediterranean cultures as well.[40]

The entire text of the *Shepherd,* especially the *Mandates,* uses frequently occurring terms and formulaic expressions. Double-mindedness (διψυχία) is an overriding concern that occurs throughout the text. Believers are referred to as οἱ δοῦλοι τοῦ θεοῦ, the servants of God, nearly fifty times in over thirty contexts throughout the *Shepherd,* an otherwise unusual expression.[41] The exhortation to "have peace among yourselves," a probable allusion to 1 Thessalonians 5:13, occurs four times in a brief space.[42] Most of the *Mandates* end with the same formula: "Therefore, do . . . [or avoid . . .], and you will live to God."[43] But the formula reappears eight

38. Philippe Henne's analyses of successive layers of interpretation following the presentation of a given image or story point in the same direction: "La Polysémie allégorique dans le *Pasteur* d'Hermas," *ETL* 65, no. 1 (1989): 131-35.

39. Ong, 38.

40. Compare the "flowery" and formulaic character of Arabic or Chinese statements translated into English. In modern experiments with persons of Anglo-American versus Greek or Turkish cultural upbringing, Americans give negative value to formulaic expressions as clichés; Greeks and Turks value them for lending an aura of wisdom: Deborah Tannen, "The Oral/Literate Continuum in Discourse," in *Spoken and Written Language,* 1-16, here 5-6. Of course, formulaic expressions also occur in literature and so must be treated cautiously as characteristics of oral structure; see the caution raised by Henaut, 80-93.

41. Peterson, 278, proposed unconvincingly that the expression referred in *Hermas* to a group of ascetics. Cf. 4 Ezra 16.35; *Did.* 11 = *Ap. Const.* 2.45.2; J. Reiling, *Hermas and Christian Prophecy: A Study of the Eleventh Mandate,* NovTSup 37 (Leiden: Brill, 1973), 32 n. 2; C. Osiek, "The Ransom of Captives: Evolution of a Tradition," *HTR* 74, no. 4 (1981): 365-86, here 371 n. 17. Peter Brown, *Augustine of Hippo* (Berkeley, Los Angeles, and London: University of California Press, 1967), 132-37, like Peterson, appropriates the expression to refer to a group of ascetics in Augustine's day, but — by his own admission in later conversation — without adequate foundation.

42. *Vis.* 3.6.3; 9.2, 10; 12.3; also *Sim.* 8.7.2; cf. *Man.* 2.3.

43. All except *Mandates* 2, 4 (but see 4.2.4), 5, 10, 11.

times in the *Similitudes* in similar paraenetic contexts, because the commandment genre is also present there. The pattern of illustration, explanation, and concluding exhortation that ends with this formula becomes so familiar that those hearing these structures read aloud could finish the line themselves. In this way, the audience is brought into participation in the narration and instruction.

Ong's third characteristic of orality is redundancy or copiousness: whereas writing establishes a sparse line of progression with brief excursuses, oral speech that is not governed by a story line has no linear progression as outline for forward movement. Even storytelling can be characterized by long digressions. The forward impetus is conveyed by repetition and expansion, so that texts written even into the Middle Ages and Renaissance "are often bloated with 'amplification', annoyingly redundant by modern standards."[44]

In the *Shepherd,* most of the explanations are wordy and expansive, often to the point of being tedious to the modern reader. The paraenetic sections of the *Mandates* are repetitive, often because the interlocutor Hermas has asked for further explanation, a device that both engages the hearer and provides the occasion to add new material. More specifically, for example, the allegory of the willow tree with its various kinds of sticks, which occupies the whole of the eighth *Similitude,* is tireless in its detailed explanations of the meaning of each kind of stick. The replay of the building of the tower in the ninth *Similitude,* first told in *Vision* 3, repeats many of the elements of the first account in a slightly different way, but also adds many new features without ever integrating them in any systematic way into the original image.

For example, the tower is now built on rock instead of on water (*Vis.* 3.3.5 and *Sim.* 9.3.1). Twelve female figures are now involved in the building of the tower (*Sim.* 9.2) instead of seven (*Vis.* 3.8). The fate of the various kinds of stones brought for the construction is laid out in detail through five long chapters (*Sim.* 9.5-9).

Fourth, oral communication is conservative or traditionalist: while writing freezes information so that it can be preserved without great effort, orality must rely on memory and repetition to preserve valuable information, and therefore gives more weight to traditional wisdom than to new ideas. "Indeed, the residual orality of a given chirographic culture can be

44. Ong, 41.

calculated to a degree from the mnemonic load it leaves on the mind, that is, from the amount of memorization the culture's educational procedures require."[45] Originality consists primarily in finding a way to interact with the given audience in the present, rather than to suggest new ideas or interpretations.

The image of the church in the *Visions* conforms to the traditional valuation of old as true and good: she is the first of creation, rejuvenated by the changed lives of the faithful (*Vis.* 3.10-13), yet always ancient. The moral teaching of the *Mandates* is not innovative, but intends to preserve traditional ideals. The proclamation of one chance for conversion before the completion of the tower (*Vis.* 3.8.9; 9.4-6; *Man.* 4.2-3; *Sim.* 10.4.4; etc.) is not something new, but is, this time with a sense of finality, a repetition of the traditional call to conversion with the sense of a final appeal.

A fifth characteristic of orality is its closeness to the human life world: facts, or even lists, cannot be used apart from a concrete situation of human action.[46] In the *Shepherd,* time and place references, besides being recognizable elements of visionary literature, bring an immediacy to the narrative: "on the way to the country,[47] at about the same time as the previous year" (*Vis.* 2.1.1); "after fifteen days" (2.2.1); "on the Via Campana" (4.1.2); "praying in the house, sitting on a couch" (5.1). Practical examples drawn from life are used for illustration, sometimes introduced briefly to illuminate a point: a blacksmith (*Vis.* 1.3.2); wormwood in honey (*Man.* 5.1.5); vinegar in wine (10.3.3); empty wine jars (11.15); stone and water pump (11.18). At other times, a scene from real life becomes the inspiration for the teaching: e.g., the elm and vine seen in a vineyard become symbols of the relationship of rich and poor (*Similitude* 2).

Sixth, oral communication is agonistically toned: knowledge is situated within a context of struggle, be it a human battle or the struggle with the spirit world. While the *Shepherd* as a whole is neither a narrative of prolonged struggle nor a saga in which a hero is pitched against his enemies,

45. Ong, 41.

46. This is one of the least satisfactory criteria offered by Ong, since all good narrative, oral or written, should fit it. Moreover, it is not clearly distinctive from the ninth criterion below.

47. Εἰς κώμας, "to the country," not εἰς Κούμας, "to Cumae," as previously conjectured from Latin *regionem Cumanorum* (see also *Vis.* 1.1.3): Antonio Carlini, "Le passeggiate di Erma verso Cuma (su due luoghi controversi del *Pastore*)," in *Studi in onore di E. Bresciani* (Pisa: Giardini, 1986), 105-9.

the antagonism that is set up in the *Mandates* is that between good and bad spirits as witnessed in the lives of believers, within the time frame of eschatological urgency dramatized by the building of the tower (*Vision* 3; *Similitude* 9). Human persons are the battleground on which the contest is played out. "Battle" may be too strong an image, but *psychomachia* and *kardiomachia* have been suggested to describe the struggle of the spirits here and in the Manual of Discipline from Qumran.[48]

Seventh, oral communication is empathic and participatory rather than objectively distanced: knowledge is relationship, and any "subjective" knowledge is incorporated within the fund of communal knowledge and experience.[49] It is a mistake to see the *Shepherd* as an unfortunate individualizing and objectifying of tiresome virtue and the practice of penitence. The purpose of Hermas's writing is not literary entertainment but a change of heart, and thus changed behavior, not of individuals as isolated entities but of a community. The teaching on the life of the virtues is unthinkable in an isolated individualized context.[50] The vision of community put forward here is fundamentally social in nature. That it should be anything else would not fit the intensely social cultural experience of the ancient Mediterranean world, in which personal identity is largely seen through social embeddedness.

The concluding formula of all the *Mandates* except 1, 6, and 11, and of *Similitudes* 5.1, 7; 6.1.4; 8.11.4 (see also vv. 1, 3); 9.20.4; 22.4; 28.8; 29.3, includes the generalization of teaching explicitly to all, usually moving from singular to plural as the addressee of the teaching shifts from Hermas to the intended hearers, from the rhetorical singular by which the individual Hermas is meant as type or example for all to the whole audience which is thus drawn into the account. The recurring concluding formula, "Do this . . . [or avoid this . . .] and you will live to God," is one of the formulaic expressions typical of oral proclamation (see second characteristic, above). Here it usually

48. Henry A. Kelly, *The Devil at Baptism: Ritual, Theology, and Drama* (Ithaca and London: Cornell University Press, 1985), 130.

49. Perhaps something like this is meant by A. Hilhorst's "disposition des mots dans l'ordre affectif" as a characteristic of oral style, in *Sémitismes et latinismes dans le Pasteur d'Hermas,* Graecitas Christianorum Primaeva 5 (Nijmegen: Dekker & Van de Vegt, 1976), 23. He adds parataxis, numerous genitive absolutes, and anacolutha as further characteristics of oral style, without citing a source.

50. Yet commentators often speak of *Hermas* as moralized individualism, e.g., Dibelius, 510-13; Leutzsch, 207.

marks a change from second-person singular to second-person plural. The plural lasts only as long as the formula. By this formula, the listening audience is brought into the story at crucial points to reinforce the instruction and evoke audience participation. In a supposed context of oral proclamation of the message (as intended at *Vis.* 2.4.3), the concluding formula would become so familiar that the listener-participants hearing the beginning of it could finish the formula themselves, thus being drawn into the recitation.

Eighth, oral communication is homeostatic: time consciousness is primarily present-oriented. The past exists for its values brought forward into the present. Whatever of the past is not of value in the present will drop off; whatever of the past is useful in the present will be retained. Both past and future exist only as imaginary time, not real time; both can only be imagined in terms of present realities or their reverse, or the perceptible future potential of present situations, e.g., pregnancy or planting of seed. This has significant consequences for an understanding of eschatology.[51]

The primary orientation to the present and a weak linear time concept mean that any discussion in the *Shepherd* about duration of time outside the present reality cannot be taken as intended to be crudely literal. For example, Hermas tries to establish with the Shepherd a schema of the duration of punishment for those who live in heedless luxury (*Sim.* 6.4-5), but exactness keeps eluding him. Punishment endures for equal time (4.1), a short time (4.2), but has the force of a ratio of real time (4.4). Eventually it becomes clear that the Shepherd is not talking about duration of time at all, but making the psychological observation that pleasure has a short memory and suffering a long one (5.3-4).

All speculation about a chronological schema applied to the end of the building of the tower, seemingly different time limits for conversion of believers and unbelievers, and Hermas's program for apocalyptic events is meaningless. The author's eschatology is not a road map to the future but an interpretation of the present. This is reinforced internally by the woman church's impatience with Hermas's own persistent questions about the interpretation of her eschatology after the revelation and explanation of the tower: "I asked her about the times, whether the end time was already here. She raised her voice and cried out: 'Senseless person! Do you not see

51. Even future eschatological statements cannot be understood to be making assertions about a concrete future. See Bruce J. Malina, "Christ and Time: Swiss or Mediterranean?" *CBQ* 51, no. 1 (1989): 1-31.

the tower still being built? Whenever the construction of the tower is completed, that is the end. But it will be built quickly. Now do not ask me anything else!'" (*Vis.* 3.8.9). The same is of course true about other apocalyptic writings of the period.

Ninth, oral communication is situational rather than abstract: identification of objects and assignment of value have to do not with abstract concepts or syllogistic thinking but with what is of immediate use.[52] The structure of the *Similitudes* is built around a series of visions and images of material objects to illustrate teaching, but the use of images as examples is not limited to the *Similitudes.* Hermas's attention is first captured by Rhoda at her bath in the Tiber and the subsequent heavenly vision of her (*Vision* 1), then by the vision of the woman church, described with close attention to detail (*Vis.* 1.2), before moving on to the tower in *Vision* 3. For the most part, images are used rather than concepts to convey meaning: tower, stones, willow sticks, mountains. The concern is more with praxis than with ideas separated from praxis. What may sometimes seem to be abstract, e.g., the listing of virtues or vices, an indication of literate thinking, is still in the service of praxis, and in fact the virtues are sometimes personified, as in the possibly contemporary *Tabula of Cebes*[53] (*Vis.* 3.8; *Sim.* 9.15).

4. Conclusion

The entire structure of this long text is very loose, as anyone who has tried to understand it knows. The argument presented here is that this loose structure is not the result of careless editing, but is an indication that the text as we have it grew out of oral performance within a basically oral culture among the ordinary Christians of first- and second-century Rome. Inasmuch as the "high" but minority culture of literacy and the "low" majority culture of

52. Ong, 49-53, relates the experiments of A. R. Luria with illiterate and barely literate persons who saw no value in categorical thinking. One, when presented the first time with a syllogism about the color of bears in different regions, resisted with a description of only what he had seen. Given the same syllogism a second time, he prefaced his syllogistically correct answer with "To go by your words . . . ," showing that he understood the logical structure but refused to take personal responsibility for a statement outside his experience.

53. Text, notes, and translation by John T. Fitzgerald and L. Michael White, SBLTT 24 (Chico: Scholars, 1983).

orality[54] coexisted side by side in this time and place — and of course, this was the case — Hermas represents the latter but has a stake in the former, for he is literate to a degree but shows more affinity with the oral than with the literate way of thinking. It may be possible to correlate these data with levels of literate or formal education, but estimates of social status or class must be based on it with caution. Even if the *Shepherd* stands in marked contrast to *1 Clement* by way of literary quality, for example, nothing can be directly concluded about the relative social status of the authors, though Clement may in fact have represented the interests of the ruling classes in a way that Hermas did not. It can be affirmed that the original text of the *Shepherd* was intended for communication in the oral world of the everyday life of people, whether of "low" or "high" status. This may be a major factor in the immense popularity it enjoyed in the first centuries after its production.[55] Elements of its form that seem annoying and pointless to modern readers can be seen as really characteristics of residual orality that were not obstacles for ancient readers. It should be compared in this regard with other long recitals of visions such as Revelation and 4 Ezra.

Most modern studies of orality in ancient texts have been done with epic poetry and narrative, and the criteria, including those developed above, have been formulated for use with those genres. In the *Shepherd of Hermas* we have evidence of an author from a predominantly oral life world who believed that he had received an oral revelation and set those parts dictated to him into writing,[56] to serve as an aid to oral proclamation of the message

54. Goody, "Alternative Paths to Knowledge," 212-14.

55. Known and used by Irenaeus, Tertullian, and Origen, the *Shepherd* was probably more widely known in early Christianity than any other noncanonical text, and probably continued to be used for oral proclamation in Christian groups for some time. Evidence of its continued popularity has been collected most recently by Brox, 55-71. On its continuing and extended use in Egypt, based on manuscript evidence, cf. Philippe Henne, "Hermas en Egypte: La tradition manuscrite et l'unité, rédactionnelle du *Pasteur*," *Cristianesimo nella Storia* 11 (1990): 237-56. Among others, one factor in its popularity was probably that it said many things that church authorities wanted said, and thus facilitated social control, so its reading was encouraged.

56. By saying it this way, I follow the implied process of formulation of the text, without making a judgment as to the "authenticity" of the author's spiritual experience, a judgment that is beyond the domain of the modern literary critic or historian. I do not believe, however, that the author simply decided to compose a document; rather, he was convinced that he had received a heavenly revelation that he was to communicate to the church.

he had received. Thus we have in this text evidence for the oral formulation not of narrative but of paraenetic material, within an apocalyptic framework.[57] This combination of eschatological images and realistic ethical instruction gives the work the ability to sustain hope and encourage conversion at the same time.

The oral character of the text is a product of the oral world that produced it. A linear, logical reading of the text reveals many inconsistencies, especially in identification of major characters. For example, if the text is taken as a coherent whole, the woman church is the tower, but also the Holy Spirit who is the Son of God! These and other internal inconsistencies and non sequiturs have in the past been seen as evidence of multiple authorship. The author's goal, however, is not theological consistency but a variety of images, each of which can have multiple referents, while each analogy stands on its own. In the process of oral proclamation, the coherence of the immediate subject with the life world of the hearers is the focus, not overall coherence with all the images and narratives presented.

The *Shepherd* reveals to us something of the thought world of the nonelites of early imperial Rome: direct, present-oriented, yet possessed of an eclectic imagination capable of bringing in bits and pieces of classical tradition: a beautiful woman at her bath, the mountains of Arcadia, allegorical virtues. It reveals, too, something of the piety of the ordinary early Christians of Rome, who were probably much like the author, and who could freely combine Greek and Jewish images and traditions into their new faith. They lived in an oral world little touched by the literate theological developments that preoccupied some of their more highly educated leaders, except in the brief references that occasionally seem to slip in and out of a document like this one.

The *Shepherd* is another example of the great diversity of early Roman Christianity, alongside Romans, Mark, *1 Clement,* and the later hints of church historians about the divergent views of the great teachers who frequented Rome later in the century, such as Valentinus and Marcion. There is no reason to think that Rome is exceptional with regard to the oral context of early Christianity, however. Probably, it is rather typical. The

57. On the question of the literary genre of *Hermas,* see C. Osiek, "The Genre and Function of the Shepherd of Hermas," in *Early Christian Apocalypticism: Genre and Social Setting,* ed. Adela Y. Collins, *Semeia* 36 (1986): 113-21.

reexamination of early Christian literature within its oral world should continue to revitalize our understanding of the people who produced it and of their faith.

PART 3

DEVELOPMENTAL STUDIES

CHAPTER 8

Romans, Jews, and Christians: The Impact of the Romans on Jewish/Christian Relations in First-Century Rome

James C. Walters

1. Introduction

Marcel Simon, in *Verus Israel*, argued that the attitudes of Christians and Jews toward one another were influenced decisively by the Roman authorities.[1] Although Simon demonstrated his thesis with evidence from a later period (135-425 C.E.), I am confident that it holds for the period of our interest as well. This paper describes the evolving relations between Christians and non-Christian Jews in Rome, and especially how administrative interventions by the Romans may have affected their interactions during the Flavian period.[2] The argument of the paper will proceed as follows: a brief analysis of the relations of Christians and non-Christian Jews during the later Julio-Claudian period will set the stage for an investigation of probable developments under the Flavians;[3] the latter portion of the paper will test my interpretation of the Flavian period by analyzing *1 Clement* for

1. Marcel Simon, *Verus Israel: A Study of the Relations between Christians and Jews in the Roman Empire*, trans. H. McKeating (Oxford: Oxford University Press, 1986 [1964]).

2. I trust that the hazards of using the (anachronistic) term "Christian" to refer to someone attached to the "Jesus movement" during this transitional period are mitigated somewhat by the content of the essay itself.

3. Because the Julio-Claudian period was the focus of my recent book *Ethnic Issues in Paul's Letter to the Romans* (Valley Forge, Pa.: Trinity Press International, 1993), more detailed treatment of the period is contained there, as well as fuller bibliographical data.

evidence of interaction between Christians and non-Christian Jews in Rome at the end of the first century.

2. The Later Julio-Claudian Period

Peter Lampe's study of the early Roman Christians has reinforced the conclusion that many scholars had already reached: earliest Christianity in Rome was an intra-Jewish phenomenon.[4] It is most probable that Christianity made its way to Rome spontaneously as the personal baggage of Jews, proselytes, and sympathizers, who brought faith in Jesus as Messiah with them from the East. They came to Rome for commercial reasons, as immigrants, or against their will as slaves. It is not surprising therefore that early Christians were concentrated within the same regions as non-Christian Jews, both residing primarily in areas where foreign peoples were concentrated.[5] Jews — and Gentile sympathizers and proselytes — who believed Jesus was Messiah not only shared a religious outlook with non-Christian Jews, but also a common socialization:[6] They were part of the Jewish *ethnos* and of the foreign population of ancient Rome.[7] They assembled in synagogues with other Jews and may not have gathered outside Jewish contexts in the earliest period.[8]

4. Peter Lampe, *Die stadtrömischen Christen in den ersten beiden Jahrhunderten,* WUNT 2/18 (Tübingen: Mohr-Siebeck, 1989), 53-63.

5. Lampe locates the Christians in Rome by means of a topographic investigation that shows the convergence of five independent lines of investigation. They were concentrated in Trastevere and along the Appian Way outside the Porta Capena but were also found in Marsfield and the Aventine (*Die stadtrömischen Christen,* 10-35).

6. For a description of this social context with bibliography, cf. Walters, 6-18 and 28-55.

7. Archaeological evidence from Jewish catacombs in Rome has provided a wealth of information regarding the Jews and their communities in Rome. The best source for these materials is still Harry J. Leon, *The Jews of Ancient Rome* (Peabody, Mass.: Hendrickson, 1995 [1960]). Although Leon (as well as Frey and others) believed that at least the Monteverde catacomb was in use in the late Republican period, recent studies suggest that none may date before the third century C.E. (Leonard Rutgers, "Überlegungen zu den jüdischen katakomben Roms," *JAC* 33 [1990]: 140-57). Consequently, these materials must be used with great caution by those whose interest is Jewish and Christian communities in the first century.

8. The Claudian edict is our only evidence for this early stage (Suetonius, *Claudius* 25.4; Acts 18:2).

However, the dissonance created by the activities and/or words of Christians provoked tension, particularly over issues related to the observance of the Law and the inclusion of Gentiles.[9] Eventually these tensions escalated into disturbances which gained the attention of the Romans, resulting in the Claudian edict of 49 C.E.[10] Christian Jews such as Aquila and Prisca were expelled from Rome, as were no doubt other Jews, both Christian and non-Christian.[11] Gentile Christians who "lived like Jews" were probably expelled as well — especially if they were involved in the disturbances — because the Romans considered a person who "lived the life of a Jew" to be a Jew.[12]

The immigration into the capital of Christians who were already accustomed to assembling outside synagogue contexts, tensions with non-Christian Jews, and an emerging self-consciousness on the part of Christians may have prompted Christian assemblies outside the synagogues prior to the Claudian edict.[13] Whether or not Christians met in

9. The beliefs of the Christians are unlikely to have occasioned conflict. As David Aune has observed, Jewish communities were more concerned with orthopraxy than orthodoxy: David Aune, "Orthodoxy in First Century Judaism?" *Journal for the Study of Judaism* 7 (1976): 1-10. It was the greater openness to Gentiles characteristic of Christian practice that invariably jeopardized the boundaries of Jewish communities. These boundaries maintained the ethnic integrity of the Jewish communities and protected them from foreign invasion (cf. Philip Francis Esler, *Community and Gospel in Luke-Acts* [Cambridge: Cambridge University Press, 1987], 22). Cf. Segal's comment: "The issue was not how the gentiles could be saved but how to eat with them and marry them" (Alan Segal, "The Costs of Proselytism and Conversion," *Seminar Papers,* Society of Biblical Literature, no. 27 [Atlanta: Scholars Press, 1988], 336-69, esp. 363).

10. The actions of Claudius relative to the Jews of Rome have been a matter of considerable scholarly debate. Most of the controversy surrounds the relationship between what ostensibly appear to be two edicts against the Jews, and with the possible association of Christianity with the disturbances that stand behind the action(s). Cf. my discussion of these issues (with bibliography) in *Ethnic Issues,* 49-53.

11. Acts 18:2. Syntax permits a reading of the Suetonius text that limits the scope of the edict to those involved in the disturbance. However, the Acts version says "all" the Jews were commanded to leave Rome. Even if all the "Jews" were ordered to leave Rome, it is unlikely that all did. Tacitus was well aware of the difference between an expulsion order and an actual eviction: "A decree of the Senate was then passed for the expulsion of the astrologers from Italy, stringent but ineffectual" (Tacitus, *Annals* 12.52).

12. Cf. especially Cassius Dio 37.17.1. For additional evidence, cf. Walters, 58f.

13. Lampe's observation regarding Aquila and Prisca suggests this possibility: "Dass Aquila und Priska sogleich nach ihrer Vertreibung aus Rom in Korinth vorbe-

their own assemblies prior to the edict, it is safe to say that they did so afterward.[14]

On account of the edict, the ethnic and socioreligious composition of these assemblies would have shifted because Christian Jews, and Gentiles who lived like Jews, were expelled (many if not most of them). The Christians who played the chief roles in defining the character of the Christian gatherings after the edict, therefore, would have been those Roman Christians who were least shaped by the Jewish context of earliest Christianity in Rome.

The Claudian edict did not create the tensions between Christians and non-Christian Jews in Rome; however, it exacerbated them. The edict in effect drove a wedge between them by dramatically communicating — especially to non-Christian Jews — that it would be in their best interests to go their separate ways. By reducing interactions between Christians and non-Christian Jews and by altering the context in which those interactions took place, the edict affected the evolution of Christian self-definition in the capital. When Jewish Christians and Gentile Christians (who lived like Jews) returned to Rome after the edict had lapsed, they encountered Christians whose socialization had changed markedly. Not only were Christians assembling in house churches that were independent of Jewish gatherings, these house churches were populated by persons who — for the most part — no longer observed Sabbath and dietary laws and who were not eager to resume such behaviors, as Romans 14:1–15:13 indicates.[15]

Hence, the path of separation from the Jewish communities is not only discernible from deductions based on the Claudian edict, it is also detectable

---

haltlos an der paulinischen Heidenmission mitarbeiteten (Apg 18; cf. Röm 16,3f), eröffnet die Möglichkeit, dass sie es bereits vom Synagogenverband Roms her gewohnt gewesen waren, mit Heidenchristen zusammenzuleben" (*Die stadtrömischen Christen,* 53).

14. The greetings in Romans 16 — written less than ten years after the edict of Claudius — indicate several house churches. A church in the house of Prisca and Aquila is mentioned explicitly (16:5), and four other groupings are suggested in 16:10, 11, 14, and 15. Because it is unlikely that the other fourteen persons greeted belonged in either of these groupings, Lampe suggests that at least two more house churches should be assumed (Peter Lampe, "The Roman Christians of Romans 16," in *The Romans Debate: Revised and Expanded Edition,* ed. Karl Donfried [Peabody, Mass.: Hendrickson, 1991], 229f.).

15. This circumstance best accounts for Paul's argument in Rom. 14:1–15:13. Cf. Walters, 84-92.

in Paul's letter to the Romans. The effects of the Claudian edict were felt most starkly by the more Law observant of the Roman Christians. After they returned to Rome — and as others immigrated into the city — many sought a middle ground through maintaining their fidelity to dietary laws and Sabbath. However, the refusal of others in the Christian house churches to follow suit jeopardized this intermediate option.[16] Although there were no doubt "reasons for Romans," one of the goals Paul had was to emphasize the common ground that existed between Jewish and Gentile Christians, and to encourage a greater willingness on the part of Gentile Christians to make room for the "Jewishness" of their observant counterparts.

Whether Paul's letter improved the situation for the more observant Christians is difficult to assess. Even if it did create more space for their "Jewishness," it did not mitigate the growing distance between the Jewish synagogues and the Christian house churches. Rather, Romans 9–11 makes it clear that Paul accepted the distance as a painful fact, though he did not accept the conclusion Gentile Christians were drawing: that God had rejected Israel.

The extent of the break between non-Christian Jews and Christians by the mid-60s is indicated indirectly by the ability of Roman administrators to move against Christians in 64 C.E. as not Jews (or at least not like the other Jews).[17] Fergus Millar is correct in noting that the ancient mate-

16. It is reasonable to assume that many of these Christians migrated to house churches that were composed of more observant Christians. Although Romans 16 gives evidence for a number of house churches, it is not possible on the basis of the information contained there to offer more than a guess concerning which ones might have been more observant. Because of their earlier involvement with Paul's Gentile mission, it is unlikely that Aquila and Prisca's house church provided any unique haven for observant Christians. Andronicus and Junia(s) were Jews and probably were among the earliest converts to Christianity (they were in Christ before Paul). How their apostolic ministry/ministries operated vis-à-vis Jews and Gentiles is unknown.

17. The only significant criticism of Lampe's book that John Elliott offers in his review (*CBQ* 51 [1989]: 560-62) involves Lampe's contention that the Christians in Rome had severed themselves from the synagogue prior to the arrival of Paul's letter. He finds this conclusion to be at odds with the material evidence Lampe surfaces in his study: "common urban location, trades, social stratification, burial customs, and uncentralized organization." However, Elliott claims too much on the basis of the material evidence. This datum does suggest that the Jews and Christians shared a common social context — that of Rome's immigrant poor — as well as certain religious customs, but the separation of the communities would leave no trace in this record whether it occurred in the 50s or the 150s, so it cannot be used to date the separation.

rials are silent regarding how Christians were identified and prosecuted in 64 C.E.; nonetheless, they were identified and prosecuted, and the implications of that datum for the existence of features which distinguished Christians from non-Christian Jews, and Christian communities from Jewish communities, should not be underplayed.[18]

How one accounts for Rome's "discovery" of the Christians affects the interpretation of what Nero's outburst might say about Jewish and Christian relations during the period. Fox has argued that it was the apostle Paul's appeal to Caesar and trial in Rome that prompted the distinction.[19] More common have been the explanations that follow the early Christian apologists in blaming the Jews. In *Martyrdom and Persecution in the Early Church,* Frend writes:

> [T]he persecution represented a triumph for the orthodox Jews, who were able, through influence at Court, to shift the odium of the outbreak on the hated schismatics, the Christian synagogue. This they hoped to destroy at a single tremendous blow. In the persons of Poppaea Sabina and the actor Tigellinus they had the ear of the Emperor, and they succeeded in so far as a great number of Christians were killed, including the leaders, Peter and Paul.[20]

Marcel Simon nuances "the Jewish factor" more carefully in his explanation but still concludes that "the Jews . . . could have been, in a sense, at the bottom of the persecution."[21]

Instead of imagining that Poppaea or some other person of influence made an eleventh hour plea in behalf of the Jews and directed or diverted the Roman fury on the Christians, historians should interpret possible Jewish involvement in light of the broader question of the Roman admin-

18. Fergus Millar, *The Emperor in the Roman World* (Ithaca: Cornell University Press, 1977), 554. Livy's account of the Bacchanal conspiracy indicates some of the resources available to the Romans when they resorted to police powers: paying informers and punishing those who harbored fugitives (Livy 39.15).

19. Robin Lane Fox writes, "After Paul's trial, the Christians were the obvious group for Nero to blame" (*Pagans and Christians* [New York: Knopf, 1986], 432). This view attaches too much significance to a trial that we know nothing about. We do not even know if it occurred. If it did, it may not have been as significant to the Romans as Christians are apt to imagine.

20. W. H. C. Frend, *Martyrdom and Persecution in the Early Church* (Oxford University Press, 1965), 164.

21. Simon, 117.

istration of non-Roman religions and the vicissitudes of the Jews under the Julio-Claudians.[22] Within this context non-Christian Jews in Rome would have begun to distance themselves from Christians following the Claudian edict, if not earlier. This would have left the Christians exposed in 64 C.E.

The dietary adjustments made by Seneca during the reign of Tiberius can be read as a firsthand commentary on how Roman administrative interventions encourage such distancing and how it could be achieved:

> I was imbued with this teaching, and began to abstain from animal food; at the end of a year the habit was as pleasant as it was easy. . . . Do you ask how I came to abandon the practice? It was this way: The days of my youth coincided with the early part of the reign of Tiberius Caesar. Some foreign rites were at that time being inaugurated, and abstinence from certain kinds of animal food was set down as a proof of interest in the strange cult. So at the request of my father, who did not fear prosecution, but who detested philosophy, I returned to my previous habits.[23]

With regard to our inquiry we must ask (1) what behaviors associated with the Christians would have put the Jews in a position similar to Seneca and (2) what actions might they have taken to accomplish the necessary distancing. The behaviors that seem to have the most capacity for putting the Jews at risk with the Romans during this period are riots, messianism, and especially proselytism. The eviction under Claudius in 49 C.E. was prompted by riots and messianism, while proselytism was a factor in the eviction under Tiberius.[24]

Proselytism stands out because under Tiberius and Claudius the Romans were exceedingly anxious about foreign cults that proselytized Romans

22. Cf. Walters, 40-55.

23. Seneca, *Epistles* 108.22. Seneca's Pythagorean diet looked like the participation of a Roman in an oriental cult that Tiberius might not tolerate (e.g., Judaism). The "Judaism" of the Christians looked like a Judaism that the Romans would not tolerate.

24. Riots and possibly messianism are indicated in Suetonius (*Claudius* 25.4), whether one reads *Christus* or *Chrestus*. On the Tiberius expulsion, cf. Josephus, *Ant.* 18.3.5; Tacitus, *Annals* 2.85; and Cassius Dio 57.18.5a. Rutgers has recently argued that the Romans were concerned about "law and order," not the religious practices of the Jews: "It was quite common for the Roman authorities to expel easily identifiable groups from Rome in times of political turmoil. Such expulsions were ordered not for religious reasons, but rather to maintain law and order" (see his essay in this volume). I doubt, however, that Roman concerns were so easily catalogued at the time.

and because Christians unabashedly sought converts.[25] Martin Goodman has argued that Judaism in the first century was not a proselytizing religion and that the desirability of embarking on a proselytizing mission occurred to third-century rabbis only because of the successes of the Christians.[26] Although I believe Goodman draws the distinction between Jews and Christians too sharply, he is correct in stressing that Jews did not operate with the same mandate for mission that was assumed by the Christians. Even if — as Goodman argues — Jews in the first century only passively accepted non-Jews who pursued Judaism, the Romans would have viewed them as proselytizers if proselytes were among their numbers; Roman administrators would not have paused to measure the level of Jewish activity or passivity, especially during times of disorder or political distress. It is precisely here that Christians posed the greatest threat: their aggressive proselytizing risked attracting the scrutiny of Roman administrators whose attention would be occupied elsewhere were it not for the Christians.[27]

If the proselytizing of Christians put non-Christian Jews in a situation roughly analogous to that of Seneca, what behaviors would have accomplished the distancing that was necessary to protect themselves and their communities? Synagogue leaders could have prescribed beatings for those who jeopardized the boundaries, as in Paul's case (2 Cor. 11:24). Christians would either submit to this discipline — as Paul did on at least five occasions — or sever relations with the community. They could have withdrawn from the common table, as some of the Jews did when visitors from Jerusalem arrived in Antioch (Gal. 2:11-13). They could have withdrawn hospitality, as the Elder prescribed to protect his communities (2 John 9-11).

25. This is not to say that riots and messianism were not similarly provocative or that they were unrelated to proselytism.

26. On the early period, cf. Martin Goodman, "Jewish Proselytizing in the First Century," in *The Jews among Pagans and Christians in the Roman Empire,* ed. Judith Lieu, John North, and Tessa Rajak (London: Routledge, 1992), 53-78. On rabbinic attitudes, cf. Goodman, "Proselytising in Rabbinic Judaism," *JJS* 40 (1989): 175-85. Though he struggles with the evidence from Rome — admitting that Jewish proselytizing in Rome "is perhaps only an exceptional and sporadic situation" ("Jewish Proselytizing," 74) — similar conclusions are drawn by Scot McKnight, *A Light among the Gentiles: Jewish Missionary Activity in the Second Temple Period* (Minneapolis: Fortress, 1991).

27. Dividing families, riots, and conversions of people with status, especially women, were notable ways of attracting Roman attention during the Julio-Claudian period. Cf. the behaviors noted by John North, "The Development of Religious Pluralism," in Lieu et al., 184.

They could have expelled the troublemakers from the community, as was the fate of Johannine Christians (John 9:22, 34; 12:42; 16:2). They could have created or at least clarified distance by lobbying public officials.[28]

It is unclear which of these (or other) actions may have been undertaken by Roman Jews. However, it is clear that in the Julio-Claudian period non-Christian Jews had much to gain by distancing themselves from the Christians and making their autonomy as clear as possible. By 64 C.E. the distance was considerable, and Nero's attack on the Christians added no new incentives for interaction.

3. The Flavian Period

Evidence for interactions between Christians and non-Christian Jews in Rome is lacking for this period; however, the Roman administrative climate provided few incentives for reversing the trends reflected in the later Julio-Claudian period. Under the Julio-Claudians, non-Christian Jews in Rome had compelling reasons to distance themselves from Christians. In the Flavian period, on the other hand, the incentives for distancing belonged equally, if not especially, to the Christians.

The Jewish rebellion in 66 C.E. and the loss of Roman soldiers in the campaign in Judea must have created or exacerbated anti-Jewish feelings in Rome.[29] When Titus traveled to Antioch following the fall of Jerusalem, he was greeted by its citizens with a request that he expel the Jews from Antioch. Although Josephus reports that Titus refused to do so, he notes that the Jews of Antioch lived in terrible fear and uncertainty regarding what would be done.[30] The Jewish temple at Leontopolis in Egypt was

28. On the lobbying of officials by the Jews, cf. Tessa Rajak, "Was There a Roman Charter for the Jews," *JRS* 74 (1984): 107-23. Esler's sociological description of how the "church-sect" model relates to tension between the Jewish and Christian communities is consonant with this conclusion. He points out that the "church" (the Jewish community) is likely to use the "state" to get at the "sect" (the Christians). The state is more likely to support the church because it is more conservative and stable (Esler, 22-23).

29. Note the generalization of Stern, "Jews are viewed unfavorably in the literature of the Flavian age" (Menahem Stern, "The Jews in Greek and Latin Literature," in *The Jewish People in the First Century,* 2 vols., ed. Samuel Safrai and Menahem Stern, CRINT [Philadelphia: Fortress Press, 1976], 2:1152).

30. Josephus, *War* 5.2.

destroyed under Vespasian, Josephus tells us, because the emperor was suspicious of the "incessant tendency of the Jews to revolution."[31]

Besides uncertainty and fear, the Jews of Rome must have felt profound humiliation in the aftermath of the fall of Jerusalem, the destruction of the temple, and the Roman army's triumphal march through the Roman Forum — with Jewish prisoners of war and spoils from the temple.[32] A triumphal arch constructed in the Forum Romanum that is still visible today,[33] coin issues in the reigns of Vespasian and Titus celebrating the Roman victory,[34] and a special Jewish tax instituted by Vespasian were abiding reminders of the defeat/victory.[35] The staggering effects of the war on Jewish history are often rehearsed, though probably never grasped — the destruction of Jerusalem, the loss of the temple, the end of sacrifices, and the end of the high priesthood. The impression the war made on the Romans, however, is seldom considered. In the winter of 69/70 — four years into the war — Vespasian left Titus a force of approximately one-seventh of the entire imperial army to complete the siege of Jerusalem. It took five months (April to September) for Titus to capture the city.[36] The impression this ordeal made on the Romans is shown by the fact that the triumph of Vespasian and Titus celebrated in Rome in 71 was, according to Millar, the "only Roman triumph ever to celebrate the subjugation of the population of an existing province."[37] Ten years after the fall of Jerusalem the Romans were still issuing coins celebrating their victory over Judea.[38]

31. Josephus, *War* 7.420.

32. Josephus offers an eyewitness account of the triumphal procession (*War* 7.116-62). Stern notes the humiliation Roman Jews would have felt (Stern, *Greek and Latin Authors on Jews and Judaism,* 3 vols. [Jerusalem: Israel Academy of Sciences and Humanities, 1976-84], 2:129).

33. Another triumphal arch commemorating the victory over the Judeans was erected in the Circus Maximus in 80 C.E. No longer extant, it is known only from an inscription (ILS 264).

34. E. M. Smallwood, *The Jews under Roman Rule: From Pompey to Diocletian* (Leiden: Brill, 1976), 330, 164.

35. The Jewish tax is known from Greek sources as the *Ioudaion telesma* or the *didrachmon* and was administered by a treasury called the *fiscus Iudaicus.* L. A. Thompson, "Domitian and the Jewish Tax," *Historia* 31 (1982): 329.

36. Fergus Millar, *The Roman Near East, 31 BC–AD 337* (Cambridge: Harvard University Press, 1993), 76.

37. Millar, *The Roman Near East,* 79.

38. Seventy-one is the date of the main issue, but it was continued in 72-73 and

Although Jews in Rome undoubtedly feared Flavian reprisals following the war, their fears were apparently unrealized until Domitian began a crack-down on Jews who were evading payment of the tax which was imposed as a consequence of the war. Ancient sources make it clear that during his reign the Jewish tax was exacted in a fashion not characteristic of the reigns of Vespasian and Titus. Suetonius reserved one of his rare personal vignettes for a description of an episode that for him epitomized Domitian's enforcement of the tax:

> Besides other taxes, that on the Jews was levied with the utmost vigour, and those were prosecuted who without publicly acknowledging that faith yet lived as Jews, as well as those who concealed their origin and did not pay the tribute levied upon their people. I recall being present in my youth when the person of a man ninety years old was examined before the procurator and a very crowded court, to see whether he was circumcised.[39]

Apparently this approach led to what Thompson has called a "witch-hunt for so-called Jewish tax-evaders."[40] Whether Domitian's policy represented any innovation in the scope of those liable for payment of the tax has been a controversial question.[41] Some have argued that the tax was extended to include proselytes and/or Jewish sympathizers in order to discourage the spread of Jewish religion, while others have speculated that it was the Christians whom Domitian aimed to bring under the tax. Still others, however, have maintained that the change was only in the rigor and harshness with which the tax was collected, not in the scope. Recently, Margaret Williams has argued convincingly that the issue was in fact tax evasion, meaning "catching and punishing people who were already deemed liable."[42]

---

revived in 77-78. A special type was issued in 80-81, apparently celebrating the tenth anniversary of the victory (R. A. G. Carson, *Coins of the Roman Empire* [New York: Routledge, 1990], 29). Smallwood notes that the evidence for a Domitianic issue of this coin type is based on one "dubious" coin. Smallwood, 330, 164.

39. Suetonius, *Domitian* 12.2.

40. Thompson, 329.

41. Cf. commentary with bibliography in Stern, *Greek and Latin Authors,* 2:128-31.

42. Margaret H. Williams, "Domitian, the Jews and the 'Judaizers' — A Simple Matter of Cupiditas and Maiestas?" *Historia* 39 (1990): 199. Those liable appear to be those who were Jews from birth and those who had "gone over" to Judaism. Since proselytes were considered to be Jewish, there is no reason to assume that Suetonius evidences any extension of the scope of the tax.

It seems, however, that the pursuit of tax evaders got completely out of hand. This would have rendered the technical question of who properly fell under the tax's liability a moot point. What counted was whether the charge of "living the life of a Jew" could be leveled against someone. It appears that in many cases these investigations were not ultimately about a person's religious identity, but rather were convenient opportunities for opponents to bring down their rivals. How widespread this charade became is graphically indicated by the Nervan coin legend *FISCI IUDAICI CALUMNIA SUBLATA.*[43] That Nerva would advertise his reversal of Domitian's policy on a coin is itself a clear indication that the "witch-hunt" had affected a significant number of people. That the legend appeared on the first three coin issues of Nerva's reign — two of these within weeks of Domitian's death — suggests not only the popularity of the move but also Nerva's grasp of its urgency.[44] I believe that Williams is correct in her contention that "false accusations for 'Jewish life' must have reached scandalous proportions by the end of Domitian's reign and upset a far more important constituency than some modern authorities would allow."[45]

Moreover, it appears that charges of "Jewish life" began to be leveled against people in Rome outside the context of enforcement of the Jewish tax. The case of Clemens and Domitilla does not seem to have been connected to the tax, but it does appear to belong to the same general context.[46] Cassius Dio writes:

43. Harold Mattingly, *Coins of the Roman Empire in the British Museum,* vol. 3 (Oxford: Oxford University Press, 1966), 15-19, nos. 88, 98, 105-6.

44. For Nerva coin dates, cf. D. C. A. Shotter, "The Principate of Nerva — Some Observations on the Coin Evidence," *Historia* 32 (1983): 218.

45. Williams, 200.

46. The evidence suggesting that Domitilla and Clemens were Christians is not persuasive. Jones finds no convincing evidence for a Domitianic persecution of the Christians; however, "The situation with the Jews was vastly different" (Brian W. Jones, *The Emperor Domitian* [New York: Routledge, 1992], 117). Archaeological evidence for the connection — recently reexamined by Jeffers (*Conflict at Rome: Social Order and Hierarchy in Early Christianity* [Minneapolis: Fortress Press, 1991], 50ff.) — is not conclusive and cannot overturn the fact that early Christian writers did not claim that Domitilla and Clemens were Christians. The first writer to claim Clemens was a Christian was Syncellus in the ninth century. Eusebius did not associate him with Christianity even though he mentioned him as a relative of Flavia Domitilla, whom he claimed was a Christian. Cf. the commentary with bibliography representing both sides of the issue in Stern, *Greek and Latin Authors,* 2:381.

> And the same year Domitian slew, along with many others, Flavius Clemens the consul, although he was a cousin and had to wife Flavia Domitilla, who was also a relative of the emperor. The charge brought against them both was that of atheism, a charge on which many others who drifted into Jewish ways were condemned. Some of these were put to death, and the rest were at least deprived of their property. Domitilla was merely banished to Pandateria. But Glabrio, who had been Trajan's colleague in the consulship, was put to death, having been accused of the same crimes as most of the others, and, in particular, of fighting as a gladiator with wild beasts.[47]

Another administrative action of Nerva, recorded by Cassius Dio as a move intended to correct abuses under Domitian's reign, offers further evidence that charges of "Jewish life" affected considerable numbers of people and extended to circumstances beyond the collection of the Jewish tax:

> Nerva also released all who were on trial for *maiestas* and restored the exiles; moreover, he put to death all the slaves and the freedmen who had conspired against their masters and allowed that class of persons to lodge no complaint whatever against their masters; and no persons were permitted to accuse anybody of *maiestas* or of adopting the Jewish mode of life.

Domitian's anti-Jewish bias was routinely exploited by *delatores.* Thus, especially for persons of high status, like Clemens and Domitilla, charges of *atheotes* could become *impietas* or *maiestas* or both.[48] In view of these broader measures, Domitian's policy regarding the tax cannot be explained by fiscal concerns alone.[49] Rather, Domitian operated with an anti-Jewish

47. Cassius Dio 67.14.1-3.

48. Paul Keresztes, *Imperial Rome and the Christians* (New York: University Press of America, 1989), 91. Brian Jones thinks that "The only Jewish sympathizers with reason to fear for their lives were men of wealth and property, those of senatorial or equestrian rank, for this was the only group to interest the *delatores,* who could make use of it to play upon the emperor's prejudices and so, perhaps, devise charges of *maiestas*" (Jones, 118).

49. In Syme's words, "the ruthless exaction of the fiscus Iudaicus is not a mere by-product of financial straits, but is something very much like a persecution" (R. Syme, "The Imperial Finances under Domitian, Nerva and Trajan," *JRS* 20 [1930]: 67).

bias observable in the *fiscus Iudaicus* as well as in contemporary literature that was dedicated to him, particularly from the pens of Martial and Quintilian.[50]

The Flavian period, particularly the reign of Domitian, was a period when Christians would have benefited from being distinguished from Jews in Rome. It is likely that a number of Christians perished as a result of Domitian's "witch-hunt" for Jewish tax evaders.[51] This is true whether the scope of the tax was extended to include them or whether the search for evaders only exposed them to proceedings where, once before a judge, their fate was all but determined.[52] Though the distance between the Jewish and Christian communities was already considerable at the end of the Julio-Claudian period, the Flavian period would have further discouraged interactions between Jews and Christians in the capital.

The only early Christian literature that can be connected to Rome with any degree of reliability during the Flavian period is 1 Peter and the letter to the Hebrews. There is general agreement that 1 Peter was written from Rome, though scholars are divided on the association of Hebrews with the city. Among those who associate Hebrews with Rome, there is division over whether the phrase "those of Italy greet you" (13:24) should be read to indicate that the Christians addressed were in Italy or whether the author wrote from Italy.[53] It is apparent that both documents make extensive use of Old Testament images and traditions. Moreover, Brown finds a connection between Paul's letter to the Romans, Hebrews, 1 Peter,

50. Williams, 197, 204ff.

51. This may explain Clement's reference to "a series of misfortunes and accidents that suddenly came upon us" (*1 Clem.* 1.1). He does not refer to any wholesale Domitianic persecution of Christians, but rather to the "accidental" impact of Domitian's policy on Christians.

52. Cf. Pliny, *Letters* 10.96-97. Trajan directed Pliny not to hunt Christians down; however, if they were brought in on some charge they either repented of their Christian faith or they were executed (regardless of their guilt or innocence relative to the charge under which they were summoned). Trajan states the policy as if it were standard procedure. Pliny's comment that he had "never been present at any trials of the Christians" suggests that he knew such trials had occurred. Presumably these would have been in Rome while Domitian was emperor.

53. On 1 Peter, cf. John Elliott, *A Home for the Homeless* (Philadelphia: Fortress Press, 1981), 21ff., and R. E. Brown and J. P. Meier, *Antioch and Rome* (New York: Paulist, 1983), 128ff. On Hebrews, cf. Paul Ellingworth, *The Epistle to the Hebrews* (Grand Rapids: Wm. B. Eerdmans Publishing Co., 1993), 21-29.

and *1 Clement* in their frequent use of Jewish cultic language, their insistence on obedience to civil authority, and their increasing articulation of church structure.[54]

Although texts transposing traditional images of Jewish self-identity to Christians are very common in 1 Peter — note especially 2:1-10 — there is no evidence of direct interaction between Christians and Jews and no indication of polemic with Jews or Judaism. In fact, as Richardson claims, the "relatively thorough transposition of attributes and titles to the Church testifies to the distance that the Church has moved away from close contact with Judaism."[55] Hence, if the language of 1 Peter offers any commentary on Roman Christianity, by virtue of the author's association with Rome, it would support the crystallizing of boundaries already suggested for the Flavian period.

Whereas 1 Peter emphasized the transposition of Jewish traditions, Hebrews stresses their supersession (e.g., the Jewish rest, the Levitical priesthood, the Mosaic covenant, the tabernacle, etc.). Also in contrast to 1 Peter, Hebrews has a polemical edge and — if (at least some of) its readers were on the brink of defecting to the synagogue, as is widely thought — the document may indicate interaction between Christians and Jews. However, although Abraham is an important figure in Hebrews, those features of the Abraham story which generally surface in conflicts with non-Christian Judaism (e.g., the implications of Abraham's call for circumcision and the inclusion of Gentiles) are noticeably absent.[56] This may suggest that the author of Hebrews was not so concerned that readers were defecting to the synagogue, but rather that they had absorbed Jewish traditions too literally and were in danger of blurring the boundaries between Christianity and Judaism.[57]

54. Brown and Meier, 136.

55. Peter Richardson, *Israel in the Apostolic Church* (Cambridge: Cambridge University Press, 1969), 171. Richardson says that "1 Peter begins to approach the position of some early apologists who imply that the Old Testament and the prophets belong especially (only) to Christians" (175).

56. Jeffrey Siker, *Disinheriting the Jews: Abraham in Early Christian Controversy* (Louisville: Westminster/John Knox, 1991), 97.

57. Cf. Brown and Meier, 155f. Cf. also J. V. Dahms, "The First Readers of Hebrews," *JETS* 20 (1977): 365-75.

4. *1 Clement*

Although *1 Clement* was written to address the problem of communal strife which threatened the Christian *politeuma* in Corinth and caused the removal of some presbyters,[58] there are indications that the letter may offer insight into Roman Christianity as well. Because the letter continually appeals to what the Corinthians and the Romans hold in common, one would expect it to provide some glimpse of Roman Christianity. The author's claim to write on behalf of Roman Christians as a whole would have put some burden on him to represent the sentiment of the larger Christian community in Rome.[59] Moreover, Clement's statement in 7.1 — "We write such things to you, beloved brethren, not only to admonish you but also to remind ourselves; for we are in the same arena and the same conflict faces us" — suggests that at least in some ways a letter adapted to the church in Corinth should mirror at least some characteristics of the church in Rome. Finally, the content and mode of argumentation of *1 Clement* tell us a great deal about the author. In the words of Barnard, "Clement interprets the problems in Corinth in light of existing Jewish or Jewish-Christian tradition which spoke of schism, sedition, persecution and martyrdom."[60] The litany of quotations and the endless stream of exempla represent neither content nor a rhetorical approach that was born when this letter was penned. This is how Clement uses Scripture. These are the materials within which Clement is at home. This

58. This statement of the problem reflects my general agreement with the conclusions of Barbara Bowe regarding the purpose and occasion of the letter (*A Church in Crisis: Ecclesiology and Paraenesis in Clement of Rome,* Harvard Dissertations in Religion, no. 23 [Minneapolis: Fortress Press, 1988], 16-32). Unless otherwise indicated, quotations from *1 Clement* are from Robert Grant and Holt Graham, *The Apostolic Fathers: A New Translation and Commentary* (New York: Thomas Nelson & Sons, 1965). Although the author of the letter from "The Church of God which sojourns in Rome to the Church of God which sojourns in Corinth" nowhere identifies himself, it seems likely that he is the same Clement referred to by the *Shepherd* (*Vis.* 2.4.3). Cf. the discussion of authorship and date in Bowe, 1-3, and Andreas Lindemann, *Die Clemensbriefe* (Tübingen: Mohr-Siebeck, 1992), 12ff., 26. I agree with most scholars that Clement was the author and that the letter was written in the mid-90s.

59. Cf. Wayne Meeks, *The Origins of Christian Morality* (New Haven: Yale University Press, 1993), 153.

60. L. W. Barnard, "The Early Roman Church, Judaism, and Jewish-Christianity," *ATR* 49 (1967): 371-84.

is how Clement makes a case. Surely this tells us something about Clement's Roman context.

What the content and rhetorical approach tell us about Clement and his Roman context is important for our purposes here. That Clement was heavily influenced by Israel's scriptures, no one can doubt. As Hagner has pointed out, approximately one-fourth of Clement's letter is composed of direct quotations from the Old Testament — cited from the LXX and including the Apocrypha — and these quotations supply the raw material for his argument.[61] However, Clement has not simply read the Old Testament in light of Christian experience; rather, *1 Clement*'s inclusion of post-testamental Jewish traditions suggests that the author's reading of the Old Testament was influenced by the Hellenistic synagogue.[62] According to Koester, *1 Clement* (and the Shepherd) "abounds with only slightly Christianized Jewish traditions, and might have been written by any hellenized Jew anywhere."[63] Whether the ethnicity of the author can be established on the basis of the content of *1 Clement* is open to debate;[64] its status as a storehouse of Christianized Jewish traditions is not.[65]

61. There are approximately 75 direct quotations, many of which are of unusual length compared to quotations in other early Christian writers (Donald Hagner, *The Use of the Old and New Testaments in Clement of Rome* [Leiden: E. J. Brill, 1973], 21ff.). The number of quotations varies significantly depending on who is counting. Harnack has 120 quotations and allusions (Adolf von Harnack, *Einführung in die alte Kirchengeschichte. Das Schreiben der römischen Kirche an die Korinthische aus der Zeit Domitians* [I. Clemensbrief] [Leipzig: Hinrichs, 1929], 66), while Mayer says, "Clement quotes the Old Testament some 166 times" (Herbert Mayer, "Clement of Rome and His Use of Scripture," *CTM* 42 [1971]: 536-40). Interestingly, the New Testament document that comes closest to *1 Clement* in the frequency of OT quotations is Paul's letter to the Romans! Although the epistle of Barnabas exceeds *1 Clement* in OT quotations, the frequency of its quotations is related to the author's intention to set the record straight on the proper interpretation of the OT. *1 Clement* is unique in its extensive dependency on the OT for paraenetic purposes (Hagner, 23, 25).

62. Cf. the concise list of texts from *1 Clement* along with their post-testamental Jewish connections and bibliography in Lampe, *Die stadtrömischen Christen*, 59.

63. James M. Robinson and Helmut Koester, *Trajectories through Early Christianity* (Philadelphia: Fortress, 1971), 275.

64. Brown finds no indication of ethnicity because the Jewish character of Christianity in Rome made these traditions generally available (Brown and Meier, 162).

65. In a very detailed study of *1 Clement* 1–7, Beyschlag found connections between *1 Clement* and late Jewish and early Jewish-Christian traditions and apologetics (Karlmann Beyschlag, *Clemens Romanus und der Frühkatholizismus: Untersuchungen zu*

Does this influence suggest interaction between the Roman Christians and the Jewish synagogues, or more specifically between Clement and non-Christian Jews? This question is very difficult to answer. A similar problem presents itself to Meeks and Wilken in Antioch:

> Sources of information about Christian-Jewish relations in the second and third centuries are fragmentary, mostly indirect, and almost entirely from the Christian side. During this period it is also difficult or impossible to distinguish between continuing direct Jewish influence on Christianity and the independent internal development of Christian exegesis of the common scriptures.[66]

Lacking other sources, we are left to comb the contents of *1 Clement* in search of any indications that Clement or other Roman Christians interacted directly with non-Christian Jews and/or their communities.

Although Jews and Judaism are omnipresent in *1 Clement,* the author refers to them only in the context of Scripture. Not only does *1 Clement* reveal no contact with Jews or Judaism, it shows no trace of or fallout from polemical encounters with Jews in the past.[67] Furthermore — and most

I Clemens 1–7 [Tübingen: Mohr and Siebeck, 1966]). Cf. also E. Nestle, "War der Verfasser des 1. Clemensbriefes semitischer Abstammung?" *ZNW* 1 (1900): 178-80. Grant thinks Clement used an anthology of Old Testament quotations — based on the criteria of Prigent — that was created in Hellenistic Jewish circles (Robert M. Grant and Holt H. Graham, *The Apostolic Fathers,* vol. 2 [New York: Nelson and Sons, 1965], 10-13).

66. Wayne Meeks and Robert Wilken, *Jews and Christians in Antioch* (Missoula: Scholars Press, 1978), 19.

67. Against Jeffers, 173, who thinks that "those who differ with us" in 47.7 are former Christians who returned to the synagogues. I find it impossible to believe that polemical issues vis-à-vis Jews and Judaism would be completely absent from *1 Clement* if "those who differ with us" were Christians who had defected to the synagogue. The phrase more likely refers simply to outsiders. It serves a rhetorical strategy similar to the one Paul employs in Rom. 2:23-24. The approach allows Clement to say that the Corinthians' internal problems represent not simply a sin against one another, but also a sin against God. Cf. the discussion of this rhetorical move in Rom. 2:23-24 and other early Christian literature in Halvor Moxnes, *Theology in Conflict: Studies in Paul's Understanding of God in Romans* (Leiden: E. J. Brill, 1980), 56-57.

The other text that is sometimes seen as a reference to Jews or Judaism in Rome is *1 Clement* 5.2. Clement's identification of jealousy and envy as the cause of the deaths of Peter and Paul has led many scholars to accuse Roman Jews (e.g., Smallwood, 218; Frend, 164). Since *1 Clement* wants to show that almost every calamity that has befallen

striking of all — Clement feels comfortable making extended moral arguments on the basis of Old Testament characters, and even argues from Levitical regulations without including Christian disclaimers. Note how Clement introduces the section of the letter that prescribes "church order" as the solution to Corinth's problems:

> Now then, since this is quite plain to us, and we have gained insight into the depths of the divine knowledge, we ought to do in order all those things the Master has ordered us to perform at the appointed times. He has commanded sacrifices and services to be performed, not in a careless and haphazard way but at the designated seasons and hours. He himself has determined where and through whom he wishes them performed, to the intent that everything should be done religiously to his good pleasure and acceptably to his will. Those then who offer their sacrifices at the appointed seasons are acceptable and blessed; for since they comply with the Master's order, they do not sin. Thus to the high priest have been appointed his proper services, to the priests their own place assigned, upon the Levites their proper duties imposed; and the layman is bound by the rules for laymen.[68]

Whereas the common approach to the Old Testament for early Christian writers was to claim the traditions while attacking the Jewish institutions, Clement used both and attacked neither.[69] He seems completely unconcerned that his approach might blur the boundary between Christianity and Judaism and result in defections to the synagogues or open the door to Judaizers.

It seems to me that either Clement did not care if Christians defected

---

the people of God resulted from envy and jealousy, room must be left for Clement to exercise some license in fitting Peter and Paul into this scheme. Furthermore, if Clement has a particular culprit in mind, it could just as easily have been a rival Christian voice; in fact, this would fit Clement's rhetorical goal better. Cf. Beyschlag's analysis of the "jealousy/envy" motif (Beyschlag, 48-134).

68. *1 Clement* 40.1-5.

69. Richardson observes that "Clement of Rome nowhere suggests that Christianity is set over against Israel, or that Christianity is a *tertium genus*" (Richardson, 24). Siker's interpretation of *1 Clement*'s use of Abraham is consistent with my point: "It remains striking, however, that neither the promises to Abraham nor his circumcision is a subject for discussion in this literature. These two topics appear to have functioned almost exclusively in Christian controversy with Judaism" (Siker, 161).

to the synagogue — a rather unlikely option — or that the distance between the Jewish and Christian communities in Rome was so great at this point that Clement felt no automatic compulsion to guard the back door. I am convinced that the latter option is in fact correct.[70]

I am left to conclude, therefore, that the Hellenistic Jewish traditions evidenced in *1 Clement* were not passed to Clement directly via the synagogue; Clement received this rich exegetical heritage within Christian circles in Rome. In spite of the fact that by the time Paul wrote Romans Jewish Christians were already a distinct minority in the Roman Christian communities, a strong synagogue tradition must have remained alive. The apostle Paul's letter appealed to that tradition and, by its use of the Old Testament and its emphasis on continuity with Israel, also extended it.[71] The fact that Clement was nurtured in the traditions of the Hellenistic synagogue is a testament to the survival of those traditions within (at least some of) the Roman churches. In Romans 11:17ff. Paul reminded Gentile Christians that the olive tree has Jewish roots; apparently, some listened![72]

70. *1 Clement*'s transposition of traditional Jewish images and attributes of self-identity also indicates distance from contemporary Judaism. Richardson found that Justin was the first of the early church Fathers to claim explicitly that the church was Israel. In this context, note his comment concerning *1 Clement:* "in all the literature (of the Church Fathers to 160 CE) only one reference to Israel approaches the force which Justin gives the word — *1 Clement* 29.2" (Richardson, 15).

71. Lampe emphasizes that even though the numbers of Jewish Christians were declining relative to Gentiles, strong Jewish Christian leaders played important teaching roles (i.e., Aquila and Prisca, Rom. 16:5; Andronicus and Junia(s), Rom. 16:7). Ultimately the Jewish synagogue traditions would be passed down by Gentile Christians who were thoroughly steeped in the traditions (Lampe, *Die stadtrömischen Christen,* 58ff.).

72. However, there is no evidence that the Roman Christians in the decades following Paul's letter anticipated with Paul that the natural branches would be grafted back into the olive tree (Rom. 11:23). Although I agree with Richardson that *1 Clement* does not deny the spiritual value of the old (speaking of continuity with Israel's traditions), I see no evidence to support his suggestion that Clement (along with Ignatius) was "hopeful of further fruitful contact with Judaism" (p. 32).

5. Conclusion

In 1985 Wayne Meeks published an essay entitled "Breaking Away: Three New Testament Pictures of Christianity's Separation from the Jewish Communities."[73] In the article Meeks analyzed the Gospel of John, the letters of Paul and his disciples, and the Gospel of Matthew in order to show that the "path of separation . . . was not single or uniform."[74] It is interesting to note that the path followed by the Christians addressed in Paul's letter to the Romans shares more in common with the paths followed by the Christians addressed in John and Matthew than those addressed in Paul's other letters. As Meeks points out, Paul's practice was to establish house churches that were fundamentally independent of Jewish communities from the start: "They were not shaped by having once been within a Jewish context."[75]

Earliest Christianity in Rome was indeed shaped in a Jewish context. However, reconstructions based on a "Jewish trajectory" for early Christianity in Rome may be problematic for two reasons: first, to speak of the "Jewishness" of Christianity in Rome in the last third of the first century is vague to the point of being unhelpful — and it may be misleading; second, to speak of a "trajectory" likely claims too much on the basis of a narrow slice of evidence. The social context of early Christianity in Rome — especially the dynamics of immigration and social status — and the ambiguity that exists regarding the extent to which the author of *1 Clement* represents the "Church in Rome" should caution us against resorting to grand schemes that ignore other "paths" which may have been followed by Roman house churches that have not survived in our sources.

73. It appeared in *To See Ourselves as Others See Us: Christians, Jews, and "Others" in Late Antiquity*, ed. Jacob Neusner and Ernest S. Frerichs (Chico: Scholars Press, 1985), 93-115.

74. Meeks, "Breaking Away," 114.

75. Meeks, "Breaking Away," 108; the situation Paul addressed in Rome has more in common with Paul's own call/conversion than it does with the churches he planted and nurtured. This may help to explain why Paul's only attempt to deal with the question of non-Christian Judaism is found in Romans, and why his discussion is so passionate and personal (Romans 9–11).

CHAPTER 9

Social Perspectives on Roman Christianity during the Formative Years from Nero to Nerva: Romans, Hebrews, *1 Clement*

William L. Lane

Preliminary Considerations

An inquiry concerning the shape and development of Roman Christianity during the period from Nero to Nerva invites a fresh evaluation of the evidence bearing on a Christian presence in Rome over the span of approximately forty years. The period in view is bracketed by Paul's letter to the Romans near its beginning and *1 Clement* near its end. These documents are the two primary Christian sources for ascertaining the character of Roman Christianity during this formative period. Their witness, however, may be augmented by evidence drawn from Hebrews. As I have argued elsewhere,[1] Hebrews provides an independent and informed witness to the state of Christianity in Rome near the end of Nero's reign. If that argument is deemed persuasive, Hebrews provides a valuable resource for tracking developments in Roman Christianity following Romans. Its witness is germane to the issue of similarity and dissimilarities in Roman Christianity between Romans and *1 Clement*. I propose to address the question of development by tracing the trajectory of Roman Christianity along a continuum from Romans to Hebrews to *1 Clement*. At each point it will be imperative to take account of the social and religious constraints that inevitably influenced an emerging self-consciousness on the part of the church at Rome.

1. W. L. Lane, *Hebrews 1–8*, WBC 47A (Dallas: Word, 1991), lviii-lxvi.

Concern with developments in Roman Christianity following Romans tends to presuppose a consensus concerning the state of Roman Christianity at the time Paul wrote his letter. In point of fact, it is commonly concluded that Romans has no direct bearing on the Roman community and its internal situation. There are vigorous disagreements concerning the occasion of the letter, its destination and integrity, its unique character, and Paul's purposes for writing. A scholarly consensus remains elusive. Although a number of suggestive proposals have been made concerning the state of Christianity on the basis of Romans,[2] there is currently no common agreement. The evidence lends itself to diverse interpretations. The issues are complex, and the proposals that have been made to resolve them have often been contradictory. Conflicting evaluations of Romans as a primary source for the state of the church in Rome near the beginning of Nero's reign lie at the heart of "the Romans debate."[3]

Methodologically, it would be preferable to begin with a fresh appraisal of this central question preliminary to an evaluation of the state of the church in Rome at the time Paul wrote Romans. Only if Romans has its genesis in Paul's awareness of the situation in Rome can clues gleaned from Romans serve as the basis for gauging developments in Roman Christianity following Romans, probing for lines of continuity and for discontinuities in that development. That tactic is beyond the scope of this paper. A brief summary of the Romans debate, and a statement of my own critical stance, will have to suffice as a response to this preliminary issue.

Suggestions concerning the character of Romans can be grouped roughly into two basic approaches: (1) proposals that claim that circumstances in the Roman community were decisive in the genesis and organization of the letter, and (2) proposals that regard Paul's own circumstances as generating the letter. The primary question is not whether Romans is a situational letter; it is the determination of the precise nature of this situation. The fundamental choice in the Romans debate is whether the letter exclusively reflects Paul's own biographical situation or whether it also

2. See, for example, K. H. Schelke, "Römische Kirche im Römerbrief," *ZKT* 81 (1959): 393-404; P. Minear, *The Obedience of Faith* (Naperville, Ill.: Allenson, 1971), 7-36; R. E. Brown, "The Roman Church near the End of the First Christian Generation (A.D. 58 — Paul to the Romans)," in R. E. Brown and J. P. Meier, *Antioch and Rome* (New York: Paulist, 1983), 105-27; among others.

3. See K. P. Donfried, ed., *The Romans Debate*, rev. ed. (Peabody, Mass.: Hendrickson, 1991), for a valuable collection of contributions to the debate.

assumes a knowledge of and concern for the problems in the Christian communities in Rome.

The first approach claims that Romans, like all of Paul's other letters, addresses an existing situation, in this case in Rome.[4] Although clues to the actual circumstances of the Roman communities are sparse, appeal may be made to the decree of Claudius in 49 C.E. expelling the Jews from Rome.[5] The imperial edict almost certainly had an impact upon the leadership of the earliest congregations in Rome. The decree appears to have been rescinded by the beginning of Nero's reign in 54 C.E., since Jewish Christians began to return to the city following Claudius's death (Rom. 16:3-5). It is plausible to suppose that their return after a five-year period of banishment generated divisions and resentments. The exiled Jewish Christians returned to a predominantly Gentile church. Their arrival exacerbated tensions and mutual suspicions, resulting in a fragmented community incapable of common worship. These divisions are reflected in Paul's appeals to the "strong" and the "weak" for mutual acceptance (14:1, 13, 19; 15:1-2, 5-7) and in his warnings against Gentile arrogance (11:13-21; 12:3-4). Accordingly, Paul wrote to prepare for his own visit to Rome, but also to seek reconciliation and unity in a fragmented church. The exegetical key to this approach is to be found in Romans 15:1-13: Roman Christians are to accept one another, just as they have been accepted by Christ. Paul addressed a troubled community struggling with an alienated constituency of Jews and Gentiles. I fully support this first approach.

The second approach argues that the character of Romans precludes the thought that Paul addresses a specific situation in Rome.[6] The obliqueness

4. Among the interpreters who regard the situation in Rome as playing some part in generating the letter, see the essays by W. Wiefel, K. P. Donfried, F. F. Bruce, and W. S. Campbell in *The Romans Debate,* 85-125, 175-94, 251-64.

5. Suetonius, *Life of the Deified Claudius* 25.4; Acts 18:2. For a recent critical discussion of the decree, with bibliography, see W. L. Lane, "The Edict of Claudius," in *Hebrews 1–8,* lxiii-lxvi. The importance of this decree for Roman Christianity will become evident below.

6. Representative of this second approach are the essays by G. Bornkamm, J. Jervell, and R. J. Karris in *The Romans Debate,* 16-28, 53-62, 65-84, 125-27. Cf. also N. A. Dahl, *Studies in Paul* (Minneapolis: Augsburg, 1977), 78, 87-88, 110; J. Bassler, "Divine Impartiality in Paul's Letter to the Romans," *NovT* 26 (1981): 43-58; Bassler, *The Impartiality of God: Paul and a Theological Axiom* (Chico: Scholars, 1982); J. Drane, "Why Did Paul Write Romans?" in *Pauline Studies,* ed. D. Hagner and M. J. Harris (Grand Rapids: Wm. B. Eerdmans Publishing Co., 1980), 208-27.

of the letter and the absence of the sense of dialogue elsewhere characteristic of Paul's letters to churches suggest that Paul was not directing his letter to any particular concern known to him about the state of Roman Christianity. The historical situation arises out of the circumstances of Paul. Paul writes this letter at a turning point in his career — shortly after the Corinthian correspondence and at a time when, by his own admission, his work in the East was completed (Rom. 15:18-24). More importantly, Paul had completed the collection for the saints in Jerusalem and was on his way there to deliver the contribution (15:25-28). The exegetical key to this approach may be found in Romans 15:30-33, which reflects anxiety on Paul's part concerning the delivery and the reception of the collection. More than famine relief was involved. The collection symbolized for Paul the ratification of the unity between Gentile and Jewish Christians.[7] The issue at stake was whether there was to be one church or two. Moreover, Jerusalem's acceptance of the gift from the Gentiles would acknowledge the equal status of the Gentile churches as well as the legitimacy of Paul's entire apostolic mission. Hence, the specific historical circumstances that provide the point of references for understanding why Paul wrote this letter at this particular time are to be found in Paul's life, *not* in the Roman church. Paul wrote to introduce himself and to dispel possible misconceptions concerning his mission, but especially to enlist their prayer for his journey to Jerusalem. In short, it is not the problems of the Christian communities in Rome but Paul's own mission that provides the framework for the development in Romans.[8]

The following considerations lend support to the first approach, which finds in Romans evidence for the state of Roman Christianity early in Nero's reign.

1. A convincing case has been made for the integrity of the letter.[9]

7. Cf. K. F. Nickle, *The Collection: A Study in Pauline Strategy* (Naperville, Ill.: Allenson, 1966), 111-29.

8. So Dahl, 78. Cf. G. Bornkamm, "The Letter to the Romans as Paul's Last Will and Testament," in *The Romans Debate,* 21: "As all other letters of Paul, this letter, too, is thoroughly related to the real historical circumstances out of which it has arisen. . . . Yet we must not look to the Christians of Rome, whom the apostle had before him as he wrote, for the individual features of this real history, but rather to the history which lay behind Paul and the churches he had established."

9. H. Gamble, *The Textual History of the Letter to the Romans* (Grand Rapids: Wm. B. Eerdmans Publishing Co., 1977). See also K. P. Donfried, "A Short Note on Romans 16," in *The Romans Debate,* 44-52.

Romans 16 provides evidence that Paul established and sustained several personal acquaintances with individuals who were now in Rome. Although it is unnecessary to assume that Paul was personally acquainted with all of the individuals he greets in Romans 16, personal acquaintance must be presumed in some instances. Despite the fact that Paul has not yet visited Rome, he may very well have possessed specific knowledge of the community. It simply does not follow that Paul's lack of direct experience of the Roman communities means that he had no acquaintance with the church, its prior history or current contingencies. It is at least possible that Paul could have possessed certain detailed information.[10]

2. The obliqueness of Romans — its lack of polemic and directness — must be acknowledged. This feature, which makes Romans unique, finds a sufficient explanation in the fact that Paul has previously had no direct contact with the church. The indirectness and careful wording in the epistolary introduction and conclusion of the letter are due, not to any alleged ignorance of Paul of the situation in Rome, nor to the fact that he is not addressing that situation, but to the fact that Paul had never visited the church. Paul imposed upon himself the rule of "non-interference" (Rom. 15:20-21; 2 Cor. 10:13-16); he determined not to preach the gospel where others had labored before him and had already laid the foundation for the church. That rule had previously kept him from visiting Rome (Rom. 15:22). Paul departed from this rule when he preached the gospel in this letter. But with this exception, he makes it

10. Particularly important is Gamble's stress on the commendatory character and function of the greetings in Romans 16. See p. 92: "Thus the greetings are invested with the function of commendation; but why is this? This peculiarity is difficult to explain on any supposition other than that of a Roman address, for it is especially striking how, in the descriptive phrases, a heavy emphasis is placed on the relationship between the individuals mentioned and Paul himself. He ties them to himself and himself to them. From these features it can be seen that Paul's commendatory greetings to specific individuals serve to place those individuals in a position of respect vis-à-vis the community; but also, by linking the Apostle so closely with them, place Paul in the same position. At the same time, those singled out for greeting are claimed by Paul as his advocates within the community. That epistolary greetings should be turned to this effect would hardly be comprehensible if they were addressed to a community whose recognition of himself Paul could have presumed. Only if addressed to the Roman church, where such recognition could not be assumed — a fact acknowledged in Paul's caution and apologetic approach to it (Rom. 15:14-21) — does the peculiar character of the greetings of Rom. 16 make any sense."

clear that he does not want to intrude upon the Roman Christians. The Roman communities had not acknowledged his authority, and Paul exercises deliberate reserve in addressing them. His approach remains tactful and diplomatic. He assures his readers that he is confident of their faith and ability to instruct each other and that he writes only as a reminder (Rom. 15:14-15). He concedes that he has written boldly on some points, but he goes on to explain his apostolic mission and plans and to inform the church that his stay in Rome will be temporary, not permanent (Rom. 15:24).[11]

3. Although "the strong" and "the weak" of Romans 14–15 do not represent strictly defined factions and parties and their precise identity remains ambiguous, these units provide evidence of a troubled church. Paul's special exhortations are not purely hypothetical. The fact that Paul's counsel repeats and echoes the arguments of 1 Corinthians 8–10 does not imply that these principles could apply to any Christian community.[12] It seems certain that some form of Jewish piety influenced the stance of "the weak."[13] This consideration, coupled with Paul's warning to the Gentiles not to display arrogance before their Jewish Christian brothers and sisters (Rom. 11:13-21), suggests that Paul's appeals for mutual acceptance addressed actual strained relationships between the Christian communities in Rome. Paul's admonitions, then, however deliberately reserved and general, address real tensions.

4. The persistent focus on the relationship of Jews and Gentiles provides the dominant framework of this letter. Paul selects the themes of his

11. Paul's reserve and careful wording in the epistolary introduction and conclusion are rightly stressed by Dahl, 75-76.

12. Cf. R. J. Karris, "Romans 14:1–15:13 and the Occasion of Romans," in *The Romans Debate,* 84, who claims that "Rom. 14:1–15:13 is better explained as general Pauline paraenesis, which is adapted and generalized especially from Paul's discussion in 1 Cor 8-10 and is addressed to a problem that may arise in any community." E. Käsemann, *Commentary on Romans* (Grand Rapids: Wm. B. Eerdmans Publishing Co., 1980), 364, points out the uniqueness of Romans 14–15, for only here does special exhortation (chaps. 14–15) follow general exhortation (chaps. 12–13). Cf. F. Watson, "The Two Roman Congregations: Romans 14:1–15:13," in *The Romans Debate,* 203-15.

13. Cf. C. E. B. Cranfield, *A Critical and Exegetical Commentary on the Epistle to the Romans,* ICC (Edinburgh: T. & T. Clark, 1977), 2:695, who identifies the "weak" with overly scrupulous Jewish Christians who continued to struggle with a sensitive conscience and dietary regulations. He points out that many Jews opted for vegetarianism whenever kosher meat was difficult to obtain.

letter with a specific aim, i.e., the reconciliation of Jews and Gentiles in one church. The theme that anticipates and undergirds the themes of justification by faith and the righteousness of God, and that persistently dominates much of the discussion of the letter (Romans 1–4; 9–11; and 14:1–15:13), is the impartiality of God's grace.[14] Unique to Romans, Paul's focus on the fact that he makes no distinction between Jews and Gentiles is fundamental to the argument of the letter, while the social corollaries of the assertion that both Gentile and Jew have equal access to God's grace are developed in the paraenetic section of the letter.

In Romans, Paul addresses a church with real tensions and struggles. He stresses the relationship of Jews and Gentiles in one church because this is a critical issue that Paul is certain will come to a head in Jerusalem. The distinctiveness of Romans lies in the fact that it reflects Paul's intense concern for the unity of Christ's church, but does so through correlation of the integrity of his own mission and lifework with a specific historical church in Rome.

I. Roman Christianity under Nero: Romans

The early years of Nero's reign were popular and benevolent. The young emperor was under the tutelage of Seneca and Burrus during the years 54-59 C.E., and the result was a five-year period of responsible government (Tacitus, *Annals* 13.51). Romans may be assigned to this period. The letter appears to have been written from Corinth during the spring of 56, just prior to Paul's journey to Jerusalem with the collection (Rom. 15:25; Acts 20:2-3). The letter implies a Christian presence in Rome for an extended period before this, since Paul states that he had desired to visit the Christians in the city "for many years" (Rom. 15:23). The origins of Roman Christianity are buried in obscurity. It is plausible that Christianity penetrated Rome through Hellenistic Jewish Christians engaged in commerce with the great Jewish colony in Rome, given the social mobility in the Roman Empire at this time.[15] This supposition is consistent with our sources, both Chris-

14. It is the merit of J. Bassler to have demonstrated this convincingly. See *Impartiality of God* and the development of the main argument in "Divine Impartiality."

15. G. LaPiana, "Foreign Groups in Rome during the First Centuries of the Empire," *HTR* 20 (1927): 183-403, esp. 341-93.

tian and pagan, that agree that the earliest Christian presence in Rome was Jewish Christian in character.

A. Early Roman Christianity

In the preface to his *Exposition of Romans,* written ca. 375 C.E., Ambrosiaster commented on the character of early Roman Christianity:

> It is established that there were Jews living in Rome in the time of the apostles and that those Jews who had believed [in Christ] passed on to the Romans the tradition that they ought to profess Christ but keep the Law. . . . One ought not to condemn the Romans, but to praise their faith, because without seeing any of the signs or miracles, and without seeing any of the apostles, they nevertheless accepted faith in Christ, although in a Jewish manner [*ritu licet Judaico*].[16]

The period to which Ambrosiaster refers would seem to be the earliest mission to Rome. The statement that these early believers embraced a tradition that Christian confession should be supported by adherence to the provisions of the Law is intriguing because it suggests a Judaizing type of Jewish Christianity associated with the strict wing of the Jerusalem church (Acts 15:1, 5; cf. Gal. 2:3-5, 12-14; 3:1-5; 5:1-12; 6:12-16).[17] While Ambrosiaster has been judged to have a good sense of history, we know little about his sources of information. Nevertheless, his assertions are congruent with other pieces of evidence that support the Jewish character of early Roman Christianity.[18]

16. *Ad Romanos,* ed. H. J. Vogels, *CSEL* 81:1 (Vindobonae, 1961), 6. On Ambrosiaster, see A. Souter, "A Study of Ambrosiaster," in *Cambridge Texts and Studies* vii, 4 (Cambridge: Cambridge University Press, 1905); Souter, *The Earliest Latin Commentaries on the Epistles of St. Paul* (Cambridge: Cambridge University Press, 1927).

17. Tacitus, *Annals* 15.44, seems to draw a connection between Christianity in Rome and its origin in Judea. Commenting on the execution of Christ by the procurator Pontius Pilate, he states, "In spite of this temporary setback, this pernicious superstition broke out again, not only in Judea (where the mischief had originated) but even in the capital city [Rome] where all degraded and shameful practices collect and become the vogue."

18. W. Wiefel, "The Jewish Community in Ancient Rome and the Origins of Roman Christianity," in *The Romans Debate,* 85-101. Cf. F. F. Bruce, "The Romans Debate — Continued," in *The Romans Debate,* 178-82.

Evidence for a committed Jewish Christian presence in Rome as early as 49 C.E. may be found in an edict of Claudius. Luke alludes to the hardships borne by Aquila and Priscilla, who had arrived in Corinth ca. 49 or 50 "because Claudius had commanded all the Jews to leave Rome" (Acts 18:2). This edict of expulsion is known from Suetonius, who published his *Lives of the Caesars* in 120 C.E. Commenting on Claudius's acts with regard to certain foreign groups in Rome, he states without elaboration, "Judaeos impulsore Chresto adsidue tumultuante Roma expulit" (*Claudius* 25.4).[19]

The statement is ambiguous, and may be translated in either of two ways: (1) "He expelled from Rome the Jews constantly making disturbances at the instigation of Chrestus"; (2) "Since the Jews constantly make disturbances at the instigation of Chrestus, he expelled them from Rome." The first translation allows the interpretation that Claudius expelled only those responsible for the disturbances among the Jews. The second translation suggests that the entire Jewish community was affected by the edict because they had been engaged in frequent rioting. The reason for favoring the first translation is that in Rome the Jewish community was divided into a number of district synagogues.[20] In all probability the decree of expulsion was directed against the members of one or two specific synagogues, who would have been forced to leave the city until there was a guarantee of no further disturbances.

The notorious confusion displayed in the words *impulsore Chresto* suggests a contemporary police record. It is well known that Suetonius merely reproduced his sources without attempting to evaluate them carefully.[21] While *Chrestus* (signifying "good," or "useful") was a very common name among Roman slaves, it was not a common Jewish name. H. J. Leon lists over 550 names used by Jews in Rome in the first century of the common era, but *Chrestus* is not among them.[22] The garbled reference to

19. For a recent critical discussion of the decree, with bibliography, see Lane, "The Edict of Claudius," in *Hebrews 1–8*, lxiii-lxvi.

20. E. M. Smallwood, *The Jews under Roman Rule* (Leiden: Brill, 1981), 138. There were some eleven to fifteen synagogues at Rome. See Harry J. Leon, *The Jews of Ancient Rome* (Peabody, Mass.: Hendrickson, 1995 [1960]), 135-66. Dio Cassius, *History* 60.6.6, specifically denies a general expulsion of the Jews at this time.

21. H. Janne, "*Impulsore Chresto,*" in *Mélanges Bidez,* AIPHO 2 (Brussels: Secrétariat de l'Institut, 1934), 537-46.

22. Leon, 93-121.

Chrestus is almost certainly evidence for the presence of Christians within the Jewish community of Rome. The source of the disruptions in the Jewish quarters was, plausibly, the propagation of the Christian message by Hellenistic Jewish Christians, and especially their insistence that the crucified Jesus was the promised Jewish Messiah. The leadership of the Jewish communities, or some portion of it, was drawn into violent debate that soon attracted the unfavorable attention of the imperial authorities. Claudius, it would seem, issued a decree of expulsion affecting those most directly involved.

The confusion between *Chrestus* and *Christus* was natural enough. At that point in time the distinction in spelling and pronunciation was negligible. In the manuscript tradition of the New Testament the confusion is reflected in the spelling of the name "Christian" in Acts 11:26; 26:28; and 1 Peter 4:16, where the uncial codex Sinaiticus reads Χρηστιανός (i.e., *Chrestianos*). Even after the distinction was known, it was quite popular among those who were not Christians to interchange the two forms. The urge to identify the founder of the new "superstition" with a common slave name may have been difficult to resist. Several of the early apologists complain that pagans often confuse the two spellings, much to the dismay of the Christians.[23]

The date of the Claudian edict is contested. Suetonius's compositional style does not permit any conclusion regarding a date for the disturbances or for the edict of expulsion. The only firm datum is provided by the fifth-century historian Orosius (*History* 7.6.15-16), who introduces the terse statement from Suetonius with the declaration that "Josephus refers to the expulsion of the Jews by Claudius in his ninth year" (i.e., 49 C.E.). Although the extant writings of Josephus do not contain such a statement, the dating of the edict to 49 is plausible. It is precisely in the period from 47 to 52 that Claudius engaged in a campaign to restore the old Roman rites and to check the growth of foreign cults.[24]

23. Cf. Justin, *Apology* 1.4; Tertullian, *Apology* 3; Lactantius, *Divine Institutes* 4.7.

24. The date of 49 is accepted by a number of responsible scholars. Among them see A. D. Nock, "Religious Developments from the Close of the Republic to the Death of Nero," in *Cambridge Ancient History*, ed. S. A. Cook et al., vol. 10 (Cambridge: Cambridge University Press, 1934), 500; V. Scramuzza, *The Emperor Claudius* (Cambridge: Harvard University Press, 1940), 145-56, 286-87; F. F. Bruce, "Christianity under Claudius," *BJRL* 44 (1961-62): 317; D. V. Melton, "The Imperial Government and Christianity during the Principate of Claudius" (diss., University of Oklahoma, 1984),

In short, when heated disputes deteriorated into riots, Claudius banished from the city synagogue and church leaders responsible for the disruption of civil peace. The Suetonian formulation suggests that it was "mainly Christian missionaries and converts who were expelled," i.e., those Jewish Christians labeled under the name *Chrestus*.[25]

The edict of expulsion undoubtedly had social as well as religious implications for the nascent Christian movement. At least in some instances, it must have created a crisis of leadership and of mission. In the absence of centralized leadership within the Jewish community of Rome,[26] Jewish Christians appear initially to have had a measure of success in propagating their message in individual synagogues, without encountering concerted resistance. After 49 C.E., however, it is likely that they would not have been welcome at many, perhaps all, of the Roman synagogues. It is also unlikely that those who had been expelled from the city would have been able to return until the relaxation of the decree at the beginning of Nero's reign. In the interim, the basic orientation of the Christian movement changed. It became predominantly Gentile. The dynamics of this reorientation are no longer recoverable, but the evidence for it may be found in Romans, written early in Nero's principate. Paul addresses himself primarily to a Gentile constituency (Rom. 1:5-6, 13; 11:13-23; 15:15-22). There was clearly also a Jewish Christian presence

---

54-63. This date has been corroborated independently by the Gallio inscription from Delphi, which has made it possible to determine when Paul entered Corinth and made the acquaintance of Aquila and Priscilla, who had arrived "only recently" (Acts 18:1-2). On the Gallio inscription see E. M. Smallwood, *Documents Illustrating the Principate of Gaius, Claudius, and Nero* (Cambridge: Cambridge University Press, 1967), 105; cf. J. Murphy-O'Connor, *St. Paul's Corinth* (Wilmington, Del.: Glazier, 1983), 129-52, 173-76, for a different reading of the evidence.

25. So Smallwood, *The Jews under Roman Rule,* 216.

26. For a careful review of the evidence in support of the thesis that the Roman *gerusiarch* presided over only the council of an individual congregation and that there was no ethnarch in Rome, see J. B. Frey, "L'ancien Judaisme, spécialment à Rome, d'après les inscriptions juives," *Corpus Inscriptionum Judaicarum* (Rome: Vatican Press, 1936), cvi-cxi. The argument has been accepted by Leon, 167-70; by S. Applebaum, "The Organization of Jewish Communities in the Diaspora," in *The Jewish People in the First Century,* ed. S. Safrai and S. Stern (Philadelphia: Fortress, 1974), 498-501; and by P. Lampe, *Die stadtrömischen Christen in den ersten beiden Jahrhunderten. Untersuchungen zur Sozialgeschichte,* 2nd ed., WUNT 2/18 (Tübingen: Mohr, 1989), 301-45, 367-68.

in the church (cf. 16:3-5, 7, 10b, 11),[27] but it is no longer possible to identify Roman Christianity with the tradition of Jewish Christianity from which it originated.[28]

B. A Social Perspective on Romans

In a discussion of Claudius's edict, W. Wiefel argued that the Jews were forbidden public assembly even after returning to Rome in 54 C.E. He holds that this synagogue prohibition affected Jewish Christians as well and contributed to the development of house churches.[29] The argument has been accepted by Donfried, who finds in the social-political situation of the returning Jewish Christians the ground for tension between the dominant Gentile constituency of the church and the Jewish Christian remnant.[30] Concern with the development of house churches, with social tensions, and with the social dynamics of a fragmented church is integral to an assessment of the state of Roman Christianity near the beginning of Nero's rule.

27. There would be little point to the appeal for mutual acceptance, with its reference to the significance of the incarnation for both Jews and Gentiles, in Rom. 15:7-13, if both groups were not represented in the church. Moreover, the repeated reference to Jews and Gentiles having the same responsibility before God (Rom. 1:16; 2:9-11, 25-29; 3:29; 10:12) and the broad discussion of the grounds for the unbelief of the majority of Israel, including the assertion of God's continuing redemptive goal for Israel (Romans 9–11), would be incomprehensible if there were no Jewish Christians in the church at Rome.

28. For a different interpretation of the evidence, and an insistence that it is essential to bring a nuanced understanding of Jewish and Gentile Christianity, see R. E. Brown, "Roman Church near the End," 105-27; Brown, "Not Jewish Christianity and Gentile Christianity, but Types of Jewish/Gentile Christianity," *CBQ* 45 (1983): 74-79.

29. Wiefel, 92-96.

30. Donfried, "False Presuppositions in the Study of Romans," in *The Romans Debate,* 105: "It is easy to perceive that both the new polity involving house churches separate from the synagogue structure and a theological situation heavily dominated by the Gentile Christians who had remained in Rome were bound to be alien to the returning Jewish Christians. The likely result was tension between the two groups."

1. The Household Setting of Roman Christianity

The primary social universe in which members of Greco-Roman society lived was the household. It provided the basic economic, political, and religious social unit of Greco-Roman civilization. In Rome the household community constituted the basic unit of society. The Roman *familia,* consisting of all the persons, free or slave, under the authority of the head of the household *(paterfamilias),* provided an emotionally and existentially satisfying social setting for its individual members.[31] The early church in Rome could not exist in such a milieu without something of that environment leaving its mark upon it.

In Romans 16:3-15 Paul shows an awareness of the existence of several house churches in Rome, one of which was associated with the Jewish Christian leaders Aquila and Priscilla, who are now back in the imperial capital after the lapsing of the decree of expulsion (Rom. 16:3-5).[32] Christians in Rome during this formative period appear to have met as "household" groups in privately owned locations scattered around the capital city. They constituted a loose network of house churches, without any central facility for worship. The absence of central coordination matches the profile of the separated synagogues in Rome during this period.[33]

An impression of what such early house churches in Rome may have been like is conveyed by the remains of buildings of several stories that date to the second and third centuries, but which have been modified over the course of time. Incorporated into the walls or preserved below the floors

31. See H. O. Maier, "The Household in the Ancient World," in *The Social Setting of the Ministry as Reflected in the Writings of Hermas, Clement, and Ignatius* (Waterloo, Ont.: Wilfrid Laurier University Press, 1991), 15-28. Maier examines the traditional Greco-Roman household and goes on to examine the role of the householder and patronage in four broad areas: the mystery religions and foreign cults, the philosophical schools, the Greco-Roman associations, and the Jewish synagogue. He marshals an abundance of evidence showing that the household idea was adapted for the use of groups that extended beyond the traditional family boundaries.

32. For the other household fellowships, see Rom. 16:10b, 11b, 14, 15. It is possible that the entire rest of the list of greetings is structured in terms of households. Cf. P. Lampe, *Die stadtrömischen Christen,* 130-31, 161, and Lampe, "The Roman Christians of Romans 16," in *The Romans Debate,* 216-30, especially 229-30; H. J. Klauck, *Hausgemeinde und Hauskirche im frühen Christentum* (Stuttgart: Verlag Katholische Bibelwerk, 1981), 27-28.

33. See above, n. 26.

of at least three of the existing titular churches in Rome are the remnants of large tenement houses.[34] The ground floors appear to have been occupied by shops, and the upper levels by prosperous families. The connection of these buildings with the social world of craftsmen and artisans is suggestive in the light of reference to the church in the house of Aquila and Priscilla (Rom. 16:5), whose property must have served as workshop, residence, and meeting place. As yet there has been no excavation of common housing from the days of the early empire in Rome, but the work of J. E. Packer and A. G. McKay on the *insulae,* or apartment buildings, points to the existence of amorphous blocks of tenements, one building abutting another, that served the vast majority of people in the capital and other large cities of the Roman Empire.[35]

A typical *insula* contained a row of shops on the ground floor, facing the street, and provided living quarters for the owners and their families over the shops or in the rear. There would be space on the premises for the manufacture of goods sold in the shops, and accommodations for visiting clients, workers, servants, or slaves. The arrangement brought together a considerable cross section of a major group in society, consisting of manual workers and tradespeople. Such households were part of an intricate social network made up of other households to which they were tied by kinship, friendship, professional advantage, and other considerations. The strategy of situating the church in the home was sound, for it provided Christians with relative privacy, a setting where identity and intimacy could be experienced, a ready-made audience as well as a social network along which the influence of the Christian movement could spread.[36] The conversion of households with their dependents helps to account for the growth of Roman Christianity.

34. See J. M. Peterson, "House-Churches in Rome," *VC* 23 (1969): 264-72; Peterson, "Some Titular Churches at Rome with Traditional New Testament Connexions," *ExpT* 84 (1973): 277-79. Cf. R. Jewett, "Tenement Churches and Communal Meals in the Early Church," *BR* 38 (1993): 24-43.

35. J. E. Packer, "Housing and Population in Imperial Ostia and Rome," *JRS* 57 (1967): 280-95; A. G. McKay, *Houses, Villas, and Palaces in the Roman World* (London: Thames & Hudson, 1975), esp. 213-14; B. Frier, *Landlords and Tenants in Imperial Rome* (Princeton: Princeton University Press, 1980).

36. See W. A. Meeks, *The First Urban Christians: The Social World of the Apostle Paul* (New Haven: Yale University Press, 1983), 29-31, 75-77; L. M. White, "Adolf Harnack and the Expansion of Christianity: A Reappraisal of Social History," *Second Century* 5 (1985-86): 97-127.

The number of house churches in a given locale such as Rome is a topic for debate. Klauck, for example, contending for a plurality of meeting places, argues that the preposition κατά in the Greek phrase κατ' οἶκον ἐκκλησίαν in Romans 16:5 (1 Cor. 16:19; Philem. 2) should be understood distributively, i.e., "the church which constitutes itself as a household."[37] M. Gielen, appealing to contemporary papyrological evidence as well as to the fact that the formula occurs in the context of a greeting, argues that the preposition should be interpreted simply as ἐν, i.e., "the church *in* the house of X."[38] Gielen is correct to point to some form of common meeting in Corinth on the basis of Romans 16:23, where Paul refers to Gaius as "the host to the whole church." But she fails to account successfully for the greetings in Romans 16:14-15, where separate groups seem to be indicated. There may well have been meetings of the whole community in some places, such as Corinth, but in other places this may not have been the case. There is no evidence for a common meeting in Rome.[39]

2. Wealth, Patronage, and the House Church[40]

There is an abundance of evidence from antiquity that patronage and leadership went hand in hand, especially when a member's generosity extended to the gift of his home for communal use. To cite only two instances, inscriptional evidence recovered from the house synagogues at Dura-Europos and at Stobi demonstrates that this was true in the Diaspora Jewish community. Epigraphic evidence from the third-century-C.E. Dura synagogue shows that the owner of the house, Samuel ben Yeda'ya, funded and supervised the conversion of his private home into a synagogue complex. The designation of Samuel as elder (πρεσβύτερος) and ruler (ἄρχων) probably indicates that he was the highest authority in the community. C. H. Kraeling, who published the evidence, argues that

37. Klauck, 21.

38. Gielen, "Zur Interpretation der paulinischen Formel ἡ κατ' οἶκον ἐκκλησία," *ZNW* 77 (1986): 109-25; cf. N. Afanassieff, "L'assemblée eucharistique unique dans l'Église ancienne," *Kleronomia* 6 (1974): 1-34.

39. Following Maier, *Social Setting*, 34.

40. Cf. J. H. Elliott, "Patronage and Clientism in Early Christian Society — A Short Reading Guide," *Forum* 3 (1987): 39-48.

Samuel continued to live in the domestic quarters of the enlarged complex.[41] At Stobi in Macedonia, in the second century C.E., Tiberius Polycharmus, who is designated "father of the synagogue," converted his villa into a household synagogue containing a prayer hall, a dining room, and a portico, reserving for himself and his successors the right to reside in the upper story of the complex.[42] In both instances, wealth and patronage were determining factors in leadership.

This was undoubtedly true for the church in Rome as well. In Romans, Paul acknowledges his own dependence upon patronage in Corinth (16:23) and Cenchreae (16:2).[43] Romans also provides evidence that leadership in Rome was a function of wealth and patronage. G. Theissen has identified four criteria for assessing the degree of wealth of individuals mentioned by Paul: (1) engagement in civil or religious office; (2) possession of a house; (3) service to Paul or the church or both; (4) ability to undertake a journey on behalf of the church.[44] To judge from Paul's commendation of Aquila and Priscilla in Romans 16:3-5 and incidental references in Acts (18:1-3, 18, 24-27), they, at least, satisfy all four criteria. Wealth and patronage were almost certainly determining factors in the leadership they provided in Rome to those who looked to them as hosts and house church patrons. This would presumably also be true of the leadership of the other house churches acknowledged in Paul's greetings in Romans 16.

We may conclude that in Rome the host who possessed the resources and initiative to invite the church into his or her home assumed major leadership responsibilities deriving from the patronage offered. These included important administrative tasks, such as the provision of the common meals of the community, the extension of hospitality to traveling

41. C. H. Kraeling, "The Synagogue," *Final Report VIII, Part I of the Excavation at Dura Europas,* ed. A. R. Bellinger,. F. E. Brown, A. Perking, and C. B. Welles (New Haven: Yale University Press, 1956), 11, 263-64, 331-32.

42. *CII* I, 694. See M. Hengel, "Die synagogen Inschrift von Stobi," *ZNW* 57 (1966): 148-83.

43. For προστάτις in Rom. 16:2 as *patrona,* see R. A. Kearsley, "Women in Public Life in the Roman East: Iunia, Theodora, Claudia, Metrodora and Phoebe, Benefactress of Paul," *Ancient Society: Resources for Teachers* 15 (1985): 124-30.

44. G. Theissen, *The Social Setting of Pauline Christianity* (Edinburgh: T. & T. Clark, 1982), 73-74. He notes that the last two criteria of themselves do not indicate wealth.

missionaries and other Christians, the representation of the community outside the domestic setting, in addition to pastoral oversight and governance. In this connection it is important to note Paul's usage of the term to refer to the person who gives aid to the congregation (ὁ προϊστάμενος) in Romans 12:8, where the context refers to the extension of material help. The term carries connotations both of patronage and leadership.[45] A plausible inference is that those who acted as patrons were in some sense also involved in governance of the community. A position of authority emerged out of the benefits that individuals of relatively higher wealth and social status could confer upon the community.[46]

How did such leaders arise? Certainly in Rome they did not owe their position to apostolic appointment, a point of some significance in the light of the later argument of *1 Clement* 42.4 and 44.2, where the first leadership of the church in Corinth is traced to appointment by Paul. In Rome, leadership was almost certainly derivative from patronage and service, as well as from the interaction between willing individuals and recognition by the wider community.[47] That said, it is important to observe the significance of the commendatory greetings in Romans 16. Paul's formulation amounts to a recommendation of certain individuals as leaders within the several Christian communities of Rome who gain their "legitimacy" from recognition by the apostle. Household leadership had emerged "from below" in the several communities in Rome, but the effect of Romans is to legitimate it "from above" by the apostle.[48]

45. See Meeks, 234 n. 75, for discussion and literature. The term in Rom. 12:8 occurs in a triad indicating the charisma of extending material help. Meeks (135) translates the triad ὁ μεταδιδούς . . . ὁ προϊστάμενος . . . ὁ ἐλεῶν as "the donor," "the patron," and "the one who shows mercy." See, however, the translation of the term in the NIV: "if it is leadership, let him govern diligently." For connotations of leadership, see 1 Thess. 5:12.

46. So Maier, *Social Setting,* 37.

47. Cf. B. Holmberg, *Paul and Power: The Structure of Authority in the Primitive Church as Reflected in the Pauline Epistles* (Lund: Gleerup, 1980), 106-9.

48. Cf. F. Laub, "Paulus als Gemeindegründer (I Thess.)," in *Kirche im Werden,* ed. J. Heinz (München: Beck, 1976), 34-35, who speaks of "eine originäare Unter und Überordnung." On the commendatory character and function of the greetings in Romans 16, see especially Gamble, 92.

3. Church Structure and Social Tensions

The fact that the church in Rome was organized structurally and socially as household units helps to explain the tensions between "the strong" and "the weak" that Paul addresses in Romans 14:1–15:13. The early house churches must have drawn whatever organizational structure they had primarily from the Hellenistic synagogues and extended family structures of the Greco-Roman households. They may also have borrowed patterns of structure from trade guilds or other voluntary associations formed by special interest groups. The impression conveyed by Paul's greetings in Romans 16:3-15 is of a number of small household fellowships not in close relationship with one another. It would have been natural for Jewish and Gentile Christians to have met in separate households for their common meal or Eucharist. One of the purposes of Paul's greetings may have been to reinforce a sense of unity at a time when the several house churches enjoyed little interrelationship with one another.

Ignatius and Hermas provide evidence that even in the first decades of the second century Rome was not centrally organized under the administrative authority of a single bishop. In six of his seven letters, Ignatius insists on the importance of the office of bishop. His silence in regard to this pastoral concern in the *Letter to the Romans* (ca. 110 C.E.) is explained best by the absence of a monarchical bishop in Rome. Hermas refers only to "the elders who preside over the church" (*Herm. Vis.* 2.43; 3.9.7). The existence of several house churches only loosely connected with one another throughout Rome suggests why diversity, disunity, and a tendency toward independence were persistent problems in the early history of the Christian communities in Rome.

C. Conclusions

The conclusions reached in the discussion of early Roman Christianity may be summarized as follows: (1) The earliest Christian presence in Rome was rooted in Judaism. The primary focus of its mission was the Diaspora Jewish community in the capital, organized in terms of district synagogues. In the absence of centralized Jewish leadership, there had been initial success in propagating the Christian message. Claudius's edict of expulsion in 49 C.E. caused disruption and created a crisis in leadership and mission for the early church. By the time Paul wrote Romans there had been a significant influx of Gentiles to Christianity, and the balance of power had shifted to Gentile leadership. (2) At the beginning of Nero's reign Jewish Christians returned to a church that had become predominantly Gentile. The reorientation of the church's leadership and mission led to mutual resentment and suspicion. Paul addressed a troubled community struggling with an alienated constituency of Jews and Gentiles. (3) The Greco-Roman household played a central role in the establishment, growth, and leadership of the early Christian communities in Rome. This is reflected in the fact that Roman Christianity was organized in terms of households, following a pattern rooted in Greco-Roman society and emulated by social groups that extended beyond the boundaries of the traditional family. (4) The church meeting in households provides the social setting for development of leadership structures in the early Roman Christian communities. Paul recognized leadership by house church hosts. They were the wealthiest members of the church who took the initiative to offer their houses and patronage to groups of Christians. There is an integral relationship between patronage and leadership. He also recognized seniority of experience and service to the community as the ground for leadership. (5) The organization of the mission of the church around the households of relatively wealthy patrons contributed to its success, but also reinforced a tendency to fragmentation and dissension. (6) One of the purposes of Romans was to urge reconciliation between alienated constituencies of Jews and Gentiles, and to reinforce unity in a fragmented church denied the privilege of common worship.

II. Roman Christianity under Nero: Hebrews

By 59 C.E. Nero had tired of restraint. He had Agrippina murdered and increasingly marginalized his two key advisers. The death of Burrus and the retirement of Seneca in 62 left him uncontrolled. His extravagance, vanity, and jealous fear of eminence, coupled with a sense of imperial power, led to a recklessly irresponsible neglect of administration and a series of judicial murders that alienated the Roman nobility, the army, and the people. When a devastating fire swept through ten of the fourteen districts of Rome in July of 64, and it was rumored that Nero had instigated the fire, he initiated repressive measures against the Christians in the city (Tacitus, *Annals* 15.44).[49] By June of 68, when Nero committed suicide, he had been deserted by the Praetorians and was hated by all classes in Rome. Hebrews belongs to the lower end of this turbulent period.

A. Hebrews and Rome

Proposals for the social location of the community addressed in Hebrews have ranged from Jerusalem in the East to Spain in the West. I hold that the intended audience is to be located in or near Rome. The ambiguity in the formulation "Those from Italy greet you" (Heb. 13:24) is well known. The fact remains, nevertheless, that in the sole parallel to ἀπὸ τῆς Ἰταλίας provided by the NT the phrase clearly means "from Italy" in the sense of outside the Italian peninsula (Acts 18:2). In Acts 18:2 "Italy" denotes "Rome." This may be the most natural way of reading Hebrews 13:24 as well. In the closing lines of Hebrews, the writer conveys to members of a house church in or near Rome the greetings of Italian Christians who are currently away from their homeland.[50]

The following evidence may be cited in support of this critical judgment. (1) The allusions to the generosity of the audience in supporting other Christians in Hebrews 6:10-11 and 10:33-34 agree with the early history of Christianity in Rome as known from other sources (cf. Ignatius, *Romans,* Salutation; Dionysius of Corinth [cited by Eusebius, *Church History* 4.23.10]). (2) The description of the early sufferings endured by the audience in Hebrews 10:32-34 is congruent with the experience of those who were impacted by the Claudian decree of expulsion in 49 C.E. Insult, public abuse, and especially the loss of property were normal under the conditions of an edict of expulsion. (3) The designation of the leadership of the community in Hebrews 13:7, 17, 24 as ἡγούμενοι points toward Rome. Subsequent to Hebrews the use of this collective term, or the com-

49. Cf. H. Fuchs, "Tacitus über die Christen," *VC* 4 (1956): 65-93; M. Dibelius, "Rom. und die Christen im ersten Jahrhundert," in *Botschaft und Geschichte,* 2 vols. (Tübingen: Mohr, 1956), 2:177-228; J. Beaujue, "L'incendie de Rome en 64 et les Chrétiens," *Latomus* 19 (1960): 65-80, 291-311.

50. So A. Harnack, "Probabilia über die Adresse und den Verfasser der Hebräerbriefs," *ZNW* 1 (1900): 16-41; E. F. Scott, "The Epistle to the Hebrews and Roman Christianity," *HTR* 13 (1930): 205-19; F. F. Bruce, "'To the Hebrews': A Document of Roman Christianity?" *ANRW* 25.4 (1987), 3513-19; among others.

pound προηγούμενοι, "chief leaders," to designate holders of community office appears to be confined to documents associated with the church in Rome (e.g., *1 Clem.* 1.23; 21.6; 37.2; *Herm. Vis.* 2.2.6; 3.9.7). (4) Hebrews was first known and used in Rome. *1 Clement* provides indisputable evidence of the circulation of Hebrews among the churches of Rome. Not only are there striking parallels to the form and statement of Hebrews throughout *1 Clement,* but Clement is literally dependent upon Hebrews in *1 Clement* 36.1-6.[51]

There is, of course, a considerable risk in assigning so definite a social location to the community addressed in Hebrews in the absence of firm evidence from the text or in early Christian tradition. The construction is one that can never be proven, yet it gives a concreteness to Hebrews that other hypotheses lack, and it affords a plausible framework for the document. What is gained in exchange for the risk is a sense of social context for the statement in Hebrews that can be tested exegetically. If the supporting detail is deemed sufficient for locating the group addressed in or near Rome, then what is known of the Jewish community and of the early house churches in Rome can be invoked in seeking to reconstruct some of the religious and social dynamics that impinged upon the life of the audience. For the purposes of this essay, Hebrews will be regarded as an independent and informed witness to developments in Roman Christianity over the course of a decade or so following Romans.

A brief sketch of my understanding of Hebrews may be helpful. The communication in Hebrews was prepared for a specific local group, who are distinguished from their leaders and from others with whom they constitute a Christian presence in the urban setting (Heb. 13:17, 24). The intended audience was almost certainly a house church, one of several scattered throughout the districts and sections of the city. The social and religious roots of this community are almost certainly to be traced to the Jewish quarters and to participation in the life of a Hellenistic synagogue. Their theological vocabulary and conceptions were informed by the rich legacy of Hellenistic Judaism.

From the beginning, sufferings had been a constituent part of their

51. See especially D. A. Hagner, *The Use of the Old and New Testaments in Clement of Rome* (Leiden: Brill, 1973), 179-95; G. L. Cockerill, "Heb 1:1-14; *1 Clem.* 36:1-6 and the High Priest Title," *JBL* 97 (1978): 437-40; P. Ellingworth, "Hebrews and 1 Clement: Literary Dependence or Common Tradition?" *BZ* 23 (1979): 262-69.

Christian experience. Shortly after coming to faith they had endured public abuse, imprisonment, and loss of property (Heb. 10:32-34). The description of the sufferings endured is appropriate to the hardships borne by the Jewish Christians when they were expelled from Rome by the emperor Claudius in 49 C.E. In the case of the Jewish Christian leaders Aquila and Priscilla, the decree had meant banishment from Rome and almost certainly the loss of property. Sporadic persecution of those who remained exposed others in the same community to humiliation, imprisonment, and deprivation.

Hebrews, of course, addresses the community at a later point in time (5:12). A new crisis has emerged, confronting the members of the house church with the threat of a fresh experience of suffering. Reference to enslavement through the fear of death (2:15), to loss of heart (12:3), and to the fact that the audience had *not yet* contended to the point of bloodshed (12:4), climaxing a section summarizing the experience of men and women of faith who endured torture, flogging, banishment, chains, and execution (11:35–12:3), suggests that the situation now facing the community is more serious than the earlier one under Claudius. It is not unreasonable to think of the sufferings endured by Christians in Rome under Nero (Tacitus, *Annals* 15.44).

Hebrews appears to be addressed to the members of a house church that had not yet borne the brunt of the persecution. Nevertheless, the targeted audience was an assembly in crisis. There had been defections from their number (10:25), and among those who remained, a loss of confidence in the viability of their convictions. The cumulative weight of this evidence indicates a crisis of faith and a failure of nerve. It is reasonable to assign a date for the composition of Hebrews tentatively to the insecure interval between the aftermath of the great fire of Rome in 64 C.E. and Nero's suicide in June of 68.[52]

B. A Social Perspective on Hebrews

The social setting of the community addressed in Hebrews is in view both in the expository and paraenetic sections of the homily. It is evoked in the

52. For supporting detail, with bibliography, see Lane, *Hebrews 1–8*, liii-lxvi; Lane, *Hebrews 9–13*, WBC 47B (Dallas: Word, 1991), 298-301, 415-19.

description of the church as the household of God (Heb. 3:6; 10:21), and it stands behind the writer's pastoral concern to mitigate tensions between the members of the assembly and their current leadership (13:17-18). It is integral to the writer's strategy to reinforce the social connection between the alienated members of the group he addressed and other Christian communities in the city (13:24). These cursory observations demonstrate the importance of bringing a social perspective to Hebrews. A social-historical approach to a document cannot generate new data. It can encourage a fresh angle of vision and generate new questions to be addressed to the text.

1. The Household Setting of Roman Christianity

There is every reason to believe that Christians continued to meet as household fellowships in privately owned homes scattered around the imperial capital a decade after Romans. The community addressed in Hebrews is clearly distinguished from their leaders and from others who constituted the church in Rome (Heb. 13:24a, "Greet all your leaders and all the saints"). They are undoubtedly a relatively small congregation, their numbers having been depleted through defections (10:25). The social setting for communal identity and life remains the extended household dependent upon the generosity of one or more individuals who host the church in the house or the tenement.

It is striking that in Hebrews the primary image for the church is "the household of God" (3:6; 10:21). The context identifies God's household as the community of faith, who maintain their Christian confidence and hope (3:6b; 10:22-25). The reference is clearly to the church, and more specifically to the community addressed. Corresponding to the image of the church as a household is the presentation of Christ as "the householder" who has been appointed by God to preside over his house (3:1-6a; 10:21). The extension of protection, the exercise of administrative responsibility, and the provision of supervision and nurture are his responsibility, analogous to the role of the head of the household in Greco-Roman society. The writer's description of the church as "the household of God" may be intentional in its implied reference to the gathering of the house church. The language gains a dimension of depth when heard in the context of the household as the basic social unit in Rome. The appeal for unwavering fidelity to Christ in Hebrews draws upon the array of social expectations that was present whenever a group met in an individual's house or was dependent upon the benefactions of the householder.

The household as the setting for Roman Christianity in this period is presupposed in the catechetical precepts of Hebrews 13:1-6. This unit conveys an essential message concerning Christian life as the worship of God (12:28) in the context of shared communal life. The social setting for the expression of fraternal love (13:1); for the extension of hospitality to itinerant teachers, missionaries, emissaries, and refugees from persecution (13:2); and for the display of compassionate concern for prisoners and others who have suffered from abusive treatment (13:3) is clearly the household. Respect for marriage and for sexual responsibility (13:4) and the cultivation of a contentment grounded in the pledge of God's constant presence (13:5-6) are intrinsic to the ethos of a Christian household. In short, all of the catechetical precepts in 13:1-6 are functions of the household setting of early Roman Christianity.[53]

2. *Structures of Leadership*

Hebrews may shed some light on the structures of leadership in the Christian communities of Rome at this time. The writer applies the term ἡγούμενοι collectively to the leadership of the church (13:7, 17, 24). The term is not technical but broadly descriptive of the role that certain persons played in the life of the community from its formative period. The term appears to have originated linguistically in official and administrative language. In a series of papyri, for example, high state officials are designated this way.[54] The term is not reserved for a specified official position or administrative task but designates a person entrusted with responsibility for leadership, who on the ground of the official position receives authority.[55]

53. See further Lane, *Hebrews 9–13*, 509-21.

54. See F. Laub, "Verkündigung und Gemeindeamt: Die Autorität der ἡγούμενοι Hebr 13, 7.17.24," *SNTU* 6-7 (1981-82): 183-84.

55. Laub, "Verkündigung und Gemeindeamt," 189-90. In the LXX, the form is used typically of political and official leaders (e.g., Deut. 1:3; Ezek. 43:7; Sir. 17:17; 30:27; 41:17; 1 Macc. 9:30; 2 Macc. 14:16).

According to Hebrews 13:7, the function of the "leaders" consisted in preaching the word of God. From this fact they may be characterized as charismatically endowed leaders whose authority derived exclusively from the word they proclaimed and whose precedence was promoted by preaching alone.[56] No other grounding and safeguarding of the position of the leaders is provided than the authority that results from the word proclaimed. The "former leaders" of the community are now deceased. As those who "spoke the word of God," their preaching belongs to the community's past. It is probable that the community was gathered in response to the word they proclaimed. It was on the ground of their preaching that the missionaries were elevated to leadership roles.[57] They were thus the original leaders or founding fathers of the community. Although deceased, they retain authority for the community because one can refer to their faith, which was validated by the solid accomplishment of their lives (13:7b).

The reference to these former leaders is intriguing precisely because it implies an authority structure based on charisma rather than patronage. There is insufficient data to determine the relationship of charismatic leadership to leadership functions derived from the role of patron and house church host, but the question is an important one. The writer's formulation in 13:7 implies a plurality of leaders from the earliest days of the community addressed.

A pastoral concern with structures of communal leadership is sustained in 13:17-18, where the writer draws attention to the current leaders of the community. The clear interest in strengthening a respect for the authority of the current leaders in 13:17 is a consequence of the theology of the word that undergirds 13:7. The members of the house church are admonished to obedience and submission to the authority of the leading men of the community. The distinctive vocabulary selected by the writer is instructive. Normally in the NT the verb ὑποτάσσεσθαι (to subject oneself, to obey) is used to call Christians to the acknowledgment of constituted ordinances and authorities (e.g., Rom. 13:1-7; 1 Cor. 14:33-36; Eph. 5:22–6:9; Col. 3:18–4:1; 1 Pet. 2:13-17; 2:18–3:7). The writer, however, defines the obligatory conduct of his audience with the verb πείθεσθαι (to be persuaded, to obey). This verb

56. Cf. O. Michel, *Der Brief an die Hebräer,* 13th ed., MeyerK 13 (Göttingen: Vandenhoeck & Ruprecht, 1975), 488-529; Laub, "Verkündigung und Gemeindeamt," 169, 171-73, 189.

57. So Laub, "Verkündigung und Gemeindeamt," 171-77.

certainly demands obedience. But the specific quality of the obedience for which it asks is not primarily derived from a respect for constituted structures of authority. It is rather the obedience that is won through persuasive conversation and that follows from it.[58]

The writer carries his injunction a step further with the second verb, ὑπείκειν (to submit to someone's authority). Although the verb occurs only here in the NT, it is used frequently in secular Greek in the sense of submission to a person of authority.[59] The community is summoned to respect the authority with which the leadership has been invested by God.

The motivation for submitting to the authority of the leaders is provided in Hebrews 13:17b. It is grounded in the quality of the leaders' response to the charge to watch for the welfare of the congregation. The members of the house church owe obedience and submission since the leaders "keep watch for your eternal life as those who intend to give an account." The clause offers a commendation, and legitimization, of the leaders as men with divinely given pastoral authority and responsibility. God has entrusted to their care the other members of the community. The leaders function as watchmen for the community, knowing that in the eschatological judgment they intend to give an accounting to God.

The implication is that they have been charismatically endowed with the gift of discernment and were prepared to exercise this gift in the service of the church. The legitimation for their authority is grounded in their responsibility before God in the final judgment. Leadership of the house churches was a form of service worthy of honor. Charismatic leaders should be shown the deference that their leadership plainly deserved.

There is no reference in Hebrews to a hierarchical structure of the community and of jurisdiction.[60] The authority of the leaders is not offi-

58. Laub, "Verkündigung und Gemeindeamt," 179-80, who points out that πείθεσθαι in the sense of obey is used in conjunction with persons of authority comparatively rarely: 4 Macc. 6:4; 8:17, 26; 10:13; 12:4-5; 15:10; cf. James 3:3.

59. Cf. 4 Macc. 6:35; Philo, *On the Special Laws* 2.232; *Moses* 1.156; *On the Sacrifices of Cain and Abel* 105. A cognate term ἑκτικῶς, which denotes a "habitual readiness" to comply, is used in describing military subordination in *1 Clement* 37.2.

60. As urged by C. Spicq, *L'Épitre aux Hébreux,* 2 vols., EBib (Paris: Gabalda, 1952-53), 2:431; H. Zimmerman, *Das Bekenntnis der Hoffnung: Tradition und Redaktion im Hebräerbrief,* BBB 47 (Cologne/Bonn: Hanstein, 1977), 12-13; G. Buchanan, *To the Hebrews,* AB 36 (Garden City: Doubleday, 1972), 238: the accounting must be given not merely to God but "to their superior officers"!

cially bestowed but derives directly from the authority inherent in the word of preaching and in the exercise of charismatic gifting on behalf of the community.[61] The fact that the writer feels obliged to call for obedience and submission to the current leaders suggests that local authority structures were relatively fluid at this time.

It is difficult, if not impossible, to determine the precise relationship that the writer enjoyed with the members of the house church. Certainly the purpose clause in 13:19, "so that I might be restored to you sooner," implies that he had been with them previously and knows these Christians personally. In 13:18 he groups himself with the "leaders" to whom the community owed obedience and submission. He is persuaded that his sphere of leadership extended to the men and women for whom he expressed such ardent concern. The suggestion that the writer actually belonged to the church addressed, and that he wrote at the instigation of the other leaders, who appealed to him "as a sort of elder statesman who [was] well known and respected by everyone in the church,"[62] moves beyond the warrant of the text.

3. Church Structure and Social Tensions

The household setting of Roman Christianity sheds light both on church structure and social tensions. In Hebrews 13:17-18 there is a clear intimation of a strained relationship between the community addressed and those recognized as their current leaders.[63] There is evident pastoral concern on the part of the writer of Hebrews to bring the two groups together in a social context of shared cordiality.

One consideration that alarmed the writer was the group's attraction to traditions that he regarded as conflicting with the word of God preached by their former leaders (13:7-9). This attraction appears to have been the primary source of unresolved tension between the community, in their desire to define their own identity, and the current leadership charged with communal vigilance. It would also account for the community's proneness

61. So rightly Laub, "Verkündigung und Gemeindeamt," 177-80.

62. See B. Lindars, "The Rhetorical Structure of Hebrews," *NTS* 35 (1989): 384-86.

63. For the detail, see Lane, *Hebrews 9–13*, 553-56.

to isolation, which left them without any sense of accountability to a larger network of household fellowships (13:24). Volatile social and religious factors combined to undermine the stability of the house church, making them vulnerable to fluctuations in the sociopolitical and religious climate. The writer could not allow the members of the house church to regard themselves as an autonomous society or to isolate themselves from other household groups in the city.

There is another suggestion that lies close at hand in the household setting of Roman Christianity. It is possible that a source of the tension between the audience and their current leaders was strained relationships between the householder, who as host and patron held prerogatives of social authority within the household and the house church, and those whom their writer recognizes as their current leaders on the basis of charismatic endowment and wider church recognition. To counter an inclination toward isolation on the part of the group, the writer asks them to convey his greetings "to all the saints throughout the city" (13:24a).

C. Conclusions

The conclusions reached in the discussions of early Roman Christianity near the end of Nero's reign may be summarized as follows: (1) Hebrews offers an independent and informed witness to developments in Roman Christianity subsequent to Romans. The focus on a single community in crisis provides a lens through which to view some of the social and religious dynamics that played an essential role in shaping the development of the church in Rome. In the aftermath of the great fire of 64 C.E., the church found itself in an insecure and hostile climate. The writer of Hebrews addressed a troubled community struggling with its own identity as well as a failure of nerve. (2) There continues to be a Jewish Christian presence in the church in Rome. Those addressed in Hebrews constitute an "old guard"; they had been Christians since the Claudian period, and had felt the impact of the edict of expulsion of 49 C.E. (Heb. 10:32-34). At that time a strong sense of community had characterized the congregation. By the end of Nero's reign, however, they have become a church at risk, questioning the viability of their convictions and exhibiting an attraction to traditions alien to the gospel. They have become a marginalized group in the loose network of Christian communities in Rome and in society at large. (3) Hebrews indicates that the household setting of Roman Christianity attested in Romans 16:3-15 at the beginning of Nero's reign persists a decade later. The community addressed is clearly distinguished from others with whom they constitute the church in Rome. The extended household, supported by the generosity of one or more individuals who host the church in the house, provides the social setting for communal identity and life. (4) Hebrews (13:7, 17, 24) sheds light on structures of leadership in Roman communities based not on patronage but on charismatic endowment and service to the congregation. At this relatively early period, it is implied that local authority structures were relatively fluid. There is no evidence in Hebrews for a hierarchical structure of community and jurisdiction. The authority of local leaders was not officially bestowed but derived directly from the authority of the word proclaimed and from the exercise of charismatic gifting on behalf of the community. Hebrews implies a plurality of leaders in each of the communities. (5) A household setting for Roman Christianity continued to be a contributing factor in the fragmentation of the church. The community addressed in Hebrews appears to have been alienated from their current leaders (13:17-18) and exhibited an inclination toward isolation from other Christian fellowships in the city. A potential for strained relationships existed in the tension between the householder, who as host and patron held prerogatives of social authority, and those who had been recognized as leaders on the basis of charismatic endowment. (6) One of the pastoral purposes of Hebrews is to bring the members of the house church and their current leaders together in a social context of shared cordiality.

III. Roman Christianity under Nerva: *1 Clement*

In the closing years of Domitian's reign, when he had become obsessed with the thought that anyone of note was his enemy, Suetonius wrote, "his poverty made him grasping and his fears made him savage" (*Domitian* 3.2). As early as 85-86 C.E. constitutional safeguards had been swept aside as Domitian became more and more despotic. Motivated by malice, jealousy, or caprice, he carefully selected his victims and struck them down one by one. Agricola was executed in 93. Christians were eligible for the reign of terror that followed, not because they were Christians but because the emperor considered them to be a threat to his status.[64] One of the most celebrated persons to have been victimized was Domitian's cousin, the consul Titus Flavius Clemens, whose children had been named by Domitian as "heirs to the Empire." He, his wife, and others were accused of atheism, with a bias toward "living a Jewish life."[65] The formulation reflects an accusation often leveled against Christians[66] and suggests that Flavius Clemens and his wife Domitilla were Christians. It would appear that Roman Christianity had by this time penetrated the highest echelons of society, including the imperial family.[67]

The reign of terror ended only with the assassination of Domitian on 18 September 96 C.E. Relief followed with the accession of Nerva, who recalled those who had been banished and proscribed the bringing of accusations of *maiestas* on "Jewish life" (Dio Cassius, *History* 68.1.1-3). The fact that he chose to issue a series of coins to mark this act of clemency indicates that he meant this measure to be regarded seriously.[68] *1 Clement*

64. In his *Letter to Trajan,* Pliny states that many Christians had been tried for their lives in Rome during his recollection, although he could not recall the procedure followed (*Letters* 10.96). The reference must be to Domitian's reign, since Pliny was an infant in the time of Nero. On Domitian and his character see L. W. Barnard, "Clement of Rome and the Persecution of Domitian," *NTS* 10 (1963-64): 252-60.

65. Dio Cassius, *History* 67.14. This part of Dio's history is found in the abridgment of Xiphilinus, an eleventh-century monk from Constantinople.

66. Cf. *Martyrdom of Polycarp* 9; Justin, *First Apology* 1.6; 2.8; Tertullian, *Apology* 10.

67. For the detail of the argument, see Barnard, 259-60, and esp. 259 n. 4, where Barnard responds to E. M. Smallwood, "Domitian's Attitude toward the Jews and Judaism," *Classical Philology* 51 (1956): 1-13. Smallwood sought to show that Flavius Clemens and his wife were God-fearers, living on the fringe of Judaism, who adopted Jewish customs to a sufficient extent to be subject to attack from Domitian. Subsequently, P. Keresztes, "The Jews, the Christians, and Emperor Domitian," *VC* 27 (1973): 1-28, argued that Flavius Clemens, his wife, and others accused of "living a Jewish life" were proselytes to Judaism, but that there was reliable evidence that some members of the Flavian family had become Christians. The evidence and secondary literature have been reviewed more recently by M. Sordi, "Christianity and the Flavians," in *The Christians and the Roman Empire* (Norman: University of Oklahoma Press, 1986), 38-54, and esp. 43-53. She concludes that some members of the Flavian dynasty were indeed Christians, among them Flavius Clemens, his wife, and niece, as were various members of the aristocracy, in particular, Acilius Glabrio.

68. H. Mattingly, *Coins of the Roman Empire in the British Museum,* vol. 3 (Oxford: Oxford University Press, 1966), 15-19, nos. 88, 98, 105-6.

appears to belong to this general period, to which there may be a reference in the opening allusion to "the sudden and successive misfortunes and accidents that have befallen us" (*1 Clem.* 1.1).[69] The language is entirely appropriate to the agony of suspense that marked the years 93-96, and to the respite that followed immediately with the enthronement of Nerva, allowing the church in Rome to direct its attention to dissension in Corinth.

A. The Date and Occasion of *1 Clement*

The question of the date for the composition of *1 Clement* was reopened by L. L. Welborn.[70] He argued that the conventional date of 95-96 C.E. had been assigned to the document on insufficient grounds. His own investigation of the internal evidence and external attestation indicated that *1 Clement* was composed at some point between 80 and 140. He conceded that the upper limits of the range were unlikely, but he was unwilling to be more precise than this.

Primary support for the date of composition must be drawn from the document itself. The author assigns the death of Peter, Paul, and others who suffered with them to "our own times," adding that they became outstanding examples "to us" (5.1–6.1). The author's language suggests that what had taken place under Nero was common living knowledge within the Roman Christian community. Yet he makes a distinction between that earlier suffering at the time of the apostles and the present struggle to which he alludes in 7.1. He is clearly writing sometime after the Neronian period. In 44.1-5 he refers to elders who were appointed by the apostles or their successors, some of whom had died. The period envisioned is most naturally interpreted as stretching over thirty or forty years. A similar deduction may be drawn from the designation of the church at Corinth, which was founded ca. 50 C.E., as firmly established and "ancient" (ἀρχαίαν). Finally, the delegates who delivered the letter to Corinth are described as men who had lived irreproachable lives in the Roman church "from youth to old age"

69. For a careful analysis of this passage, see especially Barnard, 255-58, in dialogue with R. L. P. Milburn, "The Persecution of Domitian," *CQR* 139 (1945): 154-64, who denied that there was any allusion to persecution at Rome or "anything of the kind" in the text.

70. L. L. Welborn, "On the Date of First Clement," *BR* 24 (1984): 34-54.

(63.3). These several pieces of evidence, together with the opening allusion to "the sudden and successive misfortunes and accidents" endured by the church (1.1), support a date for the composition of *1 Clement* between the years 94-97.

The occasion for the pastoral letter from Rome to Corinth would appear to be the reception of correspondence from Corinth. A. W. Ziegler has observed that the middle voice in πεποιῆσθαι in *1 Clement* 1.1 implies that Clement had a personal concern regarding the Corinthian dispute, while the perfect tense, together with the reference to the report mentioned in 47.6, suggests that the letter had a prior history. It was preceded by some form of correspondence from Corinth.[71] Clement had begun to frame a response to the Corinthian church but was disrupted by a series of unanticipated misfortunes and accidents. Only now is he able to resume the task he had set for himself sometime before. These passages considered together provide reason to suspect that Clement was relatively well informed concerning the nature of the dispute in Corinth. He does not provide a later reader with precise information concerning the dispute precisely because the substance of it was common knowledge in the Corinthian community. It was sufficient to allude to the matter obliquely, leaving us merely with clues concerning the character of the dissension.

That leadership in Corinth should turn to Rome for counsel and support may seem extraordinary. An exchange of correspondence between the Corinthian and Roman churches may be explained by the close ties that existed between Rome and the Roman colony of Corinth.[72] The cultural proximity between Rome and Corinth at least makes it possible that there was close contact between the leadership of the two churches. It may be adduced from the relocation of Aquila and Prisca from Rome to Corinth and then back to Rome (Rom. 16:3; Acts 18:2), that there were close links between the two churches a generation prior to *1 Clement*. The fact that the church in Corinth was founded by Paul, and that Paul was identified with Roman Christianity through individuals such as

71. A. W. Ziegler, *Neue Studien zum I Clemensbrief* (Munich: Kaiser, 1958), 125-27. Ziegler argues that the voice provides an instance of a dynamic middle, in which case the verb has a meaning which implies personal interest in the matter. See BDF, sec. 317 (166).

72. For the political and cultural relationship between Rome and Corinth in the early empire, see R. van Cauwelaert, "L'intervention de l'Église de Rome à Corinthe vers l'an 96," *Revue d'Histoire Ecclésiatique* 31 (1935): 267-306.

Prisca and Aquila, may have encouraged a continuing relationship between the two Christian communities. These proposals seem to offer a better explanation for the occasion of *1 Clement* than the suggestion that *1 Clement* represents the attempt of the Roman church to expand its sphere of influence.[73]

B. The Setting for the Corinthian Dispute

The variety of the proposals concerning the character of the dispute in Corinth[74] is indicative of the difficulty of determining the precise nature of the disruption. That difficulty reflects the literary form of *1 Clement* itself: the letter has been cast in the form of a highly stylized treatise, filled with apparent digressions and conflicting accounts of those responsible for the discord. The nature of the document dictates that the text be approached differently than we would approach Paul's Corinthian correspondence, where the interpreter is provided with relatively direct polemical and descriptive statements.[75]

Methodologically, it is necessary to focus on the less indirect references concerning the Corinthian dispute and to place these into a tentative framework. Clement states that the division in the church occurred because "one or two persons" (47.6) had "removed some from the ministry which they had fulfilled blamelessly" (44.6). He also states that the apostles knew through foreknowledge that there would be strife for the title of bishop (44.1). This last assertion implies that this is the core of the problem that has erupted at Corinth. These statements allow us to infer plausibly that the dissension to which Clement refers originated from the communal life of the Corinthian church. It calls for close attention to the social setting of *1 Clement* and to the evidence of the institutionalizing forces within the Corinthian and Roman communities in the generation following Paul's death.

A house church setting helps us to understand the social context of

73. In agreement with Maier, *Social Setting,* 89, 103.

74. For a convenient summary of proposals concerning the character of the dispute in Corinth, see Maier, *Social Setting,* 87-91.

75. Ziegler, 1-8, argues that not every reference which appears to describe those who have disrupted the Corinthian community necessarily presents, nor was intended to present, an accurate account of them.

the dispute more adequately. The dispute that Clement describes as arising over the title of bishop is plausibly understood as referring to an unauthorized division within one or two of the Corinthian house churches. The action to remove "a number of persons from . . . a ministry they have fulfilled with honor and integrity" (44.6) represented a concerted move for power within a household setting that could have been initiated only by one or more persons who enjoyed a relatively high social status. It is possible that the difficulties in Corinth arose as a result of well-to-do householders asserting their rights of recognition over against those who had been recognized as presbyters. The result was the establishment of an alternative place of meeting, the departure of members of the house fellowship who were sympathetic toward those who had initiated the dispute, and, presumably, the exclusion of others who opposed them. One or more house churches had formed around relatively wealthy householders who began to hold their own celebrations,[76] and who, on the ground of the patronage extended, usurped the title of bishop. From Clement's point of view, these were unauthorized celebrations and represented a breach of divinely constituted church order. That he accurately represented the interests and beliefs of the majority of the Corinthians may be inferred from the fact that *1 Clement* so quickly gained prominence as an authoritative writing in the Corinthian community.[77]

The precise reason(s) for the dispute, or the means by which recognized presbyters had been removed from office, cannot be recovered on the basis of Clement's letter. Nevertheless, a conflict between house churches and house church patrons provides a plausible setting for the Corinthian dispute.[78] This proposal can be advanced only tentatively. It finds a measure of support, as Henry Chadwick recognized, in the importance that Clement

76. R. M. Grant concluded from *1 Clement* 40.103 and 41.2 that "Clement is arguing that Christian worship cannot be conducted in private assemblies apart from the bishops, presbyters, and deacons whom he is about to discuss." See R. M. Grant and H. H. Graham, *The Apostolic Fathers: A New Translation and Commentary,* vol. 2, *The First and Second Clement* (London: Thomas Nelson, 1965), 70. Similarly, W. K. L. Clarke, *The First Epistle of Clement to the Corinthians* (London: SPCK, 1937), 25-26, argued that *1 Clement* 40–41 refer to an appointed house church.

77. This may be inferred on the basis of Dionysius of Corinth's letter to Rome (ca. 170 C.E.), which reports that *1 Clement* continued to be read publicly in the community from time to time (Eusebius, *Church History* 4.23.11).

78. With Maier, *Social Setting,* 91-94.

places on the household virtue of hospitality (1.2; 10.7; 11.1; 12.1).[79] It is consistent with the fact that to the list of vices Clement recalls from Romans 1:29-32 he adds the sin of inhospitality (ἀφιλοξενία, 35.5). It is consonant with the wider social setting of the early church. It also explains why the dispute involved only some presbyter-bishops (44.6), since not all of the house churches were directly affected by the schism.

C. Clement's Purpose in Writing

Clement's primary purpose in writing was to resolve a particular dispute involving social conflict in the Corinthian church. His intention is advanced most clearly in 57.1-2 when he urges those who initiated the schism to repent. This interpretation is consistent with Clement's development of repentance as a recurring motif throughout the letter (7.4-7; 8.1-5; 9.1; 18.2-17; 57.1). At least part of the desired end of the pastoral letter was to bring to repentance those who, in Clement's terms, have initiated the sedition. The motivation underlying Clement's letter is to respond to a request for help in moving the parties to the dispute beyond intransigence. It is not to dominate, and still less to offend or further divide alienated groups within the Corinthian community. He hoped rather to convince the Corinthians to put an end to their dispute.

In pursuit of this end, he set for himself the task of the legitimation of an already existing church order in a particular community which had been disrupted by certain individuals. He engaged in an effort to legitimate leadership structures in the Corinthian church. His contribution must be assessed primarily on the local level. Von Campenhausen is probably correct when he suggests that Clement elaborated more precisely and systematically conclusions regarding the origins of the institutional order that were already present in the Corinthian community.[80] Even the notion that the apostles arranged for the succession of leadership after their first appointees (44.2)

79. H. Chadwick, "Justification by Faith and Hospitality," in *Studia Patristica* 4, ed. F. L. Cross, TU 79 (Berlin: Akademie, 1961), 281-85, emphasized the importance of Clement's references to hospitality as clues relative to the nature of the dispute in the Corinthian community.

80. H. F. von Campenhausen, *Ecclesiastical Authority and Spiritual Power in the Church of the First Three Centuries* (London: A. & C. Black, 1969), 91.

may have been common belief in the Corinthian church. Clement's unique contribution was his integration of what appears to have been shared convictions regarding the origins of institutional order with the community's wider beliefs.[81]

D. A Social Perspective on *1 Clement*

The nature of the dispute in Corinth and of Clement's pastoral response compels an interpreter of *1 Clement* to bring a social perspective to the document. Clues concerning the social dynamics within the gathered house churches, the shape and social setting of the ministry, and the role of social conflict in institution building, for example, call for social explanation.

Clement's attention was necessarily concentrated on Corinth. Nevertheless, his pastoral letter provides important clues concerning the state of Christianity in Rome at the end of the first century. To cite only one example, Clement complains about the report he has heard from Corinth and the threat it represents to the stability of the church (47.6-7). In 7.1 he concedes that the "same struggle," i.e., "jealousy and strife" (cf. chaps. 3–6), challenged his community in Rome. Clement knew enough about the dispute in Corinth to draw analogies with divisions in his own church. This observation provides an adequate explanation for the reference to mutual admonition in 7.1. For the purpose of this essay, *1 Clement* may be appreciated as evidence of the institutionalizing forces at work within the Corinthian and Roman communities in the generation after Paul's death. Reflections of the situation in Rome in *1 Clement* constitute evidence for the state of Roman Christianity at the end of the formative period from Nero to Nerva. This evidence will provide the basis for assessing developments in Roman Christianity following Romans, probing for lines of continuity and for discontinuities in that development.

1. The Household Setting of Roman Christianity

There are no specific references to house churches in *1 Clement.* Nevertheless, a reflection of the household setting of Roman Christianity at this time

81. So Maier, *Social Setting,* 121.

may be found in the emphasis Clement placed on the household virtue of hospitality (*1 Clem.* 1.2; 10.7; 11.1; 12.1, 3).[82] These references may be placed naturally in the general setting of the church gathered in the homes of relatively wealthy persons who provided leadership for the assembled fellowship. There is ample warrant for looking in this direction because we know from Romans and Hebrews that this was the social shape of Roman Christianity just a few decades prior to the composition of *1 Clement.* This earlier evidence may now be supplemented from the *Shepherd of Hermas,* which suggests that the house church remained an important part of the Roman scene into the early second century.

After a careful analysis of the conflicting evidence for the unity and date of *Hermas,* Maier has recently concluded that this document was composed by a single author sometime near the end of the first century.[83] It is roughly contemporaneous with *1 Clement.* He has further shown that a house church setting provides a plausible background for the more serious divisions discussed by *Hermas.*[84] The community described in *Hermas* is similar to that described in *1 Clement,* and this may also imply a similar social setting for the two documents. We have evidence in *Hermas* which suggests that the Roman church that Clement served met in the homes of wealthy Christians who acted as the community's leaders.[85]

The reference to "the church of God, living in exile in Rome" in the salutation of *1 Clement* is inclusive of all the house churches now found throughout the imperial capital. It is at least plausible to assume a social setting for the church in which Christians in Rome continued to meet in the homes of house church patrons who exercised a leadership role on the ground of the patronage extended to the assembly. A house church setting not only helps us to understand the social setting of the dispute in Corinth

82. So Chadwick, 281-82; R. E. Brown, "The Roman Church at the Beginning of the Third Christian Generation (A.D. 96 — *1 Clement*)," in *Antioch and Rome,* 173. Brown calls attention as well to the attention paid to "house order" in 1.3 and 21.5-7. These passages, however, pertain to instruction concerning relationships within the domestic setting of a home, and do not necessarily imply a reference to the household setting of the church.

83. Maier, *Social Setting,* 55-58.

84. Maier, *Social Setting,* 59-65: "Wealth and House Churches."

85. Maier, *Social Setting,* 93; W. Countryman, *The Rich Christian in the Church of the Early Empire: Contradictions and Accommodations* (New York and Toronto: Edwin Mellen, 1980), 154-55.

more fully, but it reflects the state of Roman Christianity a generation after Romans as well.

If this is a plausible description of Roman Christianity at the end of the first century, we may compare it to the one addressed by Paul some forty years earlier. What social developments can we discern? Can we reconstruct some of the changes that occurred in the Roman community after Paul's death? In the nature of the case, any proposed reconstruction may be advanced only as a possible course of development. It is necessary, nevertheless, to make an attempt to identify potential sources of social development on the basis of such evidence as we possess. It should be possible to do so in relationship to structures of leadership and to the role of social conflict in institution building.

2. Structures of Leadership

One line of inquiry is to ask about developments in the experience of the early Christian communities of Rome that encouraged the emergence of the formal body of leaders discussed by Clement. A factor that has tended to be ignored is the impact of the death of Peter and Paul, who were revered by Clement's church as martyrs (*1 Clem.* 5.1–6.1). So long as they were a felt presence in the church, they must have been regarded as the highest sources of authority, overshadowing that of the leaders of the local house churches. Their martyrdom left a void in terms of the authority they had embodied. This was recognized over fifty years ago by F. V. Filson, who pointed to the role of the house church for nurturing the Christian leadership that would be capable of filling that void: "The house church was the training ground for the Christian leaders who were to build the church after the loss of 'apostolic' guidance, and everything in such a situation favoured the emergence of the host as the most prominent member of the group."[86] Filson's observation is important for recognizing the leadership gap left with the death of the apostles as well as the role of the house church and of the house church host. It was his contention that the development of leadership structures can never be understood without reference to the

86. F. V. Filson, "The Significance of the Early House Churches," *JBL* 58 (1939): 112. Cf. H. O. Maier, "The Death of Paul and the Desire to Preserve Sect Ideals," in *Social Setting,* 112-17.

house churches and their hosts. He correctly stressed that the host of a house church was almost inevitably a person "of some education, with a fairly broad background and at least some administrative abilities,"[87] qualities that were essential to church leadership.

In the light of the impact that house church hosts had on the shape of community life while the apostles were alive, it is reasonable to suggest that the influence of such individuals as those to whom Paul extends a commendatory greeting in Romans 16 would have continued after his death. It is also reasonable to hold that those who had labored with Paul and who had been commended to the church of Rome by him (Rom. 16:3-15) would have gained in stature as persons of authority within the church, especially after the death of Peter and Paul. The near contemporary evidence of *Hermas* is that several types of authority continued to be recognized in the church at Rome near the end of the first century. There is reference, for example, to the exercise of a prophetic role in the instruction of the church (*Man.* 11.1-2, 9), and a distinction is drawn between true and false prophets. The preeminent leadership role, however, was assigned to wealthy household-owners.[88] Similarities between the description of structures of leadership in *Hermas* and in *1 Clement* permit us to assume that Clement's description of structures of leadership accurately reflects the prevailing situation in Rome.[89]

The first clue regarding the level of general institutional development in Rome at this period is provided when Clement uses a more formal terminology for church offices. A generation earlier there had been a relatively fluid use of terminology to denote functions of leadership. Paul, for example, relies on general nouns in 1 Corinthians 12:28, or on articular participles in Romans 12:8. By the end of the first century there has emerged a more standardized and precise use of terminology. Terms such as ἐπίσκοποι, πρεσβύτεροι, and διάκονοι are used by Clement with reference to distinct groups of persons whom he assumes the Corinthians will recognize as well (42.4; 44.4; 47.6; 54.2; 57.1; cf. *Herm. Vis.* 3.5.1). Clement also provides evidence that particular places have been designated for common worship (40.23; cf. 41.2). It is reasonable to infer from 40.23 that the

87. Filson, 111.

88. For a discussion of the evidence, see Maier, *Social Setting*, 59-65.

89. So correctly Maier, *Social Setting*, 140 n. 107. My discussion of the structures of leadership that follows is heavily dependent upon Maier, 103-6.

reference is to certain households where the Eucharist was celebrated. There is a relatively clear reference to a distinctly liturgical role for the presbyter-bishops in 44.4. This is a marked development in contrast to the Pauline period during which arrangements for worship appear to have been more diverse. There is in *1 Clement* no evidence that a particular place was set apart for the presbyter-bishops in the worship service itself, but the reference in *Hermas, Vision* 3.9.7 (cf. 3.1.8) suggests that by this period there was in Rome a special seating arrangement distinguishing "laity" from those who had been officially recognized as leaders.[90]

Clement allows us to infer that a distinctive group of persons had been set apart from the rest of the community and had been invested with leadership (40.23; 41.1; 42.4; 43.1; 44.3, 4, 5; 54.2; 57.1; cf. 37.3; 38.1). The fact that the title "bishop" had become an object of competition in Corinth (44.1) indicates that it was not accessible to everyone. Indicative of more highly developed organizational structures is the language of appointment (καθιστάναι, 42.4; 43.1; 44.3; 54.2; ἱδρύεσθαι, 44.5). When this vocabulary is taken in conjunction with the reference to some form of ratification by the membership of the church ("with the whole church's consent," 44.3), it seems probable that there was at this date some formal act of investiture by which authority to lead the community was conferred.

While it is likely that the presbyter-bishop who celebrated the Eucharist exercised authority over the other presbyters and deacons gathered together with him, there is no explicit evidence of a hierarchy of leadership in *1 Clement.* Similarly, there is no precise information concerning the relationship of bishops and deacons to presbyters in *1 Clement* or *Hermas.* Maier has suggested cautiously, on the basis of his studies of *Hermas,* that in Rome the "presbyters" were a group consisting of Christians with seniority in the faith from whose number overseers, and perhaps even deacons, were selected.[91] Whatever the precise relationship, it is probable that these members of the communities were distinguished, at least in some cases, by certain functions, and in all cases by the degree of deference shown to them.

It is not always possible to determine the precise nuance in the term πρεσβύτεροι. In *1 Clement* 1.3 and 21.6, for example, it is not clear whether the term connotes seniority in age or seniority in faith. Maier argues that the best way to resolve the issue is to recognize that presbyters were in fact

90. Cf. von Campenhausen, 84-85.
91. Maier, *Social Setting,* 105.

elder men. Reverence for age was a norm in Greco-Roman society; age conferred authority. In the case of the church, the length of time a person had been a Christian would also be a significant factor. Presbyters were those upon whom authority was conferred both on the ground of seniority of age and of experience in the community.[92] A measure of support for this proposal may be found in the respect accorded in 63.3 to the elder members of the Roman community who served as the emissaries to Corinth. They are commended both for their irreproachable life and their seniority in the faith. These qualities clothe them with authority. The importance attached to the criterion of seniority suggests a degree of development toward a more formal structure of leadership over the period of time between Romans and *1 Clement.*

The reference to obedience in *1 Clement* 1.3 and 21.6 indicates that certain presbyters have a distinctive leadership role. Consonant with my proposal concerning the role of household leaders in the early years of the church in Rome, these passages are suggestive of a process of development toward centralized authority which had its beginning in the appropriation of household forms for shared communal life. It seems probable that in the Roman communities not all presbyters were in a position of household church leadership. But the exhortations to obedience to communal leaders, the assignment of a liturgical function, and the evidence for a form of investiture and ratification by the church of those upon whom the mantle of leadership has been bestowed are indicative of a state of affairs in which there is a degree of separation between a group of formal leaders and the other members of the Christian community in Rome.

In short, *1 Clement* indicates that authority has become centralized and functions of leadership have become formalized in Roman Christianity in accordance with recognized norms. Clement reflects a stage of communal development toward the official structures of leadership that had their inception during Paul's lifetime. But what had remained relatively fluid in Paul's day has become a more formal division of the Christian community.

92. Maier, *Social Setting,* 117. Maier suggests that seniority in the faith was one criterion for distinguishing Christians in Pauline churches from the start, appealing to 1 Cor. 16:15 (Stephanas and his household were the first converts of Achaia) and Rom. 16:5 (Epaenetus was the first convert in Asia). When Clement states in 42.4 that the apostles appointed their first converts (ἀπαρχαί) to be bishops and deacons, there is probably a kernel of historical truth present. This is the same term used in 1 Cor. 16:15 and Rom. 16:5.

As a more highly structured group, probably led by wealthy house church patrons, the church in Rome was undoubtedly making adjustments to its societal situation.

What is distinctive of Clement is the grounding of the structures of leadership in the creative will of God. Like Paul, Clement believed that all secular authority is instituted by God (61.1; cf. Rom. 13:1-7). He felt obligated to pray for its representatives (60.4). The hierarchical secular order is a response to the creative action of God (60.1; 61.1-2). For Clement, God's action in establishing the secular order is also responsible for the structures of church order (37.1–38.3).[93] This is a motif that is only germinally present in the letters of Paul, but in Clement it has become a fundamental framework for the ordered Christian life.

3. Church Structure and Social Tensions

A household setting for Roman Christianity continues to shed light both on church structure and on social tensions at the end of the first century. There is evidence for the presence of social tension in the church of Rome during this period both in *1 Clement* and in *Hermas.* Responding to the report of dissension and disunity in the Corinthian Christian communities, Clement concedes that the church in Rome is "involved in the same struggle" (*1 Clem.* 7.1). A spirit of competition and strife (*1 Clem.* 3.2–6.4; cf. *Herm. Sim.* 8.7.4) had created a climate of social unrest in some of the Christian communities in Rome, just as it had in Corinth. The household structure of the church in Rome under the leadership of wealthy patrons would tend to promote a spirit of independence reflected in a variety of Christian cells differing from one another in varying degrees.

Hermas is more explicit concerning the state of the church in Rome at this time. A plurality of leaders govern the church (*Vis.* 2.2.6; 2.4.2-3; 3.1.8; 3.9.7; *Sim.* 9.27.2). House church patronage appears to be a central feature of the Roman community addressed in the revelations of *Hermas,* where a primary concern is the use and abuse of wealth. In particular, Hermas directs attention to certain leaders of the church who have misused their wealth to cause schism in the community (e.g., *Sim.* 9.26.2; 9.31.2-6).

93. Cf. K. Wengst, *Pax Romana and the Peace of Jesus Christ* (London: SCM, 1987), 107-13.

A correlation between financial wealth and power in the church clearly exists. For example, Hermas assumes a degree of wealth on the part of church leaders when he describes the ideal bishops as a foil to those who have been negligent (*Sim.* 8.10.3; 9.27.2). Such leaders are expected to welcome other Christians into their homes and to provide a meeting place for the worshiping community. The reference is almost certainly to various house churches and their patrons, and supports the assumption that a number of house cells met in wealthier members' homes.[94]

In statements about the abuse of leadership, Hermas refers explicitly and repeatedly to schism in the Roman church (*Vis.* 3.6.3; 3.9.2, 9-10; 3.12.3; *Sim.* 8.7.2; 8.9.4; 8.10.1-2; 9.23.2-3; 9.31.4). He utters a stern warning to the leaders and prominent members of the community concerning their disagreements (*Vis.* 3.9.2, 9-10) and identifies jealousy and a concern for status as a cause for division (*Sim.* 8.7.4). Maier correctly observes that in house churches "where wealthier elders coveted the first position, one option open to them would have been to separate themselves from the house church which did not accord them the honour they felt fitting and invite sympathetic members to worship in their own households."[95] Contemporary norms of deference and support for householders' religious stance would have placed an obligation on their dependents, such as slaves and freedmen, to separate as well. In a society where patronage was extended to groups with a view to receiving honors proportionate to the gifts bestowed, it is not difficult to imagine wealthy members of the church feeling dissatisfaction with the honors received as disproportionate to the financial support they had offered. The church meeting in the houses of wealthy patrons provides a plausible explanation of the nature of the more serious disruptions in the Roman communities addressed by Hermas.[96]

Hermas exposes the disruptive and discordant aspects of social tension. The value of *1 Clement* is that it provides a case study for the significance of social conflict for crystallizing issues and fostering institution building in the early church. Clement's intervention in the dispute at Corinth may be analyzed fruitfully from the perspective of conflict theory. The implications for the role of the conflict in Corinth in increasing group structure in the church in Rome may then be drawn.

94. Following Maier, *Social Setting*, 59-63.

95. Maier, *Social Setting*, 64.

96. With Countryman, 157-63; Maier, *Social Setting*, 61-64.

Briefly, social conflict arises from disagreements between groups and within groups; it entails a struggle over values or claims to status and power in which the aims of the conflicting parties are not only attainment of the desired values or status but the neutralizing, injuring, or elimination of their rivals.[97] But social conflict can contribute in a constructive way to institutional development by providing the catalyst for the creation of new norms for addressing the new situation, or through the fresh discovery of certain norms that were dormant before the conflict arose. The application of norms and rules in response to conflict tends to lead to the growth of new institutional structures concerned with the enforcement of the norms and rules that are created or freshly discovered as a result of social conflict.[98]

Conflict resolution does not normally occur of its own accord. It requires the intervention of a "specialist" in formulating solutions to intra-group conflicts. The "specialist" is a person with authority to determine and articulate the norms that are relevant to a discordant situation, who is capable of showing how these norms pertain to the basic values and experiences of any given group. The result is almost always increased group structure and institution building as a response to the challenge of existing social arrangements.

These observations from social conflict theory provide a different angle of vision from which to view Clement's intervention in the Corinthian dispute. Clement's role as a "specialist" in conflict resolution is administrative. When Clement presented the rejection of the authority of the deposed presbyters as a rejection of divinely established community structures (*1 Clement* 40–44), he made those structures explicit. When he indicated how the community's beliefs committed them to support for those who were leading with the consent of the church, he strengthened the normative character of those leadership structures. In *1 Clement* we are exposed to a church administrator engaged in institutional building or strengthening.

In response to social unrest Clement appeals to "the glorious and venerable rule of our tradition" and to "what is good and pleasing and acceptable in the sight of our Maker" (7.2-3). Throughout the pastoral letter

97. Cf. L. A. Coser, "Conflict: Social Aspects," in *International Encyclopedia of the Social Sciences,* ed. D. L. Sills, vol. 3 (New York: Macmillan and the Free Press, 1968), 232-36.

98. Cf. L. A. Coser, *The Functions of Social Conflict* (London: Routledge and Kegan Paul, 1965), 125-27.

he attempts to identify the norms and values of the church, to show that they are consistent with the community's tradition, and to apply them to the dispute in order to resolve the conflict in the church. In short, Clement confronts the Corinthians with a normative church order that he believes had its inception with Paul and those associated with him, but which took on greater significance after Paul's death (42.1–48.1).

The nature of the conflict focused the attention of the church on existing institutional arrangements. Clement's role as a mediator engaged in conflict resolution was to conserve what Paul and the apostles had initiated by showing how the existing structures were expressions of the church's beliefs and that the values shared by Christians implied a commitment to a church order rooted in apostolic practice and grounded ultimately in the will of God. Clement holds that all order is established by God (20.1-12; 33.2-3; cf. 61.1-2) and demands the response of obedience because of its divine origin (37.1–38.4; 40.3; 41.1, 3). This is equally true for the order of church leadership established by the apostles (40.1; 41.1; 42.2-5; 44.1-2). Subjection to leaders is from another perspective subjection to God. In this way the structures of leadership in the church were strengthened and endowed with inviolability.

A positive result of the social conflict in Corinth was the identification of the values and historical events (or the interpretation of those events) that were normative for the proper functioning of shared communal life in which each individual had his or her place (cf. 38.1–41.1). It is reasonable to assume that the argument developed by Clement reflected a shared response as much to social unrest in Rome as to social conflict in Corinth. Clement's specific contribution to institutionalization in the early church was to provide a formal legitimation of certain leadership structures that constituted the prevailing pattern in Rome and in Corinth at the close of the first century.[99]

99. On the role of social conflict in crystallizing issues in the Corinthian dispute and contributing to institutional development, see especially Maier, *Social Setting*, 110-21. On 122-35 Maier extends his social analysis to show more precisely how Clement attempted to legitimate institutional leadership in the Corinthian church. By focusing on the theme of legitimation he is able to show that *1 Clement* is a relatively unified document (124-25) and that Clement was engaged in an explication of the church's symbolic universe in order to justify and validate the institutional order to his audience and to demonstrate its normative character (126-35).

E. Roman Christianity at the Time of *1 Clement*

By way of summary, it may be helpful to pull together the several strands of evidence developed through a social analysis of *1 Clement,* and, to a lesser extent, of *Hermas,* concerning the state of Roman Christianity at the close of the first century.

1. The house church, under the leadership of its host and patron, remains an integral part of the Roman scene. The church in Rome possessed the capacity to act and express itself as an inclusive entity (*1 Clem.* Salutation; 63.3-4; 65), but it is an entity composed of a social network of cells meeting in the homes of well-to-do Christians who acted as the community's leaders. In terms of the household setting of Roman Christianity, there is basic continuity in the development of the church from Romans to *1 Clement.*

2. Authority has become centralized and functions of leadership have become formalized in Roman Christianity in response to its societal situation. This reflects institutional development fostered by the death of the apostles and those associated with the founding of the church, which left a void in leadership and structures of authority. Other factors that contributed to this development include: the persecution under Nero and the more selective assault upon persons of high rank by Domitian; the presence of social unrest; and the tendency toward independence that the household structure of Roman Christianity promoted. There is in *1 Clement* and in *Hermas* a more formal terminology for church office than is found in Romans or Hebrews. The terms "bishops," "presbyters," and "deacons" denote distinct groups of persons who have been set aside from the rest of the community through a formal act of investiture involving the consent of the church. This is a marked development from an earlier period when leadership was a function of hospitality or of charismatic endowment. In the light of the Roman reverence for age, it seems plausible that the presbyters were those upon whom authority was conferred on the ground of seniority in age and of experience in the church. It would be natural for bishops, and perhaps even deacons, to be selected from this group. Not all presbyters were in a position of house church leadership. The importance attached to the criterion of seniority indicates development toward more formal criteria for leadership in the generation following Romans.

3. There is no explicit evidence for a hierarchy of leadership in the Roman church in *1 Clement. Hermas,* however, attests a desire for status

and power on the part of certain church leaders in the Roman community. Specific reference to coveting "the first place" (πρωτεῖος, *Sim.* 8.7.4) suggests that the presbyter-bishop who celebrated the Eucharist enjoyed a higher status than the other presbyters and deacons gathered around him. By this time particular places, presumably specific household churches, have been designated for the celebration of the Eucharist in Rome, encouraging a more centralized common worship (cf. *1 Clem.* 40.2-3). A special seating arrangement distinguished ordinary worshipers from their officially recognized leaders (*Herm. Vis.* 3.9.7). These developments represent discontinuity from the more informal arrangements that prevailed a generation earlier. Social arrangements that had remained relatively fluid in Paul's day have become more formally regulated and structured by the end of the first century.

4. The correlation between wealth and power evident in the leadership structures of the Roman church reflects societal norms where patronage conferred honor or status. Presbyter-bishops were expected to welcome other Christians into their home, to provide a place of meeting for the worshiping community in their district, and to minister to the poor and oppressed. The social situation envisioned is that of a network of house churches and their patrons. Prevailing societal attitudes toward patronage and the bestowal of honor are reflected in the formal structures of leadership in the church. Those same social norms exerted a disruptive influence on certain house churches in Rome where a striving for status created social tension, dissension, and even schism.

F. Conclusions

The conclusions reached in the discussion of Roman Christianity in the time of Nerva may be summarized as follows:

1. *1 Clement* was composed sometime between the years 94-97 C.E. in response to some form of correspondence from Corinth to Rome. Clement was, therefore, relatively well informed concerning the nature of the dispute. It was unnecessary for him to repeat the details, for the substance of the dispute was common knowledge in the Corinthian community. An exchange of correspondence between the Corinthian and Roman churches at this time reflects the close ties that existed between the two churches from the days of Aquila and Priscilla. This offers a better explanation for

the occasion of *1 Clement* than the proposal that the letter represents an attempt by the church in Rome to expand its sphere of influence.

2. Vying for the title of bishop was at the center of the dispute at Corinth. A house church setting sheds light on the situation; relatively wealthy patrons of the church asserted their rights of recognition over against some of those who had been officially recognized as presbyters. The action of removing from office persons who had been formally invested with authority constituted a concerted move for power within a household setting by one or more persons of relatively high social status. Conflict between house churches and house church patrons provides a plausible setting for the Corinthian dispute.

3. Clement's purpose in writing was to resolve the dispute and to legitimate an already existing form of church order. It was not to dominate, but rather to mediate between alienated communities within the church at Corinth. His unique contribution was the integration of shared convictions concerning the origins of institutional order with the church's wider beliefs.

4. A social perspective on *1 Clement* permits an interpreter to address a number of issues calling for social explanation. Although addressed to the issue of dissension in Corinth, *1 Clement* reflects the shape and social setting of the church and its structures of leadership in Rome. Its witness may be supplemented by the detail of *Hermas,* which was composed by a single author sometime near the end of the first century. The Roman community described in *Hermas* is similar to that described in *1 Clement,* and this implies a similar social setting for the two documents.

5. Evidence from *Hermas* suggests that the church in Rome that Clement served continued to meet in the homes of wealthy Christians who served as the community's leaders. A house church setting provides a plausible background for the social unrest acknowledged by Clement and for the more serious abuses of leadership exposed by *Hermas.*

6. Similarities between the description of the structures of leadership in *Hermas* and in *1 Clement* permit us to assume that Clement's discussion of the structures of leadership accurately reflects the prevailing pattern in Rome. Institutional development over the course of a generation may be recognized in the emergence of standardized and precise terminology for church office, in the designation of particular places for the celebration of the Eucharist, in the assignment of a distinctly liturgical role for the presbyter-bishop, in the arrangement of seating to distinguish leaders from the rest of the assembly, and in the conferral of authority through some formal

act of investiture. All of these aspects of shared communal life in Rome at the end of the first century reflect a more highly developed organizational structure than that which prevailed only a generation earlier. The degree of separation between a group of formal leaders and the other members of the church in Rome indicates a process of development toward centralized authority which had its inception in the appropriation of household forms for church life.

7. Clement grounds the formal structures of leadership in the creative will of God which stands behind all order. Consequently, submission to constituted leaders is ultimately subjection to God. For Clement, this is the fundamental frame of reference for resolving conflict over status and for appropriating the well-ordered Christian life.

8. Clement's intervention in the dispute at Corinth may be analyzed fruitfully from the perspective of conflict theory. Social conflict in the form of striving for status is invariably disruptive, but there is a constructive aspect as well. Social conflict serves to crystallize issues and to reinforce or create norms in response to threatened existing social arrangements. Clement's role in the dispute was essentially administrative; he functioned as a specialist in conflict resolution. His strategy was to make explicit the ground of the authority of the deposed presbyters in divinely established community structures, and so to strengthen the normative character of the structures of leadership within the church. By identifying the values and historical events that were normative for the proper functioning of ordered church life, Clement underscored that the church was committed to support the deposed elders. His special contribution to the institutionalization of the early church was to provide a formal legitimation of certain leadership structures that prevailed at Rome and in Corinth at the end of the first century.

CHAPTER 10

From Obscurity to Prominence: The Development of the Roman Church between Romans and *1 Clement*

Chrys C. Caragounis

I. Introduction: The Subject and Its Problems

This paper will be concerned with developments in Roman Christianity during the last forty years of the first century C.E. Its aim will be to examine critically the evidence bearing on the state of Roman Christianity in order to ascertain the continuities as well as the discontinuities in its development. The beginning and end boundaries of this period are set by Paul's letter to the Romans and Clement's first epistle to the Corinthians, respectively. These two letters happen to be the most important Christian evidence on the state of Roman Christianity during this period. For the *terminus a quo* the evidence of Romans may be supplemented by the notices in Acts and Philippians, while for the *terminus ad quem* the evidence of *1 Clement* may be augmented (with care) by reference to other (later) early Christian literature (e.g., Ignatius, Hermas, Eusebius). Of relevance also is such extrabiblical material as is to be found in (principally) Latin authors, inscriptions, and archaeology. In the nature of the case this extrabiblical material can only afford rather meager evidence on the subject at hand. Thus we are left with Romans and *1 Clement* as the most important sources for Roman Christianity during this period. A study of this kind is inevitably fraught with difficulties, not only because of the scarcity of sources, but also because the letter to the Romans itself constitutes a major problem per se in its witness to the Roman situation. The well-known symposium *The Romans Debate,* edited by K. P. Donfried, has not only indicated a certain welcome consensus with respect to the character of the letter, but has also highlighted the complexity of the issues to be resolved, the almost unmanageable and in certain respects contradictory solutions proposed, and finally the different evaluations of the document as a witness to Roman Christianity around 56/57 C.E. Nor are the difficulties at the other end of our period less formidable. For in spite of the fact that a century has gone since the bishop of Durham[1] brought some order out of chaos, the first epistle of Clement is in important respects still shrouded in mystery. The identity of Clement still defies solution, his position in the church of Rome continues to be a matter of speculation, and the initiative to address an epistle such as *1 Clement* to another church is not only a matter of debate but also a source of astonishment.

In this paper I propose to utilize some of the clues that can be gleaned from Romans as a basis for evaluating the developments of the mid-90s as reflected in *1 Clement.*

II. The Roman Church at the Time of Romans

A. Romans — A Situational Letter

Today the traditional view that Romans is a kind of summary of Christian doctrine, though not dead,[2] is in retreat. Scholarly opinion is moving toward

1. J. B. Lightfoot, *The Apostolic Fathers: Clement, Ignatius, Polycarp,* 2nd ed., 5 vols., pt. 1: Clement, 2 vols. (Macmillan, 1890; reprint, Peabody, Mass.: Hendrickson, 1989).

2. In modified form this view is supported by T. W. Manson, "St Paul's Letter to the Romans — and Others," in *The Romans Debate,* ed. K. P. Donfried, rev. ed. (Peabody, Mass.: Hendrickson, 1991), 4; F. F. Bruce, *The Epistle of St Paul to the Romans,* TNTC (London: Tyndale, 1963), 12; C. K. Barrett, *A Commentary on the Epistle to the Romans,* BNTC (London: A. & C. Black, 1962), 7; W. G. Kümmel, *Introduction to the New Testament* (Nashville: Abingdon, 1966), 221; C. E. B. Cranfield, *A Critical and Exegetical Commentary on the Epistle to the Romans,* 2 vols., ICC (Edinburgh: T. & T. Clark, 1975-79), 817; P. Stuhlmacher, "The Purpose of Romans," in *The Romans Debate,* 236, but see 242; and G. Bornkamm, "The Letter to the Romans as Paul's Last Will and Testament," in *The Romans Debate,* 16-28, who, though considering Romans as originating in "real historical circumstances" and "not [being] a timeless theological treatise" (21), nevertheless thinks "this letter . . . elevates [Paul's] theology . . . into the sphere of the eternally and universally valid . . . [and] is the last will and testament of the Apostle Paul" (27f.).

the consensus that Romans is an occasional letter.[3] However, scholars are divided as to whether the situation that prompted its composition is to be found in the circumstances of the Roman Christians[4] or in those of Paul.[5] The insight that Romans is an occasional letter is not only in harmony with the concerns of this letter, but is also invaluable for its interpretation. For the matter in hand this presupposition is of basic importance.

In *The Romans Debate* contributors have argued strongly — based on the view that Romans reflects Paul's own circumstances — for the occasional character of the letter and its being addressed to a concrete situation in Rome, though they have been almost as determined *not to use the clues of the letter to form an opinion about the then state of Roman Christianity.* At the same time every straw in chapter 16 has been clutched to prove that Roman Christianity consisted solely of house churches. Surely if Romans is an occasional letter, it cannot only divulge Paul's own circumstances, his fears and misgivings as he departs for Jerusalem,[6] or the arsenal of his arguments on the Jewish question.[7] If he had any understanding of the Roman church at all[8] — as he seems to have had — then not only the argumentative but also the hortatory passages of the letter must contain important information about the state of the Roman church.[9]

3. E.g., Donfried, "False Presuppositions in the Study of Romans," in *The Romans Debate,* 103ff.; J. C. Beker, "The Faithfulness of God and the Priority of Israel in Paul's Letter to the Romans," in *The Romans Debate,* 327; W. S. Campbell, "Romans III as a Key to the Structure and Thought of the Letter," in *The Romans Debate,* 264; J. Jervell, "The Letter to Jerusalem," in *The Romans Debate,* 55.

4. E.g., W. Marxsen, *Introduction to the New Testament* (Philadelphia: Fortress, 1968), 94ff.; P. S. Minear, *The Obedience of Faith: The Purposes of Paul in the Epistle to the Romans,* SBT (London: SCM, 1971), 8ff.; W. Wiefel, "The Jewish Community in Ancient Rome and the Origins of Roman Christianity," in *The Romans Debate,* 96.

5. E.g., E. Fuchs, *Hermeneutik* (Bad Cannstatt: R. Müllerschön, 1963), 191, and Jervell, 60ff., have suggested that the concerns of Romans are determined by Paul's impending journey to Jerusalem and the argumentation he will use there.

6. Jervell, 53-64.

7. Stuhlmacher, 231-42, thinks the primary reason is that Paul wants to refute the false picture of him that must have reached Rome, too.

8. If Romans 16 is an integral part of Romans, in which case Aquila and Priscilla had returned to Rome, they at least would not have left their old friend in the dark about the state of the Roman church.

9. The period between Romans and *1 Clement* may receive some light from Hebrews and 1 Peter; see R. E. Brown, in R. E. Brown and J. P. Meier, *Antioch and Rome* (New York: Paulist, 1983), 128-58, and W. Lane's chapter in this volume.

B. The Limits of the Inquiry

The ongoing Romans debate encompasses a wide variety of issues, such as the foundation and date of the Roman church, the occasion and purpose of Romans, alleged inconsistencies in Romans, and the relation of Romans to Paul's other letters, especially Galatians. Owing to lack of space, this chapter will concentrate on the composition, the structure, and the characteristics of the Roman church. The picture of Roman Christianity that will emerge will then be compared with that of *1 Clement.*

C. The Composition and Social Stratification of the Roman Church

Romans gives ample evidence of having been addressed to a church that was constituted by both Jewish and Gentile Christians. A brief account of Jewish presence in Rome is therefore in place.

1. The Jews of Rome and the Beginnings of the Roman Church

In 139 B.C.E. the praetor Hispalus (or Hispanus) expelled a number of Jews from Rome, as it would appear, on the charge of proselytizing activities.[10] When the Jews first settled in Rome is at present unknown, but the embassies mentioned in 1 Maccabees 8:17-32; 12:1-4, 16; 14:24; 15:15-24 might imply that some Jews had lived there before the mid–second-century-B.C.E. Jewish presence in Rome becomes certain in the following century, since before 61 B.C.E. Jewish money had been sent from Italy to Palestine.[11] At any rate, on his return to Rome Pompey graced his triumph (61 B.C.E.) with large numbers of Palestinian Jews, many of whom later were manumitted, and having become Roman citizens joined their compatriots in Trastevere.[12] By 4 B.C.E.

10. According to the epitomes of Valerius Maximus by Julius Paris and Januarius Nepotianus (see H. J. Leon, *The Jews of Ancient Rome* [Philadelphia: Jewish Publication Society, 1960], 2ff.).

11. Cicero, *Pro Flacco* 28.67.

12. Philo, *Embassy* 23 (155ff.). In 59 B.C.E., during his defense of Flaccus, Cicero was annoyed with the large crowds of Jews in his audience; *Pro Flacco* 28.69.

no fewer than eight thousand Roman Jews supported a Jewish embassy to Rome.[13] In 19 C.E. Tiberius, incited by the prefect Sejanus, expelled "the whole Jewish nation"[14] from Rome on account of some Jews who had embezzled the Roman matron Fulvia's money; four thousand were sent to Sardinia to fight bandits, while the rest were banished from the city.[15] Their debarment from Rome cannot have lasted long,[16] and we find that Claudius issues decrees both for their protection[17] (in the early part of his reign)[18] and for their fresh expulsion from Rome (in the latter part of his reign)[19] on account of disturbances at the instigation of *Chrestus*.[20] This is no doubt a reference to uproars caused by Jews following the introduction of Christianity to Rome. Among the victims of this persecution were Aquila and his wife Prisca (Acts 18:2). When the Jews were allowed to return to Rome — provided that the expulsion had been carried out[21] — is not known, but Romans (written 56/57 C.E.) presupposes the presence of Jews in the capital, and on arrival at Rome around 59 Paul conferred with Jewish leaders (Acts 28:17-25). Moreover, archaeology has brought to light at least six Jewish cemeteries or catacombs in and around Rome[22] and, in addition, epigraphical evidence attesting Jewish names.[23]

From this brief review of the data the conclusion is that there was a substantial Jewish community in Rome before the middle of the first century. It is also reasonable to conclude that this community became the cradle of Christianity in the capital.

13. Josephus, *War* 2.80ff.; *Ant.* 17.299ff.

14. Josephus, *Ant.* 18.83, κελεύει πᾶν τὸ Ἰουδαϊκὸν τῆς Ῥώμης ἀπελθεῖν.

15. See also Tacitus, *Annals* 2.85, and Suetonius, *Tiberius* 36.

16. Philo, *Embassy*, passim, presupposes the presence of Jews in Rome during the reign of Gaius (37-41 C.E.).

17. Josephus, *Ant.* 19.280-92.

18. On the petitions by Agrippa I and Herod, see Josephus, *Ant.* 19.279.

19. Cf. E. Schürer, *The History of the Jewish People in the Age of Jesus Christ*, new ed. by G. Vermes, F. Millar, and M. Goodman, III.1 (Edinburgh: T. & T. Clark, 1986), 77.

20. Suetonius, *Claudius* 25.

21. Cf. Dio Cassius 60.6.6, who speaks of prohibition to assemble rather than expulsion. Perhaps the latter proved too hard to enforce (completely).

22. See Schürer, III.1, 79-81.

23. See e.g., P. Lampe, *Die stadtrömischen Christen in den ersten beiden Jahrhunderten: Untersuchungen zur Sozialgeschichte*, 2nd ed., WUNT 2/18 (Tübingen: J. C. B. Mohr, 1989), 130f., and Lampe, "The Roman Christians of Romans 16," in *The Romans Debate*, 226ff.

Two things are certain about the Roman church: (a) It was not founded by an apostle;[24] Peter must have come to Rome after Paul's arrival there,[25] so, when or how Christianity was brought to Rome is not known with certainty.[26] (b) When Paul wrote his Romans around 57,[27] Roman Christianity was already established. Paul had desired πολλάκις (Rom. 1:13) to come to the Roman Christians (notice, not to pre-Christian Rome to evangelize it!) in order to help and edify them, a desire that went back to ἀπὸ πολλῶν ἐτῶν (15:23), which cannot mean fewer than five years. His urge to visit Rome may have been awakened in him by meeting Aquila and Prisca around 50, who had recently come from Rome, provided that they had been Christian already before meeting Paul.

Thus, in view of Claudius's edict in 49 and Suetonius's reference to Jewish uproars on account of *Chrestus,* the gospel must have reached Rome before 49 C.E.

2. Composition and Stratification

Since there is a strong presumption that Christianity was introduced to Rome via the synagogue, Christian believers could have shared their faith in their own homes, thus initiating the house groups. Once they had

24. See, e.g., Brown, 126; G. Klein, "Paul's Purpose in Writing the Epistle to the Romans," in *The Romans Debate,* 40ff.; J. D. G. Dunn, *Romans* I, WBC (Dallas: Word, 1988), xlviii.

25. See Brown, 98; Lightfoot, *The Apostolic Fathers,* I.1, 73.

26. But it may be surmised that some of the ἐπιδημοῦντες Ῥωμαῖοι of the Day of Pentecost (Acts 2:10) were converted and later, when compelled to flee Jerusalem (Acts 8:1), returned to Rome. *Pace* Brown, 104 n. 215, ἐπιδημοῦντας may be used of temporary residence in a foreign country; see, e.g., Xenophon, *Memorabilia* I.2, 61; Demosthenes, 1357. The fact that, for example, Andronicus and Junia[s] are said in Rom. 16:7 to have been Christians before Paul, thus going back to the very beginnings of the gospel, makes this assumption quite probable, though final certainty is not possible. Brown, 104 n. 215, regards this line of approach as "sheer imagination." He supposes, instead, that Roman Christianity derived from Jerusalem sometime in the 40s (pp. 104, 126). Brown's conclusion is based on a problematic interpretation of Rom. 15:30-32 (105, 110f.). See Dunn, *Romans* 1:xlviii.

27. So, e.g., J. A. T. Robinson, *Redating the New Testament* (London: SCM, 1976), 84; R. Riesner, *Die Frühzeit des Apostels Paulus, Studien zur Chronologie, Missionstrategie und Theologie,* WUNT 1/71 (Tübingen: J. C. B. Mohr, 1994), 286.

outgrown their homes — if they were not already united as one church — it would have been natural for them to seek out one another and to organize themselves into a community. This may have been the occasion when their endeavors for a united existence and front for a more effective impact on Rome brought them into collision with the Jewish community.[28] At the same time this would imply that Roman Christianity at its inception — as was usual everywhere — was Jewish Christianity, the Jews being in the majority. There are good reasons also to suppose that the edict of Claudius brought about a change in the composition of the church of Rome.[29] The expulsion of the Jews, even if only the most militant elements, must have had as a consequence the growth of the Gentile part of the church, so that when Paul wrote to them the majority were undoubtedly of Gentile descent.[30] More specifically, the Roman Christians at this time were mainly of Greek origin.[31] This is confirmed by the following facts: (a) the majority of names in Romans 16 are Greek; (b) with two or three exceptions, the Roman bishops of the first two centuries bear Greek names,[32] a circumstance that reveals the non-Latin character of the church; (c) Paul writes his letter to the heart of the Roman

28. We must not forget that early Christianity was a warring faith and that the Christian community was characterized by missionary zeal.

29. Wiefel, 93ff.

30. Romans certainly reflects a church that is predominantly Gentile. ἵνα τινὰ καρπὸν σχῶ καὶ ἐν ὑμῖν καθὼς καὶ ἐν τοῖς λοιποῖς ἔθνεσιν, 1:13, is decisive. Further evidence to this effect may be adduced from 1:14, which speaks of Ἕλλησίν τε καὶ βαρβάροις, but not of Jews. 1:18-32 is, apart from verses 19-20, addressed only to the Gentiles. True, chapter 2 (particularly 2:17-29) and 3:1-20 have the Jew in view, though the argumentation is diatribal, but 4:1, προπάτορα ἡμῶν, in view of 2:27-29, need not imply any Jews. The Adam typology in chapter 5 is especially applicable to the Gentiles, since Paul finds here a rationale for Gentile salvation, by going back not to Abraham, the father of the Jewish nation, but to Adam, the father of all mankind. 7:1 is often interpreted of the Jewish law, but the context does not require that. Unless we are of the opinion that Romans or Greeks could commit adultery without being imputed by their law systems, the reference is surely to any law system about such matters, and in this case to Roman law. The problem of "the strong" and "the weak" (14:1–15:6), too, seems to support this understanding. The Jewish question (Romans 9–11) has primary relevance for the Gentiles rather than for the Jews.

31. Cf. J. B. Lightfoot, *St. Paul's Epistle to the Philippians* (reprint, Peabody, Mass.: Hendrickson, 1987), 19ff.; Lampe, "Roman Christians of Romans 16," 224ff.

32. Linos, Anenkletos, [Clemens], Euarestos, Alexandros, Xystos, Telesphoros, Hyginos, [Pius], Aniketos, Soter, Eleutheros, [Victor], Zephyrinos, Kallistos.

Empire in Greek; and (d) the Roman church's literature in the first two centuries is in Greek.

Sociologically, the picture Romans offers is that there were some who could show mercy (Rom. 12:8) and some in need of that mercy (12:13); some who might be tempted to pride (ὑψηλὰ φρονοῦντες), but also some who were of low estate (12:16: ταπεινοί). Moreover, the penetration of the gospel among the higher ranks of Roman society is also witnessed. At about the time Paul wrote Romans a Roman lady of high rank, Pomponia Graecina, the wife of Plautius, victor over Britain, was accused of foreign superstition, tried by a family tribunal led by her husband, and acquitted.[33] Archaeological discoveries in the catacombs of Callistus have led to the conclusion that Pomponia Graecina had become a Christian.[34] By the time Paul wrote Philippians,[35] he could speak of the Christian message as having penetrated the Praetorium (Phil. 1:13) and send greetings from "those of Caesar's household" (Phil. 4:22).

D. The Structure of the Roman Church

In *The Romans Debate* a number of authors argue or take it for granted that the Roman Christians did not constitute one church for the whole city, but various house churches or house groups. These groups are supposed to have consisted of some fifteen to twenty members each.[36] This hypothesis may turn out to be correct, though the arguments on which it is based at present cannot be said to be decisive. Inasmuch as this issue makes an important difference on the kind of Roman church that is to be compared with that of *1 Clement*, it will be necessary to go into this matter in some detail. The hypothesis is based on three main arguments.

33. Tacitus, *Annals* 13.32.

34. See the evidence and discussion presented by Lightfoot, *The Apostolic Fathers,* I.1, 31f., and more recently by Lampe, *Christen,* 164f.

35. More recent alternatives to Rome as the place of writing are Ephesus and Caesarea, but when the pros and cons have been taken into account Rome is still the likeliest.

36. E.g., J. Murphy-O'Connor, *St. Paul's Corinth: Texts and Archeology* (Wilmington, Del.: Michael Glazier, 1983), 158; Lampe, *Christen,* 161; W. Lane, *Hebrews* I, WBC (Dallas: Word, 1991), liii.

The first argument derives from the fact that Paul addresses the Roman Christians as πᾶσιν τοῖς οὖσιν ἐν Ῥώμῃ ἀγαπητοῖς θεοῦ (1:7) but not as ἐκκλησία.[37] The reason for this, it is surmised, is that there was no church in Rome but only house groups.[38] There is no evidence for this surmise, either biblical or extrabiblical; it is merely circular reasoning from the absence of ἐκκλησία: there is no church in Rome since Paul does not use the term ἐκκλησία, and Paul does not use the term ἐκκλησία since there is no church in Rome. This reasoning is, of course, anchored on the idea that if there were a church in Rome Paul would have greeted it with the term ἐκκλησία. As a matter of fact, Paul follows no uniform practice. He uses it in 1 and 2 Corinthians and 1 (and 2) Thessalonians, and, moreover, he uses the plural in Galatians. But he greets the Philippian church without the use of this term: πᾶσιν τοῖς ἁγίοις ἐν Χριστῷ Ἰησοῦ;[39] i.e., he uses an identical greeting as the one directed to the Romans. Neither the church of Ephesus nor the church of Colosse is greeted by the term ἐκκλησία. Would this perhaps imply that Paul or his imitators did not regard these as churches? Would not the Ephesian church be one of the πάσῃ ἐκκλησίᾳ/ἐκκλησίαις πάσαις of 1 Corinthians 4:17 (written from Ephesus, 1 Cor. 16:8)? Moreover, such a supposition does not harmonize with Paul's view of the essence of the church. The idea of the church as being constituted of the elect (cf. Ephesians) is adumbrated already in such letters as, e.g., 1 Corinthians (15:9), Galatians (1:13), and Philippians (3:6), where ἐκκλησία (τοῦ θεοῦ) is used abstractly of a part of *the church.*[40] Surely, if Paul can use the term of a handful of people meeting in Aquila's house, how much more could he have used it of all such groups together in Rome. The absence of the term from the Romans' greeting, therefore, cannot positively support the above hypothesis.

The second argument builds on archaeological, and especially epigraphical, evidence bearing on the Jewish community in Rome.[41] We hear

37. See J. H. Elliott, *A Home for the Homeless: A Social-Scientific Criticism of 1 Peter, Its Situation and Strategy* (Minneapolis: Fortress Press, 1990), 264.

38. See, e.g., Dunn, *Romans* 1.liif.; Wiefel, 92ff.; Lampe, *Christen,* 301; Lampe, "Roman Christians of Romans 16," 229f.; Stuhlmacher, 241.

39. That Paul uses ἐπισκόποις καὶ διακόνοις, insignia of church life (cf. Klein, 41), is irrelevant.

40. Cf. a similar use in Acts 9:31.

41. Lampe, *Christen,* see esp. 10-67 and 301-20; Lampe, "Roman Christians of Romans 16," 216-30.

of several synagogues scattered in various parts of the capital,[42] which are believed to have had a sort of loose connection with one another but which, in the absence of an ethnarch who could hold them together, were largely independent. The evidence stops here. Thus, although Lampe presents a lot of interesting and useful material, its value as evidence always stops short of proof,[43] and in the final analysis the alleged Christian fragmentation is based on the Jewish fragmentation: "Der Fraktionierungsbefund steht vor dem Hintergrund einer *fraktionierten stadtrömischen Judenschaft:* Das stadtrömischen Judentum bestand aus mehreren selbständigen Synagogengemeinden. . . . Die Parallelität verblüfft — ob man die jüdische Struktur nun als unmittelbares Vorbild gelten lassen will oder nicht."[44] From here on it is surmised that Christianity's introduction to Rome took place through these synagogues — as it often did in other cities, according to Acts — and that therefore the Christian enclaves were also independent or loosely connected with one another, being tied up with the various synagogues — at least in the beginning, and that they continued their separatist existence even after their ties with the synagogue had been severed. Again there is no objective evidence for this; it is merely a surmise. That Christianity often took root in a place via the synagogue may be readily conceded,[45] though sometimes it did not use the synagogue.[46] The problem with this argument, however, is that it does not do justice to the explosive character of the Christian message. The Christianity preached by Paul had no chance of remaining within the Jewish fold more than a few weeks or

42. Wiefel, 89f.

43. The same is the case with B. Blue's more recent learned study "Acts and the House Church," in *The Book of Acts in Its Graeco-Roman Setting,* ed. David W. J. Gill and Conrad Gempf, The Book of Acts in Its First-Century Setting, vol. 2 (Grand Rapids: Wm. B. Eerdmans Publishing Co., 1994), 119-222, which evinces an inadequate understanding of what constitutes historical proof, and whose mainly later concerns tend to render its title a misnomer.

44. Lampe, *Christen,* 306. Furthermore, Lampe refers to Justin, *Dialogue* 47.2 and *Apology* 1.67 (*Christen,* 306), as evidencing the fragmentation of Roman Christians. It seems to me that the Justin passages prove the exact opposite. The archaeological evidence, which Lampe considers support for his thesis, is of the negative sort; that is, no buildings dedicated to Christian service have been unearthed yet. Of course, no one had expected this. But this circumstance proves nothing in particular.

45. Cf. Acts 9:20; 13:5, 14; 14:1; 17:1, 10, 17; 18:4, 19; 19:8.

46. Apart from the special circumstances of Acts 14:14-18 and 17:19-31, see 8:4ff.; 11:1, 19-20; 19:1-7.

at most a few months (cf. Acts 19:8). Paul's law-free gospel almost immediately aroused the sentiments of the Jews and led to uproars and commotions.[47] Paul represented, to be sure, the radical left wing, but all Christian endeavors — no matter how accommodating to Jewish sentiment — as soon as they put forth the claims of Christ, were bound to run into trouble. This is witnessed not only for the church of Antioch (Gal. 2:1ff.; Acts 15:1ff.), but also for Jerusalem: the deaths of Stephen and James, the imprisonment of Peter and the persecution (Acts 7:59f.; 8:1ff.; 11:19; 12:1-3). It is significant therefore that already the first (second after Damascus) church on Gentile soil (Antioch) is not connected with the synagogue. Nor do we know of any other church in the Gentile world that existed within the synagogue.[48] And if we may believe Acts 28:22, there was no connection between the synagogue(s) and the Christians of Rome. Thus, that Roman Christianity in the time of Paul lived within the synagogue I regard as quite improbable.

The third argument is based on the mention in Romans 16 of what is taken to be several groups of Christians. Romans 16 speaks of Prisca and Aquila and the κατ' οἶκον αὐτῶν ἐκκλησίαν (vv. 3-5). It also speaks of two groups as (a) τοὺς ἐκ τῶν Ἀριστοβούλου (v. 10) and (b) τοὺς ἐκ τῶν Ναρκίσσου (v. 11), as well as of two other groups as (c) τοὺς σὺν αὐτοῖς ἀδελφούς (v. 14) and (d) τοὺς σὺν αὐτοῖς πάντας ἁγίους (v. 15). It is obvious that here we have one house church. The expressions (c) τοὺς σὺν αὐτοῖς ἀδελφούς and (d) τοὺς σὺν αὐτοῖς πάντας ἁγίους may possibly refer to two similar house groups. However, the expression τοὺς ἐκ τῶν is too vague to carry such a significance; the supposition that they met in regular worship as

47. E.g., at Pisidian Antioch, Acts 13:45ff.; at Thessalonica, Acts 17:5ff.; at Beroea, Acts 17:13; at Corinth, Acts 18:5-17.

48. The case of Jerusalem is unique in this regard. Located in the stronghold of Judaism and under the leadership of James, the Jerusalem church with its "myriads of Jews who believed, all of whom were zealous of their law" (Acts 21:20) was leading a sub-Christian existence without prospects for survival. That its end was sealed a decade later could hardly come as a surprise. The days were past when Peter and John had dared defy the Jewish authorities. The Jerusalem church of the late 50s seemed to have come to an implicit agreement with Judaism for coexistence. There is no evidence that any other church experienced the constraints of Judaism in that way. Certainly the Christians of the capital need not and could not have followed suit. On the contrary, the uproar of which Suetonius speaks may be explained by the Christians of Rome seeking a form of Christianity that was free from Judaism, a matter that aroused the Jews.

churches is not a necessary or logical conclusion from this expression. Thus, according to the evidence of Romans 16, we have one house church. If we press the evidence, we may get three house churches. And if we press the evidence to its breaking point, we may get five such groups.[49] This still does not prove that Roman Christianity consisted solely of house groups. If we take Asyncritus, Phlegon, Hermes, Patrobas, and Hermas on the one hand and Philologus, Julia, Nereus, his sister, and Olympas on the other hand as being parts of the two groups consisting of τοὺς σὺν αὐτοῖς respectively, we are still left with fourteen persons (vv. 5-13) who apparently did not belong to any such house group. That they constituted at least two more groups[50] is a mere *Vermutung*. Why does Paul not say so? And why does he not greet their groups, too, in the same way he greets Aquila's house church? And why should Paul start his own (eighth) house group when Aquila, who was a Paulinist, already had a house church?

Moreover, the compositional order of Romans 16 is against this supposition. If the eight persons named in verses 5-10 represented a sixth group and the five persons named in verses 12-13 represented a seventh, to which group did Herodion, who is squeezed between "those of the household of Aristobulus" and "those of the household of Narcissus," belong? And if the Roman Christians were divided into seven (or five) groups, would not Paul have addressed (already in his prescript) all of them together, especially if one of his aims, according to the hypothesis, was to help unify the various groups?[51]

But there are more objections. Who or which house group was the recipient of the letter? Who would see to it that the letter circulated among the seven groups, especially if their relations were strained or even competitive, as we are led to believe by the theory? And what are we to make of the greetings to the persons greeted? For example, what are we to make of the following situation in which Aquila, as the leader of his house church, read to his congregation Romans 16:3: "Greet Prisca and Aquila"![52] And why is Phoebe recommended to the recipients of the letter if there was no church in Rome to take care of her, instead of to Aquila and Prisca, whose

49. Cf. W. A. Meeks, *The First Urban Christians: The Social World of the Apostle Paul* (New Haven: Yale University Press, 1983), 75.

50. Lampe, "Roman Christians of Romans 16," 230.

51. R. Jewett, "Following the Argument of Romans," in *The Romans Debate*, 266.

52. The difficulty hinted at here has led some to see Romans 16 as a covert recommendation for Paul: "Look how many people I know among you?" (e.g., Brown, 107) — hardly congruent with Paul's practice (cf. 2 Cor. 3:1: ἐξ ὑμῶν).

house group (according to the theory) was one of many such groups, when she certainly must have been personally acquainted with them and therefore would hardly have needed to go to any other house group for help?[53] On the other hand, if we can assume — as in other cities, such as Corinth, Thessalonica, Ephesus, and Colosse — that there was a main church, the church called after the city, then we can understand why Paul sends his greetings to certain individuals and groups. These groups were not schismatic but were outreach posts in different parts of the metropolis. Certainly we should not understand Aquila's house church in Ephesus as schismatic in relation to (Paul's) church there! At least Paul did not think so (1 Cor. 16:19). Nor do we have any reason to think that Philemon sabotaged his son's church in Colossae or Laodicea (?)[54] by maintaining a church in his own house (Philem. 1; cf. Col. 4:17).

Perhaps a few observations on Paul's consistent use of the term ἐκκλησία might help to set the record straight. (1) Whenever Paul addresses the Christians of a place that is larger than a city, as for example a province, he always uses the plural ἐκκλησίαι.[55] He can also refer abstractly or in general and without mention of name to various city or province churches together in the plural.[56] (2) Whenever Paul addresses the Christians of a particular city, he always uses the singular ἐκκλησία.[57]

53. The description of Phoebe in Rom. 16:1-2 implies that she had been a Christian of long standing, from the time of Aquila and Prisca's residence in Corinth.

54. Cf. J. B. Lightfoot, *St Paul's Epistles to the Colossians and Philemon* (reprint, Peabody, Mass.: Hendrickson, 1987), 42f., 244, 308-10. Cf. also C. F. D. Moule, *The Epistles of Paul to the Colossians and to Philemon*, CGTC (reprint, Cambridge: Cambridge University Press, 1980), 14-21; F. F. Bruce, *The Epistles to the Colossians, to Philemon, and to the Ephesians*, NICNT (Grand Rapids: Wm. B. Eerdmans Publishing Co., 1984), 185f., 199f., 206; P. O'Brien, *Colossians, Philemon*, WBC (Waco: Word, 1982), 259, 273; J. Gillman, "Archippus," *ABD*, I, 368f.

55. Note ταῖς ἐκκλησίαις τῆς Γαλατίας (1 Cor. 16:1; Gal. 1:2); ταῖς ἐκκλησίαις τῆς Ἀσίας (1 Cor. 16:19); ταῖς ἐκκλησίαις τῆς Μακεδονίας (2 Cor. 8:1); ταῖς ἐκκλησίαις τῆς Ἰουδαίας (Gal. 1:22).

56. Rom. 16:4: πᾶσαι αἱ ἐκκλησίαι τῶν ἐθνῶν; Rom. 16:16: αἱ ἐκκλησίαι τοῦ Χριστοῦ; 1 Cor. 11:16: αἱ ἐκκλησίαι τοῦ θεοῦ; 1 Cor. 14:33: αἱ ἐκκλησίαι τῶν ἁγίων.

57. Note τῆς ἐκκλησίας τῆς ἐν Κεγχρεαῖς (Rom. 16:1); τῇ ἐκκλησίᾳ ἐν Κορίνθῳ (1 Cor. 1:2; 2 Cor. 1:1); τῇ ἐκκλησίᾳ Θεσσαλονικέων (1 Thess. 1:1; [2 Thess. 1:1]). In 1 Cor. 14:34 ἐκκλησίαις refers abstractly to the *gatherings* of the believers, which was also the original meaning of the term in Greek society and remains the basic, dynamic meaning of it in the NT.

(3) Whenever Paul refers to the Christians at Corinth, he refers to them in the singular as one ἐκκλησία. Thus, the Corinthians are expected to set up the lowliest members of the church as judges.[58] They are chided for dividing themselves into groups (σχίσματα) in their assembling together as a church (1 Cor. 11:18), which again could hardly apply to the small numbers of a house group. In their public appearances they are to edify the church (14:4, 5, 12), and Paul prefers to speak in the church five words with his mind than one myriad in tongues (14:19). That their women are to keep quiet (14:34f.) is readily explained by his having in mind the whole congregation rather than household members or the few friends of the neighborhood meeting in homely atmospheres. Further, the plurals "women" and "their husbands" imply a number of married couples. Moreover, the house group model with its dominant householder would have been a stifling atmosphere for the charismatic exercise of gifts and leadership.[59] That throughout chapter 14 Paul has in mind the whole church at Corinth becomes obvious from verse 23: ἐὰν οὖν συνέλθῃ ἡ ἐκκλησία ὅλη ἐπὶ τὸ αὐτό.[60] Here Paul presupposes that the entire city church was gathered together in one place (ἐπὶ τὸ αὐτό).[61] In line with this public character of

58. 1 Cor. 6:4, which could hardly apply to a house group. For the above interpretation ἐὰν ἔχητε and καθίζετε are decisive.

59. Cf. Meeks's sobering remarks, 77.

60. R. Banks, *Paul's Idea of Community* (Grand Rapids: Wm. B. Eerdmans Publishing Co., 1980), 38, gives ὅλη a novel (and un-Greek) interpretation, making it refer to a multiplicity of groups, not to the entire city church.

61. Ἡ ἐκκλησία ὅλη must be understood in principle and representatively — not inclusively — like the use of πᾶς and ὅλος often in the NT: Matt. 3:5; 27:27; Mark 1:33; Acts 10:22; Rom. 1:8; 16:23. Although the earliest Christian basilicas were erected in Constantine's time (Christian churches were apparently erected from the time of Alexander Severus [222-35 C.E.]; see *Larousse Encyclopedia of Byzantine and Mediaeval Art* [New York: Excalibur Books, 1981], 38) and archaeology has not brought to light any first-century buildings that might have been erected by Christians as meeting places (probably because of the poor materials that might have been used), there were assembly halls available which the Christians could have rented or in some other way procured for their meetings. In Corinth, for example, three Roman basilicas have been excavated, one from the first century (64.75 × 22.87 m.) on the Lechaeon Road (see *Ancient Corinth*, American School of Classical Studies at Athens, 1954, 21) near the place where the inscription of the Jewish synagogue was found (see *Corinth, Results of Excavations Conducted by the American School of Classical Studies at Athens*, vol. VIII, pt. I, *Greek Inscriptions, 1896-1927*, ed. B. D. Meritt [Cambridge: Harvard University Press, 1931], no. 111, 78f.) and a second one from the time of Augustus (pp. 45f.). Such buildings

the church meeting, there is an expectation that unbelievers will venture into the meetings (and hopefully be converted; 14:24-25), something that could hardly be expected to happen in a private house.[62]

This brief scrutiny of the theory that Roman Christianity consisted entirely of separate house groups has hopefully indicated that the theory lacks sure foundation.[63] On the contrary, house churches found in other cities than Rome existed side by side with the main city church, and their existence was not owing to divergencies in belief or to conflicting standpoints, but rather to zealous initiative to evangelize, to win one's neighbors. Such house churches were to be found in Ephesus (1 Cor. 16:19), Colosse (apparently two: Nympha's [Col. 4:15] and Philemon's [Philem. 2]), and, on the analogy of Romans 16:10-11 (τοὺς ἐκ), perhaps also in Corinth (1 Cor. 1:11: ὑπὸ τῶν).[64] Thus, even though house groups existed in the

---

"served as a social or commercial meeting-place" (*Oxford Classical Dictionary,* s.v. "basilica"). We may here recall that "basilica" was the name given to the first Christian church buildings, a connection that has not yet been satisfactorily settled (see *RGG,* 3rd ed., 1910). Might the hypothesis be hazarded that the Christians took over the name "basilica" from such places which they had once used for their meetings? The basilica, which was a purely Roman architectural creation, was to be found throughout Italy (see also *Der Kleine Pauly: Lexikon der Antike,* vol. 1 [Stuttgart: Alfred Druckenmüller, 1964], 836f.). If Paul was in a position to live in his own rented apartment (Acts 28:30; cf. B. Rapske, *The Book of Acts and Paul in Roman Custody,* The Book of Acts in Its First-Century Setting, vol. 3 [Grand Rapids: Wm. B. Eerdmans Publishing Co., 1994], 236ff.) (indicating economic ability by the Christians), and furthermore to rent Tyrannus's school for two years in Ephesus (Acts 19:9f.) for the purpose of holding his meetings (indicating freedom to make public appearances; the persecutions were sporadic, not continuous), might we not have reason to suppose that similar locales were used by him and others both in Corinth (where one of his Christian friends was none other than the influential Erastus, the οἰκονόμος τῆς πόλεως, the *aedilis* of the inscription, according to which he had laid a pavement in the city at his own expense [cf. *Ancient Corinth,* 74f.]) and other places, and therefore Rome, too? It is important to underline that what is being argued for here is the constitution of all the believers of a particular city into one church, with one administration, as was the case with the mother church of Jerusalem.

62. Εἰσέλθῃ implies that the unbeliever goes to the meeting of his own accord!

63. Cf. Elliott, 265: "Taken on the whole, however, the evidence at best allows rather than demonstrates that the household constituted the basic form of organization among the Christians in Rome."

64. According to Acts 16:40, the Philippian church started as a house church in Lydia's house. Whether the house church continued to exist after the development of the Philippian church, we cannot tell.

different cities, there was but one church for each city: e.g., Corinth, Ephesus, Antioch. We have no concrete evidence that the situation in Rome was different.

E. The Characteristics of the Roman Church

1. "Your Faith Is Proclaimed in the Whole World"

Paul's initial, complimentary words in Romans 1:8 that "your faith is proclaimed in the whole world" and his closing words in 16:19 that "your obedience is known to all" probably have some basis, though their character of *captatio benevolentiae*, coming from one unknown to the church, and, moreover, one who normally exhibits a measure of tact, cannot tell us much about the state of the Roman church. This characterization is neither unique for this church,[65] nor can we draw from it any conclusions about "the high quality of the Christianity that exists in Rome."[66] Precisely because Paul is a stranger to them, his exhortations are a much safer index of the Romans' spiritual or moral state. Consequently, we must look in these passages for the state of Roman Christianity.

2. Contempt of the Jews

The Jewish disturbances of 49 C.E. or earlier must have caused the Gentile part of the church, which now increased rapidly and became the majority, to rethink its relation to Judaism. The gradual decrease of Jews accepting the gospel cannot but have widened the gap. This could not fail to lead to conclusions that God had rejected his people, replacing them with a new one, Gentiles (11:1; 9:30-31). Under the circumstances it is understandable, too, that Gentile Christians might look down upon the Jews, thus forgetting that it was the root that bore the branches and not the other way round (11:18). Thus from Paul's point of view the Gentiles needed to be put in their place. Hence, even if Romans 9–11 in particular should have been composed in view

65. The characterization of the Corinthian church (1 Cor. 1:5ff.) is at least as flattering, while that of 1 Thess. 1:3-8 surpasses all others in praise.

66. Brown, 115.

of Paul's coming defense in Jerusalem,[67] or as a defense in the face of accusations against Paul,[68] or to set forth Paul's revised views of Judaism,[69] the interpretation of this section would lose an important dimension unless it were interpreted against a concrete background in the Roman church: the problem of Judaism in the minds of the Roman Gentile Christians.

3. *Obedience to the Authorities*

Romans 13 takes up the problem of obedience to the secular authorities. The second person singular (vv. 3, 4) might be interpreted as diatribal, but the switch to the second person plural and the concrete references to the payment of taxes (vv. 6-8) indicate that the exhortation ought to be real and applicable to the recipients of the letter. Paul's command that πᾶσα ψυχὴ ἐξουσίαις ὑπερεχούσαις ὑποτασσέσθω may imply that there were tendencies of rebellion among the Roman Christians. This may have been owing to influences from the general tendency among the Roman populace, which needed bread and spectacles to keep quiet; to the constant propensity of the Jews to rebellion; or to the Christian claims about Jesus as king, who could not brook another rival (emperor worship). A concrete occasion for this paraenesis may be found in the disturbances of 49 C.E.[70] Though Suetonius blames the Jews for what happened, the Christians, too, may have answered the Jewish attack in kind and not have been entirely innocent. The detail with which Paul goes into this problem in 13:1-7 surely makes it impossible to explain this as a general, timeless, academic treatment. It makes best sense if it is taken as a much needed admonition.[71]

4. *The "Weak" and the "Strong"*

The terms "weak" (ἀσθενοῦντες, ἀδύνατοι) and "strong" (δυνατοί) are evaluative terms, and they are being used from Paul's standpoint. Paul's use

67. Jervell, esp. 60-64.
68. Stuhlmacher, 236.
69. Brown, 120.
70. Or under Nero; cf. Riesner, 283.
71. Cf. the similar thought in 1 Pet. 2:13-17.

of δυνατοί in 1 Corinthians 1:26 might predispose us to see sociological significance here. However, his juxtaposition of δυνατός with ἀσθενέω (2 Cor. 12:10; 13:9) shows that no such distinction is made between the two stems. Romans 15:1 shows, moreover, that the ἀδύνατοι are "weak" in respect of their ἀσθενήματα. Thus, the exact meaning of these words can be obtained from Paul's use of these and equivalent terms elsewhere (e.g., Gal. 6:1f.; 1 Cor. 2:14–3:3; Phil. 3:12-16; and esp. 1 Cor. 8:7-13; 9:22).[72] A closer look at the above passages shows that these terms have not a sociological but a theological orientation. They express the Godward relation of the individual. Even the horizontal relation between the members of the church is determined by their vertical relation. More than one chapter (14:1–15:7) is devoted to the problem of the "weak" and the "strong," which is indicative of the importance of the topic for the Roman Christians.[73] The weak have been understood in more ways than one,[74] but the details of eating herbs rather than meat (14:2, 21) and the observance of special days (14:5) would seem to have in view Jewish-inspired objections to eating meat offered to idols[75] and Sabbath keeping. In other words, the "weak" represent those elements in the church that are acting under the restraints of the Jewish law and traditions. Paul identifies himself with the "strong," who in this case happen to be mainly the Gentile part of the church. These Gentiles are not "strong" in themselves, but on account of the liberty in Christ which they have accepted. At the same time this limitation of "weak" to persons characterized by Jewish food behavior perhaps reflects also the waning presence and influence of the Jewish element in the church of Rome. Paul is here making one more attempt to support his compatriots by inducing the dominant Gentile part of the church to accept them as equals in Christ. Indeed, this appears to be at least partly the reason for Romans 9–11. This impression is corroborated by 15:25-27, in which the Gentiles

72. Cf. Cranfield, 2:691f.

73. Otherwise R. J. Karris, "Romans 14:1–15:13 and the Occasion of Romans," in *The Romans Debate*, esp. 71-84, who thinks the topic is not applicable to the Romans.

74. Karris, 65-84, who thinks the Romans text is adapted from 1 Corinthians 8–10, and F. Watson, "The Two Roman Congregations," in *The Romans Debate*, 203-15, who thinks of two congregations hostile to each other.

75. Cf. the similar argumentation in 1 Cor. 8:1-13. P. D. Gooch, *Dangerous Food: 1 Corinthians 1–8 in Its Context* (Waterloo, Ontario: Wilfrid Laurier University Press, 1993), 115-18, denies the connection. But cf. Cranfield, 2:690-98, and Dunn, *Romans* II, WBC (Dallas: Word, 1988), esp. 801-2.

are made "debtors" to the Jews. It was the last straw that Paul was clutching to help the "weak" element, as he saw the increasing falling away of Israel from the long-awaited promise of salvation which now finally had arrived.[76]

5. Dissensions

Romans 16 reveals that the Roman church was plagued by dissension. Paul describes the culprits as τοὺς τὰς διχοστασίας καὶ τὰ σκάνδαλα . . . ποιοῦντας, who ἐξαπατῶσιν τὰς καρδίας τῶν ἀκάκων, and behind whom he sees the working of Satan (16:17-20). The term διχοστασία, "dissension" in particular, implies the existence of divisive elements in the community.[77] The reference to the διδαχή, "which you have learned" — referring no doubt to 6:17 — and the assurance that "God will soon crush Satan under your feet" leave no doubt that the passage deals with real dissensions in the church of Rome and is not expressive of any reflections on Paul's own opponents. The letter to the Philippians presumably has the same persons in view when it describes Paul's antagonists in Rome as preaching Christ out of φθόνον, ἔριν, and ἐριθείας (1:15, 17) (the last word being used along with διχοστασίαι in Gal. 5:20), though the identification of these persons with the Judaizers of Philippians 3:2ff., 18f., in spite of the common κοιλία, is not certain.[78]

F. Conclusions

The conclusions from the above discussion may be summarized as follows: (1) Recent research is increasingly inclining to the conclusion that Romans is an occasional letter. Its information about the addressees must therefore be taken seriously in any attempt to reconstruct the character of Roman Christianity at the time of Romans. (2) In the 30s and 40s there was a sizable Jewish community in the capital, which probably became

76. Cf. 9:1-3, 32; 10:1; 11:7, 14-24.

77. In Gal. 5:20, the only other occurrence in the NT, διχοστασίαι is flanked by ἐριθεῖαι (selfish ambitions) and αἱρέσεις (factions).

78. Lightfoot, *Philippians,* 17f., 26, has no doubt that they are Judaizers; the matter, however, is not so straightforward.

the cradle of the new faith. (3) Initially the church of Rome was dominated by the Jewish factor. Following 49 C.E., however, the Jewish element declined and the Gentile element became predominant. The Christian faith seems to have made discreet inroads into the higher strata of society, though the majority of Christians belonged to the lower or lowest strata of society. The church was Greek-speaking. (4) A relatively recent but influential viewpoint is that Roman Christianity consisted solely of house churches — some eight of them. This conclusion is found to rely on a questionable interpretation and a one-sided presentation of the evidence. The damaging evidence in Paul's epistles has not been properly heeded. The conclusion is drawn that house churches existed, but only side by side with the city church. (5) Although the letter is not devoid of remarks complimentary to the Roman Christians (e.g., on faith, obedience), safer pointers to the state of Roman Christianity are the various exhortations Paul addresses to the church, showing that it is beset by many problems and in need of apostolic instruction. Among the problems that surface are the Gentile Christians' negative attitude toward the Jews; the waning presence and influence of the latter; divisions in the church over food laws, etc., inspired by the Jewish factor; opposition to the secular authorities; and divisiveness. (6) In other words, at the time of Paul's writing we have in Rome a church that has existed for at least one decade, perhaps two; that has felt the heavy hand of the emperor — even if not in regular persecution — but has stood fast; and that, although lacking the fatherhood of an apostle and his strong guiding hand, nevertheless has continued in its witness. The hortatory sections of Romans, the absence of apostolic activity, and Acts 28:22 indicate that the Roman church up to the time of Romans must have led a relatively obscure existence.

III. The Roman Church at the Time of *1 Clement*

A. The Date and Occasion of *1 Clement*

1 Clement 5 speaks of the deaths of Peter and Paul, and hence of the Neronian persecution, as belonging to "our generation" (γενεᾶς ἡμῶν). In 42.4, however, the author speaks of the ἐπισκόπους and διακόνους whom the apostles appointed, and in 44.3-5 of the presbyters whom the apostles or their successors appointed as well as of the death of some of these. Finally, the envoys who bear the letter to Corinth are said to have lived an exemplary life in the Roman church from their youth to old age (63.3). These references would seem to place *1 Clement* in the last decade of the first century. *1 Clement* 1.1 has been taken to refer to Domitian's refined, sporadic persecutions; hence the change of circumstances which makes possible the writing of this letter is generally taken to be the year of Domitian's death, 96 C.E.[79]

Ostensibly the occasion for the writing of the letter was that news had reached the Roman church that certain young members of the church of Corinth had brought about the deposition from their office of a number of old presbyters. This act was looked upon with alarm by the Roman church, which no doubt feared that the toleration of such conduct might encourage similar actions in other churches as well. Hence the Roman church adopted the novel procedure of addressing to the Corinthians a letter in which every fiber is bent to persuade the culprits to desist from their action, to restore the old presbyters to their posts, and to withdraw from the church. The situation at Corinth, however, hardly provides an adequate basis for the form and content of this letter.

B. The Author of *1 Clement*

1 Clement is anonymous, having the church of Rome as its sender. However, since early times the letter was believed to have been written by a certain Clement.[80] The *Shepherd of Hermas*[81] speaks of a Clement in the church of Rome who was to send the booklet which Hermas was bidden to write to

79. This dating is supported by, e.g., Lightfoot, *The Apostolic Fathers,* I.1, 67; Brown, 160; A. Lindemann, *Die Apostolische Väter I: Die Clemensbriefe,* HNT 17 (Tübingen: J. C. B. Mohr, 1992), 12. L. L. Welborn, "First Epistle of Clement," *ABD,* I, 1059, interprets the αἰφνιδίους καὶ ἐπαλλήλας . . . συμφορὰς καὶ περιπτώσεις (1:1), not of Domitian's persecutions, but rhetorically as *captatio benevolentiae* to gain the sympathy of the Corinthians, and dates the letter between 80 and 140.

80. The earliest witnesses — if somewhat dubious (cf. Lightfoot, *The Apostolic Fathers,* I.1, 358f.) — are Hegesippus (†180-192; Eusebius, *Hist. Eccl.* 4.22.1); Dionysius bishop of Corinth (†190; Eusebius, *Hist. Eccl.* 4.23.11; J. Quasten, *Patrology* I [Utrecht-Antwerp: Spectrum Publishers, 1966], 280-82); and Irenaeus (†202; *Adv. Haer.* 3.3.3), though the first clear ascription of the letter to Clement is by Clement of Alexandria, *Stromateis* 1.7; 4.17-19.

81. *Vis.* 2.4.3.

the cities outside Rome, with the motivation ἐκείνῳ γὰρ ἐπιτέτραπται. This expression has often been construed as revealing Clement's position as a kind of foreign secretary writing Rome's communications to other churches.[82] However, neither the verb nor its perfect tense says anything about any recurrence of what Clement is expected to do on this particular occasion, nor do we have any evidence that he wrote any more letters.[83] An additional problem here is the dating. The Clement of *Hermas* was contemporary with Hermas himself, who, according to the *Muratorian Fragment,* wrote during his brother Pius's episcopate, i.e., between 140-155 C.E., whereas the Clement with whom *1 Clement* is connected must have died at about the end of the first century.

Following Lightfoot's researches, the current view is that Clement probably was a freedman of the house of Titus Flavius Clemens,[84] cousin of Emperor Domitian and consul of Rome in 95 C.E. Before[85] or upon the termination[86] of his office as consul, he was executed on Domitian's orders on "the most trivial of charges,"[87] while his wife, Flavia Domitilla, Domitian's niece, was exiled. To emphasize that the consul constituted no danger to the emperor, Suetonius dubs him a man of the "most contemptible indolence."[88] The charges against Clemens and Domitilla given by Dio Cassius are ἔγκλημα ἀθεότητος,[89] and are connected with Judaism. This may be an indication that Clemens and Domitilla had become Christian.[90] Lightfoot conjectured that the author of *1 Clement* was third bishop of Rome[91] and

82. E.g., Lightfoot, *The Apostolic Fathers,* I.1, 54, 348, 359f.; Brown, 160, 164.

83. *2 Clement* is obviously not by him, and it is even suggested that it might have been written by the Corinthian elders themselves (K. P. Donfried, *The Setting of Second Clement,* NovTSup 38 [Leiden: Brill, 1974]). Brown's remarks (p. 164) cannot prove the contrary, since Ignatius, *Rom.* 3.1, ἄλλους ἐδιδάξατε, does not prove reference to any letters in addition to this one.

84. Lampe, *Christen,* 173, questions this.

85. Dio Cassius 67.14.1, ὑπατεύοντα.

86. Suetonius, *Domitian* 15.1, *tantum non in ipso eius consulato.*

87. Suetonius, *Domitian* 15.1, *tenuissima suspicione.*

88. Suetonius, *Domitian* 15.1, *contemptissimae inertiae.*

89. Dio Cassius 67.14.2.

90. So Lightfoot, *The Apostolic Fathers,* I.1, 34f. The existence of a cemetery of Domitilla (Lightfoot, *The Apostolic Fathers,* I.1, 35f.; Brown, 161) leaves no doubt about Domitilla's Christian standing (cf. Eusebius, *Hist. Eccl.* 3.18.4).

91. After Linus and Anacletus (Cletus), according to Irenaeus, *Adv. Haer.* 3.1.1 (and Hegesippus). See the list in Lightfoot, *The Apostolic Fathers,* I.1, 63ff., 326, 335. However,

of Jewish descent,[92] a conclusion accepted by Brown and others.[93] This is evident from his deep acquaintance with the OT Scriptures, though he also exhibits a smattering of classical knowledge.[94]

C. The Roman Church at the Time of *1 Clement*

1. Some Preliminary Remarks

Although *1 Clement* apparently addresses a situation that had arisen in Corinth, it tells us extremely little of the circumstances. We know nothing about who the troublemakers were; they are merely designated as "young men." We know nothing about the cause of their rebellion against the older presbyters.[95] We know nothing about their teaching or their views of church government. We are not told explicitly about the church's view on the matter, though it appears that the church had sanctioned the deposition. In other words, all the important matters of what constitutes an historical problem are omitted. In fact, we can know very little about the church of

---

Lightfoot is careful to indicate the kind of episcopal office (synonymous with that of presbyter) which Clement could have held at this early time (*The Apostolic Fathers,* I.1, 67-72, esp. 69; Lightfoot, *Philippians,* 95-99, 196). Brown agrees (163f.).

92. Lightfoot, *The Apostolic Fathers,* I.1, 61. Lampe, *Christen,* 172-82, thinks that it is not possible to define Clement sociohistorically.

93. Brown, 161f.

94. Note his utilization of the Phoenix myth (25.2) as well as his obscure reference to the Danaids and Dircae (6.2). On the Phoenix traditions in antiquity, see Lindemann, 263-77.

95. Welborn's suggestion (p. 1059) on the basis of ἐφόδια in 2.1 and Eusebius, *Hist. Eccl.* 4.23.10, that the younger generation was dissatisfied with the supposed provisions sent by the Roman church, is unsubstantiated and precarious. There is no evidence that Corinth ever received financial help from Rome. Eusebius speaks of the Romans helping those in need and in the mines. The reference more naturally would suit Italian cities (κατὰ πᾶσαν πόλιν is clearly an hyperbole) and a later time. It can hardly be supposed that members of the Roman church would sell themselves to slavery to support their own needy, while the Roman church sent financial assistance to Corinth. Besides, *1 Clement* 2.1 does not say that the ἐφόδια Χριστοῦ came from Rome! In view of the concerns of the letter, it is more pertinent to think that the deposition of the older presbyters was a measure taken to check the institutionalization of leadership by the younger generation which was convinced that the Pauline legacy was the pattern of charisma and renewal.

Corinth and its state from this letter. On the other hand, the letter gives us a rare glimpse of the church of Rome.

2. The Genre

There are two passages that give a characterization of this letter: in 58.2 the author describes it as a συμβουλή, while in 63.2 he describes it as ἔντευξις περὶ εἰρήνης καὶ ὁμονοίας. In Ptolemaic papyri ἔντευξις is used frequently in the technical sense of a petition to the king;[96] in Roman times it is used less frequently of a petition to the *strategus.*[97] Lindemann[98] is of the opinion that this description fits best the *Gattungsbestimmung* of *1 Clement.*[99] In this case the letter is not an accusation but an appeal to the Corinthian church, which is herself the judge who decides over her own fate.[100] But note the important difference, that the request to the king concerns not himself but other persons or things, whereas in our case the request to the Corinthians concerns the Corinthians themselves, making this understanding of *1 Clement* difficult.

The ἔντευξις is said to have been made ἐν τῇδε τῇ ἐπιστολῇ, which may imply that the ἔντευξις is understood as being only a part of the letter. This opens the way to considering the other description, that of συμβουλή,[101] as the broader genre of the letter within which the ἔντευξις forms an important part. The probability for this is enhanced by the fact that the συμβουλευτικὸν γένος was one of the three γένη which Greek rhetoric, following Aristotle, recognized: συμβουλευτικόν (deliberative), δικανικόν (forensic), and ἐπιδεικτικόν (epideictic).[102]

96. The term ἔντευξις occurs hundreds of times in the papyri and inscriptions; see, e.g., P Par 26^5; P Flor $I.55^{18}$.

97. See MM, s.v.

98. Lindemann, 13.

99. Since the ἔντευξις normally is addressed to a person of higher rank, there must be a development of the meaning here (cf. BAGD, s.v.).

100. Lindemann, 14: "Aus der Sicht Roms stünde die korinthische Kirche aber nicht einfach unter einer Anklage, sondern sie wäre als Empfängerin der ἔντευξις zugleich Richterin in eigener Sache. Die römische Kirche teilt der korinthischen also nicht ein schon (gleichsam in absentia) gefälltes Urteil mit, sondern sie überläßt die Entscheidung der Adressatin."

101. In 56.2 the Roman church seems to consider its letter as a νουθέτησις, a synonym of συμβουλή.

102. *Ars Rhetorica* 1.3.3.

A very brief account of Aristotle's system will be given, taking up the salient points, particularly those that are of relevance for *1 Clement.* The task of the συμβουλευτικὸν γένος is to exhort or to dissuade (τὸ μὲν προτροπὴ τὸ δὲ ἀποτροπή).[103] In distinction to forensic and epideictic oratory, which are concerned with the past and present respectively, the συμβουλευτικὸν γένος is concerned with the future (ὁ μέλλων), and its objective is that which is expedient or harmful (τὸ συμφέρον καὶ βλαβερόν).[104] Moreover, the συμβουλευτικὸν γένος deals only with matters that are contingent and under our control.[105] Of the five subject matters with which this kind of rhetoric is concerned,[106] the one about war and peace (περὶ πολέμου καὶ εἰρήνης) fits *1 Clement* best. This means that the situation in Corinth is understood as a kind of στάσις,[107] which, perhaps with political overtones, might be compared with a situation of danger in a city arising out of sedition from within or threat of war from without.

There are two kinds of proofs — example (παράδειγμα) and *enthymeme* (ἐνθύμημα)[108] — of which the former is more suitable to the συμβουλευτικὸν γένος.[109] There are two kinds of παραδείγματα, one in relating things that have occurred, the other in inventing examples oneself, like fables. *1 Clement* is full of the first type (cf. its OT examples), while we might assign the story of the Phoenix to the second type.

Style (περὶ τῆς λέξεως) is concerned with the effective presentation of the subject matter.[110] The chief qualities of style are perspicacity (σαφή)

103. *Ars Rhetorica* 1.3.3.

104. *Ars Rhetorica* 1.3.4-5.

105. *Ars Rhetorica* 1.4.3: ἀλλὰ δῆλον ὅτι περὶ ὅσων ἐστὶ τὸ βουλεύεσθαι. τοιαῦτα δ' ἐστὶν ὅσα πέφυκεν ἀνάγεσθαι εἰς ὑμᾶς, καὶ ὧν ἡ ἀρχὴ τῆς γενέσεως ἐφ' ἡμῖν ἐστίν.

106. Περι; (i) πόρων, (ii) πολέμου καὶ εἰρήνης, (iii) φυλακῆς τῆς χώρας, (iv) τῶν εἰσαγομένων καὶ ἐξαγομένων, and (v) νομοθεσίας (*Ars Rhetorica* 1.4.7).

107. Cf. *1 Clement* 57.1: ὑμεῖς οἱ τὴν καταβολὴν τῆς στάσεως ποιήσαντες; 63.1: ὅπως ἡσυχάσαντες τῆς ματαίας στάσεως.

108. A kind of syllogism based on probable premises, which lacks a clause that is easily deduced and thus mentally supplied, e.g.:

ἡ δικαιοσύνη ἀρετὴ ἐστί,
ἄρα ἡ δικαιοσύνη ἀξιέπαινος ἔστι.

The missing clause, on which the conclusion is based, is: ἡ ἀρετὴ ἀξιέπαινος ἔστι.

109. *Ars Rhetorica* 2.20.1-2; 3.17.5.

110. *Ars Rhetorica* 3.1.1-2.

and propriety (πρέπουσα).[111] The latter consists of a diction that is emotional, ethical, and proportionate to the subject matter.[112] *1 Clement* certainly conforms to these demands, except perhaps to the last one. That is, one may wonder whether the arguments (examples) do not stand out of all proportion to his stated purpose. The συμβουλευτικὸν γένος is the least finished of the three kinds of rhetoric.[113]

With regard to the arrangement of the parts (μέρη τοῦ λόγου), Aristotle recognizes two main parts as absolutely necessary: presentation, or statement of the problem (πρόθεσις), and proof (πίστις).[114] Proem (προοίμιον), comparison (ἀντιπαραβολή), and recapitulation (ἐπάνοδος) may occur only if there is contradiction (ἀντιλογία).[115] Narrative (διήγησις) is difficult to fit into this kind of rhetoric,[116] having limited scope because deliberative rhetoric (συμβουλευτικόν, δημηγορική) is concerned chiefly with the future. However, if there is narrative, it will be concerned with things past ἵν' ἀναμνησθέντες ἐκείνων βέλτιον βουλεύσωνται περὶ τῶν ὕστερον.[117] Here, too, *1 Clement* keeps to the rules, in that it contains a recapitulation (ἐπάνοδος) (62–65), but extremely little narrative (i.e., the background of the conflict) and a wealth of protreptic examples (proof).

The above remarks do not imply that the author of *1 Clement* had Aristotle's manual in front of him as he penned his letter. They imply rather an awareness of the rhetorical devices suitable to his purpose and that these can be readily explained from Aristotle's work on rhetoric.

3. *The Addresser and the Addressees*

Unlike Paul, who in his letter to the Romans addresses the church of Rome as an apostle, dwelling at great length on his call and extraordinary qualifications (1:1-5), the author of this letter does not even mention his name

111. *Ars Rhetorica* 3.1.2.

112. *Ars Rhetorica* 3.7.1: Τὸ δὲ πρέπον ἕξει ἡ λέξις, ἐὰν ᾖ παθητική τε καὶ ἠθικὴ καὶ τοῖς ὑποκειμένοις πράγμασιν ἀνάλογον.

113. *Ars Rhetorica* 3.12.1-2, 5: ἡ μὲν οὖν δημηγορικὴ λέξις καὶ παντελῶς ἔοικε τῇ σκιαγραφίᾳ. Here, as further on, δημηγορική takes the place of συμβουλευτικόν.

114. *Ars Rhetorica* 3.13.1, esp. 4.

115. *Ars Rhetorica* 3.13.1-3.

116. *Ars Rhetorica* 3.13.3; 3.16.11.

117. *Ars Rhetorica* 3.16.11.

in the address or, indeed, anywhere else. There is thus an immense difference between Paul and the author of *1 Clement* in the way they envisage their respective relationships to the churches they address. Paul writes in his own name and with the authority of an apostle. The author of *1 Clement* writes in the name of the Roman church. In fact, the unpretentious designation "The church of God which sojourns in Rome" writing to "The church of God which sojourns in Corinth" indicates the total equality between the two churches. This is in line with the constant use of the first person plural and the extreme tact the author exhibits in the earlier part of the letter to gradually assume a more authoritarian tone.

4. The Composition of the Roman Church

The first thing to note here is that *1 Clement* gives no evidence of any house groups, but speaks not only of the Christians in Corinth but also of the Christians in Rome as one entity, not only theologically but also sociologically and administratively. He speaks of both churches as ἐκκλησία. This goes counter to Lampe's claim[118] that during the first two centuries the Roman church consisted solely of house groups. Indeed, more than that, if at the time Paul wrote Romans there had been seven house groups and Paul, instead of uniting them, had added his own (eighth) group,[119] it may be asked when the Roman church was united, say, between the sixties and the nineties. There is no evidence for such an event. Neither Hebrews nor 1 Peter gives any evidence.

Second, the Roman church at the time of *1 Clement* was composed mainly of Gentiles, and was still predominantly of Greek character. The Latin element will not make its presence appreciably felt until some considerable time later.[120]

Third, the Roman church had been put hard to the test since Paul had written his letter to it. Nero's savagery and Domitian's refined sadism had harvested countless Roman Christians, among them the great apostles Peter

118. Lampe, "Roman Christians of Romans 16," 229.

119. Lampe, "Roman Christians of Romans 16," 229f.

120. To the four points mentioned under II.C.2 and nn. 31 and 32 above may be added: (a) that their Scripture, as is witnessed by *1 Clement,* is the LXX, and (b) that they, too, write their letter to Corinth in Greek, and in rather good Greek at that.

and Paul. How much these two apostles — the only ones connected by tradition with the Roman church — had contributed to the formation of the church is difficult to say. However, their steadfastness to death became an example for others to follow. Along with them there perished a great multitude (6.1) of Roman Christians. *1 Clement,* dwelling upon the motif of womanly weakness or delicacy (6.2, echoing 1 Pet. 3:7), alludes to terrible and indecent indignities suffered by women, who are thus praised for their heroic faith. In other cases the Christian faith of its members led to the disruption of the marriage union, which must have caused great pain to the church (5.2-3).

Fourth, sociologically the picture cannot have changed appreciably since Romans. We saw, above, that according to Romans the church included rich and poor, exalted and of low estate. In the Roman church of *1 Clement* we find a similar situation: "Let the strong care for . . . the weak reverence; the rich bestow . . . the poor give thanks; the wise . . . the humble . . ." (38.2).[121] In the closing prayer, which is often understood to be a part of the Roman liturgy, fervent prayer is directed to God to help and succor "the afflicted . . . the lowly . . . the needy . . . the hungry . . . the prisoners . . . the sick . . . the faint-hearted" (59.4). This cross section of Roman Christian society gives a good picture of the situation. More concretely, we are told specifically of many believers (ἐπιστάμεθα πολλούς) who delivered themselves up to imprisonment or bondage (δεσμά) in order to redeem or save (λυτρώσονται) their fellow Christians, and of many others who sold themselves to slavery (ἑαυτοὺς παρέδωκαν εἰς δουλείαν) in order to provide bread for their fellow Christians (ἐψώμισαν) (55.2). The first group may be a reference to those who refused to betray their fellow Christians during the persecutions, and may be giving the positive side of a complex situation, of which Tacitus gave the negative side when he described the leading Christians as giving up to the persecutors the names of their fellow Christians.[122] The second group, however, shows, as Lampe has pointed out, (a) that these Christians could not have been Roman citizens, (b) that the need of the poor was so great and that no other means were available to relieve it than this extreme measure, and

121. Though this is directed to the Corinthian church, the first person plural and the general reference of the statement indicate personal acquaintance with the condition.

122. Tacitus, *Annals* 15.44. See Lightfoot, *The Apostolic Fathers,* I.2, 160, and Lindemann, 155f., who, however, do not appear to recognize two groups. See also Lightfoot, *The Apostolic Fathers,* II.2, 305f. (on Ignatius, *Smyrn.* 6).

(c) that the church was socially integrated and solidified.[123] In my opinion this whole action presupposes, furthermore, the integration and solidarity of the Roman Christians at large, and at the same time it constitutes further evidence for the unity of the Roman church and disproof of the theory that Roman Christianity consisted of small, divided, and even competing groups of Christians.

Fifth, we saw above that the gospel had begun to make itself felt in the higher strata of society, as in the case of Pomponia Graecina and, following Paul's arrival, among "those of Caesar's household." Nearer the time of *1 Clement* we have the case of the consul Titus Flavius Clemens and his wife Domitilla, both related to the imperial Flavian family. The Christian standing of the consul is questioned, but that of Domitilla is accepted as certain.[124] In addition to these, it has been argued that Rome's envoys to Corinth, Claudius Ephebus and Valerius Biton, who had had a high reputation for their faith since their youth, have been chosen because of their authoritative position in the Roman church.[125] Lightfoot[126] surmised that these persons might be freedmen, associated with the houses of Claudius and his wife Messalina, who was a Valerian.[127] But as Lindemann points out,[128] these are uncertain conclusions. However, we ought not to think of the Roman church as composed to any appreciable degree of slaves. The impression gained from the Corinthian correspondence is that Paul is addressing ordinary, free persons, not slaves. Sociologically, it is fairly improbable that a church with a slave's outlook could have addressed such a letter as *1 Clement* to a church composed of free people.

There are other personalities that might be considered here, such as the author of the letter himself, but these examples suffice to show that the

123. Lampe, *Christen*, 68f.

124. See the long discussions in Lightfoot, *The Apostolic Fathers*, I.1, 33-51; Lampe, *Christen*, 166-72.

125. Lampe, *Christen*, 155, "Das die stadtrömischen Christen in Claudius und Valerius Autoritätspersonen sahen, sie zu ihren Repräsentanten gegenüber den Korinthern bestellten, gegen die sonstigen Gepflogenheiten urchristlicher Briefliteratur ihre Gentilicia besonders hervorhoben, sind m. E. drei Indizien dafür, das Claudius und Valerius soziologisch zu den 'Spitzen' des stadtrömischen Christentum im 1. Jh. zählten, zu denen die meisten übrigen Christen in Rom 'aufsahen'."

126. Lightfoot, *The Apostolic Fathers*, I.1, 27-29.

127. Inscriptions associate the two names, even in the relationship of parent and child. See, e.g., *CIL* X.2271; VI.4548; 15174; 15304; 15351.

128. Lindemann, 180.

church of Rome could number among its members — if often in a rather discreet manner — persons who were drawn from the higher strata of society. Nevertheless, the great majority of Roman Christians were recruited from the lower or sometimes even lowest strata of society, and in this respect this church was not any different from the church of Corinth to which Paul had written βλέπετε . . . τὴν κλῆσιν ὑμῶν . . . ὅτι οὐ πολλοὶ σοφοί . . . δυνατοί . . . εὐγενεῖς . . . etc. (1 Cor. 1:26ff.). These words do not imply slaves, but people of a very ordinary standing.

5. The Structure of Authority in the Roman Church and the Question of Obedience and Harmony

1 Clement uses three words to describe church officials: ἐπίσκοπος (bishop, two times: 42.4, 5), διάκονος (deacon, two times: 42.4, 5), and πρεσβύτερος (presbyter, four times: 44.5; 47.6; 54.2; 57.1). The ἐπίσκοπος and the πρεσβύτερος refer to the same office, the office of elder or overseer.[129] The terms themselves are all "Pauline," but the force behind them is original to this letter. Taking its cue from Titus 1:5, "appoint elders in every city," *1 Clement* lays down that the apostles, who were sent out by Christ, who in turn had been sent out by God, "in every district . . . and every city . . . appointed their first converts . . . as bishops and deacons" (κατὰ χώρας . . . καὶ πόλεις . . . καθίστανον τὰς ἀπαρχὰς αὐτῶν . . . εἰς ἐπισκόπους καὶ διακόνους) (42.1-4). This is carried a decisive step further in 44.1-2, which claims that the apostles, foreseeing that there would be strife about the office of bishop κατέστησαν τοὺς προειρημένους, καὶ μεταξὺ ἐπινομὴν δεδώκασιν, ὅπως, ἐὰν κοιμηθῶσιν, διαδέξωνται ἕτεροι δεδοκιμασμένοι ἄνδρες τὴν λειτουργίαν αὐτῶν. The meaning of the word ἐπινομή is problematic;[130] however, in view of Titus 1:5, ὡς ἐγώ σοι διεταξάμην, from which this idea derives its biblical support, it should be taken in the sense of "directive" or "instruction."[131] The great difference

129. See Titus 1:5-7; cf. also 1 Tim. 3:1 and 5:17. See further Lightfoot, *The Apostolic Fathers,* I.1, 69; I.2, 129, and Lindemann, 126-28.

130. Lightfoot, *The Apostolic Fathers,* I.2, 132f., emends to ἐπιμονή (permanence), and gives the linguistic options as well as the older discussion. See also BAGD, s.v.

131. Similarly, Lindemann, 130, who, without referring to Titus 1:7, renders with "Anweisung"; K. Lake, *Apostolic Fathers* (Loeb), renders with "codicil."

between the model passage (Titus 1:5-7) and *1 Clement* is that the former says nothing about any succession. Titus is merely to appoint presbyters or bishops, but they are not taking Paul's place in any way. In fact, they cannot.[132] In the *1 Clement* passage, however, the thus appointed bishops "succeed to their [i.e., the apostles'] ministry" (διαδέξωνται . . . τὴν λειτουργίαν αὐτῶν). There is thus an inconsistency in *1 Clement*. On the one hand the writer — assuming him to be Clement, the third bishop of Rome — totally effaces himself, the letter being sent by and having the authority of the whole church, while on the other hand he seeks here to establish an apostolic succession between the apostles and his own office! This he does, however, only indirectly. For his apparently primary reason for positing this apostolic succession is to establish the God-given right of the old presbyters of Corinth and thus show the heinousness of the action of the rebels in deposing them. Thus, although the bishop still does not have monarchical powers but functions simply as the mouthpiece of the whole church, *1 Clement* lays the foundation for such a development.

Whence, then, does this imperious tone come in addressing a sister church, which could make an even greater claim to apostolic foundation and contact than Rome? The answer must be sought not in apostolic succession — this was put forth for Corinthian consumption — but within the church of Rome itself. One factor must be that the Roman church had emerged victorious from "the sudden and repeated misfortunes and calamities" (1.1) which it had experienced under Nero and Domitian. This "victory" had no doubt boosted Roman confidence and given it a sense of strength. But another and even more potent factor seems to have been its being the church of the capital.[133] Living in the most important city of the empire, it was easy for the Roman Christians to exchange the principles at work in the kingdom of God for the principles at work in the kingdom of the Romans. A breach of order and a revolt against legitimate authority in a provincial city must be met decisively and inexorably. In spite of the use of the first person plural and the pleading tone of the letter, the indisputable fact is that the Roman church is not giving simply a fraternal counsel to the church of Corinth.[134] It is surprising that it is not asking for any explanations, nor for the general opinion of the church of Corinth. Uni-

132. Cf. N. Brox, *A History of the Early Church* (London: SCM Press, 1994), 74ff.
133. To the same effect, Brox, 83ff.
134. Similarly Welborn, 1059.

laterally it takes the side of the deposed elders, although it is implicitly clear that the church of Corinth has endorsed the deposition (44.6), and in effect demands that the Corinthian church comply with its request. For this reason it sends not one but three representatives — witnesses, we might say — and so to speak, "draws the circle" around the Corinthian Christians as C. Popillius Laenas once had done with Antiochus Epiphanes.[135] Its "συμβουλή" sounds more like an ultimatum: ἐὰν δέ τινες ἀπειθήσουσιν τοῖς ὑπ' αὐτοῦ δι' ἡμῶν εἰρημένοις, γινωσκέτωσαν ὅτι παραπτώσει καὶ κινδύνῳ οὐ μικρῷ ἑαυτοὺς ἐνδύσουσιν (59.1). And again, θεμιτὸν οὖν ἐστίν . . . ὑποθεῖναι τὸν τράχηλον καὶ τὸν τῆς ὑπακοῆς τόπον ἀναπληρῶσαι . . . χαρὰν γὰρ καὶ ἀγαλλίασιν ἡμῖν παρέξετε, ἐὰν ὑπήκοοι γενόμενοι τοῖς ὑφ' ὑμῶν γεγραμμένοις διὰ τοῦ ἁγίου πνεύματος . . . (63.1-2). What is demanded is nothing less than the bowing of the neck and unconditional obedience.

But the Roman church has no formal right to demand these things. Hence the arguments used to achieve this end are, in line with the συμβουλευτικὸν γένος, the example.[136] The attempt is made by means of manifold examples from the OT to "rub in" the order established by God, an order which had prophetically even foreshadowed the NT offices of bishop and deacon (42.5–44.4). These examples are reinforced by NT examples, chief of which are those of Peter and Paul (5.3-7; 47), who suffered on account of the same ζῆλος which now plagues the Corinthians. But above all the letter is dominated by two key words: εἰρήνη and ὁμόνοια. The first occurs fifteen times, the second eight times, and the two together an additional six times. The first is a NT word; the second is not. But though both words might well describe the NT idea of peace and unity or like-mindedness in the church, it would appear that the peace and concord of *1 Clement* is more akin with the Pax Romana. Peace and concord are understood as obtaining when the establishment is intact, when the offices of those who rule are secure, when the challengers are in exile. For this reason the idea of concord is forced upon a number of OT passages (e.g., 9.4; 11) and becomes even a characteristic of love, as in 49.5, a passage patterned on 1 Corinthians 13, from which it is absent. Welborn, who shares

135. Livy, 45.12.

136. Similarly Welborn, 1056: "That the author did not possess the authority he claims is evident from the rhetorical character of the letter: He must persuade by argument and induce by example; that is, it is not yet his to command."

my analysis, pursues the matter in more detail, showing by specific references to ancient literature how the Roman church patterned its treatment of other churches on the model of the Roman Empire.[137]

This leads finally to the relation of *1 Clement* to the Roman authorities. If Paul had counseled "submission" to the authorities on account of conscience (Rom. 13:1-7), *1 Clement* shows a harmonious relationship to the Roman imperium: thus in 37.1 "the soldiers under our generals" are an example of obedience and order to be emulated by the Christians, while in the liturgical prayer God's help is petitioned in order to "do the things that are good and pleasing before . . . our rulers" (60.2), "that we may be obedient . . . to our rulers and governors on earth" (60.4). It is thus obvious that for *1 Clement* the glory, honor, and dominion of the empire are God-given (61.1-2).

IV. Comparisons with Romans, Conclusions, and Further Reflections

1. *1 Clement* has the authority of the whole Roman church behind it, not that of one or more house groups. Since the church was also one at the time of Paul, continuity, not development, is discernible here.

2. The persecutions by Nero and Domitian had left indelible marks on the church of Rome, but Roman Christianity emerged victorious, strong, unified. The trials and privations which the members of the church had endured had helped unite and solidify it. The problems characterizing the church at the time of Paul are no longer apparent. The leaders (bishop-presbyters and deacons) have a firm grip on the church.

3. Sociologically, the church continues to penetrate the higher strata of society, though the large masses are still drawn from the lower or even lowest classes. The author of *1 Clement* as well as the three envoys sent to Corinth may have been freedmen or descendants of freedmen, and thus represent a church sector of a higher rank. The church is still Greek-speaking and in its majority still non-Latin; the Jewish element can hardly have been more than negligible.

4. The LXX dominates the thinking of the church — inasmuch as this

137. Welborn, 1055-60. Similarly Brox, 83ff.

is reflected in *1 Clement* — being regarded as the authoritative word of God, but is at times interpreted tendentiously.

5. The structure of the church shows considerable advance since the time of Paul. Romans does not mention any church officials. The great difference with *1 Clement* is not that it does, but that these officials are invested with rights and powers proceeding from a succession, which has no basis in Romans or elsewhere in the NT.

6. In similarity with the above line of development (or discontinuity) in regard to the structure of the Roman church since the time of Paul, the church of the capital is becoming conscious of its position and has begun to assume the airs that befit such a position. In spite of the use of the first person plural, *1 Clement* reveals a church that is inspired by the order of the Roman imperium and aspires to power over the churches of the provinces. The wishes of the Corinthian Christians are of no consequence. The problem of Corinth gives an opportunity for intervention. The Roman church's inexorable line must be carried through, and to this intent all possible means are put to use. Using the ultimate (psychological) weapon that failure to comply with its directions is tantamount to opposing God's will and order, it tries to coax and coerce the dissidents into submission. We do not know what the result was. The letter was read and esteemed at the time of Dionysius, who himself sent similar letters to other churches, but it was always distinguished from the canonical books of the NT[138] and was criticized by the learned Photius, chiefly for its imprecise Christology.[139]

7. *1 Clement* also shows that the time of creative Christian writing is over.[140] The letter has nothing new to offer. Its strength lies in its mastery of the OT and its ability to marshal appropriate examples (though often slanted) for its argumentation. The Christianity it represents is not of the Pauline type; it is a Jewish type, heavily influenced by the OT cultus.[141]

8. The above point may imply that the trouble in Corinth was the desire for a renewal, perhaps, of a charismatic (Pauline) type of church government, which led to the deposition of the old presbyters, who repre-

138. See Lightfoot, *The Apostolic Fathers,* I.1, 366-78.

139. Photius, *Bibliotheca* (Codex 125), 94b. Cf. also Lightfoot, *The Apostolic Fathers,* I.1, 375.

140. Similarly Lightfoot, *The Apostolic Fathers,* I.1, 103. See also some interesting remarks in F. W. Farrar, *The Early Days of Christianity* (London: Cassell, 1888), 57f.

141. See Brown, 169ff.

sented a static authority. If this is correct, *1 Clement* represents the Roman repudiation of Pauline Christianity and its definite embracing of a more static, sacerdotal type of Christianity, patterned on the OT and Judaism. Perhaps after all, what we have in *1 Clement* is that beneath the Corinthian problem and the Roman church's reaction lies the triumph of the Jewish-Christian point of view over the Pauline understanding of Christianity, and this may imply also the long-term failure of Paul's letter among the Roman Christians. This also shows that the Roman church is no longer the weak, dissentient, problematic, obscure church of the time of Romans. It has assumed a position of prominence.

Bibliography

Afanassieff, N. "L'assemblée eucharistique unique dans l'Église ancienne." *Kleronomia* 6 (1974) 1-34.

Andreau, Jean. *Les affaires de monsieur Jucundus.* Collection de l'Ecole Française de Rome 19. Rome, 1974.

Applebaum, S. "The Organization of Jewish Communities in the Diaspora." In *The Jewish People in the First Century.* S. Safrai and S. Stern, eds. Philadelphia: Fortress, 1974, 498-501.

———. *Jews and Greeks in Ancient Cyrene.* Leiden: Brill, 1979.

Arrupé, Pedro. "Letter to the Whole Society on Inculturation." In *Other Apostolates Today: Selected Letters and Addresses of Pedro Arrupé.* J. Aixala, ed. Vol. 3. St. Louis: 1981 (1978), 172-81.

Aune, David. "Orthodoxy in First Century Judaism?" *Journal for the Study of Judaism* 7 (1976) 1-10.

Balch, David L. *Let Wives Be Submissive: The Domestic Code in I Peter.* Chico, CA: Scholars Press, 1981.

Banks, R. *Paul's Idea of Community.* Grand Rapids: Eerdmans, 1980.

Barnard, L. W. "Clement of Rome and the Persecution of Domitian." *New Testament Studies* 10 (1963-64) 252-60.

———. "The Early Roman Church, Judaism, and Jewish-Christianity." *Anglican Theological Review* 49 (1967) 371-84.

Baron, S. W. *A Social and Religious History of the Jews.* Philadelphia: The Jewish Publication Society of America, 1952.

Barr, David L. "The Apocalypse of John as Oral Enactment." *Interpretation* 40 (1983) 243-56.

Bibliography

Barrett, C. K. *A Commentary on the Epistle to the Romans.* Black's New Testament Commentary. London: A. & C. Black, 1962.

Bassler, J. "Divine Impartiality in Paul's Letter to the Romans." *Novum Testamentum* 26 (1981) 43-58.

———. *The Impartiality of God: Paul and a Theological Axiom.* Chico, CA: Scholars Press, 1982.

Bauman, R. A. "The Suppression of the Bacchanals: Five Questions." *Historia* 39 (1990) 334-48.

Beard, Mary. "Ancient Literacy and the Function of the Written Word in Roman Religion." In *Literacy in the Roman World.* J. H. Humphrey, ed. *Journal of Roman Archaeology* Supp. Ser. 3. Ann Arbor: Department of Classical Studies, University of Michigan, 1991, 35-58.

Beaujue, J. "L'incendie de Rome en 64 et les Chrétiens." *Latomus* 19 (1960) 65-80, 291-311.

Becatti, Giovanni. *Scavi di Ostia, Volume VI. Edificio con Opus Sectile fuori Porta Marina.* Rome: Instituto Poligrafico dello Stato, 1967.

Beker, J. C. "The Faithfulness of God and the Priority of Israel in Paul's Letter to the Romans." In *The Romans Debate.* K. P. Donfried, ed. 2nd ed. Peabody, MA: Hendrickson, 1991, 327-32.

Ben-Rafael, Eliezer. *The Emergence of Ethnicity: Cultural Groups and Social Conflict.* Westport CT: Greenwood Press, 1982.

Berger, P., and T. Luckmann, *The Social Construction of Reality.* Garden City, NY: Doubleday, 1966.

Bernhardt, R. *Polis und römische Herrschaft in der späteren Republik (149-31 v. Chr.).* Berlin: de Gruyter, 1985.

Beyschlag, Karlmann. *Clemens Romanus und der Frükatholizismus. Untersuchungen zu I Clemens 1–7.* Tübingen: J. C. B. Mohr (Paul Siebeck), 1966.

Bickermann, E. "The Altars of the Gentiles: A Note on the Jewish 'Ius Sacrum.'" In Studies in Jewish and Christian History 2. Leiden: Brill, 1980, 324-46.

Blake, M. E. *Roman Construction in Italy from Tiberius through the Flavians.* Washington: Carnegie Institute, 1959.

Blue, B. "Acts and the House Church." In *The Book of Acts in Its First Century Setting.* Vol. 2. Grand Rapids: Eerdmans, 1994, 119-222.

Boersma, J. S. *Amoenissima civitas.* Leiden: Brill, 1987.

Bornkamm, G. "The Letter to the Romans as Paul's Last Will and Testament." In *The Romans Debate.* K. P. Donfried, ed. 2nd ed. Peabody, MA: Hendrickson, 1991, 16-28.

Bosch, David J. *Transforming Mission.* Maryknoll, NY: Orbis, 1991.

Boswell, John. *The Kindness of Strangers: The Abandonment of Children in Western Europe from Late Antiquity to the Renaissance.* New York: Pantheon, 1988.

Bovini, Giuseppe. *Ravenna: An Art City.* Ravenna: Edizioni A. Longo, 1967.

Bowe, Barbara. *A Church in Crisis: Ecclesiology and Paraenesis in Clement of Rome.* Harvard Dissertations in Religion 23. Minneapolis: Fortress, 1988.

Bowsky, M. W. Baldwin. "M. Tittius and the Jews of Berenice." *American Journal of Philology* 108 (1987) 495-510.

Bradley, Keith R. *Slavery and Rebellion in the Roman World, 140 BC–70 BC.* London: Oxford University Press, 1989.

Brooten, Bernadette J. *Women Leaders in the Ancient Synagogue: Inscriptional Evidence and Background Issues.* Brown Judaic Studies 36. Chico, CA: Scholars Press, 1982.

Brown, Peter. *Augustine of Hippo.* Berkeley/Los Angeles/London: University of California Press, 1967.

Brown, R. E. "Not Jewish Christianity and Gentile Christianity, but Types of Jewish/Gentile Christianity." *Catholic Biblical Quarterly* 45 (1983) 74-79.

———, and John P. Meier. *Antioch and Rome.* New York: Paulist Press, 1983.

Brox, Norbert. *Der Hirt des Hermas.* Ergänzungsreihe zum Kritisch-exegetischen Kommentar über das Neue Testament 7. Göttingen: Vandenhoeck and Ruprecht, 1991.

———. *A History of the Early Church.* London: SCM Press, 1994.

Bruce, F. F. "Christianity under Claudius." *Bulletin of the John Rylands Library* 44 (1961-62) 309-26.

———. "The Romans Debate — Continued." In *The Romans Debate.* K. P. Donfried, ed. 2nd ed. Peabody, MA: Hendrickson, 1991, 178-82.

———. " 'To the Hebrews': A Document of Roman Christianity?" *Aufstieg und Niedergang der römischen Welt* 25.4 (1987) 3513-19.

———. *The Epistle of St Paul to the Romans.* Tyndale New Testament Commentary. London: Tyndale, 1963.

———. *The Epistles to the Colossians, to Philemon, and to the Ephesians.* New International Commentary on the New Testament. Grand Rapids: Eerdmans, 1984.

Bruun, Patrick. "Symboles, signes et monogrammes." In *Sylloge inscriptionum christianarum veterum musei vaticani.* H. Zilliacus, ed. Acta instituti Romani Finlandiae 1, 1-2. Helsinki, 1963, 73-166.

Buchanan, G. *To the Hebrews.* Anchor Bible 36. Garden City, NY: Doubleday, 1972.

Bush, Archie C. *Studies in Roman Social Structure.* Washington, DC: University Press of America, 1982.

Calderone, S. "Superstitio." *Aufstieg und Niedergang der römischen Welt* 2.1.2 (1972) 377-96.

Cameron, A. "*THREPTOS* and Related Terms in the Inscriptions of Asia Minor." In *Anatolian Studies Presented to William H. Buckler.* W. M. Clader and Josef Keil, eds. Manchester: Manchester University Press, 1939, 27-62.

Campbell, W. S. "Romans III as a Key to the Structure and Thought of the Letter."

In *The Romans Debate.* K. P. Donfried, ed. 2nd ed. Peabody, MA: Hendrickson, 1991, 251-64.

Carcopino, Jérôme. *Daily Life in Ancient Rome.* New Haven: Yale University Press, 1963.

Carlebach, A. "Rabbinic References to Fiscus Judaicus." *Jewish Quarterly Review* 66 (1975) 57-61.

Carlini, Antonio. "Le passeggiate di Erma verso Cuma su due luoghi controversi del *Pastore.*" In *Studi in onore di E. Bresciani.* Pisa: Giardini, 1986, 105-9.

———, ed. *Erma. Il Pastore Ia-IIIa visione, Papyrus Bodmer 38.* Cologny-Genève: Fondation Martin Bodmer, 1991.

Carson, R. A. G. *Coins of the Roman Empire.* New York: Routledge, 1990.

Chadwick, H. "Justification by Faith and Hospitality." In *Studia Patristica* 4. F. L. Cross, ed. Texte und Untersuchungen 79. Berlin: Akademie, 1961, 281-88.

Charlesworth, James H., ed. *Jesus' Jewishness: Exploring the Place of Jesus in Early Judaism.* New York: Crossroad Publishing, 1996 (1991).

Childe, Vere Gordon. *The Danube in Prehistory.* Oxford: Clarendon, 1929.

Cirillo, Luigi. "Il pastore di Erma e la storia," *Miscellanea di Studi storici* 2 (1982) 35-58.

Clark, Gillian. "Roman Women." *Greece and Rome* 28 (1981) 193-212.

Clarke, W. K. L. *The First Epistle of Clement to the Corinthians.* London: SPCK, 1937.

Coarelli, F. "I monumenti dei culti orientali in Roma." In *La soteriologia dei culti oriental nell'impero romano.* U. Bianchi and M. J. Vermaseren, eds. Leiden: Brill, 1982, 33-67.

Cockerill, Gareth L. "Heb 1:1-14, *1 Clem.* 36:1-6 and the High Priest Title." *Journal of Biblical Literature* 97 (1978) 437-40.

Cohen, S. J. D. "Crossing the Boundary and Becoming a Jew." *Harvard Theological Review* 82 (1989) 13-33.

Coser, L. A. "Conflict: Social Aspects." In *International Encyclopedia of the Social Sciences.* Vol. 3. D. L. Sills, ed. New York: Macmillan and the Free Press, 1968, 232-36.

———. *The Functions of Social Conflict.* London: Routledge and Kegan Paul, 1965, 125-27.

Costa, Ray O., ed. *One Faith, Many Cultures: Inculturation, Indigenization, and Contextualization.* Maryknoll NY: Orbis, 1988.

Cotter, Wendy. "Collegia." In *Voluntary Associations in the Ancient World.* John S. Kloppenborg and S. G. Wilson, eds. London: Routledge, 1996, 74-89.

Countryman, W. *The Rich Christian in the Church of the Early Empire: Contradictions and Accommodations.* New York/Toronto: Edwin Mellen, 1980.

Cowley, A. *Aramaic Papyri of the Fifth Century B.C.* Oxford: Oxford University Press, 1923.

Cramer, F. H. "Expulsion of Astrologers from Ancient Rome." *Classica et Mediaevalia* 12 (1951) 9-50.

Cranfield, C. E. B. *A Critical and Exegetical Commentary on the Epistle to the Romans.* 2 vols. International Critical Commentary. Edinburgh: T. & T. Clark, 1975-79.

D'Alès, Adhémar. *L' édit de Calliste. Etudes sur les origines de la pénitence chrétienne.* Paris: Beauchesne, 1914.

D'Arms, John H. *Commerce and Social Standing in Ancient Rome.* Cambridge: Harvard University Press, 1981.

Dahl, N. A. *Studies in Paul.* Minneapolis: Augsburg, 1977.

Dahms, J. V. "The First Readers of Hebrews." *Journal of the Evangelical Theological Society* 20 (1977) 365-75.

de Ste Croix, G. E. M. "Why Were the Early Christians Persecuted?" *Past and Present* 26 (1963) 24-28.

Dewey, Joanna. "Mark as Aural Narrative: Structures as Clues to Understanding." *Sewanee Theological Review* 36 (1992) 45-56.

———. "Mark as Interwoven Tapestry: Forecasts and Echoes for a Listening Audience." *Catholic Biblical Quarterly* 53 (1991) 221-36.

———. "Oral Methods of Structuring Narrative in Mark." *Interpretation* 53 (1989) 32-44.

Dexter, Caroline E. "The Casa di L. Cecilio Giocondo in Pompeii." Ph.D. diss., Duke University, Durham, NC, 1974.

Dibelius, Martin. "Rom. und die Christen im ersten Jahrhundert." In *Botschaft und Geschichte.* 2 vols. Tübingen: J. C. B. Mohr, 1956, 2.177-228.

———. *Der Hirt des Hermas.* Handbuch zum Neuen Testament Ergänzungsband. Apostolischen Väter 4. Tübingen: J. C. B. Mohr (Paul Siebeck), 1923.

Dinkler, Erich. "Shalom–Eirene–Pax: Jüdische Sepulkralinschriften und ihr Verhältnis zum frühen Christentum." *Rivista Archeologia Christiana* 50 (1974) 121-44.

Dixon, Suzanne. *The Roman Mother.* Norman, OK: University of Oklahoma Press, 1988.

Donfried, K. P. "False Presuppositions in the Study of Romans." In *The Romans Debate.* K. P. Donfried, ed. 2nd ed. Peabody, MA: Hendrickson, 1991, 102-24.

———. ed., *The Romans Debate.* Peabody, MA: Hendrickson, 2nd ed. 1991.

Downing, F. Gerald. "A bas les aristos: The Relevance of Higher Literature for the Understanding of the Earliest Christian Writing." *Novum Testamentum* 30 (1988) 212-30.

Drane, J. "Why Did Paul Write Romans?" In *Pauline Studies,* D. Hagner and M. Harris, eds. Grand Rapids: Eerdmans, 1980, 208-27.

Duncan-Jones, Richard. *Structure and Scale in the Roman Economy.* Cambridge: Cambridge University Press, 1990.

———. *The Economy of the Roman Empire: Quantitative Studies.* Cambridge: Cambridge University Press, 1974.

Dunn, J. D. G. *Romans 9–16.* Word Biblical Commentary 38B. Waco, TX: Word, 1988.

Eck, Werner. "Inschriften aus der vatikanischen Nekropole unter St. Peter." *Zeitschrift für Papyrologie und Epigraphik* 65 (1986) 245-93.

———. "Inschriften und Grabbauten in der Nekropole unter St. Peter." In *Die Antike im Brennpunkt.* P. Neukam, ed. Munich: Bayerischer Schulbuch-Verlag, 1991, 26-58.

———. "Römische Grabinschriften. Aussageabsicht und Aussagefähigkeit im funerären Kontext." In *Römische Gräberstrassen.* H. von Hesberg and P. Zanker, eds. Abhandlungen des Bayerischen Akademie Wissenschaftliche. Munich: Akademie Verlag, 1988, 61-83.

Ellingworth, P. "Hebrews and 1 Clement: Literary Dependence or Common Tradition?" *Biblische Zeitschrift.* n.s. 23 (1979) 262-69.

———. *The Epistle to the Hebrews.* Grand Rapids: Eerdmans, 1993.

Elliott, J. H. "Patronage and Clientism in Early Christian Society — A Short Reading Guide." *Forum* 3 (1987) 39-48.

———. *A Home for the Homeless: A Social- Scientific Criticism of 1 Peter, Its Situation and Strategy.* Minneapolis: Fortress, 1990.

Esler, Philip F. *Community and Gospel in Luke-Acts.* Cambridge: Cambridge University Press, 1987.

Ettinger, S. "The Beginnings of the Change in the Attitude of European Society towards the Jews." *Scripta Hierosolymitana* 7 (1961) 201.

Eyben, Emiel. "Fathers and Sons." In *Marriage, Divorce, and Children in Ancient Rome.* Beryl Rawson, ed. Oxford: Clarendon, 1991, 117-23.

Farrar, F. W. *The Early Days of Christianity.* London: Cassell, 1888.

Favro, D. G. "The Urban Image of Augustan Rome." Ph.D. diss., University of California, Berkeley, 1984.

Feldman, L. H. "Jewish Proselytism." In *Eusebius, Christianity, and Judaism.* H. W. Attridge and G. Hata, eds. Leiden: Brill, 1992, 372-408.

———. *Josephus and Modern Scholarship.* Berlin: de Gruyter, 1984, 273-76.

Filson, F. V. "The Significance of the Early House Churches." *Journal of Biblical Literature* 58 (1939) 105-12.

Franklin, Jr., James L. "Literacy and the Parietal Inscriptions of Pompeii." In *Literacy in the Roman World.* J. H. Humphrey, ed. *Journal of Roman Archaeology* Supp. Ser. 3. Ann Arbor: Department of Classical Studies, University of Michigan, 1991, 77-98.

Frey, J. B. *Corpus Inscriptionum Iudaicarum.* 2 vols. Rome: Pontificio Instituto di Archeologia Cristiana, 1936.

Frier, B. *Landlords and Tenants in Imperial Rome.* Princeton: Princeton University Press, 1980.

Frohnhofen, H., ed., *Christlicher Antijudaismus und jüdischer Antipaganismus. Ihre Motive und Hintergründe in den ersten drei Jahrhunderten.* Hamburg: Steinmann & Steinmann, 1990.

Fuchs, E. *Hermeneutik.* Bad Cannstatt: R. Müllerschön, 1963.

Fuchs, H. "Tacitus "Über die Christen." *Vigiliae Christianae* 4 (1956) 65-93.

Fuks, Gerhard. "Where Have All the Freedmen Gone? On an Anomaly in the Jewish Grave-Inscriptions from Rome." *Journal of Jewish Studies* 36 (1985) 25-32.

Funk, R. *Greek Grammar of the New Testament.* Cambridge: Cambridge University Press, 1961.

Gager, J. G. *The Origins of Anti-Semitism: Attitudes toward Judaism in Pagan and Christian Antiquity.* Oxford: Oxford University Press, 1983.

Gamble, H. *The Textual History of the Letter to the Romans.* Grand Rapids: Eerdmans, 1977.

Garnsey, P. "Religious Toleration in Classical Antiquity." In *Persecution and Toleration.* W. J. Sheils, ed. *Studies in Church History* 21 (1984) 1-27.

———. *Social Status and Legal Privilege in the Roman Empire.* Oxford: Clarendon, 1970.

Gauger, J.-D. *Beiträge zur jüdischen Apologetik. Untersuchungen zur Authentizität von Urkunden bei Flavius Josephus und im ersten Makkabäerbuch.* Cologne: Hanstein, 1977.

Gee, James Paul. "Orality and Literacy: From *The Savage Mind* to *Ways with Words.*" *TESOL Quarterly* 20/21 (1986/87) 719-46.

Geertz, Clifford. *The Interpretation of Cultures: Selected Essays.* New York: Basic Books, 1973.

Gielen, M. "Zur Interpretation der paulinischen Formel ἡ κατ' οἶκον ἐκκλεσία." *Zeitschrift für die Neutestamentliche Wissenschaft* 77 (1986) 109-25.

Gillman, J. "Archippus." In *Anchor Bible Dictionary.* D. N. Freedman, ed. New York: Doubleday, 1992, 1:368-69.

Gooch, P. D. *Dangerous Food: 1 Corinthians 1–8 in Its Context.* Waterloo, ON: Wilfrid Laurier University Press, 1993.

Goodenough, Erwin R. *Jewish Symbols in the Graeco-Roman Period.* 13 vols. New York: Bollingen, 1952-65.

Goodman, Martin. "Jewish Proselytizing in the First Century." In *The Jews among Pagans and Christians in the Roman Empire.* J. Lieu, J. North and T. Rajak, eds. London, New York: Routledge, 1992, 53-78.

———. "Proselytising in Rabbinic Judaism." *Journal of Jewish Studies* 40 (1989) 175-85.

———. *The Ruling Class of Judaea: The Origin of the Jewish Revolt against Rome. AD 66-70.* Cambridge: Cambridge University Press, 1987.

Goody, Jack. "Alternative Paths to Knowledge in Oral and Literate Cultures." In *Spoken and Written Language: Exploring Orality and Literacy.* Deborah Tannen, ed. Advances in Discourse Processes 9. Norwood, NJ: Ablex, 1982, 201-15.

———. *The Domestication of the Savage Mind.* Cambridge: Cambridge University Press, 1977.

———. *The Interface between the Written and the Oral.* Cambridge: Cambridge University Press, 1987.

———. *The Logic of Writing and the Organization of Society.* Cambridge: Cambridge University Press, 1986.

———, ed. *Literacy in Traditional Societies.* Cambridge: Cambridge University Press, 1968.

Grant, Robert M., ed. *The Apostolic Fathers: A New Translation and Commentary.* Vol. 2: *First and Second Clement.* New York: Nelson, 1965.

Hagner, Donald A. *The Use of the Old and New Testaments in Clement of Rome.* Leiden: Brill, 1973.

Harnack, A. "Probabilia über die Adresse und den Verfasser der Hebräerbriefs." *Zeitschrift für die Neutestamentliche Wissenschaft* 1 (1900) 16-41.

Harrill, J. Albert. *The Manumission of Slaves in Early Christianity.* Tübingen: J. C. B. Mohr (Paul Siebeck), 1995.

Harris, William V. *Ancient Literacy.* Cambridge, MA: Harvard University Press, 1989.

Havelock, Eric. *The Literate Revolution in Greece and Its Cultural Consequences.* Princeton, NJ: Princeton University Press, 1982.

———. *The Muse Learns to Write: Reflections on Orality and Literacy from Antiquity to the Present.* New Haven: Yale University Press, 1986.

———. *Preface to Plato.* Cambridge, MA: Harvard University Press, 1963.

Hellholm, David. *Das Visionenbuch des Hermas als Apokalypse. Formgeschichtliche und texttheoretische Studien zu einer literarischen Gattung.* Vol. 1: *Methodologische Vorüberlegungen und makrostrukturelle Textanalyse.* Lund: Gleerup, 1980.

Hempel, H. L. "Synagogensfunde in Ostia Antica." *Zeitschrift für die Alttestamentliche Wissenschaft* 74 (1962) 72-73.

Henaut, Barry W. *Oral Tradition and the Gospels: The Problem of Mark 4.* Sheffield: JSOT, 1993.

Hengel, M. "Die synagogen Inschrift von Stobi." *Zeitschrift für die Neutestamentliche Wissenschaft* 57 (1966) 148-83.

———. *Zur urchristlichen Geschichtsschreibung.* 2nd ed. Stuttgart: Calwer, 1984.

Henne, Philippe. "A propos de la christologie du *Pasteur* d'Hermas." *Revue des Sciences Philosophiques et Théologiques* 72 (1988) 569-78.

———. "La polysémie allégorique dans le *Pasteur* d'Hermas." *Ephemerides theologicae lovanienses* 65.1 (1989) 131-35.

———. "La véritable christologie de la *cinquième Similitude* du *Pasteur* d'Hermas." *Revue des Sciences Philosophiques et Théologiques* 74 (1990) 182-204.

———. *L'unité, du Pasteur d'Hermas.* Paris: Gabalda, 1992.

Hilhorst, A. "Hermas." *Reallexikon für Antike und Christentum* 108/109 (1988) 682-701.

Hoffmann, C. *Juden und Judentum in den Werken deutscher Althistoriker des 19. und 20. Jahrhunderts.* Leiden: Brill, 1988.

Holmberg, B. *Paul and Power: The Structure of Authority in the Primitive Church as Reflected in the Pauline Epistles.* Lund: Gleerup, 1980.

Hopkins, Keith. "Conquest by Book." In *Literacy in the Roman World.* J. H. Humphrey, ed. *Journal of Roman Archaeology* Supp. Ser. 3. Ann Arbor: Department of Classical Studies, University of Michigan, 1991, 133-58.

———. *Conquerors and Slaves.* Cambridge: Cambridge University Press, 1978.

Horsley, G. H. R. *New Documents Illustrating Early Christianity* 3. New South Wales: Macquarie University, 1983.

Idowu, E. Bolaji. *Towards an Indigenous Church.* London: Oxford University Press, 1965.

Janne, H. "*Impulsore Chresto.*" In *Mélanges Bidez.* Annuaire de l'Institut de philologie et d'histoire orientales et slaves 2. Brussels: Secrétariat de l'Institut, 1934, 537-46.

Jarrett, Dennis. "Pragmatic Coherence in an Oral Formulaic Tradition: I Can Read Your Letters/Sure Can't Read Your Mind." *Coherence in Spoken and Written Discourse.* Deborah Tannen, ed. Advances in Discourse Processes 12. Norwood, NJ: Ablex, 1984, 155-71.

Jeffers, James S. *Conflict at Rome: Social Order and Hierarchy in Early Christianity.* Minneapolis: Fortress, 1991.

Jervell, J. "The Letter to Jerusalem." In *The Romans Debate.* K. P. Donfried, ed. 2nd ed. Peabody, MA: Hendrickson, 1991, 53-64.

Jewett, R. "Following the Argument of Romans." In *The Romans Debate.* K. P. Donfried, ed. 2nd ed. Peabody, MA: Hendrickson, 1991, 265-77.

———. "Tenement Churches and Communal Meals in the Early Church." *Biblical Research* 38 (1993) 24-43.

———. *A Chronology of Paul's Life.* Philadelphia: Fortress, 1979.

Johnson, Luke Timothy. *The Real Jesus: The Misguided Quest for the Historical Jesus and the Truth of the Traditional Gospels.* San Francisco: HarperCollins, 1995.

Joly, Robert. *Hermas le Pasteur.* Sources Chrétiens 53. Paris: Cerf, 1958.

Jones, Brian W. *The Emperor Domitian.* New York: Routledge, 1992.

Jongman, Willem. *The Economy and Society of Pompeii.* Amsterdam: Gieben, 1988.

Kajanto, Iiro. "Les Noms." In *Sylloge inscriptionum christianarum veterum musei vaticani Acta instituti romani finlandiae* 1, 1-2. H. Zilliacus, ed. Helsinki: Distributor Akateeminen Krjakauppa, 1963, 68-71.

Kant, Lawrence H. "Jewish Inscriptions in Greek and Latin." *Aufstieg und Niedergang der römischen Welt* 2.20.2: 672-713.

Kaplan, Steven. *The Beta Israel Falasha, in Ethiopia: From Earliest Times to the Twentieth Century.* New York: New York University Press, 1992.

Karrer, M. *Der Gesalbte. Die Grundlagen des Christustitels.* Göttingen: Vandenhoeck & Ruprecht, 1991.

Karris, R. J. "Romans 14:1–15:13 and the Occasion of Romans." In *The Romans Debate.* K. P. Donfried, ed. 2nd ed. Peabody, MA: Hendrickson, 1991, 65-84.

Käsemann, E. *Commentary on Romans.* Grand Rapids: Eerdmans, 1980.

Kearsley, R. A. "Women in Public Life in the Roman East: Iunia, Theodora, Claudia, Metrodora and Phoebe, Benefactress of Paul." *Ancient Society: Resources for Teachers* 15 (1985) 124-30.

Kee, Howard Clark. "The Transformation of the Synagogue after 70 C.E.: Its Import for Early Christianity." *New Testament Studies* 36 (1990) 1-24.

Kelber, Werner. *The Oral and the Written Gospel.* Philadelphia: Fortress, 1983.

Kelly, Henry A. *The Devil at Baptism: Ritual, Theology, and Drama.* Ithaca/London: Cornell University Press, 1985.

Keresztes, Paul. "The Jews, the Christians, and Emperor Domitian." *Vigiliae Christianae* 27 (1973) 1-28.

———. *Imperial Rome and the Christians.* 2 vols. New York: University Press of America, 1989.

Klauck, H.-J. *Hausgemeinde und Hauskirche im frühen Christentum.* Stuttgart: Verlag Katholisches Bibelstudien, 1981.

Klein, G. "Paul's Purpose in Writing the Epistle to the Romans." In *The Romans Debate.* K. P. Donfried, ed. 2nd ed. Peabody, MA: Hendrickson, 1991, 20-43.

Konikoff, Adia. *Sarcophagi from the Jewish Catacombs of Ancient Rome: catalogue raisonné.* Stuttgart: Steiner-Verlag-Wiesbaden-Gmbh, 1986.

Kraabel, A. T. "The Diaspora Synagogue: Archaeological and Epigraphic Evidence since Sukenik." *Aufstieg und Niedergang der römischen Welt* 2.19.1 (1979) 477-510.

———. "Impact of the Discovery of the Sardis Synagogue." In *Sardis from Prehistoric to Roman Times: Results of the Archaeological Exploration of Sardis, 1958-1975.* G. M. A. Hanfmann, ed. Cambridge, MA: Harvard University Press, 1983, 178-90.

———. "The Roman Diaspora: Six Questionable Assumptions." In *Essays in Honor of Yigael Yadin.* G. Vermes and J. Neusner, eds. *Journal of Jewish Studies* 33.1-2 (1982) 445-64.

———. "The Social Systems of Six Diaspora Synagogues." In *Ancient Synagogues:*

The State of Research. J. Gutmann, ed. Brown Judaic Studies 22. Chico, CA: Scholars Press, 1981, 79-93.

———. "Unity and Diversity among Diaspora Synagogues." In *The Synagogue in Late Antiquity.* L. I. Levine, ed. Philadelphia: ASOR, 1987, 49-60.

Kraeling, C. H. "The Synagogue." In *Final Report VIII, Part I of the Excavation at Dura Europas.* A. R. Bellinger, F. E. Brown, A. Perking, and C. B. Welles, eds. New Haven: Yale University Press, 1956, 11, 263-64, 331-32.

Kraemer, Ross S. "A New Inscription from Malta and the Question of Women Elders in Diaspora Jewish Communities." *Harvard Theological Review* 78 (1986) 431-38.

———. "Non-Literary Evidence for Jewish Women in Rome and Egypt." *Helios* 13 (1986) 85-101.

Kümmel, W. G. *Introduction to the New Testament.* Nashville: Abingdon, 1966.

Kunkel, W. *Kleine Schriften: Zum römischen Strafverfahren und zur römischen Verfassungsgeschichte.* Weimar: Böhlaus, 1974.

La Piana, George. "Foreign Groups in Rome during the First Centuries of the Empire." *Harvard Theological Review* 20 (1927) 183-403.

Lake, Kirsopp. "The Shepherd of Hermas and Christian Life in Rome in the Second Century." *Harvard Theological Review* 4 (1911) 25-46.

———. "The Shepherd of Hermas." In *The Apostolic Fathers.* Vol. 2. Loeb Classical Library. London/Cambridge, MA: Harvard University Press, 1913.

Lampe, Peter. *Die stadtrömischen Christen in den ersten beiden Jahrhunderten.* 2nd ed. Wissenschaftlichen Untersuchungen zum Neuen Testament 2.18. Tübingen: J. C. B. Mohr (Paul Siebeck), 1989.

Lane, W. L. *Hebrews 1–8.* Word Biblical Commentary. Waco, TX: Word, 1991.

Last, H. "The Study of the Last 'Persecutions.'" *Journal for Roman Studies* 27 (1937) 84-88.

Latte, K. *Römische Religionsgeschichte.* Munich: Beck, 1960.

Laub, F. "Paulus als Gemeindegründer (I Thess.)." In *Kirche im Werden.* J. Hainz, ed. Munich: Beck, 1976, 17-38.

———. "Verkündigung und Gemeindeamt: Die Autorität der ἡγούμενοι Hebr 13, 7.17.24." *Studien zum Neuen Testament und seiner Umwelt* 6-7 (1981-82) 183.

Le Glay, M. "Sur l'implantation des sanctuaires orientaux à Rome." In *L'urbs: Espace urbain et histoire.* Centre national de la recherche scientifique et de l'école française de Rome 98. Rome: École Française, 1987, 545-57.

Leon, Harry Joshua. *The Jews of Ancient Rome.* Peabody, MA: Hendrickson, 1995 (1960).

Leutzsch, Martin. *Die Wahrnehmung sozialer Wirklichkeit im "Hirten des Hermas."* Göttingen: Vandenhoeck & Ruprecht, 1989.

Lichtenberger, H. "Josephus und Paulus in Rom. Juden und Christen in Rom zur Zeit Neros." In *Begegnungen zwischen Christentum und Judentum in Antike und Mittelalter. Festschrift für Heinz Schreckenberg.* D.-A. Koch and H. Lichtenberger, eds. Göttingen: Vandenhoeck & Ruprecht, 1993, 245-61.

Liebeschütz, J. H. W. G. *Continuity and Change in Roman Religion.* Oxford: Clarendon, 1979.

Lifshitz, Baruch. *Donateurs et Fondateurs dans les Synagogues juives.* Cahiers de la Revue Biblique 7. Paris: Gabalda, 1967.

Lightfoot, J. B. *The Apostolic Fathers: Clement, Ignatius, Polycarp.* 2nd ed. 5 vols. Part One: Clement, 2 vols. Reprint. Peabody, MA: Hendrickson, 1989.

———. *St. Paul's Epistles to the Colossians and the Philemon.* Reprint. Peabody, MA: Hendrickson, 1987.

———. *St. Paul's Epistle to the Philippians.* Reprint. Peabody, MA: Hendrickson, 1987.

Lindars, B. "The Rhetorical Structure of Hebrews." *New Testament Studies* 35 (1989) 384-86.

Linder, A. *The Jews in Roman Imperial Legislation.* Detroit: Wayne State University Press and Jerusalem: The Israel Academy of Sciences and Humanities, 1987.

Luis-Font, Pedro. "Sources de la doctrine d'Hermas sur les deux esprits." *Revue d'Ascétique et de Mystique* 39 (1963) 83-98.

Lohr, Charles H. "Oral Techniques in the Gospel of Matthew." *Catholic Biblical Quarterly* 23 (1961) 403-35.

Lord, Albert B. "Characteristics of Orality." *Oral Tradition* 2.1 (1987) 54-72.

Luria, Aleksandr R. *Cognitive Development: Its Cultural and Social Foundations.* Cambridge, MA: Harvard University Press, 1976.

Mack, Burton. *Who Wrote the New Testament?: The Making of the Christian Myth.* San Francisco: HarperCollins, 1995.

MacMullen, Ramsay. "Notes on Romanization." *Bulletin of the American Society of Papyrologists* 21 (1984) 167.

———. *Roman Social Relations.* New Haven: Yale University Press, 1974.

Maier, Harry O. *The Social Setting of the Ministry as Reflected in the Writings of Hermas, Clement and Ignatius.* Dissertations SR 1. Waterloo, ON: Wilfrid Laurier University Press, 1991.

Malaise, M. *Les conditions de pénétration et de diffusion des cultes Égyptiens en Italie.* Leiden: Brill, 1972.

Malina, Bruce J. "Christ and Time: Swiss or Mediterranean?" *Catholic Biblical Quarterly* 51.1 (1989) 1-31.

Manson, T. W. "St Paul's Letter to the Romans — and Others." In *The Romans Debate.* K. P. Donfried, ed. 2nd ed. Peabody, MA: Hendrickson, 1991, 3-16.

Marasco, G. "Tiberio e l'esilio degli ebrei in Sardegna nel 19 d.C." *In L'Africa romana: Atti del VIII convegno di studio, Cagliari, 14-16 XII 1990.* A. Mastino, ed. Sassari: Gallizzi, 1991, 649-59.

Martin, Dale B. "Slavery and the Ancient Jewish Family." In *The Jewish Family in Antiquity.* Shaye J. D. Cohen, ed. Atlanta: Scholars Press, 113-29.

Marxsen, Willi. *Introduction to the New Testament.* Philadelphia: Fortress, 1968.

———. *Jesus and the Church: The Beginnings of Christianity.* Philadelphia: Trinity Press International, 1992.

Mattingly, Harold. *Coins of the Roman Empire in the British Museum.* Vol. 3. Oxford: Oxford University Press, 1966.

Mayer, Herbert. "Clement of Rome and His Use of Scripture." *Concordia Theological Monthly* 42 (1971) 536-40.

McKay, A. G. *Houses, Villas and Palaces in the Roman World.* London: Thames & Hudson, 1975.

McKnight, Scot. *A Light among the Gentiles: Jewish Missionary Activity in the Second Temple Period.* Minneapolis: Fortress, 1991.

Meeks, Wayne A. *The First Urban Christians: The Social World of the Apostle Paul.* New Haven: Yale University Press, 1983.

———. *The Origins of Christian Morality.* New Haven: Yale University Press, 1993.

Meeks, Wayne, and Robert Wilken. *Jews and Christians in Antioch.* Missoula, MT: Scholars Press, 1978.

Meiggs, Russell. *Roman Ostia.* 2nd ed. Oxford: Clarendon, 1973.

Melton, D. V. "The Imperial Government and Christianity during the Principate of Claudius." Ph.D. diss., Norman, OK: University of Oklahoma, 1984.

Meritt, B. D., ed. *Corinth, Results of Excavations Conducted by the American School of Classical Studies at Athens.* Vol. VIII, Part I: *Greek Inscriptions, 1896-1927.* Cambridge, MA: Harvard University Press, 1931.

Meyers, Eric M., and Alf Thomas Kraabel. "Archaeology, Iconography, and Nonliterary Written Remains." In *Early Judaism and Its Modern Interpreters.* R. A. and G. W. E. Nickelsburg, eds. Atlanta: Scholars Press, 1986, 175-210.

Milburn, R. L. P. "The Persecution of Domitian." *Church Quarterly Review* 139 (1945) 154-64.

Millar, Fergus. *The Roman Near East, 31 BC–AD 337.* Cambridge, MA: Harvard University Press, 1993.

———. *The Emperor in the Roman World, 31 B.C.–A.D. 337.* Ithaca, NY: Cornell University Press, 1977.

Minear, P. S. *The Obedience of Faith: The Purposes of Paul in the Epistle to the Romans.* London: SCM, 1971.

Mitteis, L. *Reichsrecht und Volksrecht in den östlichen Provinzen des römischen Kaiserreichs.* Hildesheim: Olms, 1963.

Moehring, H. R. "The *Acta pro Judaeis* in the *Antiquities* of Flavius Josephus." In *Christianity, Judaism and Other Greco-Roman Cults: Studies for Morton Smith at Sixty.* J. Neusner, ed. Leiden: Brill, 1975, 124-58.

Momigliano, A. "Freedom of Speech and Religious Tolerance in the Ancient World." In *Anthropology and the Greeks.* S. C. Humphreys, ed. London, 1978, 177-92.

———. In *Ottavo contibuto alla storia degli studi classic e del mondo antico.* Rome: Edizioni di storia e letteratura, 1987.

Mommsen, T. *Gesammelte Schriften.* Vol. 3. Berlin: Weidmann, 1907.

———. *Römische Geschichte.* 8th ed. Berlin: Weidmannsche Buchhandlung, 1889.

———. *Römisches Strafrecht* Graz: Akademische Druck- und Verlagsanstalt, 1955.

Moon, Warren G. "Nudity and Narrative Observations on the Frescoes from the Dura Synagogue." *Journal of the American Academy of Religion* 60.4 (1992) 587-658.

Moule, C. F. D. *The Epistles of Paul to the Colossians and to Philemon.* Cambridge Greek Testament Commentary. Reprint. Cambridge: Cambridge University Press, 1980.

Moxnes, Halvor. *Theology in Conflict: Studies in Paul's Understanding of God in Romans.* Leiden: Brill, 1980.

Murphy-O'Connor, J. *St. Paul's Corinth: Texts and Archeology.* Wilmington, DE: Michael Glazier, 1983.

Mussies, Gerard. "Jewish Personal Names in Some Non-Literary Sources." *Studies in Early Jewish Epigraphy.* J. W. van Henten, ed. Leiden: Brill, 1994, 242-76.

Narni, T. G. "Threptoi." *Epigraphica* 5-6 (1943-44) 45-84.

Nestle, Ehud. "War der Verfasser des 1. Clemensbriefes semitischer Abstammung?" *Zeitschrift für die Neutestamentliche Wissenschaft* 1 (1900) 178-80.

Netzer, Ehud. *Masada III.* Jerusalem: Israel Exploration Society, 1991.

Neusner, Jacob, ed. *Jewish Symbols in the Greco-Roman Period.* Princeton: Princeton University Press, 1988.

———. *Symbol and Theology in Early Judaism.* Minneapolis: Fortress, 1991.

Neusner, Jacob, and Ernest S. Frerichs, eds. *To See Ourselves as Others See Us: Christians, Jews, and "Others" in Late Antiquity.* Chico, CA: Scholars Press, 1985.

Nickle, K. F. *The Collection: A Study in Pauline Strategy.* Naperville: Allenson, 1966.

Nielsen, Hanne Sigismund. "The Physical Context of Roman Epitaphs and the Structure of the Roman Family." *Analecta Romana instituti Danici* 23 (1996) 35-62.

Nock, A. D. "Religious Developments from the Close of the Republic to the Death of Nero." In *Cambridge Ancient History.* Vol. 10. S. A. Cook, F. E. Adcock, and M. P. Charlesworth, eds. Cambridge: Cambridge University Press, 1971, 465-511.

North, J. A. "Religious Toleration in Republican Rome." *Proceedings of the Cambridge Philological Society* 25 (1979) 85.

North, John. "The Development of Religious Pluralism." In *The Jews among Pagans and Christians in the Roman Empire.* Judith Lieu, John North, and Tessa Rajak, eds. London: Routledge, 1992, 174-93.

Noy, David. *Jewish Inscriptions of Western Europe.* Vol. 1. Cambridge: Cambridge University Press, 1993.

Noy, David, and William Horbury. *Jewish Inscriptions of Graeco-Roman Egypt.* Cambridge: Cambridge University Press, 1992.

O'Brien, Peter T. *Colossians, Philemon.* Word Biblical Commentary. Waco, TX: Word, 1982.

Ong, Walter. *Orality and Literacy: The Technologizing of the Word.* London/New York: Methuen, 1982.

Orosius, Paulus. "*Historiarum Adversum Paganos Libri VII:* Dating the Claudian Expulsions, of Roman Jews." *Jewish Quarterly Review* 83 (1992) 127-44.

Osiek, Carolyn. "The Genre and Function of the Shepherd of Hermas." In *Early Christian Apocalypticism: Genre and Social Setting.* Adela Yarbro Collins, ed. *Semeia* 36 (1986) 113-21.

———. "The Ransom of Captives: Evolution of a Tradition." *Harvard Theological Review* 74.4 (1981) 365-86.

———. *Rich and Poor in the Shepherd of Hermas: An Exegetical-Social Investigation.* Washington, DC: Catholic Biblical Association, 1983.

Overman, J. Andrew, and Robert S. Mclennan, eds., *Diaspora Jews and Judaism: Essays in Honor of, and in Dialogue with, A. T. Kraabel.* Atlanta: Scholars Press, 1992.

Packer, J. E. "Housing and Population in Imperial Ostia and Rome." *Journal of Roman Studies* 57 (1967) 280-95.

Packer, James E. *The Insulae of Imperial Ostia.* Rome: American Academy, 1971.

Pailler, J. M. *Bacchanalia: Répression de 186 av. J.-C. à Rome et en Italie: Vestiges, Images, Tradition.* Bibliothèque des écoles françaises d'Athène et de Rome 270. Rome: École Française, 1988.

Paramelle, J. "Hermas." In *Dictionnaire de spiritualité.* Paris: Beauchesne, 1969, 7:316-34.

Pavolini, Carlo. "OSTIA Roma: Saggi lungo la via Severiana." In *Notizie degli Scavi di Antichità.* VIII.35. Accademia nazionale dei Lincei, 1981, 115-43.

Penna, Romano. "Les Juifs a Rome, au temps de l'apotre Paul." *New Testament Studies* 28 (1982) 321-47.

Peterson, Erik. "Kritische Analyse der fünften Vision." *Frühkirche, Judentum, und Gnosis.* Freiburg: Herder, 1959.

Peterson, J. M. "House-churches in Rome." *Vigiliae Christianae* 23 (1969) 264-72.

———. "Some Titular Churches at Rome with Traditional New Testament Connexions." *Expository Times* 84 (1973) 277-79.

Pomeroy, Sarah. *Goddesses, Whores, Wives, Slaves: Women in Classical Antiquity.* New York: Schocken Books, 1975.

Poschmann, Bernhard. *Paenitentia Secunda. Die kirchliche Busse im ältesten Christentum bis Cyprian und Origenes.* Bonn: Hanstein, 1940.

Rajak, Tessa. "Inscription and Context: Reading the Jewish Catacombs of Rome." In *Studies in Early Jewish Epigraphy.* Jan Willem van Henten and Pieter Willem van der Horst, eds. Leiden: Brill, 1994, 232-33.

———. "Jewish Rights in the Greek Cities under Roman Rule: A New Approach." In W. S. Green, ed. *Approaches to Ancient Judaism.* Vol. 5: *Studies in Judaism in Its Greco-Roman Context.* Atlanta: Scholars Press, 1985, 19-35.

———. "Was There a Roman Charter for the Jews?" *Journal of Roman Studies* 74 (1984) 107-23.

Rapske, B. *The Book of Acts in Its First Century Setting.* Vol. 3: *The Book of Acts and Paul in Roman Custody.* Grand Rapids: Eerdmans, 1994.

Rawson, Beryl L. "The Roman Family." In *The Family in Ancient Rome: New Perspectives.* Beryl L. Rawson, ed. London: Croon Helm, 1986, 1-51.

Redfield, Robert. *The Little Community.* Chicago: University of Chicago Press, 1955,

Reifenberg, A. *Ancient Jewish Coins.* 3d ed. Jerusalem: Rubin Mass, 1963.

Reiling, J. "Hermas." *Reallexikon für Antike und Christentum* 108/109 (1988) 682-83.

———. *Hermas and Christian Prophecy: A Study of the Eleventh Mandate.* Novum Testamentum Supplements 37. Leiden: Brill, 1973.

Reinhartz, Adele. "Parents and Children: A Philonic Perspective." In *The Jewish Family in Antiquity.* Shaye J. D. Cohen, ed. Atlanta: Scholars Press, 1993, 61-88.

Rengstorf, Karl-Heinrich. *Mann und Frau im Urchristentum.* Köln: Westdeutscher, 1954, 25-46.

Reynolds, J., and R. Tannenbaum, *Jews and Godfearers at Aphrodisias.* Cambridge Philological Society Suppl. Vol. 12. Cambridge: Cambridge University Press, 1987.

Richardson, Lawrence, Jr. *Pompeii: An Architectural History.* Baltimore: Johns Hopkins, 1988.

Richardson, Peter. "Early Synagogues as Collegia in the Diaspora and Palestine." In *Voluntary Associations in the Ancient World.* John S. Kloppenborg and S. G. Wilson, eds. London: Routledge, 1996, 90-109.

———. "Herod's Architectural-Religious Policy in the Diaspora." In *Second Temple Studies: The Roman Period.* Sheffield: JSOT Press, 1998.

———. *Herod, King of the Jews and Friend of the Romans.* Columbia, SC: University of South Carolina Press, 1996.

———. *Israel in the Apostolic Church.* Cambridge: Cambridge University Press, 1969.

Riesner, Rainer. "Synagogues in Jerusalem." In *The Book of Acts in Its First Century Setting.* Vol. 4: *Palestinian Setting.* Richard Bauckham, ed. Grand Rapids: Eerdmans, 1995, 179-211.

———. *Die Frühzeit des Apostels Paulus. Studien zur Chronologie, Missionstrategie und Theologie.* Wissenschaftliche Untersuchungen zum Neuen Testament 1.71. Tübingen: J. C. B. Mohr, 1994.

Robinson, J. A. T. *Redating the New Testament.* London: SCM, 1976.

Robinson, James, and Helmut Koester. *Trajectories through Early Christianity.* Philadelphia: Fortress, 1971.

Rockhill, Kathleen. "Gender, Language, and the Politics of Literacy." *Cross-cultural Approaches to Literacy.* Brian V. Street, ed. Cambridge Studies in Oral and Literate Cultures. Cambridge: Cambridge University Press, 1993, 156-75.

Ruggini, L. Cracco. "Note sugli ebrei in Italia dal IV al XVI secolo." *Rivista storica italiana* 6 (1964) 932.

Rutgers, Leonard Victor. "Archaeological Evidence for the Interaction of Jews and Non-Jews in Late Antiquity." *American Journal of Archaeology* 96 (1992) 101-18.

———. "Inscriptions grecques de Side." *Revue philosophique* 32 (1958) 36-47.

———. "Überlegungen zu den jüdischen katakomben Roms." *Jahrbuch für Antike und Christentum* 33 (1990) 140-57.

———. *The Jews in Late Ancient Rome: Evidence of Cultural Interaction in the Roman Diaspora.* Leiden: E. J. Brill, 1995.

Saller, Richard P. "Men's Age at Marriage and Its Consequences in the Roman Family." *Classical Philology* 82 (1987) 21-34.

Saller, Richard P., and Brent D. Shaw. "Tombstones and Roman Family Relations in the Principate: Civilians, Soldiers and Slaves." *Journal of Roman Studies* 74 (1984) 124-56.

Salway, Benet. "What's in a Name? A Survey of Roman Onomastic Practice from c. 700 BC to AD 700," *Journal of Roman Studies* 84 (1996) 124-51.

Sanders, E. P. *Paul, the Law, and the Jewish People.* Philadelphia: Fortress, 1983.

Sanneh, Lamin. *Translating the Message: The Missionary Impact on Culture.* Maryknoll, NY: Orbis, 1989.

Saulnier, C. "Flavius Josèphe et la propaganda flavienne." *Revue Biblique* 96 (1986) 545-62.

———. "Lois romaines sur les juifs selon Flavius Josèphe." *Revue Biblique* 87 (1981) 161-98.

Savage, S. M. "The Cults of Ancient Trastevere." *Memoirs of the American Academy in Rome* 17 (1940) 26-56.

Scheiber, A. *Jewish Inscriptions in Hungary: From the Third Century to 1686.* Leiden: Brill, 1983.

Schelke, K. H. "Römische Kirche im Römerbrief." *Zeitschrift für katholische Theologie* 81 (1959) 393-404.

Schineller, Peter. *A Handbook on Inculturation.* New York: Paulist, 1990.

Schreiter, Robert. *Constructing Local Theologies.* Maryknoll, NY: Orbis, 1985.

Schürer, Emil. *The History of the Jewsh People in the Age of Jesus Christ.* New ed. by G. Vermes, F. Millar, and M. Goodman. Vol. 3.1. Edinburgh: T. & T. Clark, 1986.

Scott, E. F. "The Epistle to the Hebrews and Roman Christianity." *Harvard Theological Review* 13 (1930) 205-19.

Scramuzza, V. *The Emperor Claudius.* Cambridge, MA: Harvard University Press, 1940.

Seager, Andrew R. "Ancient Synagogue Architecture: An Overview." In *Ancient Synagogues.* J. Gutmann, ed. Brown Judaic Studies. Chico, CA: Scholars Press, 1981, 39-47.

Segal, A. F. *Paul the Convert: The Apostolate and Apostasy of Saul the Pharisee.* New Haven: Yale University Press, 1990.

Segal, Alan. "The Costs of Proselytism and Conversion." *Seminar Papers.* Society of Biblical Literature, no. 27. Atlanta: Scholars Press, 1988, 336-69.

Shanks, Hershel. *Judaism in Stone: The Archaeology of Ancient Synagogues.* New York: Harper, 1979.

Sherwin-White, A. N. *Roman Foreign Policy in the East, 168 B.C. to A.D. 1.* Norman, OK: University of Oklahoma Press, 1983.

———. *The Roman Citizenship.* 2nd ed. Oxford: Clarendon, 1973.

Shorter, Aylward. *Toward a Theology of Inculturation.* Maryknoll, NY: Orbis, 1988.

Shotter, D. C. A. "The Principate of Nerva — Some Observations on the Coin Evidence." *Historia* 32 (1983) 215-26.

Siker, Jeffrey. *Disinheriting the Jews: Abraham in Early Christian Controversy.* Louisville: Westminster/John Knox, 1991.

Simon, Marcel. "Jupiter-Yahvé." *Numen* 23 (1976) 40-66.

———. *Verus Israel: A Study of the Relations between Christians and Jews in the Roman Empire.* H. McKeating, tr. Oxford: Oxford University Press, 1986 (1964).

Slingerland, D. "Chrestus: Christus?" In *The Literature of Early Rabbinic Judaism: Issues in Talmudic Redaction and Interpretation.* New Perspectives on Ancient Judaism 4. A. J. Avery-Peck, ed. Lanham, MD: University Press of America, 1989, 133-34.

———. "Suetonius *Claudius* 25.4 and the Account in Cassius Dio." *Jewish Quarterly Review* 79 (1989) 305-22.

Smallwood, E. Mary. "Some Notes on the Jews under Tiberius." *Latomus* 15 (1956) 314-29.

———. *Documents Illustrating the Principate of Gaius, Claudius and Nero.* Cambridge: Cambridge University Press, 1967.

———. *The Jews under Roman Rule: From Pompey to Diocletian.* Leiden: Brill, 1976.

Smelik, K. A. D. "Tussen tolerantie en vervolging." *Lampas* 22 (1989).

Smith, Jonathan Z. "Fences and Neighbors: Some Contours of Early Judaism." In

Approaches to Ancient Judaism. Vol. 2. W. S. Green, ed. Brown Judaic Studies. Missoula, MT: Scholars Press, 1980, 1-25. Reprinted in Smith's *Imagining Religion: From Babylon to Jonestown.* Chicago: University of Chicago Press, 1982, 1-18.

Snyder, Graydon F. "Early Christian Art." In the *Anchor Bible Dictionary.* D. N. Freedman, ed. New York: Doubleday, 1962, 1:454-61.

———. *Ante Pacem: Archaeological Evidence of Church Life before Constantine.* Macon, GA: Mercer University Press, 1985.

———. *The Shepherd of Hermas.* Apostolic Fathers 6. Robert M. Grant, ed. Camden, NJ: Nelson, 1968.

Solin, Heikki. "Juden und Syrer im westlichen Teil der römischen Welt: Eine ethnisch-demographische Studie mit besonderer Berücksichtigung der sprachlichen Zustände." *Aufstieg und Niedergang der römischen Welt* 2.29.2. Berlin, 1983, 587-789 and 1222-49.

———. "Die Namen der orientalischen Sklaven in rom." In *L'Onomastique latine.* N. Nuval, ed. Paris: Centre Nationale de la Recherche Scientifique, 1977, 205-9.

Sordi, M. "Christianity and the Flavians." In *The Christians and the Roman Empire.* Norman, OK: University of Oklahoma Press, 1986, 38-54.

Souter, A. "A Study of Ambrosiaster." In *Cambridge Texts and Studies.* Cambridge: Cambridge University Press, 1905.

———. *The Earliest Latin Commentaries on the Epistles of St. Paul.* Cambridge: Cambridge University Press, 1927.

Spicq, C. *L'Épitre aux Hébreux.* 2 vols. Paris: Gabalda, 1952-53.

Squarciapino, Maria Floriani. "Plotius Fortunatus archisynagogus." *Rassegna mensile di Israel* 36 (1970) 183-91.

———. "La sinagoga di Ostia." *Bolletino d'Arte* (1961) 326-37.

———. "La sinagoga recentemente scoperta ad Ostia." *Rendiconti della Pontificia Accademia Romana di Archeologia.* Ser. 3, 34. 1961-62.

———. "La sinogaga di Ostia. secondo campagna di scavo." In *Atti di VIû Congresso internazionale di archeologia cristiana, 1962.* Rome: Pontifical Press, 1965, 299-315; also published as *La sinagoga di Ostia.* Rome, 1964; an extensive English summary of this same article was published as "The Synagogue at Ostia." *Archeology* 16 (1963) 194-203.

———. "Die Synagoge von Ostia antica." *Raggi. Zeitschrift für Kunstgeschichte und Archäologie* 4 (1962) 1-8.

Stambaugh, John E. *The Ancient Roman City.* Baltimore: Johns Hopkins University Press, 1988.

Stegemann, E., and W. Stegemann. *Urchristliche Sozialgeschichte. Die Anfänge im Judentum und die Christusgemeinden in der mediterranen Welt.* Stuttgart: W. Kohlhammer, 1995.

Stern, Menahem. "Sympathy for Judaism in Roman Senatorial Circles in the Period of the Early Empire." *Zion* 29 (1964) 155-67 (Hebrew).

———. "The Jews in Greek and Latin Literature." In *The Jewish People in the First Century.* Samuel Safrai and Menahem Stern, eds. Compendia Rerum Ioudaicarum ad Novum Testamentum. Philadelphia: Fortress Press, 1976.

———. *Greek and Latin Authors on Jews and Judaism.* 3 vols. Jerusalem: Israel Academy of Sciences and Humanities, 1974-84.

Strock, A. W. "The Shepherd of Hermas: A Study of His Anthropology as Seen in the Tension between Dipsychia and Hamartia Repentance." Unpub. diss., Atlanta: Emory University Press, 1984.

Stuhlmacher, P. "The Purpose of Romans." In *The Romans Debate.* K. P. Donfried, ed. 2nd ed. Peabody, MA: Hendrickson, 1991, 231-44.

Syme, R. "The Imperial Finances under Domitian, Nerva and Trajan." *Journal of Roman Studies* 20 (1930) 55-70.

Tannen, Deborah. "The Oral/Literate Continuum in Discourse." In *Spoken and Written Language: Exploring Orality and Literacy.* Deborah Tannen, ed. Advances in Discourse Processes 9. Norwood, NJ: Ablex, 1982, 1-16.

Tcherikover, V. A., et al. *Corpus Papyrorum Judaicarum.* Cambridge, MA: Harvard University Press, 1960.

Theissen, G. "Social Stratification in the Corinthian Community: A Contribution to the Sociology of Early Hellenistic Christianity." In *The Social Setting of Pauline Christianity.* Philadelphia: Fortress, 1982.

Thompson, L. A. "Domitian and the Jewish Tax." *Historia* 31 (1982) 329-42.

Tolmach, Robin. "Some of My Favorite Writers Are Literate: The Mingling of Oral and Literate Strategies in Written Communication." In *Spoken and Written Language: Exploring Orality and Literacy.* Deborah Tannen, ed. Advances in Discourse Processes 9. Norwood, NJ: Ablex, 1982, 239-60.

Tomson, Peter J. *Paul and the Jewish Law.* Compendia Rerum Ioudaicarum ad Novum Testamentum 3.1. Assen: Van Gorcum; Minneapolis: Fortress, 1990.

Treggiari, Susan. *Roman Freedmen during the Late Republic.* Oxford: Clarendon, 1969.

———. *Roman Marriage: Iusti Coniuges from the Time of Cicero to the Time of Ulpian.* Oxford: Clarendon Press, 1991, 509-10.

Trigger, Bruce. *Gordon Childe: Revolutions in Archaeology.* New York: Columbia University Press, 1980.

Urman, Dan, and Paul V. M. Flesher, eds. *Ancient Synagogues: Historical Analysis and Archaeological Discovery.* 2 vols. Leiden: Brill, 1995.

van Cauwelaert, R. "L'intervention de l'Église de Rome à Corinthe vers l'an 96." *Revue d'Histoire Ecclésiatique* 31 (1935) 267-306.

Van Deemter, Roelof. *Der Hirt des Hermas. Apokalypse oder Allegorie?* Delft: W. D. Meinema, 1929.

van der Horst, P. W. *Ancient Jewish Epitaphs.* Kampen: Kok-Pharos, 1991.

Vermaseren, Maarten J. *Corpus Inscriptionum et Monumentorum religionis mithriacae.* 2 vols. The Hague: Martinus Nijhoff, 1956-60.

Verner, David C. *The Household of God: The Social World of the Pastoral Epistles.* Chico, CA: Scholars Press, 1983.

Vogelstein, Hermann. "The Jews in Ancient Rome." Book I in *Rome.* M. Hadas, tr. Philadelphia: Jewish Publication Society of America, 1941.

von Campenhausen, H. F. *Ecclesiastical Authority and Spiritual Power in the Church of the First Three Centuries.* London: A. & C. Black, 1969.

von Harnack, Adolf. *Einführung in die alte Kirchengeschichte. Das Schreiben der römischen Kirche an die Korinthische aus der Zeit Domitians.* I. Clemensbrief, Leipzig: Hinrichs, 1929.

von Ström, Ake. *Der Hirt des Hermas, Allegorie oder Wirklichkeit?* Arbeiten und Mitteilungen aus dem neutestamentlichen Seminar zu Uppsala 3. Uppsala: Wretmans, 1936.

Vygotsky, Lev S. *Mind and Society: The Development of Higher Psychological Processes.* Cambridge, MA: Harvard University Press, 1978.

———. *Thought and Language.* Rev. ed. Cambridge, MA: MIT Press, 1986 (1962).

Walters J. C. *Ethnic Issues in Paul's Letter to the Romans.* Valley Forge, PA: Trinity Press International, 1993.

Wardman, A. *Religion and Statecraft among the Romans.* London: Granada, 1982.

Wardy, B. "Jewish Religion in Pagan Literature during the Late Republic and Early Empire." *Aufstieg und Niedergang der römischen Welt* 2.19.1 (1979) 604ff.

Watson, A. *Roman Slave Law.* Baltimore: Johns Hopkins University Press, 1987.

———. *The State, Law and Religion.* Athens: University of Georgia Press, 1992.

Watson, F. "The Two Roman Congregations: Romans 14:1–15:13." In *The Romans Debate.* K. P. Donfried, ed. 2nd ed. Peabody, MA: Hendrickson, 1991, 203-15.

Weaver, P. R. C. "The Status of Children in Mixed Marriages." In *The Family in Ancient Rome.* Beryl Rawson, ed. Ithaca, NY: Cornell University Press, 1986, 145-69.

———. "Where Have All the Junian Latins Gone? Nomenclature and Status in the Early Empire." *Chiron* 20 (1990) 275-305.

Wedderburn, A. J. M. *The Reasons for Romans.* Edinburgh: T. & T. Clark, 1988.

Welborn, L. L. "First Epistle of Clement." In the *Anchor Bible Dictionary.* D. N. Freedman, ed. New York: Doubleday, 1992, 1:1055-60.

———. "On the Date of First Clement." *Biblical Research* 29 (1984) 35-54.

Wengst, K. *Pax Romana and the Peace of Jesus Christ.* London: SCM, 1987.

Westenholz, Joan Goodnick. *The Jewish Presence in Ancient Rome.* Jerusalem: Bible Lands Museum, 1995.

White, L. Michael. "Adolf Harnack and the Expansion of Christianity: A Reappraisal of Social History." *The Second Century* 5 (1985-86) 97-127.

———. "The Delos Synagogue Revisited." *Harvard Theological Review* 80 (1987) 133-60.

———. "Finding the Ties That Bind: Issues from Social History." In *Social Networks in the Early Christian Environment: Methods and Issues for Social History.* L. M. White, ed. *Semeia* 56. Atlanta: Scholars Press, 1991, 3-22.

———. *Building God's House in the Roman World: Architectural Adaptation among Pagans, Jews, and Christians.* Baltimore: The Johns Hopkins University Press, 1990.

———. *The Social Origins of Christian Architecture.* 2 vols. Harvard Theological Studies. Philadelphia: Trinity Press International, 1996.

Wiefel, Wolfgang. "The Jewish Community in Ancient Rome and the Origins of Roman Christianity." In *The Romans Debate.* K. P. Donfried, ed. 2nd ed. Peabody, MA: Hendrickson, 1991, 85-101.

Williams, Margaret H. "Domitian, the Jews and the 'Judaizers' — A Simple Matter of Cupiditas and Maiestas." *Historia* 39 (1990) 196-211.

———. "The Expulsion of the Jews from Rome in A.D. 19." *Latomus* 48 (1989) 765-84.

———. "*Theosebes gar en* — The Jewish Tendencies of Poppaea Sabina." *Journal of Theological Studies* 39 (1988) 97-111.

Wilson, William Jerome. "The Career of the Prophet Hermas." *Harvard Theological Review* 20 (1927), 21-62.

Wischnitzer, Rachel. *The Architecture of the European Synagogue.* Philadelphia: Jewish Publication Society, 1974.

Wolff, H. "Die Juden im antiken Rom." In *Minderheiten im Mittelmeerraum.* K. Rother, ed. Passau: Passavia Universitätsverlag, 1989, 35-62.

Yarbrough, O. Larry. "Parents and Children in the Jewish Family of Antiquity." In *The Jewish Family in Antiquity.* Shaye J. D. Cohen, ed. Atlanta: Scholars Press, 1993, 39-59.

Ziegler, A. W. *Neue Studien zum I Clemensbrief.* Munich: Kaiser, 1958.

Zimmerman, H. *Das Bekenntnis der Hoffnung: Tradition und Redaktion im Hebräerbrief.* Cologne/Bonn: Hanstein, 1977.

Contributors

Rudolf Brändle is Professor of New Testament and History of the Early Church in the Theological Faculty, University of Basel, Nadelberg 10, CH-4051 Basel, Switzerland.

Chrys C. Caragounis is Associate Professor of New Testament Exegesis in the Department of Theology and Religious Studies, Lund University, 223 62 Lund, Sweden.

Karl P. Donfried is Professor in the Department of Religion and Biblical Literature, Smith College, Northampton, Massachusetts 01063.

James S. Jeffers is Lecturer in Interdisciplinary Studies, California State University, Dominguez Hills, Carson, California 90747.

William L. Lane is Paul T. Walls Professor of Wesleyan and Biblical Studies in the Department of Religion, Seattle Pacific University, Seattle, Washington 98119-1997.

Carolyn Osiek, R.S.C.J., is Professor of New Testament in the Catholic Theological Union at Chicago, 5401 South Connell Avenue, Chicago, Illinois 60615-5698.

Peter Richardson is Professor of Christian Origins in the Centre for the Study of Religion, University of Toronto, Toronto, Ontario M5S 1A1, Canada.

Leonard Victor Rutgers is Research Fellow in the Royal Dutch Academy of Arts and Sciences in the Faculty of Theology, University of Utrecht, Utrecht 3508 TC, POB 80105, the Netherlands.

Graydon F. Snyder is Professor of New Testament in Chicago Theological Seminary (retired), 5757 South University Avenue, Chicago, Illinois 60637.

Ekkehard W. Stegemann is Professor of New Testament in the Theological Faculty, University of Basel, Nadelberg 10, CH-4051 Basel, Switzerland.

James C. Walters is Resident Research Fellow, Heartbeat Inc., 35 South Main Street, Hanover, New Hampshire 03755.

L. Michael White is Professor of Classics and Christian Origins in the Department of Classics, and Director of the Religious Studies Program of the University of Texas at Austin, Austin, Texas 78712.

Index of Ancient Texts

Index of Modern Authors

Index of Names

Index of Places

Printed in the United States
42851LVS00007B/156